M. Douglas Smith

A CLASS-BOOK OF
OLD TESTAMENT HISTORY

A CLASS-BOOK

OF

OLD TESTAMENT HISTORY

BY

THE REV. G. F. MACLEAR, D.D.

WITH MAPS

WM. B. EERDMANS PUBLISHING COMPANY
GRAND RAPIDS   MICHIGAN

*Reprinted in 1952
by special arrangement
with the Macmillan Company
Sixth printing, 1967
Eighth printing, November* 1971

NOTICE

THE present Volume forms a Class-Book of Old
Testament History from the Earliest Times to those
of Ezra and Nehemiah.

In its preparation the most recent Authorities *
have been consulted, and wherever it has appeared
useful, Notes have been subjoined illustrative of
the Text, and, for the sake of more advanced
students, references added to larger Works.

The Index has been so arranged as to form a
concise Dictionary of the Persons and Places mentioned in the course of the Narrative, while the
Maps, which have been prepared with considerable
care at Stanford's Geographical Establishment, will,
it is hoped, materially add to the value and useful-
ness of the Book.

* The Edition of Dr Robinson's *Biblical Researches* referred to is the second American Edition, 3 Vols. 1860 ; that
of Dean Stanley's *Sinai and Palestine*, the 3rd, 1856.

London, Christmas, 1864.

SYNOPSIS OF CONTENTS

BOOK I

From the Creation to the Dispersion of Mankind.

BOOK II

The Patriarchal Age.

BOOK III

From the Settlement of the Israelites in Egypt to the Giving of the Law.

BOOK VI
Joshua and the Conquest of Western Palestine.

BOOK VII
Period of the Judges.

BOOK VIII
From the Time of Samuel to the Accession of David.

BOOK IX

The Reigns of David and Solomon.

BOOK X

Kingdoms of Judah and Israel.

PART I

Period of Mutual Hostility.

PART II

Period of Mutual Alliance, and Hostility to Syria.

MAPS

BOOK I

FROM THE CREATION TO THE DISPERSION OF MANKIND.

CHAPTER I

THE CREATION.

GEN. I. II. B. C. 4004.

IN the beginning God created the heavens and the earth. With these simple but sublime words commences the History contained in the Scriptures of the Old Testament, teaching us that the Universe did not exist from all eternity, but owed its origin to the creative act of God. To us this truth appears so elementary and self-evident that we can hardly appreciate the dim and uncertain notions on this point, which the best and wisest of the heathen possessed. Certain it is, however, they were very much in the dark respecting the origin of the world. Some philosophers held that it existed from all eternity: others taught that there are two independent Causes, the one Light, and the other Darkness, and that out of the unending struggle between them the Universe had its origin; others imagined that all the marvellous order and harmony we see around us was the result of Chance; others, again, conceived that the world was an emanation from Deity, and a part of Deity. Distinct from all these guesses and conceptions is the *declaration* of the Scripture Narrative. It affirms that the world is not eternal; that it had its

1

origin with time and in time; that it owed its beginning neither to Chance, nor Necessity, but the Creative will of a Personal God, infinitely exalted above it, the Maker and Sustainer of all things. (Comp. Joh. i. 1—3, Rom. xi. 36, 1 Cor. viii. 6, Col. i. 15, 16, Heb. i. 2, 3).

The creation, however, of the present order of things was not instantaneous, but progressive, and took place in six Days, or vast Periods of time. On the *first* day light was created, and divided from the darkness; on the *second*, the firmament, or atmosphere encircling the globe; on the *third*, a separation was made between the water and the land, and the surface of the earth was covered with vegetation, with *the herb yielding seed, and the tree yielding fruit after its kind.* On the *fourth*, the sun, moon and stars were bidden *to give light upon the earth, and to be for signs and for seasons, and for days and years.* On the *fifth*, animal life appeared in its lowest forms, the waters brought forth the various marine tribes after their kind, and this was succeeded by the creation of every *winged fowl.* The *sixth* day was marked by the production of land animals, *cattle, and creeping thing, and beast of the earth,* which, like all the preceding products of Creative Power, received the Divine approval, and were pronounced to be *very good.*

But the work of Creation was not yet complete. A being higher than any yet created was to be called into existence. Accordingly *God said, Let* us *make* Man *in* our *image, after* our *likeness, and let them have dominion over every living thing, and over all the earth; and the Lord God formed Man of the dust of the ground, and breathed into his nostrils the breath of life, and Man became a living soul.* Then having seen that all things He had made were *very good* God ended His work, and *rested on the seventh day*, sanctifying it as a day of Rest for man. (Gen. i. 2—26).

The language here employed in reference to the creation of man deserves attention. It teaches us that man did not, as some have taught, slowly emerge by his own efforts from a brutish state. Unlike other created objects, he was originally made in the *image* and *after the likeness* of God. Endowed not only with a body, but also with an immortal soul, he was to combine intellectual power with liberty of will, and the faculty of conscience. And as he was great himself, so also was the work to which he was called. His was to be universal dominion *over the fish of the sea, and over the fowl of the air, and over every living thing that moveth upon the earth.* As God's vicegerent, he was to exercise lordship over nature, and guide it towards its destined perfection (Gen. i. 26).

But though the first man ADAM, was endued with those high prerogatives, he was not destined to attain immediately to the end for which he was created. His activity was to commence in a particular spot, and thence to extend in all directions, until all the earth was subdued and moulded to the will of its Creator. The Almighty, therefore, planted a garden in a region of the East, corresponding probably to the high table-land of the modern Armenia, and watered by four streams. Of two of these, Pison and Gihon, the situation is absolutely unknown, the others were the Tigris and Euphrates. Here, then, in a spot endued with everything pleasant to the sight and good for food, man's work was to commence. Action and not contemplation only was essential to his nature, hence a charge was given to him to *dress* and *keep* the garden. Nor amidst everything to gratify his senses and supply material for his understanding and reflection was he left alone. A responsible being, *bone of his bone, and flesh of his flesh,* was created a *help-meet for him.* The Lord *caused a deep sleep to fall upon Adam,* and taking one of his ribs, He made

1—2

thereof a woman, and brought her unto him, and EVE, *the mother of all flesh,* one with himself in nature and in origin, was united to him in holy bonds, which HE, Who thus instituted them in Paradise, afterwards adorned and hallowed with His own presence and first miracle at Cana of Galilee (Joh. ii. 1; Eph. v. 23—33).

CHAPTER II

THE FALL.

GEN. III. B. C. 4004.

OF the life of the first human pair in Paradise we are told but little. We know, however, that it was not only a state of innocence, and therefore of happiness, but also, like all human life since, of *probation.* Besides the charge to dress and keep the fair enclosure in which they had been placed, our first parents received but one additional command. It was couched in negative terms, and forbade in the most distinct and solemn manner possible the eating of the fruit of a mysterious tree growing in the midst of the Garden, and called the *tree of knowledge of Good and Evil.* Of the fruit of every other tree they might eat freely, of the fruit of this tree the Almighty said to them, *Ye shall not eat, for in the day ye eat thereof ye shall surely die.* In this single prohibition lay the test of their loyal obedience to their Creator, on it depended their innocence and their happiness temporal and eternal. How long they were faithful and obedient we are not told. But whether the period was long or short, certain it is that it came to a close.

The Tree of *the Knowledge of Good and Evil,* implies that Evil was already present in God's world, and therefore in part prepares us for the dark shadow that now gathers round the sacred page. The creation of man had been watched by a supernatural Being of infinite subtilty and malignity, the Enemy of God and of all goodness. Respecting this mysterious Being, though the Sacred Narrative does not gratify our curiosity with any lengthened details, yet to his existence and his unceasing hostility to man, it bears direct and explicit testimony. The name under which the supernatural Tempter appears in the earliest and latest portions of the Bible is the same (comp. Gen. iii. 1, with 2 Cor. xi. 3; Rev. xii. 9, xx. 2), and though but seldom mentioned in the Old Testament (Job i., ii.; 1 Chron. xxi. 1; Zech. iii. 1, 2), the same attributes are uniformly ascribed to him. Created originally good, like all the works of God, he *abode not in the truth* (Jn. viii. 44), but rebelled against his Maker and fell from his high estate (1 Tim. iii. 6), and henceforth, at the head of numerous other spirits (Matt. xxv. 41), whom he had dragged down with him in his fall (2 Pet. ii. 4; Jude 6), he arrayed himself in conscious hostility to the Supreme.

This Being, then, here called the Serpent, in other places Satan, i.e. the *Enemy*, and the Devil, i.e. the *Slanderer*, approached the woman, as being the weaker vessel, for the purpose of seducing her, and so her husband, from their allegiance to their Creator. With affected solicitude he began by enquiring, *Yea, hath God said, Ye shall not eat of every tree of the garden?* To this the woman replied by repeating the Divine prohibition respecting the fruit of one particular tree. Thereupon the Tempter proceeded to declare that the penalty of death would not follow the eating of this fruit, nay that the Almighty knew that in the day they ate thereof, her eyes and those of her husband would be opened, and they would *become as gods*, knowing good and evil. A more subtle scheme for shaking her allegiance to the Almighty, and her confidence in His goodness and His love, could not have been devised.

A prohibition hitherto regarded as a solemn but merciful warning was now invested with an arbitrary character, and a selfish motive. In mere envy, so the Tempter affirmed, the Almighty had denounced an impossible penalty; what she had been taught to observe as the condition of innocence and happiness was nothing more than the expedient of One, who grudged His creatures their rightful advancement, lest they should approach too nearly to Himself[1]. The idea of an envious God, of a *hard taskmaster*, was thus instilled into the mind of Eve, sapping the foundations of all real faith and trust, and rendering the more irresistible the temptation to disobey the command of Him, who had thus enviously set these bounds to her freewill. In an evil hour she believed the Tempter's words, and seeing that the *tree was good for food, that it was pleasant to the eyes, and a tree to be desired to make one wise,* she took of the fruit, and did eat, and gave also unto her husband with her, and he did eat. Thus the fell counsels of the Tempter were accomplished. Through want of faith in God's word, through a longing for independence, through a vain desire to become gods unto themselves, our first parents were beguiled into sin, and when *their eyes were opened,* instead of greater happiness they now experienced the strange and hitherto unknown consciousness of shame, and degradation, and unmeetness for God's presence (Gen. iii. 1—7.).

Brief and summary as is the information here given us respecting the enigma of enigmas, the origin of Evil, it is yet of unspeakable importance. For it teaches us that Sin is not a *part* of man's nature, but *the fault and corruption*[2] of it, that it did not spring from his nature by any inevitable necessity, but in consequence

---

[1] Hence the idea of an *envious* and jealous God so common in heathenism, as in Herodotus, I. 32, III. 40, VII. 46.

[2] The Ninth Article of the Church of England.

of his yielding to the seductions of a powerful and malignant Foe. He did not, like his Tempter, choose sin for its own sake, but was *beguiled* into it. Hence, though he became liable to all the penal consequences of his disobedience, though his being was *poisoned* with sin, yet it was not *converted* into sin. He did not lose all remembrance of his former state of purity and innocence; the shame which overwhelmed him and made him hide himself from the presence of God, testified to his consciousness of transgression, and in this sense of guilt lay the possibility of his restoration [1].

For now the Sacred Narrative, while it refuses to gratify our curiosity respecting a subject which doubtless passes our understanding, proceeds to do what is for us of far greater practical importance, namely, to place the inroad of sin in immediate connection with the Divine Counsels of Redemption. We learn that God in infinite mercy now intervened between His creatures and their Tempter. For them, indeed, it remained to taste the bitter fruits of their disobedience and mistrust. Eve was informed that sorrow and pain must henceforth be the condition of her existence; *in sorrow should she bring forth children, her desire should be to her husband, and he should rule over her* (Gen. iii. 16). Adam learnt that with himself henceforth nature too must undergo a change; *thorns and thistles* must grow upon the face of the earth, toil must be the price of his existence, and his end the silence of the grave, for *dust he was, and unto dust he must return.* Even thus, however, Justice was tempered with sweet Mercy, and Love mingled blessings with the bitterness of man's cup. If pain and multiplied

---

[1] Kurtz's *History of the Old Covenant*, I. 49: "However weakened and darkened by sin, the divine image in man is not wholly destroyed (Gen. ix. 6, James iii. 9), and even after the Fall man continues the offspring of God (Acts xvii. 28)."

sorrow was to be woman's lot, yet through pain she was to know a mysterious joy, and her anguish should be no more remembered, when she knew that *a man was born into the world.* And if grievous toil and irksome labour were to be the conditions of man's existence, yet in the provision of these effectual antidotes to idleness and many other sins was truest mercy. But these gracious purposes extended only to man, they tempered not the judgment denounced on his Seducer. Utterly *cursed was he above all cattle, and above every beast of the field.* The very creature, over whom he had seemed to triumph, should prove his ultimate Conqueror. *I will put enmity,* said the Almighty to the Tempter, *between thee and the woman, and between thy seed and her seed; it shall bruise thy head, and thou shalt bruise his heel.* In these words we trace the *first* distinct *Promise* of man's ultimate Redemption. The state of degradation, into which he had suffered himself to be seduced, was not to last for ever. " In conformity with the Divine Equity, the deceiver was to be judged by the deceived, the Conqueror was to be overcome by the conquered[1]." Man need not give himself up to despair; there was still room for hope; in infinite mercy the Almighty had espoused his cause, and He would Himself provide a remedy for his fall.

We need not venture on any profitless speculations touching the precise amount of hope the early generations of the human family were likely to have derived from this first Gospel, this "first Promise" of a Saviour. In terms it was undoubtedly indefinite. Neither the time, nor the method, nor the precise mediating cause of man's deliverance was made known. It was not revealed whether the promised "Seed" should be one or many, the collective Race, or a single Deliverer. On these points greater light was to be shed as time

[1] Kurtz's *Sacred History,* p. 48.

rolled on, and many things were to be revealed, which now man could not comprehend. But of the final *Victory*, and of its *certainty*, direct and explicit assurance was given. "Since religion cannot so much as exist without *hope*, the earliest intimation of Prophecy was adapted to the support of that essential feeling in the heart of man. It was clearly a promise of relief, an antidote to perfect despair. It contained the prediction that some one should be born of the Seed of the Woman, who 'should bruise the head of the Tempter,' by whom, therefore, the penal effect of man's transgression should be in some way reversed. With all its uncertainty as to the mode in which this End should be effected, the Promise had within it a principle of *Hope* and *Encouragement*, and the materials of a religious trust fitted to keep man still looking to his Maker[1]."

In the encouraging assurance thus given to Adam, in this first Promise of a Saviour, Sacred History finds its definite starting-point, and the Old Testament becomes a true introduction to the New, because it reveals the several steps whereby the Divine Wisdom provided for its fulfilment. From first to last Sacred History is "instinct with life and hope;" it ever points onward to the future; its key-note is ever preparation for the Coming of HIM, who was to be the true "Seed of the Woman," in whom the Father counselled before the worlds to *gather together in one all things, both which are in heaven, and which are on earth* (Eph. i. 10; Phil. ii. 9, 10).

[1] Davison, *On Prophecy*, p. 55.

CHAPTER III.

THE FLOOD.

THE FLOOD.

Gen. iv.—ix. B. C. 4004—2348.

THOUGH thus assured of ultimate restoration, the first man, as a fallen being, could not be permitted to remain in the region, which had been the scene of his trial and his failure. He might take of the fruit of another Tree, that grew in the midst of the Garden, the *Tree of Life*, and eat, and live for ever, and thus prevent the possibility of his recovery. Accordingly he was sent forth from the Garden, at the east of which were stationed Cherubim, a particular order, in all probability, of Angels (Comp. Ex. xxv. 17—22 ; Ezek. i. 5, Rev. iv. 6), while a *flaming Sword which turned every way* guarded the approach to the Tree of Life.

Thus driven forth from Eden, and re-commencing under new and altered circumstances their course of probation, Adam and Eve in due time became the parents of two sons, CAIN (*gotten*, or *acquired*), and ABEL (*breath, transitoriness*). From their earliest years the most opposite tendencies distinguished the brothers. The mysterious rite of sacrifice, which meets us at the very threshold of Sacred History, and which, it is supposed, not without probability, the Almighty Himself instituted, when He made for the first pair *coats of skins, and clothed them* (Gen. iii. 21), became the occasion of a fatal quarrel between them. Cain brought of the fruit of the ground, Abel of the firstlings of his flock, an offering unto the Lord. The offering of Abel was accepted, that of Cain rejected. The reason for this distinction cannot be pronounced with absolute certainty. Either the offering of Abel was a free and bounteous presentation of the best that he had, while that of Cain was merely commonplace and perfunctory, or Abel brought his offering in a spirit of faith, and trustful acquiescence in a divinely-instituted though mysterious command (Heb. xi. 4), a motive which the offering of his elder brother lacked. Whatever was the precise reason of the distinction, it roused all Cain's latent jealousy, and he became his brother's murderer (1 Joh. iii. 12). For thus shedding *righteous blood* (Matt. xxiii. 35) he was condemned by the Almighty to perpetual banishment from the region of Eden. Fearful of vengeance from the other children of Adam, whose family we may infer from the mention of Cain's wife had largely increased, he feared to depart before he received from the Almighty a special sign or pledge of security in the land of his banishment[1]. This having been granted, he removed into the region of Nod (*exile*), and there became the ancestor of numerous descendants, the heads of whom are enumerated to the sixth generation, under the names of Enoch, Irad, Mehu-jael, Methusael, and Lamech. In this region, too, he built the earliest city of which we have any record, and called it *Enoch*, after the name of his eldest son. The Cainite families were distinguished for their attention to the development of the arts and pleasures of life. As Cain built the first city, so Lamech instituted polygamy, while of his three sons JABAL introduced the nomadic life, JUBAL the use of musical instruments, and TUBAL-CAIN the art of working in metals (Gen. iv. 16—24).

Meanwhile with another son SETH (*substituted*), who had been given to Adam in place of Abel, commenced a line distinct in its social and religious tendencies from that of Cain. The heads of this family are enumerated

---

[1] This seems to be the true meaning of the expression, *the Lord set a mark upon Cain.* Compare the sign given to Noah (Gen. ix. 13), to Moses (Ex. iii. 2, 12), to Elijah (1 Kings xix. 11), to Hezekiah (Isai. xxxviii. 7, 8).

to the tenth generation under the names of Seth, Enos, Cainan, Mahalaleel, Jared, Enoch, Methuselah, Lamech, Noah. While the descendants of Cain advanced indeed in civilization, but were addicted to luxury and violence, the descendants of Seth were distinguished for pastoral simplicity. They *called upon the name of the Lord* (Gen. iv. 26); they were the chosen repositories of the Promise of Redemption, and the witnesses for a God of Righteousness in the midst of a generation which already began to become corrupt, and in the seen to forget the unseen. An eminent type of the characteristic virtues of this line was ENOCH, the son of Jared, *the seventh from Adam* (Jude 14). All his life long he walked in closest communion with the Most High and the spiritual world. Faith (Heb. xi. 5), implicit trust in a Righteous Ruler of the Universe, was the principle of his life, and the secret spring of his holiness. One day he vanished from the society of his fellowmen. *He was not,* for the God whom he served *took him* to Himself, and translated him to the unseen world, without undergoing the penalty of death (Gen. v. 21—24).

A peculiar feature of this period was the great length to which human life was prolonged. Adam attained to the age of 930 years, Methuselah to that of 969, the others nearly as long. From this accrued many advantages to the race. It tended to promote its speedy increase, it preserved uninterrupted such knowledge as men were able to acquire, and pre-eminently the original revelation respecting the one true God, the remembrance of Paradise, and the hope of ultimate Redemption. But the great longevity of the men of this period did not tend to hinder their increasing alienation from the paths of righteousness, and obedience to the Supreme. Amidst the extreme brevity of the sacred narrative it is clear that the wickedness of men reached a desperate pitch, *the earth was filled with violence,*

and *all men corrupted their way* upon it. At length
this alienation from God reached its culminating point
in a catastrophe, to which the Sacred Record attaches
a peculiar and mysterious importance. *When men began
to multiply on the face of the earth, and daughters
were born unto them, the sons of God saw the daughters of men that they were fair, and they took them
wives of all that they chose.* Whatever be the true
meaning of the expression *sons of God,* whether it
refers to the Angels, as some have thought, or the
descendants of Seth, certain it is that a superhuman
spirit of wickedness broke out at this period. From
these mixed marriages sprang men remarkable for
strength and power, for violence and arrogant wickedness, through whom both races speedily became hope-
lessly corrupt. The salt even in the line of Seth lost
its savour, and *the wickedness of man was great on
the earth, and every imagination of the thoughts of
his heart was only evil continually* (Gen. vi. 1—5).

In this awful crisis one man only found favour with
God, NOAH, the son of Lamech, in whom at his birth,
with prophetic glance his father beheld a pledge of that
rest and *comfort,* which the men of faith felt they so
sorely needed from the burden of weary and irksome
labour on *the ground which Jehovah had cursed*
(Gen. v. 29). When Noah was 500 years old, he became
the father of three sons, SHEM, HAM, and JAPHETH.
Like Enoch he was a *righteous and perfect man in
his generation,* and in this age of universal apostasy
maintained an unflinching trust in the Righteous Ruler
of the Universe, and at length, when the cup of man's
iniquity was full, he received intimation from the Almighty of His intention to bring an awful judgment
upon the world. *Behold I, even I,* said God, *do bring
a flood of waters upon the earth, to destroy all flesh,
wherein is the breath of life, from under heaven; and*

everything that is in the earth shall die. From the general catastrophe Noah and his family alone were to be preserved, and he was directed to construct an Ark, a huge vessel of enormous dimensions, into which, when completed, he was to repair with his wife, his three sons and their wives, and also two of every species of beasts and birds accounted "unclean" or unfit for sacrifice, and seven of every species accounted "clean." The vessel thus ordered was to be constructed of gopherwood, probably cypress, and was to be overlaid within and without with pitch or bitumen; in length it was to be 300 cubits, in breadth 50, in depth 30. But though the impending Judgment was thus announced, and a visible pledge of it directed to be constructed, the Doom itself was not to be as yet. He who afterwards waited 400 years till the *cup of the iniquity of the Amorites* was full, who gave the Ninevites forty days for repentance, now *waited* (1 Pet. iii. 20), *with much long-suffering,* for a space of 120 years.

During this period *according to all that God commanded Noah, so did he.* Though the things, of which he was warned, *were not yet seen* (Heb. xi. 7), nay, must have seemed to the men of his generation in the extremest degree improbable, *moved with fear* he yet persevered in his awful task, and by this act of faith, as well as by his own works, continued to warn his fellowmen of what was to come. But his warnings fell on unheeding ears. The men of his generation set at naught all his counsel and mocked at his reproofs: they *did eat, they drank, they married wives, they were given in marriage* (Matt. xxiv. 38; Lk. xvii. 26, 27), until the day of Doom arrived. On the seventeenth day of the second month of the 600th year of Noah's life he and his family entered into the Ark, and *the Lord shut them in.* Then, after a solemn pause of seven days, the elements of destruction were bidden to do their work. *The fountains of the great deep were broken up, the windows of heaven were opened,* and the rain descended, till the waters covered the highest hills, *and all flesh wherein was the breath of life died, of fowl, of cattle, of wild beast, and of every creeping thing which creepeth upon the earth, and every man.*

In these simple but impressive words the Sacred Narrative describes the appalling catastrophe. Written for a far higher purpose, it paints no scenes as a human writer would have done. " We see nothing of the death-struggle; we hear not the cry of despair; we are not called upon to witness the frantic agony of husband and wife, of parent and child, as they fled in terror before the rising waters. Not a word is said of the sadness of the one righteous man who, safe himself, looked upon the destruction, which he could not avert. But one impression is left upon the mind with peculiar vividness, from the very simplicity of the narrative, and it is that of utter desolation[1]." All flesh died, Noah only was left, and they that were with him in the ark. For 150 days the waters prevailed, till at length on the 17th day of the 7th month the Ark rested on one of the peaks of Ararat. From this time the waters gradually decreased till the first day of the 10th month, when the tops of the mountains having begun to appear, Noah sent forth a raven, which returned not to the Ark. A week afterwards he sent forth a dove, to see if the waters were abated from the lower and more level country. But the dove finding *no rest for the sole of her foot* returned unto the Ark. Again he waited seven days, and once more sent her forth, when she returned with a fresh olive-leaf *pluckt off in her mouth,* a sign that the waters had still further subsided. Yet again, after a similar interval, Noah sent her forth. This time, how-

[1] Smith's *Bibl. Dict.* Art. *Noah.*

ever, she did not return, having found on the earth *a rest for the sole of her foot,* and then he knew that the awful Judgment had indeed come to a close, and at the Divine command left the Ark, and set foot on the dry land[1] (Gen. viii. 1—19).

CHAPTER IV

THE CONFUSION OF TONGUES.

Gen. x.—xi.   B.C. 2347—2233.

THE first act of Noah on leaving the Ark was to build an altar, and offer burnt-offerings unto the Lord *of every clean beast, and of every clean fowl.* His sacrifice was accepted, and now for the first time a solemn Covenant was ratified between the Almighty and the Patriarch, to which definite promises were annexed, and "an outward and visible sign." From its baptism of water the Earth had risen once more to be the habitation of man, and Noah and his sons were solemnly assured that all flesh should never again be cut off by the waters of a Flood, but that *while the earth remained, seed-time and harvest, cold and heat,*

---

[1] The traditions of many nations preserve the recollection of the Flood. They may be found in the Chaldæan and Phœnician mythology, among the Persian, Indian, Chinese, and American nations. The Greeks had their tradition of Deucalion and Pyrrha. Among the Phrygians was a legend of a King Annakos or Nannakos in Iconium, who lived to the age of 400 years, foretold the Flood, and in prospect of the destruction awaiting them, wept and prayed for his people. As late as the time of Septimius Severus, a medal was struck at Apamea commemorating this event. On it is the representation of a square vessel floating on the water, and through an opening in it two persons, a man and a woman, are visible. On the top a bird is perched, while another is flying towards it carrying a branch between its feet. In front of the vessel the same pair stand as though they had just landed on dry ground. On some specimens the letters ΝΩ or ΝΩΕ have been found. See Kurtz's *Sacred History,* p. 56.

summer and winter and day and night should not cease. Again too the blessing of Paradise was bestowed, sovereignty and dominion over the animal creation were assured, and once more men were bidden to *be fruitful, and multiply, and replenish the earth.* At the same time animal food was expressly allowed, while the sanctity of human life was as solemnly enforced, *whoso shed man's blood, by man should his blood be shed.* Of this covenant the Rainbow was the visible pledge, assuring man that he might enter afresh on his course of probation, nor dread its interruption by any catastrophe like that with which the earth had been so lately visited (Gen. ix. 8—17).

The elevation of the Armenian plateau, in the neighbourhood of which the Ark had rested, being equidistant between the Black and Caspian Seas on the north, the Persian Gulf and Mediterranean Sea on the south, being also the region in which all the great rivers of Western Asia, the Tigris, the Euphrates, the Araxes, and the Halys take their rise, formed a natural and convenient centre whence the descendants of Noah might overspread the whole earth. But on this migration they did not set out, before an unseemly incident revealed the natural character of his sons, prophetic of their future destinies. Noah began to practise agriculture, and planted a vineyard, and through ignorance, as it has been supposed, of its properties, drank of the wine in excess, and lay exposed in his tent. Ham, his youngest son, mocked him while he lay in this condition, but Shem and Japheth, with more filial feeling, averting their eyes covered their father with a garment. Awaking from his slumbers Noah became conscious of what his youngest son had done, and justly angry at the irreverence he had displayed, brake forth into prophetic utterances of blessing and cursing, foreshadowing the diverse destinies of the descendants of his family. Upon CANAAN, the fourth son of Ham, and probably a partaker in his father's transgression, he pronounced the doom of perpetual servitude to his brethren[1]. Shem he declared to be *the chosen one of Jehovah*, from whom the promised Salvation should proceed, while Japheth, *multiplied* and *enlarged* should *dwell in his tents*[2], and be received as a partaker in his spiritual privileges.

With their future destinies thus foretold, the sons of Noah went forth, and took up their abode for some time on the rich alluvial plain of Shinar between the Tigris and Euphrates. Here their descendants began to form a great fraternal community, which it was the more easy to do, seeing that they all proceeded from the same parental home, and *had all one language*. But here, in defiance of the Divine command, which bade them disperse themselves abroad and *replenish the whole earth*, they resolved to make a City and a huge Tower *whose top might reach unto heaven*, to serve as a central point of union, and a great World-Metropolis. But their design was counteracted. The Almighty interposed, and by confounding their language, so that they could not understand one another's speech, rent the closest bond of human society. Unable to continue the erection of their City and Tower, which was henceforth

[1] This prediction that Canaan should become the servant of Shem is thought to have been primarily fulfilled, when the nations of Palestine were conquered by Joshua (Josh. xviii. 10; xxiii. 4; 2 Chron. viii. 7, 8), when Tyre fell before the arms of Alexander, and, again, when the Carthaginians were subdued by the Romans.

[2] The words *he shall dwell in the tents of Shem* are somewhat obscure. If they denote that God would dwell in his tents, they probably refer to the fact that the "promised Seed" was restricted to this line, and the special presence of God with the Jews (Rom. ix. 4, 5); if they mean that Japheth should dwell in his tents, they probably point to the occupation of Palestine and the surrounding countries by the Romans, and in a spiritual sense to the adoption of the Gentiles into the Church of God (Eph. iii. 6).

called Babel or *Confusion,* they were scattered abroad over the face of the earth, and thus constrained to fulfil the eternal designs of Him, who has *determined the times before appointed, and the bounds of the habitations* of the sons of men (Acts xvii. 26)[1].

Before, however, it leaves them to pursue their own ways, the Sacred Narrative presents to us a Genealogical Table, in which the names of the several nations descended from Noah, and their geographical distribution, have been preserved. With this Table antiquity has handed down nothing that can be compared for accuracy or comprehensiveness. " It exposes the fallacies of the mythical genealogies of pagans, contradicts their fables respecting gods, heroes, and periods of millions of years, and also affords a firm foundation for investigations concerning the origin and the traditions of nations." From this Table, then, it appears that

(i) The descendants of JAPHETH (*enlargement*) after leaving the original cradle of the human race, occupied chiefly *the isles of the Gentiles,* or the coast-lands of the Mediterranean Sea in Asia Minor and Europe, and thence spread chiefly in a northerly direction over the entire European Continent, and a great portion of Asia. Thus GOMER was the ancestor of the Cymmerians or Cimbri, MAGOG of the Scythians, MADAI of the Medes, JAVAN of the Ionians and Greek race, TUBAL and MESECH of the Tibareni and Moschi, two Colchian tribes, and TIRAS of the Thracians.

(ii) The descendants of HAM ("*heat*") proceeded in a southerly direction, and occupied the whole of Africa, and the Southern peninsulas of Asia, India, and Arabia. Of his four sons CUSH extended his settlements from

---

[1] An approximate indication of the Time when this Dispersion took place is afforded in Gen. x. 25, where we find one of the descendants of Shem named Peleg (" *Division*"), *for in his days was the earth divided.*

Babylonia to Ethiopia, MIZRAIM colonized Egypt, PHUT Libya, and CANAAN the land called by his name.

(iii) The descendants of SHEM established themselves in Central Asia, and thence extended in an easterly and westerly direction, ARAM colonising the country afterwards known as Syria, LUD Lydia, ARPHAXAD Chaldæa, ASSHUR part of Assyria, ELAM Persia, JOKTAN a portion of the Arabian peninsula (Gen. x. 1—26).

Thus He, *who hath made of one blood all nations of men for to dwell on all the face of the earth* (Acts xvii. 26), directed the repeopling of the world by the descendants of Noah. Like prodigal sons they were to go into far countries, and learn by bitter experience that neither human strength nor human wisdom can work out *the righteousness of God*, or win back for man his lost inheritance. But the preservation of their names in this Table of Nations is a proof that no one of them was forgotten by a God of Love; that though they might forget Him He yet guided their destinies, and overruled their counsels only to the accomplishment of His gracious purposes of Redemption. The Day of Pentecost in the New Testament corresponds to the Confusion of Tongues in the Old. Then, not till then, did men hear, each in their tongue wherein they were born, the Glad Tidings of ONE, very God and very Man, in whom *there is neither Jew nor Gentile, neither bond nor free, neither male nor female* (Gal. iii. 28).

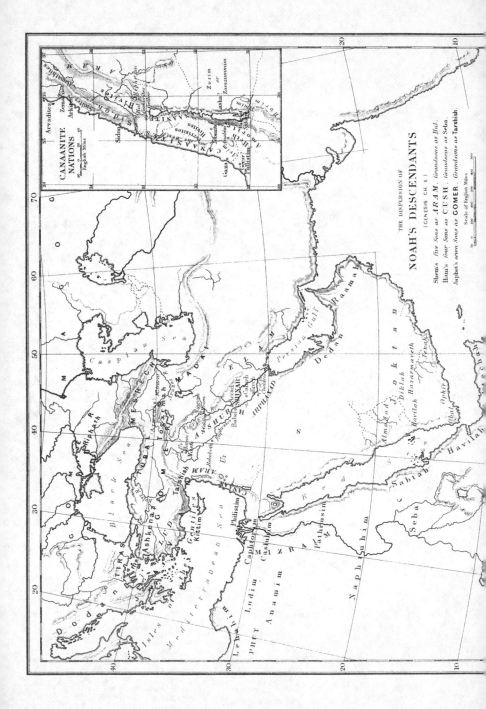

THE DISPERSION OF

NOAH'S DESCENDANTS

(GENESIS CH. X.)

Shem's *five Sons as* ARAM. *Grandsons as* Hul.
Ham's *four Sons as* CUSH. *Grandsons as* Seba.
Japhet's *seven Sons as* GOMER. *Grandsons as* Tarshish.

Scale of English Miles

CANAANITE
NATIONS

English Miles

CHAPTER V

RISE OF IDOLATRY—THE PATRIARCH JOB.

Gen. x. 6—12.   Job.

SACRED History does not record many facts connected with the immediate descendants of Noah.
The scene of the Confusion of Tongues continued to attract around it a large number of the early inhabitants
of the world, and here was established one of the earliest
of the great empires of the earth by Nimrod, a son of
Cush, and grandson of Ham. Of great powers and
gigantic stature, he first obtained wide-spread renown
by his exploits as *a mighty hunter*, and the services he
rendered the surrounding populations by ridding them
of the terror of noxious and terrible animals. In process of time, however, he combined with his exploits as
a hunter the conquest of men, and founded a great
empire on the plains of Shinar, the chief towns of which
were Babel, Erech (*Edessa*), Accad (*Nisibis*), and Calneh
(*Ctesiphon*). Thence (for such seems to be the meaning
of Gen. x. 11) he extended his dominions along the
course of the Tigris into Assyria, amongst the descendants of Shem, where he founded a second group of
cities, Nineveh, Rehoboth, Calah, and Resen. At a
period when men's lives were prolonged so far beyond
the period now allotted them, it is probable that this
great conqueror may have carried on his successful inva-
sions for nearly 200 years, and after death was worshipped under the title of Belus, or Bel, *the Lord*.
Certainly the vast ruins that overspread the site of the
ancient Babylonian empire seem to tell of the days when
there were great heroes in the earth; and to Nimrod
the modern Arabs ascribe all the great works of ancient times, the *Birs-Nimrûd*, near Babylon, *Tel Nim-*

rûd, near Baghdad, and the *Mount of Nimrûd,* near Mosul[1].

Whether the practice of idolatrous worship was introduced, as some have supposed, by this great hero of the ancient world, or not, certain it is that mankind became more and more addicted to idolatry. Though the knowledge of the one true God, and the promise of salvation, had been handed down by tradition, and though His invisible attributes, *even His eternal power and Godhead,* were clearly to be discerned in the works of creation (Rom. i. 19, 20), yet mankind *glorified Him not as God, neither were they thankful.* They began *to worship and serve the creature rather than the Creator.* The sun, moon, and stars, the principle of fire, even the inferior animals and departed heroes, came to be regarded with veneration, and usurped the worship due only to the Supreme. With idolatry came its usual consequences, a deep moral degeneracy, cruelty, tyranny, and licentiousness.

One of the earliest allusions to the worship of the heavenly bodies occurs in the Book of Job (xxxi. 26—28). The age and writer of this book are alike unknown; by some it is ascribed to Job himself, by others to Moses, by others to some writer who lived at a still later period. As, however, the scenes therein described had with great probability been referred to a period very little removed from that at which we have now arrived, it may be well to speak of them here. Job was an eminent Eastern chief, dwelling in very early times in the land of Uz (Job i. 1), probably Arabia Deserta, or, as some suppose, Mesopotamia. Greatest among "the sons of the East," endowed with all the riches of his age, he ruled piously and wisely over a happy and numerous household, having seven sons and three daughters. To

---

[1] Smith's *Dictionary of the Bible,* Article *Nimrod.*

considerable mental attainments he added a moral
uprightness, which preserved him blameless in all the
relations of life, and was declared by the Lord Himself
to be *without his like in all the earth, a perfect and an
upright man, one that feared God, and eschewed evil*
(Job i. 8). With large and liberal hand he distributed to
the necessities of the poor, so that whenever *the ear
heard him then it blessed him, when the eye saw him it
gave witness to him; the blessing of him that was ready
to perish came upon him, and he caused the widow's
heart to sing for joy.* But in the midst of this almost
perfect temporal happiness he was suddenly overwhelmed
with the heaviest misfortunes that can befall the sons of
men. He who slandered God to Eve slandered Job before
God, and affirmed that he did not fear Him for naught;
that if he were stripped of all his possessions he would
be as other men, and curse the Lord to His face (i. 11).
To put, therefore, the patriarch's faith to the most certain test, the Accuser of mankind received mysterious
permission to cast him down, and try him with the
most grievous afflictions. Blow after blow descended
upon him. From being the lord of a numerous and
attached household he suddenly became childless, for
the storm of the desert swept over the house where
his sons and daughters were assembled, and crushed
them all beneath its ruins. From being the richest of
the sons of the East he suddenly became a beggar, for
the thunderbolt, "the fire of God," fell and struck down
all his sheep, as they were grazing quietly with their
shepherds, while his camels were carried off by a band of
Chaldean robbers, and his oxen and asses by a horde of
Sabeans. And not only did he become a childless,
beggared, ruined man, but upon his own body the
black leprosy of the East set its awful mark, making
him an object hateful and loathsome to look upon.
Smitten with sores *from the sole of his foot even unto*

his crown, he sat apart, forsaken by his friends and even by his wife. But amidst these awful trials his faith was not prostrated. When the terrible tidings reached him of the fate of his household he said, in words of sublime resignation, *The Lord gave, and the Lord hath taken away, and blessed be the name of the Lord;* when his wife, utterly unable to bear up, bade him curse his Maker and die, he replied, *What? shall we receive good at the hand of God, and shall we not receive evil?* (Job i. 21, ii. 10).

Before long the news of his terrible affliction was noised abroad, and three of his old friends, Eliphaz from Teman, Bildad from Shuah, and Zophar of Naamath, came *to mourn with him and to comfort him.* In their presence Job at length brake forth into desperate words, and *cursed the day of his birth* (Job iii. 1). The storm of his soul was not calmed by the sympathy of his friends. Instead of pouring in the oil of comfort, they only heightened his griefs by ascribing his calamities to some great sin, some secret guilt, if not committed by himself at least by his children, for which he was now punished. A distinct question was thus propounded, Is great suffering a proof of great guilt? Job's friends affirmed it was, and exhorted him to repent and confess. Job denied, and at great length laboured to refute this (Job iv. 5—xxxii). At the close of their dialogue, Elihu, another and younger friend of the patriarch, intervened, to moderate between the disputants. Unable to solve the problem of Job's calamities, he declared that afflictions, even when not the direct consequences of sin, were intended for good, and he reproved his friend for justifying himself rather than the Almighty, and speaking unadvisedly of His works (Job xxxii—xxxvii). At length the Lord Himself condescended to interpose in the controversy. From the midst of a whirlwind, in words of incomparable grandeur and sublimity, he silenced the murmurs of his servant, bidding him reflect on the glory of creation, and learn from the marvels of the animal kingdom the stupendous power and wisdom of Him with whom it is useless for a created being to contend (Job xxxviii—xli). Thereupon, in deep contrition, Job acknowledged his error and supplicated the Divine pardon for the bitterness and arrogance of his complaints. This penitent acknowledgment was accepted, and Job's three friends were severely reproved for their uncharitable surmises respecting the origin of his misfortunes. On the intercession, however, of the patriarch they were pardoned; and He who had suffered him to be thus sorely tried, when his trials had served the purpose for which they had been sent, once more showered down upon him the riches of His goodness, restoring him to still greater prosperity than he had even enjoyed before, and made him the father of seven sons and three daughters[1], celebrated for their beauty above all the maidens of the East. Job survived his altered fortunes upwards of 140 years, and then, having seen his children to the fourth generation, died in a good old age, an instructive example of integrity (Ezek. xiv. 14, 20), and of patience under the most trying calamities (Jas. v. 11).

[1] Jemima = *day* or a *dove*, Kezia = *cassia*, a sweet aromatic plant, and Keren-Happuch = either *horn of antimony*, the pigment used by Eastern ladies to colour the eye-lashes, or, according to the LXX., *horn of plenty*.

BOOK II

THE PATRIARCHAL AGE.

CHAPTER I

THE CALL OF ABRAHAM.

Gen. xi. B. C. 1921.

THERE will always, perhaps, be a doubt as to the exact period after the Flood when Job lived, but there can be no doubt that neither his constancy nor his faithfulness to the one true God, were the characteristics of the age succeeding the Flood. Within ten generations after that event mankind had again become forgetful of their Maker, and corrupted their way, threatening a fresh outbreak of violence and irreligion. Now, however, it was not the purpose of the Almighty to visit the earth with any universal judgment. In the counsels of Redemption it was His will to select a man, and through him, a nation, to be His witness upon earth, to withdraw this nation from contact with the surrounding world, to place it under a special and peculiar constitution, to entrust to it the guardianship of ancient truths and of future hopes, and out of it to bring, *in the fulness of time* (Gal. iv. 4), the promised Saviour of the human race.

At this point, then, Sacred History becomes more full, and its stream hitherto slender widens into a broad river. Mighty empires and great nations seem for a while to be forgotten, but only because we are now to be more especially concerned with the history of that particular nation, in and through which *all nations of the earth were to be blessed* (Gen. xii. 3).

The man selected by the Almighty to be the ancestor of a people destined to exert so momentous an influence on the salvation of the world was ABRAHAM, or, as he was first called, *Abram*, the son of Terah, who lived in the eighth generation from Shem, in Ur of the Chaldees. Besides Abram, Terah had two other sons, Nahor and Haran, but Abram, though mentioned first, was in all probability the youngest of the three. From Ur, which may perhaps be identified with the modern *Orfah*[1], in upper Mesopotamia, where his family had become tainted with the generally prevailing idolatry (Josh. xxiv. 2, 14), Terah removed, and travelling in a southerly direction arrived at Haran or Charran[2], where he stayed. In this journey he was accompanied by his son Abram, his daughter-in-law Sarai, and his grandson Lot, and seems to have intended to go into the land of Canaan (Gen. xi. 31), but this was prevented by his death at Haran, when he had reached the age of 205. After this event, a still more distinct intimation of the

---

[1] Called by the Greeks Edessa, and Callirrhoe, "the Beautiful Spring," from a "pool of transparent clearness" hard by. Others place Ur at *Mugheir*, much further to the south, and on the right bank of the Euphrates, about six miles from the present course of the stream.

[2] Haran, or Charræ, now *Harrán*, in N.W. Mesopotamia, situated "on the point of divergence between the great caravan routes towards the various fords of the Euphrates and the Tigris," was afterwards celebrated for its temple of Luna, the Moon-goddess, and still more as the scene of the famous defeat of Crassus by the Parthian general Suræna. Here the descendants of Abraham's brother Nahor settled, so that Haran is called *the city of Nahor* (Gen. xxiv. 10; xxvii. 43).

Divine Will was made to his son Abram, bidding him leave his country, his kindred, and his father's house, and go to a land which God would shew him. *There,* said the Almighty, *I will make of thee a great nation, and make thy name great, and in thee shall all the families of the earth be blessed.* Severe as were the hardships which this call involved, painful as it must have been to flesh and blood to sever the ties which bound him to his family and his people, Abram did not refuse to follow the Hand which promised him guidance, protection, and a mighty future. At the age of 75, with his wife Sarai, his nephew Lot, and all that he possessed, he left Haran, crossed the Euphrates, and commenced his journey southward and westward towards the *Land of Promise* (Acts vii. 4, 5).

This country, the future home of the great nation destined to spring from his loins, was in many respects eminently adapted for its special mission in the history of the World. In extent, indeed, it was but a narrow strip of country, but a little larger than the six northern counties of England, being nearly 180 miles in length[1], and 75 miles in breadth, and having an area of about 13,600 English square miles. Bounded on the west by the Mediterranean Sea, on the north by the mountains of Lebanon, on the east by the Syrian desert, on the south by the wilderness of Arabia, it was situated at the meeting-point of the two continents of Asia and Africa, "on the very outpost, on the extremest

---

[1] The distance from London to York or Exeter. The limits here taken are the parallels of 31^0 and $33\frac{1}{2}^0$ north latitude, and the meridian of 34^0 to that of 36^0 east longitude. "In Palestine, as in Greece, every traveller is struck with the smallness of the territory. He is surprised, even after all that he has heard, at passing, in one long day, from the capital of Judea to that of Samaria; or at seeing within 8 hours, three such spots as Hebron, Bethlehem, and Jerusalem." Stanley, *Sinai and Palestine,* 114; see Note below, p. 367.

western edge of the East." It was a secluded land. A wilderness encompassed it on the east and south, mountains shut it in on the north, and the "Great Sea" which washed its western shore was the terror rather than the thoroughfare of ancient nations. "Unlike the coast of Europe, and especially of Greece, it had no indentations, no winding creeks, no deep havens[1]," but one small port—that of Joppa—with which to tempt the mariner from the west. But while thus eminently adapted to be the "silent and retired nursery of the Kingdom of God[2]," it was in the very centre of the activity of the ancient world, *in the midst of the nations, and the countries that were round about it* (Ezek. v. 5). On the South was the great empire of Egypt, on the Northeast the rising kingdom of Assyria. Neither of these great nations could communicate with the other without passing through Palestine, and so learning something of its peculiar institutions and religion; and when the *fulness of time was come* no country was better suited, from its position at the extremest verge of the Eastern World, to be the starting-point whence the glad tidings of Redemption might be proclaimed to all nations[3]. Moreover, narrow as were its limits, and secluded as

---

[1] Stanley's *S. and P.* p. 113.

[2] Kurtz's *History of the Old Covenant*, I. 147, 8.

[3] "All the *routes*—both by land and water—which connected the three parts of the ancient world, passed through Palestine. The commerce between Asia on the one, and Europe and Africa on the other hand, had its centre in the great mercantile cities of Phœnicia and Philistia. Towards the South the Araba led to the Gulf of Elath, and the Shephelah to that of Heroopolis, while toward the East the ordinary caravan road led to the neighbouring Euphrates, to the Persian Gulf, and thence to the important countries of Southern Asia. Even the highways which connected Asia and Africa touched Palestine. A much frequented commercial route led from Egypt to Gaza, and from Damascus over the plain of Jezreel to the Phœnician coast." Kurtz, I. 149.

was its position, it yet presented a greater variety of
surface, scenery and temperature than is to be found in
any other part of the world, and needed not to depend
on other countries for anything that either the luxuries
or actual wants of its inhabitants required. Four
broadly marked longitudinal regions divided its surface.
(i) First, there was the *low plain* of the western sea-
coast, broad towards the south, and gradually narrowing
towards the north, famous for the Shephelah (*the low
country*) with its waving corn-fields, and the vale of
Sharon (*level country*), the garden of Palestine. From
this was an ascent to (ii) *a strip of table-land*, every part
of which was more or less undulating, but increasing in
elevation from north to south[1], and broken only by the
plain of Jezreel or Esdraelon. To this succeeded a rapid
descent into (iii) *a deep fissure or valley*, through which
the Jordan (*the descender*), the only river of importance
in the country, rushes from its source at the base of
Hermon into the Dead Sea, the surface of which is no
less than 1316 feet below that of the Mediterranean[2].
Hence was a second ascent to (iv) a *strip of table-
land* on the east similar to that on the west, and
seeming with its range of purple-tinted mountains to
overhang Jerusalem itself. Crowned by the forests and

---

[1] Hence the cities of Judah are higher than the summits
of many mountains of Samaria and Galilee. Thus while
Tabor is 1865 feet above the sea-level, and Carmel 1800, as
high as the Peak in Derbyshire, Jerusalem is 2610 feet, or
higher than Plynlimmon, and Hebron 3029 feet, or nearly as
high as Helvellyn.

[2] While the lake of Cinneroth (or as it is called in the
New Testament *Tiberias*), is only 653 feet below the same
level. The two principal features in the course of the Jordan are its *descent* and its *sinuosity*. From its fountain-head
it rushes down one continuous plane, only broken by a series
of rapids or precipitous falls, traversing, in a space of 60
miles of latitude and 4 or 5 miles of longitude, at least 200
miles. See Smith's *Bib. Dict.* Article *Jordan*.

upland pastures of Gilead and Bashan, this eastern
table-land gradually melted into the desert which
rolled between it and the valley of Mesopotamia. Thus
within a very small space were crowded the most
diverse features of natural scenery, and the most varied
products. It was *a good land, a land of brooks of
water, of fountains and depths that spring out of
valleys and hills, a land flowing with milk and honey*
(Deut. viii. 7—9; xi. 10—12). The low plains yielded
luxuriant crops of wheat and barley, of rye and maize;
on the table-lands with their equable and moderate
climate grew the vine, the olive, the fig, the almond, the
pomegranate; in the tropical neighbourhood of Jericho
flourished the palm-tree and the balsam; while the
noble cedar waved on the mountains of Lebanon.

Such was the Land, secluded and yet central, narrow
and yet wonderfully diversified alike in its natural
features and its products, whither the Almighty now
bade Abram direct his steps. Striking across the great
Syrian desert, the patriarch kept on his southward
course, and having crossed the Jordan, *passed through
the land,* till he came to Shechem[1], situated between
the mountains Ebal and Gerizim. This spot, destined
afterwards to be so celebrated, was then only marked
by the majestic oak of Moreh, probably a Canaanitish
chief, but its many fountains, rills, and water-courses[2]

---

[1] " Shechem " (now *Nablous*) = " shoulder," " ridge," like
dorsum in Latin, was situated on the " saddle" or " shoulder"
of the heights which divide the waters there that flow to the
Mediterranean on the west and the Jordan on the east.

[2] "Here there are no impetuous torrents, yet there is
water ; water, too, in more copious supplies than any where
else in the land ; and it is just to its many fountains, rills,
water-courses, that the valley owes its exquisite beauty."
Van de Velde, I. 386. Stanley, *S. and P.* 142, 235. "The
whole valley," writes Dr Robinson, "was filled with gardens
of vegetables, and orchards of all kinds of fruits, watered by

made it then, as it ever has been since, a natural
pasture-ground for flocks and herds; and here Abram
halted, and learnt that he had reached the goal of his
long journey. *This land,* said God, *I will give unto
thy seed;* and at Shechem the patriarch built his first
altar to the Lord in the "Land of Promise[1]"(Gen. xii. 6,7).

Thence he afterwards removed southward a distance
of about twenty miles, to the strong mountain country
east of Bethel, or as it was then called Luz; one of the
finest tracts of the land for pasturage, and here he
erected his second altar unto the Lord. During his
sojourn in this neighbourhood he learnt that, though
the heir of mighty promises, he was not to be exempt
from his share of trials and disappointments. The first
that befell him was a grievous famine, caused probably
by a failure of the usual rains; in consequence of

fountains, which burst forth in various parts and flow westwards in refreshing streams," *Bibl. Res.* II. 275.

[1] " *The Canaanite was then in the land,*" Gen. xii. 6. Of
these seven Canaanitish nations, descended from Canaan the
son of Ham (Gen. x. 15—19), (i) the JEBUSITES inhabited
Jerusalem (Jebus) and its neighbourhood (Num. xiii. 29;
Josh. xi. 3; xv. 8, 63); (ii) the HITTITES, Hebron and its
vicinity (Gen. xxiii. 7, 10; Num. xiii. 29); (iii) the HIVITES
were located (*a*) north of the Jebusites about Gibeon and
Bethel (Josh. xi. 19) and Shechem (Gen. xxxiv. 2), (*b*) in the
neighbourhood of Hermon (Josh. xi. 3; Judg. iii. 3); (iv) the
AMORITES, or "*highlanders,*" the most powerful and warlike
tribe, occupied the country (*a*) between the Hittites and the
Dead Sea (Gen. xiv. 7, 13; Judg. i. 34—36); (*b*) at a later period, the east of Jordan, where they founded two great kingdoms, that of Og in Bashan and Sihon in S. Gilead (Num. xxi.
13—26; Deut. iii. 8; Judg. xi. 13, &c.); (v) the CANAAN-
ITES, "*lowlanders,*" were distributed along the sea-coast (Gen.
xv. 21; Exod. xxiii. 23; Josh. xi. 3) and the valley of the
Jordan (Num. xiii. 29), thus encircling (vi) the PERIZZITES,
who probably inhabited the high plains of the west country
under the range of Carmel (Gen. xiii. 7; Josh. xi. 3); the
position of (vii) the GIRGASHITES (Gen. x. 16; Deut. vii. 1)
is uncertain.

which, finding himself unable to support his numerous dependents, he resolved, though without direct Divine suggestion, to go down into Egypt, then, as always, the fertile granary of the neighbouring nations. As he drew near the land of the mighty Pharaohs, he reflected that the beauty of his wife might expose her to danger from the sensual, voluptuous Egyptians, and under the influence of these apprehensions persuaded her to stoop to an unworthy equivocation, and give herself out as his sister. What he anticipated came to pass. The princes of Egypt *beheld the woman that she was fair,* and recommended her to their monarch, by whom she was taken into his palace, while numerous presents of cattle and sheep were sent to her supposed brother. But the monarch found that the coming of the stranger into his palace involved him in serious troubles, *the Lord plagued Pharaoh with great plagues,* till, having ascertained the true relation between her and Abram, he sent her back to her husband, with a strong rebuke to the latter for the deception he had practised.

How long after this Abram stayed in Egypt we are not told. But at length his wealth in cattle, and gold and silver, having materially increased, he quitted the country, and once more took up his abode on his former camping-ground between Bethel and Ai. Hitherto his nephew Lot had accompanied him in all his wanderings, but now the increasing numbers of their flocks and herds generated a quarrel between their respective herdsmen, and it was plainly necessary that they should separate. With characteristic generosity Abram bade his nephew take the first choice, and select for himself, whether on the left hand or the right, a place for his new abode. From the high mountain-range[1] to the east of Bethel, where they were then encamped, Lot *lifted up his eyes* and looked down upon the wide and well-watered plain

[1] Stanley's *S. and P.* 218.

3

south of the Jordan, then a very *garden of the Lord*, *like the land of Egypt* (Gen. xiii. 10) they had so lately left. As yet no terrible convulsion had effaced the site of Sodom and Gomorrah and the other cities of the plain. Fair and fertile the coveted possession stretched onwards unto Zoar, and in spite of the notorious wickedness of the inhabitants Lot chose it for his abode, and the two *separated themselves the one from the other.* Though Abram was thus left to wait alone for the fulfilment of the Promise, he was not forgotten by the God in whom he trusted. A more full and more definite promise was now vouchsafed to him. *Lift up thine eyes*, said the Almighty, *and look from place to place where thou art, northward, and southward, and eastward, and westward; all the land which thou seest to thee will I give it, and to thy seed for ever; and I will make thy seed as the dust of the earth, so that if a man can number the dust of the earth, then shall thy seed also be numbered* (Gen. xiii. 14—17).

Thus encouraged, *the Friend of God* (Jas. ii. 23) removed his tent, and travelling southward took up his abode under the spreading terebinth[1] of Mamre, an Amorite prince (Gen. xiv. 13, 24), near Hebron, or as it was then called Kirjath-Arba, *the City of Arba* the father of Anak and the progenitor of the giant Anakim (Gen. xxiii. 2 ; xxxv. 27 ; Josh. xiv. 15). While dwelling peacefully in this neighbourhood, which like all other places he hallowed with an altar to Jehovah, he received one day unexpected tidings of his nephew Lot. The chiefs of the five cities in the tropical valley of the Jordan, SODOM, GOMORRAH, ADMAH, ZEBOIM, and BELAH, had for twelve years been subject to CHEDOR-LAOMER, a powerful king of Elam or Mesopotamia. But they had lately united together to throw off his yoke. Thereupon the King of Elam, aided by three other

---

[1] See Article *Oak*, in Smith's *Bibl. Dict.*

confederate chiefs, proceeded to make war against the southern kings. Sweeping down on a sudden foray, he smote the countries on the eastern uplands of the Jordan and the southern region of Mount Seir. Returning thence he ravaged all the country of the Amalekites, and with his allied chiefs met the kings of Sodom and Gomorrah in pitched battle in the Vale of Siddim, probably at the north-west corner of the Dead Sea. The five southern kings were utterly routed, and with much spoil and many captives the Assyrian invader commenced his return northwards. It was the news of this sudden invasion which now reached the ears of Abram. Without losing a moment he instantly armed his 318 trained servants, and, aided by the confederate chief Mamre and his brothers Eshcol and Aner, arose and pursued the Assyrians by night. The latter had in the meantime reached the neighbourhood of the Sidonian Laish, far up in the northern mountains. Thither, however, Abram pursued them, and falling upon them suddenly, while all unconscious of coming danger, he smote them and chased them to Hobah, on the left of Damascus. Thence, with the recovered captives, amongst whom was Lot, he returned, and at the *King's Dale*, not far from Hebron, was met by the King of Sodom, accompanied by a mysterious personage, who now meets us for the first and only time, named MELCHISEDEC, a king of Salem and priest of the Most High God. The sudden appearance of one thus uniting the kingly and priestly functions, of whose origin and family we know nothing, has led to much speculation. Putting aside more improbable conjectures, we may perhaps conclude that he was an eminent Canaanitish prince in the line of Ham, who had maintained the pure worship of the One true God, and who, according to a custom not uncommon in patriarchal times, was at once king and priest[1]. A sufficient

[1] For other notices of Melchisedec see Heb. vii. 1—21;

proof of his high dignity is afforded by the fact that to him the patriarch Abram reverently gave tithes of all that he had taken in his late successful expedition, and received his solemn blessing (Heb. vii. 2, 6). Before they parted the King of Sodom pressed Abram to take a portion of the spoil as his reward. This, however, the latter with his usual generosity firmly declined; he would take nothing, *from a thread even to a shoelatchet* (Gen. xiv. 23), save only a portion for his allies, the chiefs Aner, Eshcol, and Mamre, and then returned to the shade of the oak or terebinth near Hebron.

CHAPTER II

LIFE OF ABRAHAM CONTINUED.

Gen. xv.—xxv.　B. C. 1913—1822.

WE now enter on another and a different scene in the history of Abram. He had been victorious over the Assyrian kings; he had gotten him honour as the prompt avenger of injustice and oppression before the chiefs of the land in which he was a pilgrim and a sojourner; he had been solemnly blessed by the *King of Righteousness;* but where was the fulfilment of the promise for which he had so long been waiting? He had no son, no single pledge of the mighty nation destined to spring from his loins. When, therefore, his all-merciful Guide appeared to him again in vision, to assure him of safety and protection, he could not restrain the deep sorrow of his heart, and mournfully complained that in place of a son, *one born in his house*, probably Eliezer of Damascus, *would be his heir*. On this occasion the

Psalm cx. 4. His relation to Christ, as type and antitype, consists in the fact that each was a priest, (i) not of the tribe of Levi, (ii) superior to Abraham, (iii) whose beginning and end are unknown, (iv) and not only a priest, but a priest-king, of righteousness and peace.

Almighty not only solemnly assured His desponding servant that a son should be born to him, an earnest of a seed as numerous as the stars of heaven, and that the land on which he walked should undoubtedly be their inheritance, but, as in the case of Noah after the Flood, he vouchsafed to him *an outward and visible sign* to strengthen and support his faith. He bade the patriarch take a heifer, a ram, and a she-goat, each three years old, together with a turtle-dove and a young pigeon, and after dividing them all, except the birds, to lay them piece by piece over against the other. Familiar, doubtless, with this ancient method of ratifying a covenant, Abram did as the Lord had told him, slew the victims, and laid the divided portions in order. Then from morning until evening he watched them, and from time to time drove away the birds of prey which hovered over them. At length the sun went down, and a deep sleep fell upon him, and a horror of great darkness gathered around him. Amidst the deepening gloom there appeared to him a Smoking Furnace and a Burning Lamp passing along the space between the divided victims. Presently a Voice came to him telling him that *his seed should be a stranger in a land that was not theirs, that there they should suffer affliction* 400 *years; that afterwards, in the fourth generation, when the cup of the Amorites was full, they should come out with great substance, return to the spot where the patriarch now was, and enter on their promised inheritance.* Thus, amidst mingled light and gloom, the ancestor of the elect nation was warned of the chequered fortunes which awaited his progeny, while at the same time he was assured of the ultimate fulfilment of the Promise, and the actual boundaries of the lands of his inheritance were marked out from the river of Egypt to the distant Euphrates; and in this confidence Abram was content to *possess his soul in patience* (Lk. xxi. 19).

As yet, it will be observed, it had not been expressly said that his wife Sarai was the destined mother of the long-promised son. As the prospect, therefore, of her contributing to the fulfilment of the Promise became more and more remote, she seems to have concluded that this honour was not reserved for her, and accordingly persuaded her husband to take her handmaid, Hagar, an Egyptian, as a secondary wife, that by her he might obtain what was denied herself. Abram complied with her suggestion, and Hagar conceived; but the consequences did not tend to increase the patriarch's happiness. In a moment of elation Hagar mocked her mistress, and Sarai dealt hardly with her, till she fled from her into the southern wilderness, on the way that led to her native land. There, as she halted near a fountain of water, an angel of the Lord met her, and bade her return and submit herself to her mistress, assuring her at the same time that she should give birth to a son, whom she was to call Ishmael (*whom God hears*). Though the *son of a bondwoman* (Gal. iv. 22, 23), no mean future lay before him; he should become the ancestor of a numerous seed, who, like himself, would be true roving sons of the desert, *their hand against every man, and every man's hand against them.* In remembrance of this incident Hagar named the fountain *Beer-lahai-roi,* (*the well of the God that appeareth*), and returned to the tents of Sarah, where, in process of time she gave birth to Ishmael, when Abram was 86 years old.

Again thirteen years rolled away, and still the Promise was not fulfilled. But when hope might almost have ceased to hope, God appeared once more to Abram, recapitulated the main outline of the Covenant-Promise, changed his name from Abram (*a high father*), to Abraham (*the father of a multitude*), and assured him that at length the long-expected time was well-nigh come. But in prospect of the peculiar blessing about to be bestowed upon him, he himself, and all his seed after him, must carry about with them a perpetual pledge of their covenant relation to Jehovah. The rite of Circumcision must now be adopted by him, and instead of being the badge of any favoured class amongst the nation destined to spring from his loins, was, on pain of excommunication, to be open to the lowliest member of the Hebrew commonwealth, even to the bond-servant and the stranger. At the same time it was intimated to the patriarch that his wife Sarai, whose name also was now changed to SARAH (*princess*), and no other, was to be the mother of the promised child, that it would be born during the next year, and be called Isaac (*Laughter*); while Ishmael also, for whom Abraham had prayed, would not be forgotten, but be a partaker in the Divine blessing, and become the father of twelve princes, the ancestors of a great nation. Thereupon Abraham complied with the Divine command, and was circumcised, together with Ishmael, now thirteen years of age, and all the male members of his household.

Shortly after this, as the patriarch sat, in the heat of the day, under the oak of Mamre, he received a visit from three mysterious Strangers, whom he entertained with becoming hospitality. The meal over which he had hastily prepared, one of them inquired for his wife, and formally announced that within the year she would be the mother of a son. His words were overheard by Sarah, and she laughed incredulously at the possibility of such an event, but was thereupon reproved by the Speaker, and assured in a still more confident manner of the fulfilment of His word. Then the Three left the tent and turned their steps eastward towards Sodom. Abraham accompanied them, and on the way one of them, in whom he recognised no other than the *Angel of the Covenant*, informed him of the real purport of this visit to the cities where his nephew Lot had taken up his abode. The sin of these cities was very great, and their cup was now full; their inhabitants had wearied themselves with wickedness, and their licentiousness and iniquity called to Heaven for a visible revelation of Divine wrath, and judgment was now *even at the door*. Informed of the impending doom the *Friend of God* drew near, and with marvellous boldness blended with the deepest humility pleaded with the Almighty for the guilty cities. Peradventure there might be found therein at least fifty, or forty-five, or forty, or thirty, or twenty, or even ten righteous souls, would the *Lord of all the earth spare* them for ten's sake? Thereupon he was assured that if only ten righteous souls could be found the cities should be spared. While he was thus pleading with God, the two other angels entered Sodom, and were hospitably entertained by Lot. But their celestial beauty only served to excite the wickedness of the inhabitants, who surrounded Lot's house, and, in spite of his earnest expostulations, would have offered them personal violence had they not been suddenly stricken with blindness. As the night wore on, his visitors assured Lot of the certain destruction of the city, and warned him to gather together with all speed every member of his family if he would save them from the impending judgment. Lot did as he was advised; but his warning was lost upon his sons-in-law and his daughters-in-law, and he seemed unto them *as one that mocked*. When the day dawned, the angels broke off any further delay by laying hold on him, and his wife, and his two daughters, and having dragged them forth beyond the city, bade them flee to the neighbouring mountain range if they would not be consumed. But thither Lot was afraid to flee, and in compliance with his urgent entreaty was permitted to betake himself to the town of Bela, or Zoar (*Little*), on the southern extremity of the Dead Sea. The sun rose as he entered this city of refuge, and then *the*

Lord rained upon Sodom and Gomorrah brimstone and fire out of heaven, and utterly swept away by an awful convulsion every trace of the guilty cities and their inhabitants, the site of which became henceforth a perpetual desolation. Few as were the remnants of this fearful overthrow, yet one of these few failed to reach the little city of refuge. In spite of the Angel's reiterated warning, Lot's wife lingered, looked back, and, caught by the advancing sulphurous tide, was smothered as she stood, and became a *pillar of salt* (Gen. xix. 26; Lk. xvii. 32). As for Lot himself, afraid to dwell even in Zoar, he fled with his two daughters to the eastern mountains, and became the father of two sons, Moab and Ben-Ammi, the ancestors of two powerful nations—the Moabites and Ammonites.

Shortly after this terrible judgment, Abraham left the oak of Mamre, where he had so long encamped, and journeyed in a southerly direction towards Gerar, between Kadesh and Shur, at that time the principal seat of the Philistines, whose chief was known by the hereditary title of Abimelech, or *Father-King*[1]. Under the same apprehensions which he had felt when drawing nigh to Egypt, Abraham wished that Sarah should pass for his sister, and again exposed her to imminent risk. But, as before, the Lord mercifully intervened, and the Philistine chief restored his wife to the patriarch, together with ample presents (Gen. xx. 14—16). At length the time had come for which Abraham, now upwards of 100 years of age, had so long waited. Either at Gerar or Beersheba, Sarah gave birth to the *child of promise*, who was duly circumcised on the eighth day, and named ISAAC (*Laughter*) according to the Divine command. At the feast given on the occasion of his weaning, Ish-

---

[1] Corresponding to *Padishah* (*father-king*) the title of the Persian kings, and *Atálih* (father) the title of the Khans of Bucharia. Smith's *Bibl. Dict.* Art. *Abimelech.*

mael mocked, or in some way insulted the child. This act, observed by Sarah, roused all her animosity, and she demanded the instant dismissal of the boy and his mother. Though sorely against his will, Abraham, advised by God, yielded to his wife, and early on the following morning Hagar and her son were sent away to wander in the wilderness of Beersheba. In a short time the water in her skin-bottle was spent, and the boy tormented with thirst seemed at the point of death. Unable to endure the sight of his sufferings, Hagar laid him under the shade of the desert shrubs, and sat down about a bowshot off. But the boy was not thus to die; God heard his cry, and the angel of the Lord called to Hagar out of heaven, and bade her not despair. At the same time her eyes were opened to discern a well of water, with which she filled her bottle and gave the lad drink. Thus his life was preserved, and he grew and prospered, and dwelt in the wild desert of Paran, near Mount Sinai, and was renowned for his skill in the use of the bow. Marrying an Egyptian he became the father of twelve sons and one daughter (Gen. xxv. 13—15; xxviii. 9; xxxvi. 3), the ancestors of the chief portion of the wild Arab tribes, living by warlike forays and plunder, *their hand against every man, and every man's hand against them.*

Meanwhile Abraham was living in peace and security, feared and respected by his Philistine neighbours in the south country, near Beersheba, when a far keener trial befell him than any he had yet experienced. The call from his own country, the famine that drove him into Egypt, the desertion of Lot, the long deferring of the promised seed, the separation from Ishmael, all these had been sore trials to flesh and blood. But now, when the hope of his life seemed at length to have been gained, he was commanded to take *his son, his only son Isaac* a three days' journey into the land of Moriah, and offer him up as a burnt-offering on one of the mountains that should be shown him. Utterly inexplicable as this command must have seemed, and indescribably painful to his feelings, the patriarch's trust in God did not falter. Assured that He who had called him into being could, if it pleased Him, *raise up* his son *even from the dead* (Heb. xi. 19), he rose up early in the morning, clave the wood for the sacrifice, saddled his ass, and with two young men and Isaac commenced his journey. On the third day he lifted up his eyes, and beheld the spot afar off; thereupon leaving the young men behind, he laid the wood upon his son, and with the fire in his hand, and a knife, ascended the mountain to the spot[1] of which God had told him. Marvelling that no victim had been brought, but assured that *a lamb would be provided for a burnt-offering*, Isaac accompanied his father to the summit, and when the altar had been built and the wood laid thereon, submitted without a murmur to be bound and placed upon it. Another moment and the father's hand was actually outstretched to slay his son, when a voice from heaven arrested him, and bade him forbear to proceed further, seeing that the end for which this mysterious trial had been sent was now gained, for Abraham had not withheld his only son, but given proof of his willingness to surrender even him to the Divine call. At the same moment the patriarch looked, and beheld behind him a ram caught in a thicket by its horns, which he took and offered as a burnt-offering instead of his son. In memory of this eventful day he named the place *Jehovah-Jireh*, i.e. *Jehovah will see or provide*, and again received the assurance of the Divine blessing upon himself and his future descendants,

---

[1] Either, (1) according to the prevailing belief, the hill at Jerusalem on which the Temple was afterwards built, or (2) Mount Gerizim, near Sychem. See Stanley's *S. and P.* 251; and compare Thomson's *Land and the Book*, 474, 475.

who should be *multiplied as the stars of heaven, and as the sand upon the seashore,* and become the channel of blessings to *all the nations of the earth.*

This is the culminating point in Abraham's life. Implicit trust in the Most High, unfaltering obedience to His will, had never been more signally displayed, and his faith *was counted to him for righteousness* (Rom. iv. 3, 9). From this time his course was calm and peaceful. Leaving Beersheba he turned northwards, and once more abode under the oak of Mamre. Here he lost the partner of his long and eventful career. At the age of 127 (the only instance in which the age of a woman is recorded in Scripture) Sarah died, and was laid in the *cave of the field of Machpelah,* a spot now covered by the Mosque of Hebron, which Abraham bought for 400 shekels of silver, *for a possession of a burying-place,* of Ephron the Hittite. So deep was the respect of the children of Heth for *the mighty prince* who had so long lived among them, that in spite of the usual Oriental jealousy on this point they would willingly have permitted him to bury his dead in the choicest of their own sepulchres. But this Abraham declined, and the Cave of Machpelah with the surrounding field was made over to him for a possession for ever[1].

Three years afterwards, anxious to prevent an alliance between his son and any of the Canaanitish nations, he sent the eldest servant of his house, probably Eliezer of Damascus, into Mesopotamia, to the city of Nahor his brother, to procure from thence a wife for him. His servant faithfully discharged his commission, and the

[1] "The tomb of Machpelah is a proof, standing to this day, of the long predetermined assurance that the children of Abraham should inherit the land in which this was their ancestor's sole, but most precious possession. It is like the purchase of the site of Hannibal's Camp by the strong faith and hope of the besieged senators of Rome." Stanley, *Lectures on the Jewish Church,* p. 40.

piety he displayed reflecting the goodness of the patriarch himself was rewarded. At a well outside the city
of Haran he met REBEKAH, the daughter of Bethuel[1]
the son of Nahor, going forth with her pitcher on her
shoulder to draw water. In answer to his inquiries she
told him who she was, and conducted him to the house
of her brother Laban. There he recounted all that had
befallen his master in the land of his pilgrimage, and
made known the purpose of his errand. Rebekah, when
asked by her brother and mother, announced her readiness to accompany the servant to the tents of Abraham,
and in the course of time became Isaac's wife (Gen.
xxiv.).

Before long Abraham himself also married again,
and by KETURAH his second wife, became the father of
six children, Zimran, Jokshan, Medan, Midian, Ishbak,
and Shuah (Gen. xxv. 2), the ancestors of Arabian and
Midianitish tribes. Lest they should dispute the inheritance with Isaac, the prudent patriarch, while he yet
lived, presented them with gifts, and sent them away
into the south-east country (Gen. xxv. 6) where their descendants settled along the borders of the Elanitic
Gulf in considerable numbers. And then the *Father
of the Faithful, the Friend of God*, being 175 years
old, had reached the term of life allotted to him. In *a
good old age, and full of years*, he was gathered unto
his people, and was laid by Isaac and Ishmael also, who
had come up from the wild desert of Paran to assist in
these last sad offices, by the side of his beloved Sarah,
in the cave of Machpelah[2].

---

[1] On the consistent insignificance of Bethuel in this affair,
see Blunt's *Coincidences*, p. 32.

[2] On Abraham's character, see below, p. 76.

CHAPTER III

THE HISTORY OF ISAAC.

Gen. xxv.—xxvii. B. C. 1822—1760.

FOR nineteen years after their marriage Isaac and
Rebekah were childless. But at length, in answer
to earnest prayer, Rebekah became the mother of twin
sons, Esau (*hairy, rough*) and Jacob (*he that holds by
the heel,* or *supplanter*). The bitter enmity afterwards
to exist between the brothers was foreshadowed even
before their birth, and as they grew the difference in
their characters became still more prominent. Esau
became a *cunning hunter,* wild and daring, even as his
rough and robust frame betokened, revelling like a true
son of the desert in the excitement of the chase. Jacob,
on the other hand, was a quiet domestic youth, *dwelling
in tents,* the favourite of his mother, while Esau, by a
not uncommon caprice of affection, was the favourite
of the gentle retiring Isaac, whose keen relish for
savoury food was gratified by his success in the hunt-
ing-field (Gen. xxv. 24—28).

It is in connection with his favourite pursuit that
Esau first attracts our notice. As the eldest son he
had several important privileges. He held superior
rank in the family (Gen. xlix. 3), and would succeed
to a double portion of his father's property (Gen. xlviii.
22; Deut. xxi. 17); his also was, in all probability, the
priestly office (Num. viii. 17—19), and the Covenant-
Blessing (Heb. xii. 16, 17; Gen. xxvii. 28, 29, 36). These
were the privileges of his birthright, and by an Oriental
patriarch were held as dear as life itself. On one occasion
Esau returned faint and weary from the chase, and saw
his brother Jacob preparing some dark red pottage of

lentiles[1]. Famished and exhausted, he longed for the fragrant mess, and implored his brother to let him have it. Seeing his distress, Jacob determined to avail himself of it for his own ends, and agreed to give his brother the pottage on condition that he sold him his birthright. Unable to control the pangs of hunger, bent on the immediate gratification of his appetite, Esau was willing to barter all his privileges for a single meal. But words were not sufficient for his artful brother. He must have an oath solemnly attesting the exchange. *Swear unto me,* said he, and Esau swore, and sold his birthright *for one morsel of meat* (Heb. xii. 16), and ate and drank, and rose up and went his way[2].

At a subsequent period, in consequence of a grievous famine, Isaac left Lahai-roi, and journeyed southward to Gerar, within the fertile coast-line of Philistia. While here he received a warning from the Almighty against going down into Egypt, and was assured of the continuance of the same blessing which his father had enjoyed (Gen. xxvi. 1—5). Thus encouraged he continued to dwell at Gerar, but, like his father, was not always proof against temptations to distrust his Almighty Protector. He persuaded Rebekah to represent herself as his sister, and subjected himself to a cutting rebuke from Abimelech for this unworthy equivocation.

---

[1] The red lentile is still a favourite article of food in the East. "I can testify," writes Dr Thomson, "that when cooking, it diffuses far and wide an odour extremely grateful to a hungry man. It was, therefore, no slight temptation to Esau, returning weary and famished from an unsuccessful hunt in this burning climate." *Land and the Book,* p. 587. See also Robinson, *Bib. Res.* 1. 246.

[2] From this transaction Esau acquired the name of EDOM, or "*Red,*" though the name is more usually applied to the land of his descendants. "The ruddy hue of the mountain-range given to Esau would at once suggest the word *Edom,* and cause it to be preferred to the better known Esau." Comp. Obad. 8, 9, 21.

At Gerar his wealth increased exceedingly, and he made the first advance beyond the purely pastoral life. He *sowed in that land,* and reaped within the year an hundred fold (Gen. xxvi. 12). But his wealth and prosperity in time provoked the jealousy of the Philistines, and they stopped up the wells which his father had dug; nor did the patriarch feel himself secure till he had moved still further southward to Beersheba. Here, like Abraham before him, he built an altar unto Jehovah, and called upon His Name, and was rewarded by a second confirmation of the covenant Promise, while his contentions with the Philistines were brought to a close, and a mutual compact ratified between them (Gen. xxvi. 26—31). But his domestic happiness was not equally secured. To the great grief of both his parents, Esau, now 40 years of age, contracted an alliance with Judith the daughter of Beeri, and Bashemath, the daughter of Elon, both of the race of the Hittites, to whom he afterwards added Mahalath, a daughter of Ishmael (Gen. xxvi. 34; xxviii. 9).

Of the greater portion of Isaac's life at Beersheba the Scripture narrative tells nothing, nor is any incident recorded till we hear that *he waxed old and his eyes grew dim so that he could not see.* Then reminded of the uncertain tenure of life, he resolved by a solemn act to bestow the patriarchal blessing upon his eldest son. Summoning Esau before him, he bade him go forth to the hunt and bring him venison such as he loved, promising the blessing as his reward. His words did not escape the quick ears of Rebekah. Eager to obtain this important privilege for her favourite Jacob, she bade him, during the absence of his brother, slay two kids, with which she prepared savoury meat such as Isaac loved. Then arraying him in garments belonging to his brother, and placing the skins upon his hands and neck, she directed him to go into the presence of his father, and pass himself off as his wild, rough brother Esau. After some hesitation, Jacob fell in with her plan, and in the disguise she had prepared presented himself before his father. But Isaac, though old and dimsighted, was not free from his suspicions. To Jacob's assurance that he had been to the chase and brought of the prey, he replied by enquiring how he had found it so quickly. Nor did the ready but untruthful answer that the Lord had brought it to him relieve his mind. *Come near*, said he, *that I may feel thee, whether thou be my very son Esau or not.* And Jacob went near, and his father felt him. Another question, and another falsehood followed; and at length Jacob was bidden to present the venison that he had taken, and the old man ate and drank, and then bestowed upon him in all its fulness the Covenant Blessing. He prayed that God would *give his son of the dew of heaven, and the fatness of the earth, and plenty of corn and wine; that He would make people to serve him, and nations to bow down to him, so that he might be lord over his brethren, and see his mother's sons bow down to him, a blessing to all that blessed him, a curse to all that cursed him* (Gen. xxvii. 28, 29).

Thus successful in his shameful artifice, Jacob had scarcely gone forth from his father's presence, when the true Esau returned from the chase. With savoury meat he too presented himself before Isaac, and besought his blessing. The old man trembled very exceedingly when he heard the voice of his eldest son, but told him that he had come too late. His brother, *the Supplanter*, had been before him, and the irrevocable words had been spoken. With *a great and exceeding bitter cry* Esau implored his father for one blessing which perchance might be left; and at length Isaac assured him that *his dwelling would be of the fatness of the earth, and of the dew of heaven from above; but he must live*

4

by his sword and serve his brother, till the day when he too should gain the dominion, and should shake his brother's yoke from off his neck[1] (Gen. xxvii. 39, 40).

Enraged at the deception which had been practised upon him, Esau did not conceal his design of revenging himself by putting Jacob to death, and only deferred it till the days of mourning for his father were ended, whose death he deemed to be near at hand. But his dark threat became known to Rebekah. Anxious to save her favourite son, she persuaded him to undertake a journey to his uncle Laban at Padan-Aram, promising, when a few days were over, and his brother's wrath was appeased, to send for him again. Without communicating her real motive in urging this journey, she at the same time secured the acquiescence of Isaac, by pretending anxiety that Jacob should marry one of the daughters of Laban, rather than follow his brother's example, and contract an alliance among the Hittites. Accordingly Isaac sent for his son, and bade him go to Padan-Aram, urging him to take thence a wife from amongst his own kindred, and then consciously and purposely transferred to him and his seed after him the blessing of Abraham (Gen. xxviii. 1—5).

CHAPTER IV

LIFE OF JACOB.

GEN. XXVIII.—XXXV. B. C. 1760—1716.

THUS solemnly assured of the Covenant Blessing, Jacob bade farewell to his mother, whom he was never to see again, and set out a solitary traveller for the Eastern uplands of Aram, where in place of a few days he was destined to spend many weary years, and

[1] For the fulfilment compare 2 Kings viii. 20—22; 2 Chron. xxi. 8—10, and see below, p. 327.

amidst many trials and vicissitudes to find the same
measure that he had measured to his brother measured
also to himself. As the sun went down on the first evening of his journey, he reached the site of one of Abraham's
encampments, the stony soil[1] near the Canaanite town
of Luz. Taking of the stones that lay around, he put
them for his pillow, and lay down to sleep. As he slept,
there appeared to him a vision of the night. A ladder
seemed to rise up from the bare ground on which he
lay, and the top of it reached even unto heaven, and on
it he saw angels ascending and descending. Moreover
from above there came the Voice of God assuring the
wanderer of His protection, renewing to him the promise of Abraham, and encouraging him with the hope
of return from exile. Jacob awoke trembling and afraid,
Surely, said he, *the Lord is in this place, and I knew
it not; how dreadful is this place! This is none other
but the house of God, and this is the gate of heaven.*
Then rising early, he took the stone that had formed his
pillow, poured oil upon it, and set it up for a memorial,
calling the spot BETHEL, the *House of God.* At the
same time he made a solemn vow that, if Jehovah would
indeed sustain him in all his ways, and bring him back
as He had promised, he would not only dedicate the
spot as His House, but would give Him the tenth of
all that he possessed (Gen. xxviii. 18—22).

Then he continued his journey, and striking in a
north-easterly direction, at length reached a well in
Padan-Aram, round which were gathered three flocks
with shepherds from Haran. As he was conversing
with them, RACHEL, the daughter of his uncle Laban,

---

[1] Bethel lay in the direct thoroughfare of Palestine. "...The
track of this thoroughfare winds through an uneven valley,
covered, as with gravestones, by large sheets of bare rock;
some few here and there standing up like the cromlechs of
Druidical monuments."—Stanley, *S. and P.* 219.

approached, and with true courtesy Jacob went near, rolled the stone from the well's mouth, and watered the flocks. He then kissed the maiden, and told her he was Rebekah's son, whereupon she ran and told her father, who welcomed Jacob to the tents of Haran. After a stay of one month, Laban proposed that the wanderer should serve him as a shepherd, to which Jacob assented, and promised to serve him seven years on condition of receiving the hand of Rachel. The seven years passed away, and he who had *supplanted* his brother twice, now learnt what it was to be *supplanted* himself. On the evening of his marriage Laban substituted her sister Leah in place of Rachel; nor was the deceit discovered till the following morning, when, in answer to Jacob's reproaches, he informed him that it was not customary to give the younger before the elder daughter, and that if he would have Rachel he must serve seven more years for her. To these hard conditions Jacob assented, and in the course of time became the father of a numerous family, eleven sons and one daughter. Of these, Reuben, Simeon, Levi, Judah, Issachar, Zebulun, and a daughter Dinah, were born to Leah; Dan and Naphtali to Bilhah Rachel's maid, whom the latter, finding she had no children, gave to Jacob as a secondary wife; Gad and Asher to Zilpah, Leah's maid; and Joseph to Rachel.

Shortly after the birth of this last son, Jacob having completed his time of service, proposed to Laban that he should return into his own country. But the latter, who had found by experience that his son-in-law had brought a blessing to his house, prevailed upon him to continue in his service, on condition of receiving a certain portion of the flocks as his hire. Six years longer, therefore, Jacob staid with his father-in-law, and prospered, and became himself the owner of numerous herds. But on Laban's side the covenant was not

strictly kept. Again and again he changed the wages
of his faithful servant, till at length finding any longer
stay rendered impossible by the envy and jealousy of
his father-in-law and his sons, and encouraged by the
Word of Jehovah, Jacob determined to set out for his
native land. Accordingly, availing himself of Laban's
absence at a sheep-shearing, he gathered together all
his goods, and with his wives and family crossed the
river, the great river Euphrates (Gen. xxxi. 21), and
set his face towards the uplands of Gilead, on the east of
Jordan. Three days after his departure, news of his flight
reached the ears of Laban, who forthwith pursued after
him a seven days' journey, and overtook him as he was
encamped in the range of Gilead. Warned by God in a
dream against using any violence towards his son-in-law,
Laban contented himself with reproaching him for his
secret flight, hypocritically complaining that he had not
given him time to send him away with due formality,
and accusing him of stealing his household gods, the
teraphim or images, which Rachel had taken and concealed in the camel's furniture. After some altercation
it was resolved to come to terms. Stones were gathered
together, and set up as a Pillar of Witness, in token of
their agreement that neither party to injure the other
would cross over what was henceforth to be the boundary between their respective territories; after which
Laban returned to his home in the distant East (Gen.
xxxi. 43—55).

Thus relieved from pressing danger, Jacob continued
his journey westward. The twenty years of exile was
over, and he was bound for his native land. As if to
welcome him thither, and to remind him of the fulfilment of God's Promise, the angels, whom he had seen
twenty years before in vision at Bethel, now met him
in two hosts, to commemorate which event he named
the spot Mahanaim (*two hosts*). He was now on the

brink of the river which divided him from his father's home, and the remembrance of his brother Esau and the uncertainty of the reception he might meet with from him caused the deepest anxiety. Sending messengers into the land of Seir, he informed his *lord* Esau of his return from the land of exile, and of the success that had attended him. The messengers went, and returned with the alarming intelligence that Esau was coming to meet him with four hundred men. Jacob's distress was extreme, and he poured forth his whole soul in fervent prayer to God for protection. Then selecting a valuable present from his flocks and herds, he sent them to meet and propitiate his approaching brother, and at midnight dispatched his wives and sons, and all that he had, across the ford Jabbok, but staid himself behind to renew his earnest supplications for the Divine protection. Through the night, even to the breaking of the day, there wrestled with him One (Hos. xii. 3,4), whom he knew not, and whose Name he could not prevail upon Him to reveal, but who left upon him a palpable mark of their mysterious conflict, for He *touched the hollow of his thigh so that it was out of joint.* But in memory of this same crisis in his life another sign was given him His name was changed. No more was he to be called Jacob, *the Supplanter.* During the long years of his weary exile old things had passed away, and all things were becoming new. Henceforth he was to be known as Israel, *the Prince of God,* for *as a Prince had he power with God and with man, and had prevailed* (Gen. xxxii. 28). The site of this memorable conflict Jacob named Peniel (*the face of God*). When the day broke he looked up, and saw Esau approaching with his retinue. Thereupon in long procession he went forth to meet him ; first advanced the handmaids Bilhah and Zilpah with their children, then followed Leah and her children, last of all Rachel and Joseph. Jacob himself led the way,

bowing to the ground seven times until he came near to
his brother, who ran to meet him, and fell upon his
neck and kissed him. The reconciliation was complete.
After mutual converse, Esau agreed to leave to Jacob
the land of his inheritance, and retired himself to the
rugged mountains of Seir[1], whence he and his descendants expelled the aboriginal tribes, and dwelt in their
stead in the land henceforth known as Edom or Idumæa,
a race of hunters living by the sword.

Meanwhile Jacob continued his journey towards the
valley of the Jordan, and for a while settled at Succoth,
where he puts up booths (*Succoth*) for his cattle, as
well as a house for himself. Thence he moved westwards, and crossing the Jordan, advanced into the very
heart of Palestine, and pitched his tent before the city
of Shechem. Of Hamor its chief he subsequently bought
a portion of the rich plain, east of the city, and here he
settled down, and, like Abraham before him, erected an
altar to Jehovah. During his stay at this place, which
appears to have been somewhat protracted, an unfor-
tunate occurrence caused him for a time the greatest
anxiety, and eventually drove him from the neighbourhood. One day, on the occasion, it is not improbable, of
some local festival, Dinah the daughter of Leah, at this
time from thirteen to fifteen years of age, went out *to
see the daughters of the land*, and was dishonoured by
Shechem, the Hivite chieftain, in whose territory the
patriarch had settled. His father Hamor thereupon

---

[1] Mount Seir ("rough" or "rugged," see Jer. xlix. 16,
Obad. 4) extended along the east side of the Arabah, from
the Dead Sea to the Elanitic gulf, and "was originally inhabited by the Horites, or 'troglodytes,' who were doubtless
the excavators of those singular rock-dwellings found in such
numbers in the ravines and cliffs around Petra." These Horites
were dispossessed by the descendants of Esau, who gave to
the country the name of Edom, and were divided into tribes
under a sheikh or duke (Gen. xxxvi. 15—19).

proposed that his son should pay a certain sum, by way
of reparation, to her father and mother for the injury
he had done to the maiden and marry her, and that
this should be followed by a general intermarriage between the two peoples. To this proposition the brothers
of Dinah assented, but demanded, as the single condition of the treaty, that the people of Shechem should
consent to be circumcised. These terms were unwittingly accepted by the Shechemites, and three days
afterwards, Simeon and Levi, Dinah's own brothers, at
the head of their households, attacked the city, slew the
chiefs and all the males in the place, spoiled it of every
article of value it contained, and took captive even
the women and little children. This bloody and treacherous act excited Jacob's deepest indignation, and
shortly afterwards, fearful lest the neighbouring tribes
should gather together and slay him and all his house, in
accordance with a Divine warning, he determined to
repair to Bethel and dwell there and perform the vow,
which till now he seems almost to have forgotten. The
journey partook somewhat of a religious pilgrimage, and
was preceded by a general purification on the part of
the patriarch's followers, and a collection of the *teraphim* or strange gods, which had been brought from
Mesopotamia, and were now hidden under an oak at
Shechem. Arrived once more at the scene of his wondrous Vision, Jacob erected an altar, which he called El-
Bethel, and here he was again visited by the Almighty,
who renewed to him his name of Israel, and assured
him of his share in the blessings of the Covenant (Gen.
xxxv. 9—15). During his stay at Bethel his intimacy
with his father Isaac, who was still alive, appears to
have been renewed; for we are told that Deborah Rebekah's nurse died, and was buried under an oak, henceforth known as Allon-Bachuth, the *Oak of Tears*. But
his departure from the same place a day's journey south-

wards was saddened by a grievous trial. As he drew
near to Ephrath, the Canaanitish name of Bethlehem,
Rachel his favourite wife died in giving birth to a son,
whom she called Ben-oni, *the son of sorrow*, but whom
his father named BENJAMIN, *the son of my right hand.*
Over her grave the sorrowing husband erected a pillar,
and moving southward pitched his tent beside Edar, or
the watch-tower of the flocks, and subsequently beneath
the oak of Mamre before Hebron, where Isaac died, in
the 180th year of his age, and was committed to the
tomb by Jacob and Esau (Gen. xxxvi. 27—29).

CHAPTER V/

HISTORY OF JOSEPH.

GEN. XXXVII.—XLII.   B. C. 1727—1707.

IT was while he was sojourning in the neighbourhood
of Hebron, where, like his father, he united agricultural with pastoral occupations (Gen. xxxvii. 7) that
the saddest trial of his life befell Jacob. Of all his
sons none was dearer to him than Joseph, the child of
his beloved Rachel. In token of his affection he bestowed upon him *a coat of many colours*, probably a
tunic furnished with sleeves and reaching down to the
ankles, worn by youths of the richer class[1]. By some
this is supposed to indicate his intention of transferring
to him, as being the *eldest son of the favourite Rachel*,
the right of primogeniture. Whether this was so or
not, it roused much jealousy and ill-feeling amongst
Joseph's brothers, already incensed by the circumstance
of his bearing to his father, when seventeen years of
age, an evil report of the sons of Zilpah and Bilhah,

[1] See Smith's *Bib. Dict.* I. 452 *b.*

with whom he kept the flocks. Another incident fanned
the flame of ill-feeling. Joseph unwittingly told his
brethren of two dreams he had dreamt, in one of which
he had seemed to see them binding sheaves in the field,
and lo! his sheaf rose and stood upright, while their
sheaves stood round about and made obeisance to his
sheaf; in the other he beheld the sun, moon, and the
eleven stars making obeisance to him. Even Jacob rebuked his favourite son for his seeming self-exaltation,
though he observed the saying (Gen. xxxvii. 11).

After a time an opportunity was presented to the
brothers of taking a cruel revenge. Though Jacob was
settled in the vale of Hebron, a portion of his numerous
flocks and herds were kept by his sons on the rich
pasture-grounds near Shechem. Thither on one occasion Jacob sent his favourite son to see how his brethren
fared, and bring him word again. Joseph set out, and
being directed by a man whom he met, to Dothan[1], or
"*the Two Wells*," a place about twelve miles north of
Shechem, famous for its pasturage, he went thither in
quest of them. From the rising ground, where they
were keeping their flocks, the brothers descried the
Dreamer approaching, and straightway resolved to slay
him and cast him into a pit, and then report to his
father that he had been devoured by wild beasts. From
actually putting him to death they were, however,
dissuaded by Reuben, and contented themselves with
stripping him of his coat of many colours, and casting
him into an empty cistern, intending probably to let
him die by hunger. But when they had done this, and
had sat down to eat, a company of Ishmaelite or Mi-

---

[1] Dothan has been discovered by Van de Velde and Dr
Robinson, "still bearing its ancient name, and situated at the
S. end of a plain of the richest pasturage, 4 or 5 miles S. W.
of En-gannim or *Jenin*, and separated only by a swell or two
of hills from the plain of Esdraelon."—Smith's *Bib. Dict.*

dianite merchants (for the two names are used inter-
changeably) approached, mounted on camels, and bearing spicery and balm, going down the high road[1] which
passed near from Gilead to Egypt. Thereupon Judah
proposed that they should sell him to these traders, and
he was taken up from the pit, and sold to the Ish-
maelites, who paid for him twenty pieces of silver, the
usual price of a male slave from five to twenty years of
age. Reuben was not present when the cruel bargain
was struck, and was greatly distressed when, on his
return, he found that his brother was gone. But the
others killed a kid, dipped Joseph's coat of many
colours in its blood, and brought it to Jacob, with the
hypocritical enquiry whether it was his son's coat or no,
and informing him that they had found it thus smeared
with blood. Even Reuben did not reveal the true state
of the case, and Jacob, supposing that his favourite son
had been slain by wild beasts, put sackcloth upon his
loins, and refusing every proffered consolation, mourned
for him many days (Gen. xxxvii. 29—35).

Meanwhile the Midianitish caravan kept on its southward course, and eventually reaching Egypt, sold Joseph
to POTIPHAR[2], an officer of Pharaoh, and *Captain of the
Executioners* (Gen. xxxviii. 36 *margin*). In his house,
Joseph though a foreigner and a slave, gradually won

---

[1] Close to the large mound, on which Dothan stood, "is
an ancient road running N. and S., the remains of the massive pavement of which are still visible. The great road from
Beisân to Egypt also passes near *Dothân*." Rob. III. 122.
The caravan coming from the spice-district of Gilead would
cross the Jordan below the Sea of Galilee, pass over the plain
of Jezreel, and thence proceed along the sea-shore to Egypt.
Thomson's *Land and the Book*, 466.

[2] Also written Potipherah = the Egyptian PET-P-RA or
PET-PH-RA, "*belonging to the sun.*" Compare Pharaoh = P-RA
or PH-RA, "*the sun,*" as the representative on earth of the
god RA, "*the sun.*"

the confidence of his master, who appears to have been a wealthy man, and possessed of property in the field as well as in the house, so that before long, in the capacity of overseer, he was entrusted with the entire possessions of the Egyptian, and the Divine blessing rested upon his house for Joseph's sake.

But this period of happiness and prosperity was destined to come to an abrupt termination. With the profligacy for which the Egyptian women were notorious, the wife of Potiphar on one occasion tempted Joseph to commit adultery with her, and when he resisted all her seductions, charged him to her husband with the very crime she had ineffectually tempted him to commit. Thereupon Potiphar, fully believing her story, without bringing his faithful steward before any public tribunal, cast him into the prison in his own house. But amidst this grievous trial Joseph was not forsaken. *The Lord was with him, and gave him favour in the sight of the keeper of the prison,* who, convinced of his fidelity and uprightness, entrusted him with the care of all the prisoners there confined. Amongst these there soon appeared the *Chief of Pharaoh's Cupbearers,* and the *Chief of his Bakers,* two high officers of the Egyptian court, on whom Joseph was specially directed to wait. During their imprisonment each of them dreamt a dream. The Chief of the Cupbearers dreamt that *a vine was before him, on which were three branches; that it was as though it budded, and its blossoms shot forth, and its clusters brought forth ripe grapes, that of these he took and pressed them into Pharaoh's cup which was in his hand, and gave it to that monarch.* The Chief of the Bakers dreamt that *he had three white baskets on his head, the uppermost full of all manner of bakemeats for Pharaoh, which the birds ate out of the baskets on his head.* Convinced that these dreams portended events of great importance in their lives, and unable to interpret them, these high officers were filled with sadness. But Joseph, being informed of the cause, by virtue of his prophetic gifts interpreted the dreams, and announced to the *Chief of the Butlers* that within three days, on the anniversary of Pharaoh's birthday, he should be restored to his office, while, within the same period, his fellow-prisoner would be hanged upon a tree, where *the birds would eat his flesh from off him.* As he had predicted, so it came to pass. Within the specified period, the one of these grandees was executed, and the other restored to his former high position. But though the Hebrew Captive had told the *Chief of the Butlers* his own sad story, in the hour of prosperity the restored grandee forgat his benefactor, and his touching request that he would intercede with Pharaoh on his behalf (Gen. xl. 12—23).

Two more years, therefore, of tedious imprisonment passed over Joseph's head, when one night Pharaoh himself was troubled with two mysterious dreams. In the first he seemed *to stand by the banks of the Nile, and behold out of it there came seven well-favoured kine and fatfleshed, and fed in the marsh grass that lined the banks. And behold after them there came up seven poor, ill-favoured, leanfleshed kine, and they ate up the seven well-favoured and fat kine, and when they had done so, it could not be known that they had eaten them, for they were still as ill-favoured as at the beginning.* In his second dream, the monarch beheld *seven ears of corn growing upon one stalk, full, fat, and good, and after them seven thin ears and blasted with the east wind, which devoured the seven full and fat ears.* Troubled with these visions of the night he awoke, and sent for all the magicians of Egypt and all the wise men thereof, and told them his dream, but they were unable to give him any interpretation. In this difficulty the *Chief of the Butlers* bethought him of his youthful benefactor in the prison, and told Pharaoh what had befallen him there, and how a young man, a Hebrew, servant to the Captain of the Executioners, had interpreted his dream. Upon this the monarch sent for Joseph, who was brought into the royal presence, and having been told the nature of the dreams, informed Pharaoh that they were sent by the great God to forewarn him of what He was about to do. The seven good kine and the seven good ears denoted *seven years of plenty;* the seven thin ill-favoured kine and the seven empty ears of corn denoted *seven years of very grievous famine*, about to befall the entire land of Egypt. The doubling of the dreams denoted that the event was certain and imminent. He advised, therefore, that without delay the monarch should set over the land a man *discreet and wise*, with overseers under him, to take up the fifth part of the land during the seven years of plenty, and lay up corn and food in various cities against the seven years of famine, which were assuredly to come (Gen. xli. 14—36).

This advice found favour in the eyes of Pharaoh, and deeming no other so well fitted for the post as the interpreter of his dreams, he appointed him to fill it, and, in token of his freedom, placed on his hand his own signet ring and a gold collar about his neck, and arraying him in vestures of fine linen, he caused him to ride in the second chariot that he had, preceded by heralds crying *Bow the knee.* Joseph was thus invested with the dignity of an Oriental Vizier, and could act in the name of the king. Besides these marks of honour, Pharaoh changed his name to Zaphnath-paaneah [1], or *the Revealer of Secrets*, and united him in

---

[1] The Greek translation of the Septuagint, which was made in Egypt, has here the word "*Psonthomphanech*" = "the preserver of the world" or "of the land."

marriage with Asenath[1], the daughter of Poti-pherah (*devoted to Ra*, or *the Sun*), priest or prince (Gen. xli. 45 *margin*) of On, the later Heliopolis, and the religious capital of the country.

Thus at the age of thirty, after thirteen years of painful vicissitudes, the son of Jacob was elevated to the highest position next to the sovereign himself in the great kingdom of Egypt. In accordance with the plan he himself had indicated, he straightway commenced a tour throughout the land, and during the seven years of plenty bought up a fifth part of the corn in the country, and laid it up in granaries in the various cities. During the same period he became the father of two sons, to whom, though born of an Egyptian wife, he gave Hebrew names, calling the first-born Manasseh, "*a Forgetter;*" *for God*, said he, *hath made me* forget *all my toil and all my father's house.* The second he named Ephraim, "*Fruitful;*" *for God hath caused me to be* fruitful *in the land of my affliction.* At the close of the seven years of plenty, the seven years of dearth drew on, and its effects were felt not only in Egypt, but in all the neighbouring lands. During the first part of this period, the wants of the people were relieved by the abundance which the foresight of the Vizier had stored up. He opened all his granaries and sold unto the Egyptians, delivering over the money into Pharaoh's exchequer. When money failed, barter was resorted to, and the Egyptians obtained bread in exchange for their horses, cattle, and flocks. When at length these means were exhausted, they sold him their land, except that of the priests, who, being provided from the royal treasury, did not feel the horrors of the famine. Thus possessed of the entire country, Joseph improved the

---

[1] Asenath, interpreted by some "*the servant of Neith,*" the Egyptian Minerva. Others take it to be a Hebrew word, denoting "*storehouse.*"

opportunity to place the relations between the Egyptian monarch and his people on a settled and legal footing. He made them, indeed, vassals of their sovereign, but in place of allowing them to be taxed according to royal caprice, he disposed of the land to them, on the understanding that four parts were to be their own, for seed of the field, and for food for them and their families, while a fifth part was to be paid annually to the king in place of ground-rent; an arrangement by no means oppressive, when it is considered that the soil sometimes yielded thirty-fold, or even a greater increase (Gen. xli. 46—57).

At an early period during the seven years of famine, ten of Joseph's brethren went down into Egypt at the suggestion of their father, and presented themselves before him with the petition to be allowed to buy corn. In the Viceroy, second only to the great Pharaoh, they did not for a moment recognize the boy whom twenty years before they had lowered into the dry pit at Dothan. But though Joseph knew *them*, and recognized the fulfilment of his early dreams, he did not reveal himself to them. Through an interpreter he spake roughly unto them, pronounced them to be spies who had come down to see the nakedness of the land, and when they denied the charge, declared they should be imprisoned till one of them had brought down their youngest brother. For three days he actually kept them in ward, and finally, on condition that one remained behind as a hostage, permitted them to return with corn for their families. Stricken with remorse, and not imagining that the Viceroy could understand their language, they acknowledged that their sin had found them out, and recalled the day when they saw the anguish of their brother, and turned a deaf ear to his beseeching entreaties that they would not deal hardly with him. Then Simeon was bound before their eyes, and sad and sorrowful they commenced their return. But on the road they had fresh cause for alarm and confusion. On opening their sacks they discovered not only that corn had been supplied them, but that their money had been restored to them. Marvelling at this strange circumstance, they reached home, and recounted to their father all that had befallen them, and how he could not hope to see Simeon again till they returned with their youngest brother Benjamin into the presence of the Viceroy of Egypt. On hearing this hard condition, Jacob burst forth into bitter complaints, and though Reuben offered the life of his two children as a pledge for Benjamin's safe return, absolutely refused to allow him to accompany them; *his brother*, said he, *is dead, and he is left alone; if mischief befall him by the way, then shall ye bring down my grey hairs with sorrow to the grave* (Gen. xlii. 38).

CHAPTER VI

JACOB'S DESCENT INTO EGYPT—DEATH OF JOSEPH.

Gen. xliii.—l.   B. C. 1707—1635.

BUT as time went on, and the corn the Brothers had brought from Egypt was consumed, it became absolutely necessary to go thither a second time, if they would live and not die. Without Benjamin, however, they knew the journey would be useless, and Benjamin their father would not send. At length Judah stood forward as spokesman for the rest, and offered to bear for ever in his own person the blame, if any evil befell him, till after a struggle Jacob consented. With a present of such things as the land afforded, *a little balm, a little honey, spices, and myrrh, nuts, and almonds,*

5

with double money also in their hand, the brothers took Benjamin from his sorrowing father, and once more commenced their journey to Egypt. Arrived there they were again presented to the Viceroy, who perceiving that Benjamin was with them, ordered the steward of his house to conduct them home, and to slay and make ready, that they might dine with him at noon. Full of fear, the brothers followed the steward, and on the way informed him of their surprise, when on their return from their previous visit, they found their money in their sacks. The steward, however, answered them kindly, restored Simeon to them, and brought them water to wash their feet. At noon Joseph returned, and the brothers spread out the present their father had sent, bowing themselves before him to the earth. After some questions touching the welfare of the *old man* they had left in the land of Canaan, he *lifted up his eyes, and saw his brother Benjamin, his mother's son*, and his whole soul yearned towards him, and he entered into his chamber and wept there. Thence having washed his face he returned, commanded the attendants to set on bread, and the brothers sat down ranged each according to his age. Joseph sat at a table by himself, and the Egyptians in his retinue by themselves; for to eat bread with the Hebrews was regarded by them as an abomination. Then from Joseph's table portions were sent to his brethren, but Benjamin's portion was five times as great as any of theirs, and *they drank and were merry with him* (Gen. xliii. 34).

The next morning, as soon as it was light, with sacks replenished, and rejoicing at the successful termination of their journey, the sons of Jacob commenced their return to Canaan. But they had proceeded only a little way from the city, when the Steward of Joseph overtook them, and charged them with returning evil

for all the good they had received, and stealing the silver
divining cup[1] (Gen. xliv. 5) belonging to his master.
In the full assurance of their innocence, the brothers
not only denied the charge, but declared their willingness that the guilty one should die, and the rest become
bondmen to the Viceroy. The sacks were, therefore,
taken from the asses, and lo! in Benjamin's sack,
where it had been purposely placed by Joseph's command, the cup was found. Horror-struck at the discovery, the brothers returned to the house, and flinging
themselves on the ground before Joseph, expressed
their resolution to become slaves with Benjamin rather
than return without him to his heart-broken father.
In the dialogue that ensued Judah was again the chief
speaker. *God*, he owned, *had found out their iniquity,
and they and he with whom the cup had been found
would become Joseph's bondmen.* To this, however,
Joseph would not consent ; he with whom the cup had
been found, he alone need remain behind in servitude,
the rest might return in peace to their father. Then
Judah went near to him, *who was even as Pharaoh*
(Gen. xliv. 18), and in words of utmost pathos related
how in obedience to his command, their father had
with great difficulty been prevailed on to suffer the
child of his old age to accompany them, and how, if he
failed to return, he would certainly die, for his life was
bound up in the life of his favourite son. Nay, more,
he continued, he himself had become surety for the lad,
and was now ready, rather than *bring down* the old

[1] Divining out of cups was practised in Egypt. "The
soothsayer drew his auguries either from the rays of light
which played upon the water in the cup, or threw in pieces
of gold and silver with jewels, and then pretended to see
signs of future events from the figures which appeared on the
surface, after an incantation had been pronounced." For
instances of a similar mode of divination in the South Sea
Islands, see Kitto's *Daily Biblical Illustrations*, I. 424.

*man's *grey hairs with sorrow to the grave,* to remain
alone in the land of Egypt a bondman unto his lord, if
only Benjamin and the rest might return into the land
of Canaan (Gen. xliv. 18—34).

As Judah proceeded with his moving tale, Joseph
could restrain himself no longer. He desired every man
to leave the chamber, and he and his brethren were
left alone. Then, amidst many tears, he at length
broke forth with the astounding words *I am Joseph,*
coupling the revelation with the enquiry *Doth my
father yet live?* But the brothers were too terrified to
answer him a word. Thereupon he bade them come near
unto him, and again assured them that he was *Joseph,
their brother,* whom they had sold to the Midianitish
caravan. Let them not, he said, be grieved that they
had sold him into Egypt. God, who orders all things,
had sent him thither before them to preserve their
lives, and had made him *a father unto Pharaoh, and
ruler throughout all the land of Egypt.* Instead of re-
pining for the past, let them return to the *old man,
their father,* and tell him of all his glory in Egypt, and
bring him down, and settle, they and their children,
their flocks and their herds, and all that they had, in the
goodly country of Goshen, *frontier.* Having thus at
length poured forth his pent up feelings, Joseph fell
upon Benjamin's neck, and wept, and kissed him, and
likewise all his brethren. Tidings of what had occurred
soon reached the ears of Pharaoh, who readily assented to Joseph's wish that his father should be suffered
to settle in the land. Waggons were then made ready
to bring him and all that he had; ample provisions
were supplied for the journey, and rich presents bestowed upon all the brothers, but especially on Benjamin. Then with a parting charge to see that they
fell not out by the way (Gen. xlv. 24), the sons of Jacob
returned to their father, and recounted to him all the

strange events that had befallen them. The long lost Joseph, the son of the beloved Rachel, was *alive*, nay, *he was governor over all the land of Egypt.* At the first announcement Jacob's heart failed him, nor could he believe their words. But when the waggons that Joseph had provided came in sight, then at length his spirit revived, and he exclaimed, *It is enough, Joseph my son is yet alive, I will go and see him before I die* (Gen. xlv. 28).

To forsake, however, the familiar pasture grounds of Hebron, to leave the soil promised to him and to his seed for ever, required of the patriarch no little resolution. Abraham had gone down to Egypt, but only to involve himself in great difficulties; Isaac had been on the point of going thither, when he was restrained by the hand of God (Gen. xxvi. 2). Did the Divine Blessing rest on that journey, which an imperious necessity now induced him to essay? Jacob was not long left in doubt. On reaching Beersheba the Almighty appeared to him in vision, and bade him lay aside all apprehensions. In Egypt, in the land of the mighty Pharaohs, He would not fail to protect him, there He would make him a great nation, and thence in the fulness of time He would bring his seed back to the *Land of Promise.* Thus encouraged Jacob arose from Beersheba, and with his sons, their wives, and their little ones, their herds, their flocks, and all the goods they had gotten in the land of Canaan, commenced his journey. Judah led the way, and on the frontier of Egypt the patriarch met his long lost son, and *fell upon his neck, and wept on his neck a good while.* Arrived in the land of the Pharaohs, five of Joseph's brethren were introduced to the reigning monarch. They told him that they were shepherds, that they had come down into Egypt in consequence of the severity of the famine, and requested permission to settle as strangers and foreigners in Goshen, the most easterly frontier-land of Egypt, and offered to become guardians of the royal herds. Permission was granted, and Jacob himself was introduced to Pharaoh, and bestowed his blessing upon the monarch (Gen. xlvii. 1—10).

The period of Jacob's own sojourning in the *land of Ham* (Ps. cv. 23) was limited to seventeen years, at the close of which he had reached the age of 147, and perceived that his end was nigh. Informed that his father was sickening, Joseph brought his two sons Ephraim and Manasseh and placed them before his bedside. *Guiding his hands wittingly,* the aged patriarch stretched out his right hand and laid it on Ephraim's head, though he was the younger, and his left hand on Manasseh's head, though he was the firstborn. At this Joseph was displeased, and would have altered the disposition of his father's hands. But Jacob refused, and with his hands as they were, bestowed upon the young men and their father his solemn and abiding blessing. Though born in Egypt, Ephraim and Manasseh were to be reckoned as his own sons, and would both grow into great tribes. But as it had been in Jacob's own case, so would it be with them; *the younger brother would be greater than the elder, and his seed should become a multitude of nations.* Then turning to Joseph the Patriarch bestowed on him a special mark of affection, even *one portion above his brethren,* a piece of land which with *his sword and his bow* he had conquered from the Amorites, probably outside the green vale of Shechem (Gen. xlviii. 22, Josh. xvii. 14, &c.).

And now the day drew nigh when the Patriarch's eventful life must close. Wishing by virtue of the gift of prophecy, which gained greater power the nearer he approached the borders of the eternal world, to tell them that *which should befall them in the last days,* he desired that his sons might be summoned to his bedside. Obedient to his word, they gathered round him, and then in prophetic trance " but having his eyes open," he beheld the mighty vision of the future, and predicted their several fortunes in the land, through which he himself had wandered as a pilgrim for more than one hundred years. First, before him stood Reuben, over whom in the tents of Laban he had rejoiced as *his firstborn, his might,* and *the beginning of his strength.* To him by the law of primogeniture belonged the headship of the family, and the double inheritance. But he had proved unworthy of his vocation. *Unstable as water, he should not excel.* Next in order of their birth came Simeon and Levi. Brethren of one mother, they had been also brethren in cruelty and deceit. In their conduct towards the Shechemites they had proved the fierceness of their anger, and the cruelty of their disposition. Unworthy were they to be the head of a nation which was to be a blessing and not a curse to all peoples of the earth, therefore were they to be *divided in Jacob, and scattered in Israel.* Next came Judah, and to him the patriarch could assign a portion at least of the blessing of the firstborn. His should be the pre-eminence in power and dignity, him should *his brethren praise,* before him should *his father's children bow down;* his should be the *Sceptre and the Lawgiver,* nor *from beneath his feet should they ever depart, till* Sʜɪʟoʜ, *the Peaceable* or *Peace-maker came*[1] (Gen. xlix. 1—10).

Having thus transferred the privileges of the firstborn to Judah and predicted the fortunes of his other sons, the dying Patriarch once more solemnly adjured them, as he had already adjured Joseph, not to leave his bones in Egypt, but to carry them into the land of

[1] Comp. Is. ix. 6. Others, not understanding the word to have a personal reference, translate it " Rest."

Hope and Promise, and lay them in the cave of Machpelah, in the family-grave of his fathers, and then he
*gathered up his feet into the bed, and yielded up the
ghost.* Obedient to such reiterated commands, Joseph
caused his father's body to be embalmed in the Egyptian fashion by the physicians, and obtained permission
from Pharaoh to accompany his remains to the burial-
place he had marked out for them. Then at the head
of a numerous retinue, composed not only of the members of his own family, but also of the court-officers of
Pharaoh, and the grandees of the empire, and accompanied by chariots and horsemen, he set out. The nearest
road would have been by Gaza, and through the territory of the Philistines. Instead of this, the funeral
procession took a long circuitous route round Mount
Seir[1] and the eastern side of the Dead Sea, and halted
at the threshing-floor of Atad, on the east side of
the Jordan, opposite Jericho. Here seven days were
spent in solemn mourning, and so grievous was the
lamentation that the Canaanites of the Jordan valley
called the spot Abel-Mizraim, *the Meadow,* or *the
Mourning of the Egyptians.* Further than this point
the Egyptian retinue do not seem to have proceeded.
The sons of Jacob alone crossed the Jordan, into the
land of Canaan, and laid their father in the cave of
Machpelah, by the side of Abram, Isaac, and Sarah
(Gen. l. 1—13).

[1] "The reason of this may be attributed to political circumstances, with which we are unacquainted. So large a
procession, attended by an armed guard, would probably have
met with difficulties from the contentious Philistines. It is a
remarkable coincidence, however, that Jacob's corpse should
have taken, or have been compelled to take the same road,
which his descendants were afterwards obliged to follow in
their journey to the Promised Land." Kurtz, *History of the
Old Covenant,* II. 91. Abel-Mizraim is placed by some on
the east, by some on the west of the Jordan.

The funeral over, Joseph and his brethren returned to Egypt. Fearful now their father was dead that the Viceroy would requite them for all the evil they had done towards him, the sons of Jacob sent a messenger to intercede in their behalf. But Joseph calmed their fears, and assured them of safety and protection. Together, then, they dwelt in peace and security in the land of Goshen ; and Joseph *saw Ephraim's children of the third generation, and the children of Machir the son of Manasseh brought up upon his knees.* At length, when he had reached the age of 110, perceiving that his end was near, he sent for his brethren, and having assured them that God would certainly visit them, and bring them up out of Egypt into the land which He had promised to their forefathers, and taken an oath of them that they would remove his bones into the same Good Land, he died, and was embalmed, and laid in a coffin in Egypt (Gen. l. 26).

NOTE.

SURVEY OF THE PATRIARCHAL AGE.

WITH the death of Joseph the Patriarchal Age of Israel's history may be said to close. The *Family* had now thrown out many branches, and was on the point of merging into the *Nation.* At this juncture, then, it may be well to look back, and review some of the chief features of Patriarchal Life.

i. And the first of these that claims attention is its *Nomadic character.* Unlike the founders of Egypt, of Babylon, of Nineveh, the Patriarchs were not the builders of cities and towns, but *pilgrims and sojourners, dwellers in tents* (Heb. xi. 9). But they were very different from rude hordes, like the Amalekites and other "sons of the desert," abhorring any higher mode of life. Abraham was no stranger to the highest form of civilization that his age afforded. He was acquainted with Ur, with Nineveh, with Damascus, with Egypt; he had left his home in one of the chief cities of Mesopotamia, not from choice, but in consequence of a direct personal call from God. Moreover, so far from regarding his

present mode of life as an ultimate end, he and Isaac and
Jacob, were ever looking forward to a time when it would
close, when their descendants should be *settled* in the Land of
Promise, and become a great *nation*, when the portable *tent*
should give way to the *city that had foundations* (Heb. xi. 10,
13—16; comp. Gen. xxiv. 7; xxviii. 4; xlix. 1—27; l. 24).
Hence, from time to time, as opportunity offered, we see the
wandering life freely and willingly laid aside.   Lot settled in
Sodom (Gen. xiii. 10—12); Abraham in Egypt went direct
to Pharaoh's court (Gen. xii. 14); at Hebron he settled and
became a "prince of God" in the midst of the Hittites (Gen.
xxiii. 6); Isaac not only lived near the Philistines, but occupied a *house* opposite the palace (Gen. xxvi. 8), and practised
agriculture (Gen. xxvi. 12); and Joseph's *dream of the sheaves*
points out that this was also continued in the time of Jacob
(Gen. xxxvii. 7)[1].

ii.   The *Family* was the centre of the Patriarchal commonwealth.   Its head was the source of authority and jurisdiction; he possessed the power of life and death (Gen.
xxxviii. 24); he united in himself the functions of chief and
priest; he offered the burnt-offering; he had his armed retainers (Gen. xiv. 14; xlviii. 22; xxxiv. 25; xxxiii. 20); his
intercourse with his wives (for polygamy was not forbidden)
was free and unrestrained; the wife's consent was asked before wedlock (Gen. xxiv. 57, 58); love hallowed the relations
of Abraham with Sarah, of Isaac with Rebekah, of Jacob
with Leah and Rachel; woman, indeed, did not occupy the
position since conceded to her, but her position was far from
degraded, and the sanctity of the marriage-bond was defended
by severe laws, which made death the punishment for adultery (Gen. xxxviii. 24).   Slavery, it is true, existed, but in
the tents of Abraham the slave was ever treated with consideration, and not excluded from, but made a partaker of religious privileges (Gen. xvii. 13).   The fidelity and attachment
of Eliezer the steward of Abraham's house, the mourning for
Deborah Rebekah's nurse (Gen. xxxv. 8), are pleasing proofs
of the peace that reigned in the Patriarchal household.

iii.   *Civilization.*   The life of the Patriarchs was chiefly
that of the shepherd, and their wealth mainly consisted in
their flocks and their herds.   But besides practising agriculture they were not unacquainted with money and the
precious metals.   Abraham paid for the field of Machpelah

---

[1] See Kurtz, *History of the Old Covenant*, II. 115.

with coin (Gen. xxiii. 9—20), and the sons of Jacob took money with them into Egypt (Gen. xlii. 25, 35); while the gold ring and armlets presented to Rebekah by Eliezer (Gen. xxiv. 22), the bracelet and signet ring of Judah (Gen. xxxviii. 18), the ear-rings of Rachel (Gen. xxxv. 4), the many-coloured coat of Joseph, indicate an acquaintance with the luxuries of life.

iv. *Religion.* While other nations were rapidly learning to deify the powers of nature, the Patriarchs believed not only in a God above and beyond nature, but in a God Personal, Omnipotent, and Holy. The God of Abraham, Isaac, and Jacob was no mere abstraction, no mere law. He could and did reveal Himself by angelic appearances, by visions, by dreams; He could console, strengthen, encourage; He could punish, rebuke, and on repentance forgive. Abraham, the *Friend of God* (Jas. ii. 23), intercedes with Him in behalf of Sodom and Gomorrah (Gen. xviii. 23—33); Isaac is warned by Him against going down into Egypt (Gen. xxvi. 2); Jacob is consoled by Him at Bethel when setting out into the land of exile (Gen. xxviii. 13—15), and wrestles with Him by the fords of Jabbok till the break of day (Gen. xxxii. 24); Joseph believes in His invisible but ever-present help in prison and in a strange land, and ascribes to Him all his wisdom in the interpretation of dreams (Gen. xli. 16). The Divine Promise of a great future Abraham believed under circumstances of greatest trial, and his faith was *counted to him for righteousness* (Rom. iv. 3). Moreover the God of the Patriarchs was no mere "national or household God." His sphere of operation was not restricted to the Patriarchs and their families; He is the God of all the earth (Gen. xxiv. 3), the God of Righteousness and Holiness. He punishes the people of Sodom and Gomorrah (Gen. xix. 24, 25); He plagues Pharaoh's house (Gen. xii. 17); He is the God of the priest-king Melchizedek (Gen. xiv. 18), and of the Philistine Abimelech (Gen. xx. 3); He protects not only Isaac the "child of promise," but the outcast Ishmael the "child of the bondwoman" (Gen. xxi. 13); He is with Joseph in prison, but He sends dreams to Pharaoh, and through Joseph He saves Egypt from famine (Gen. l. 20).

v. The *Religious Worship* of the Patriarchs was in keeping with the simplicity of their creed. The head of the family was also the priest of the family. Whenever Abraham, Isaac, or Jacob, reached any new spot in their pilgrimage, they invariably erected an altar, generally of stone and on a high situation (Gen. xxii. 9; xxvi. 25; xxxv. 7); there they called on the name of Jehovah, there they presented their burnt sacrifice, there they offered up their prayers. Their history also proves the existence of offering covenant-sacrifices, and celebrating covenant-feasts (Gen. xv. 9—18; xxi. 32); the making and paying of vows (Gen. xxviii. 23); the erection of memorial pillars, and the consecration of them by pouring upon them oil and wine (Gen. xxviii. 18); the rite of circumcision (Gen. xvii. 10—14); and the paying of tithes (Gen. xiv. 20)[1].

vi. The *Character of the Patriarchs* is never represented as perfect, their faults are freely exposed, theirs is no ideal history. If we compare the four most eminent amongst them, we seem to trace in (i) *Abraham,* "the faith that can remove mountains" in its power and in its fulness, revealing itself in unfaltering trust and unquestioning obedience under the most trying circumstances conceivable; in (ii) *Isaac,* the faith that can possess itself in patience, and discharge the ordinary duties of life in quietness and waiting; in (iii) *Jacob,* the violent contest of faith with the flesh, the higher with the lower nature, till by hard discipline the latter is purified, and the "Supplanter" becomes the "Prince," the "Prevailer with God;" in (iv) *Joseph,* the fidelity and perseverance of faith, revealed not only in the patient endurance of the most grievous trials, but in energetic action, and at length crowned with victory. "He unites in himself the noble trust and resolution of Abraham, with the quiet perseverance of Isaac, and the careful prudence of Jacob." He is moreover an eminent historic type of Christ, in (1) his persecution and sale by his brethren, (2) his resisting temptation, (3) his humiliation and exaltation, (4) his dispensing to a famine-stricken people the bread of life, (5) in the fulness of his forgiving love[2].

[1] Blunt's *Scriptural Coincidences,* Pt. I. 1.
[2] Smith's *Bibl. Dict.* I. 1140 b.

A MAP OF
CANAAN, EGYPT & SINAI
to illustrate the
PATRIARCHAL HISTORY
and
THE EXODUS.

English Miles

0 10 20 30 40 50 60 70 80 90 100

G R E A T   S E A
(Mediterranean Sea)

SEA OF THE PHILISTINES

Mᵗ SINAI ENLARGED

Note * The 'Wanderings' from
Kadesh to Esiongeber
cannot be traced.

Stanford's Geographical Establiʳ

London: Macmillan & Co Lᵗᵈ

BOOK III

FROM THE SETTLEMENT OF THE ISRAELITES IN EGYPT TO THE GIVING OF THE LAW.

CHAPTER I

THE BIRTH AND CALLING OF MOSES.

Exod. i.—vi. B. C. 1706—1491.

THE district of GOSHEN (*frontier*), also called the *Land of Rameses* (Gen. xlvii. 11), where the Is-raelites were settled during the period of their sojourn in the land of the Pharaohs, was the most easterly border-land of Egypt. It was scarcely included within the boundaries of Egypt proper, and was inhabited by a mixed population of Egyptians and foreigners (Exod. xii. 38). Eminently a pasture land and adapted to the rearing of flocks and herds, it included also a consider-able portion of fruit-bearing soil, which owed its fertility to the overflowing of the Nile, called by the Egyptians Hapi-Mu, *the genius of the waters,* by the Israelites Sihor, or Shihor, *the black* (Is. xxiii. 3; Jer. ii. 18). Touching on the west the green valley of this wondrous river, and stretching onwards to the yellow sands of the Arabian desert immediately south of Palestine, it was then, as it has always been, the most productive part of Egypt, yielding luxuriant crops of wheat and millet, and abounding in cucumbers and melons, gourds and beans, and other vegetable growths (Num. xi. 5).

Sacred History does not reveal to us many particulars respecting the early portion of the period during which the sons of Jacob sojourned in *the land of Ham*. We know that they were *fruitful and multiplied and waxed exceeding mighty*, so that when the time came for them to go forth from Egypt they could scarcely have numbered less than two million souls. We need not, however, suppose that these were all the direct descendants of the seventy immediate relatives of Jacob. When that Patriarch and his sons went down into Egypt they would naturally take with them not only their flocks and herds, but their menservants and maid-servants (Gen. xlv. 10, 11). Of the number of these we can form some calculation by remembering the 318 *trained servants*, who accompanied Abraham at the rescue of Lot[1] (Gen. xiv. 14); the *great store of serv-ants* possessed by Isaac (Gen. xxvi. 13, 14), two-thirds at least of whom passed into the possession of Jacob, and must be added to the *two hosts* which he brought from Mesopotamia (Gen. xxxii. 7, 8). But even thus their increase was marvellous, and must be ascribed to the direct superintending Hand of God. The effect, however, of their stay was perceptible in other respects. They not only increased in numbers, but became ac-quainted with many arts and sciences, and thus fitted for their future national existence. One portion, indeed, of the nation seems to have retained its pastoral habits even to the end. The descendants of Reuben, Gad, and Manasseh (Num. xxxii. 1) probably tended their large flocks and herds on the eastern border of Goshen, but others settled in the cities and villages on the confines of the land of Goshen, and not only adopted more gene-

---

[1] This, with the keepers of his flocks and herds, would make the adult males in his service certainly not less than 500 or 600, "implying a household of about 2000." See Kurtz, II. 149.

rally agricultural pursuits (Deut. xi. 10), but became acquainted with many useful arts, with writing, the working of precious and common metals, the grinding and engraving of precious stones, with carpentry, byssus-weaving, and pottery (1 Chr. iv. 14, 21, 23), with fishing, gardening (Num. xi. 5), and artificial irrigation (Deut. xi. 10)[1]. On the other hand, they could not fail to become acquainted with forms of religious worship hitherto utterly unknown to them. Now, for the first time, could they witness the gorgeous and mysterious ceremonies that attended the worship of Ra, the "Sun-God," or of Isis and Osiris. Now, for the first time, they might behold the incense burnt three times every day[2], and the solemn sacrifice offered once a month to the sacred black calf Mnevis at On (*Heliopolis*), or to his rival the bull Apis at Memphis. Now they saw, as they could scarcely have seen elsewhere, the adoration of *the creature rather than the Creator* carried to its furthest point, and divine honours paid not only to the mighty Pharaoh, the Child, the representative of the Sun-God, but to almost everything *in the heaven above, and the earth beneath, and the waters under the earth,* to the crocodile and the hawk, the cat and the dog, the hippopotamus and the serpent. That the simple patriarchal faith of the descendants of Abraham and Isaac and Jacob would suffer from contact with such diverse forms of idolatry might naturally be expected. The worship of the sacred calf exercised over them a peculiar fascination. *Your fathers worshipped other gods in Egypt,* says Joshua afterwards (Josh. xxiv. 14), *they forsook not the idols of Egypt,* is the accusation of Ezekiel (Ezek. xx. 7, 8; xxiii. 3). But an important event exercised a still greater influence on their social and religious condition. A change

---

[1] Kurtz's *History of the Old Covenant*, II. 156—161.
[2] Stanley's *Jewish Church*, p. 90.

took place in the reigning dynasty. *There arose a new king over Egypt* (Ex. i. 8; Acts vii. 18) *that knew not Joseph*, who regarded with no friendly feelings the strange community with alien rites and traditions, settled on the eastern outskirts of his realm. He viewed with alarm their rapid increase, and dreaded lest, in the event of a war, instead of guarding his kingdom against, they might join the enemies of Egypt, the roving tribes of the East, "the terror of the inhabitants of the Nile valley," and fight against his own people, and effect their escape from the land. Accordingly he determined to reduce them to the condition of public serfs or slaves; and in order to crush their free and independent spirit, set taskmasters over them, and employed them in gigantic works, making bricks for his treasure cities, PITHOM and RAAMSES. Day after day, therefore, their lives were made bitter with hard bondage, while beneath a burning rainless sky, naked and in gangs, they toiled under the lash in the quarry or the brick-field. But this expedient did not produce the effects the monarch desired. The more they were afflicted, the more this strange people grew and multiplied, and *waxed exceeding mighty.* Thereupon instructions were given to the Hebrew midwives to destroy in some secret way every Hebrew man-child. And when this too proved ineffectual, from the unwillingness of the midwives to obey so cruel a decree, an order was issued that every Hebrew boy should be flung into the waters of the Nile. What Abraham had seen in mystic vision was now fulfilled (Gen. xv. 12); *a horror of great darkness* had settled upon his descendants; strangers in a strange land, they were suffering grievous affliction, they *sighed by reason of their bondage, and their cry came up unto God* (Ex. ii. 23).

But it was at this juncture, when every thing seemed at the worst, that the future Deliverer of Israel was

born. Amram, a man of the house of Levi, married
Jochebed, a woman of the same tribe, and became the
father of a daughter Miriam, a son Aaron, and a boy
remarkable from his childhood for peculiar beauty (Ex
ii. 2; Acts vii. 20). For three months his mother succeeded in eluding the vigilance of Pharaoh's inquisi-
tors, and concealing her child. But at the close of that
period, finding further concealment impossible, she constructed an ark or boat of papyrus stalks, and having
protected it with pitch or bitumen, placed the child
therein among the reeds of the Nile. There the mother
left it, but Miriam the sister stood afar off to watch her
brother's fate. As the ark floated with the stream, the
daughter of Pharaoh, attended by her maidens, came
down to bathe in the waters of the sacred river, and as
she walked by the bank, her eye lit upon the basket,
and she sent one of her attendants to fetch it. It was
brought, and when opened, *behold! the babe wept.*
Struck with compassion the Egyptian princess, though
she perceived it was *one of the Hebrews' children,*
determined to rear it for her own. At this moment
Miriam approached, and asked permission to call a
nurse for the child. Permission was given, and Jochebed once more saw her boy restored to her, with the
command to rear it for its preserver. The child grew,
and after a while was brought to the Princess, and she,
in memory of its preservation, named it Moses, or in
its Egyptian form Mo-she, from *Mo,* "water," and *Ushe,*
"saved" (Ex. ii. 10).

The Foundling of the Nile was now formally brought
up as the adopted son of Pharaoh's daughter, and, in
conformity with his high position, received a suitable
education. He became *learned,* St Stephen tells us
(Acts vii. 22), *in all the wisdom of the Egyptians;*
in all therefore, we may believe, that the science of that
day could teach him of arithmetic, writing, astronomy,

6

medicine, and sacred symbolism.   On the same authority
we further learn that Moses became mighty not only *in
words, but also in deeds* (Acts vii. 22).   What these
deeds were is not known[1], but it is certain that the
Hebrew youth was in a position to have achieved a
splendid career.   He might have *enjoyed* to the full
the pleasures of the Egyptian court (Heb. xi. 25), and
amassed much of its accumulated treasures.   But the
traditions, the hopes, the creed of his own nation had
not, we may believe, been concealed from him by his
mother.   Hence when he came to the age of forty, chanc-
ing to go forth from On or Memphis to the land of
Goshen, he beheld one of his countrymen not only
toiling amidst the shadeless brick-fields, but suffering
the bastinado from his Egyptian taskmaster.   Filled
with indignation Moses *looked this way and that way*,
and seeing no one by, slew the Egyptian, and hid the
corpse in the white sand of the desert.   The next day,
seeing two of the Hebrews quarrelling, he tried to act
as arbiter between them.   His good offices, however,
were not only rejected by the one he decided to be in
the wrong, but he discovered that the murder of the
Egyptian was no secret.   He imagined that his countrymen would have recognised in him a Deliverer sent
from the God of their fathers, but they did not.   Before long, news of the murder reached the ears of
Pharaoh, and Moses perceiving that his life was no
longer safe fled from Goshen in a south-easterly direction to the land of Midian, or the peninsula of Sinai
in Arabia, peopled by the descendants of Abraham by
Keturah (Gen. xxv. 2).

He was sitting on a well in Midian, when he per-

---

[1] Josephus tells us that he became a distinguished military commander, and led an expedition against Meroe, and
married an Egyptian princess.   *Ant.* Lib. II. 10. 1.

ceived the approach of the seven daughters of JETHRO[1], the chief and priest of that country, to draw water for their flocks. They were in the act of filling the troughs, when certain Arabian shepherds rudely tried to drive them away. Thereupon, with the same zeal he had shown in behalf of his own countrymen, Moses intervened, and defended the maidens against the intruders. Their unusually early return prompted the enquiries of their father, and led to his introduction to the chivalrous stranger. Moses was contented to dwell with the Midianitish chief, and kept his flocks, and afterward married his daughter ZIPPORAH, by whom he became the father of two sons, GERSHOM (*stranger*) and ELIEZER (*God is my help*). And here amidst "the granite precipices and silent valleys of Horeb," in quiet and seclusion, forty years of his life passed away (Acts vii. 30). Here, as nowhere else, he could commune alone with God, and know himself, and learn the lessons of patience and self-control, and dependence on the Unseen, while the daily duties of his shepherd life made him acquainted with every path and track and fountain in a region, which he was afterwards to revisit under such different circumstances.

Meanwhile, though there was a change of ruler, the lot of the Israelites experienced no alteration. Still they toiled in cruel bondage, still their cry went up to the God of their fathers. At length the time drew near when the Promise made to Abraham was to be fulfilled, the oppressing nation *judged*, and the people delivered (Gen. xv. 14). One day Moses was leading the flocks of Jethro some distance from the spots, where he seems to have usually tended them, *to the back of the wilderness,* and came to *the mountain of God,*

---

[1] Called also Jether "*excellence,*" Ex. iv. 18 (marg.), Hobab "*beloved,*" Num. x. 29, and Reuel or Raguel, Ex. ii. 18.

even to Horeb, when a marvellous sight arrested his
attention. He looked, and behold! before him burning
with fire was a bush of wild acacia[1], "the shaggy
thorn-bush of the desert." But though enveloped in
flames, it was not consumed! It remained unsinged
and uninjured by the fiery element which played around
it! Astonished at the prodigy, Moses determined to
draw near and ascertain the cause of this *great sight*,
and as he approached, lo! a Voice, the Voice of God,
called unto him out of the midst of the bush, saying,
Moses, Moses! The awe-struck shepherd answered
the Voice, and then was directed to draw not nearer,
but take his shoes from off his feet, for the place on
which he stood was *holy ground*. Moses complied, and
hiding his face, for *he dared not look upon God*, listened, while the Lord spake again, assuring him that He
was the God of Abraham, the God of Isaac, the God of
Jacob; He had not been unmindful of the sufferings
of His people in Egypt; He had seen their affliction;
He had heard their cry; He had come down to deliver them from their oppressors, and to bring them
up into a land *flowing with milk and honey*, and He
had appointed no other than Moses himself to be their
Deliverer, and bring them forth from the land of Egypt.
Filled with awe and misgiving, Moses at first sought in
every way to excuse himself from the tremendous commission. *Who am I*, said he, *that I should go unto
Pharaoh, and that I should bring forth the children
of Israel out of Egypt? I will be with thee*, was the
reply. But who was this *I?* When Moses went to the
children of Israel, and assured them of the commission
he had received, what was the Name he was to announce

---

[1] "The wild acacia (*Mimosa Nilotica*) under the name of
'sont,' everywhere represents the 'seneh' or 'senna' of the
Burning Bush."—Stanley's *S. and P.* p. 20.

to them as his authority? *Thus shalt thou say unto the children of Israel,* replied the Almighty, *I AM* —Jehovah, the Eternal, the Self-existent—*hath sent me unto you* (Ex. iii. 14).

But this did not satisfy Moses. What outward and visible assurance could he give the people of his divine mission? This difficulty was also met. The Lord invested him with a threefold miraculous power, whereby to attest his authority, alike before the people and before Pharaoh. First, he should cast his staff, his shepherd's crook, upon the ground, and it would become a serpent, and on taking the creature by the tail it would resume its former state. Then he should put his hand into his bosom, and it would become leprous, but on returning it to his bosom would become as his other flesh. Thirdly, if they believed neither the first nor the second sign, he was to take of the water of the Sacred Nile, and pour it upon the dry land, and it should become blood. But now Moses pleaded another obstacle. He was not *eloquent,* he was *of a slow speech, and a slow tongue;* no words had he wherewith to bend the awful Pharaoh on his throne. *Who hath made man's mouth?* was the reply; *Who maketh the dumb, the deaf, the blind? Have not I the Lord? Go, and I will be with thy mouth, I will teach thee what thou shalt say.* Still Moses made another effort to roll off from himself the awful responsibility of the commission. *O my Lord,* he cried, *send, I pray Thee, by the hand Thou shouldest send.* This last proof of distrust provoked even the Lord to anger, but it was the anger of Love, the Love that remembers mercy and sustains the weak. The Lord had already provided a spokesman. Aaron his brother was at this moment on his way to meet him, and he was known to be able to speak well. Together, like the Apostles afterwards, the Brothers should go in before Pharaoh; Aaron should be *instead of a mouth,* and Moses should be to him *instead of God,* and with his rod he should perform the prescribed signs. Then, at last, his timidity was removed ; he consented to go, and the object of the Vision of the Burning Bush was thus far attained (Ex. iv. 1—17).

CHAPTER II

SIGNS AND WONDERS IN EGYPT.

Exod. iv.—xi. B. C. 1491.

THE first step Moses took towards fulfilling the trust thus confided to him was to request of his father-in-law permission to revisit his brethren in Egypt. Jethro gave his consent, and then, having received the Divine assurance that *all the men were dead which sought his life,* accompanied by Zipporah and her two sons, Gershom and Eliezer, Moses commenced his return to Egypt[1]. He had not proceeded far before he encountered his brother Aaron coming forth to meet him, to whom he explained their commission, and the signs that were to attest it. On arriving in the land of Goshen the Brothers gathered together all the clans of the nation. Aaron, as spokesman, rehearsed *the words which the Lord had spoken to Moses, and did the signs in the sight of the people.* His announcement had the desired effect. The Israelites believed that the Lord God of their fathers had indeed interposed in their behalf, *and bowed their heads and worshipped.* The next step was to procure from Pharaoh the necessary permission for the departure of the people. But now, even as the Almighty had forewarned

[1] On account, however, of the incident related in Ex. iv. 24—26, Zipporah and her sons returned to Midian.

them, the difficulties of the Brothers commenced. On presenting themselves before Pharaoh, and informing him of the will of Jehovah, the God of Israel, that His people should be permitted to go three days' journey into the wilderness, there to offer sacrifice unto Him (Ex. v. 3), the monarch haughtily asked, *Who is Jehovah, that I should obey His Voice to let Israel go?* Conceiving the God of Israel to be merely a national god, it seemed to him inexplicable that One who had suffered His worshippers to endure a lengthened and degrading bondage, could demand of him, the mightiest monarch of the earth, to let His people depart. Concluding, therefore, that it was only an expedient to excite aspirations for freedom among the bondslaves, in contemptuous mockery of them and their God, he ordered that the severity of their toil should be doubled. Hitherto straw had been found them, wherewith to make bricks for the treasure-cities and other gigantic works then in progress; but now it was ordered that they must go and gather straw for themselves, and yet the tale of bricks must not be diminished; what it was before, that it was to remain, and to be completed also. To comply with this tyrannical command was impossible, and the Israelitish officers, who had been set over the people by the Egyptians were beaten, and their complaints to Pharaoh were utterly disregarded. This produced a great change of feeling towards Moses and Aaron, at whose announcement of speedy deliverance the people had so lately *bowed the head and worshipped.* They heaped reproaches upon them, and openly charged them with being the cause of their now accumulated miseries, of *having made their savour to be abhorred in the eyes of Pharaoh* (Ex. v. 1—21).

Thus the first attempt of Moses to execute his commission ended in complete failure. In deep dejection he laid before Jehovah the ineffectual issue of his efforts,

and in reply not only received a second assurance of
protection and ultimate triumph, but was told that as
Pharaoh had rejected the *word* of God, God would
now speak to him in *deeds*, and multiply His *signs and
wonders* in the land of Egypt, till the Egyptians knew
that He was the Lord. But the contest, in which
Moses was now to engage, was not to be fought with
carnal weapons. As the accredited servant of Jehovah, he was to contend against the gods of Egypt,
against those arts, the very lifeblood of heathenism, in
which Egypt deemed itself so strong, its magic and
necromancy, its priests and conjurers. Accordingly
the Brothers went a second time into Pharaoh's presence, and renewed their request. The monarch demanded a miracle in attestation of their claim. Thereupon Aaron threw down his rod before the king and his
courtiers, and straightway it became a serpent. But
snake-charming was an art in which Egypt bore off the
palm from every other country of the world. Pharaoh,
therefore, summoned his magicians[1], who cast down
their rods, and they likewise became serpents. But
though Aaron's rod swallowed up their rods, the monarch would not acknowledge that his servants had
been defeated; he hardened his heart, and refused to
recognise in this miracle an authoritative warning to let
the people go. The "signs," therefore, were now to
become *Plagues* (Ex. vii. 8—14).

(i) Accordingly, on the morrow, at the command of
God, Moses made his appearance before Pharaoh, just
as he was going to offer sacrifice to, or perform his religious ablutions in the sacred waters of the Nile, the
"Father of Life," the "Father of the Gods[2]," as it

---

[1] Their names are given in 2 Tim. iii. 8, as *Jannes* and
Jambres. The same names are also found in the Targum and
the Talmud.

[2] As Oceanus, or the "Watery Element," the Nile was a

was called by the Egyptians. In words few but decisive he announced the reason of his coming, and then
the word was given; Aaron lifted up his rod, and in a
moment, before the very eyes of the monarch and all
his servants, the waters of the sacred, fructifying river,
not only in the stream itself, but in the "canals and
tanks, in the vessels of wood and vessels of stone, then,
as now, used for the filtration of the water from the
sediment of the river bed," were turned into blood.
The fish, though similarly objects of religious reverence,
died in incredible numbers, and the "Father of Waters," the source of health and blessing, stank, nor
could the Egyptians drink thereof, for there was blood
throughout all the land of Egypt. But again the magicians were summoned ; with their enchantments, they
caused other water, probably obtained by digging about
the river, to assume the same blood-red appearance,
and Pharaoh turned into his house, and hardened his
heart, neither *would he let the people go* (Ex. vii. 14—25).

(ii) After an interval, therefore, of seven days,
Moses and Aaron again presented themselves before
him, and when their request was again denied, inflicted

member of the first Ogdood of the Egyptian theology, and the
opponent of Phtah or the "Element of Fire ;" its sacred
emblem was the "tame crocodile." On the monuments it is
still called the god Nile, "the life-giving Father of all that
exists," "the Father of the Gods," &c. "What the heart is
to the body," says an Egyptian, "the Nile is to Egypt ; it is
one with Osiris and the Supreme God." Herodotus (II. 90)
speaks of priests of the Nile, and at Nilopolis there was a
temple to it. "Flowing, as it did, between sand and rock,
the sole giver and sustainer of life in that valley of death,
it was both in its increment and its decrease, in its course
through vast solitudes and thronged populations alternately,
the most expressive and suggestive of emblems for a religion
which represented in such marked contrast the realms of
creation and destruction, of Osiris and Typhon."—See Kurtz,
II. 273, 4, and Article *Nile* in Smith's *Bibl. Dict.*

the *second* plague. From the streams, the rivers, the ponds of Egypt, *Frogs*[1] came up over the whole land, penetrating into the royal palace, the houses of the courtiers and of the people, defiling bed-chamber and bed, oven and kneading-trough, with their loathsome touch. Again the magicians were summoned, and though they were utterly unable to counteract, they succeeded in imitating this plague also. Pharaoh was more deeply moved than before; he not only condescended to beg of Moses and Aaron that they would intreat Jehovah to remove this plague from his people, but undertook to allow the Israelites to depart and do sacrifice to the Lord. But no sooner had the desired deliverance been vouchsafed, than he again hardened his heart and refused to fulfil his word (Ex. viii. 1—15).

(iii) For the *third* time, therefore, Aaron uplifted his rod, and now, not from the "Father of Waters," but from the fertile soil of Egypt itself, came forth innumerable swarms either of *Lice* or of *Gnats*[2], which afflicted both man and beast with intolerable discomfort. This plague all the spells and incantations of the court magicians were unable to imitate, and they were fain to confess to Pharaoh, *This is the finger of God*, but he hardened his heart, and *hearkened not unto them* (Ex. viii. 16—19).

(iv) On the morning after, as he went forth to the waters of the river, which he had lately seen so grievously dishonoured, he was met by Moses, and refused

---

[1] Frogs were regarded as sacred by the Egyptians; like the crocodile they were included in the second class of objects of worship. Smith's *Bibl. Dict.* Article, *Plagues of Egypt*.

[2] The meaning of the Hebrew word is doubtful. The LXX. has σκνῖφες, and the Vulgate *sciniphes*, mosquitos; which Herodotus (II. 95) mentions as an intolerable plague in Egypt. Josephus (*Ant.* II. 14. 3) makes them lice; if so, this would have been especially humiliating to the priests, who regarded cleanliness as a religious duty.

for the *fourth* time to relieve the people of their bondage. On this the servant of Jehovah spake the word, and there came innumerable *Flies* of various kinds[1], usually a fearful torment in Egypt, but now attacking with unwonted fury both man and beast, and swarming in every house of the Egyptians, while they touched neither house nor person of the Israelites in Goshen. Such was the intolerable severity of this plague that Pharaoh so far relented as to permit the people to sacrifice to Jehovah *in the land itself,* but with the proviso that they should not leave it. This Moses would not concede. Therefore the monarch extended his concession to a journey some little way into the wilderness, but on the removal of the judgment revoked it, and retained the nation in bondage (Ex. viii. 20—32).

(v) The *fifth* Plague was now inflicted. A grievous *Murrain* broke out amongst the horses, the asses, the camels, the oxen, the sheep of the Egyptians, so that all the cattle of Egypt, including not only the useful beasts, but probably "the sacred goat of Mendes, the ram of Ammon, the calf of Heliopolis, the bull Apis[2]," died, while in the land of Goshen, as Pharaoh himself ascertained, there was not one of the cattle of the Israelites dead. But even this had no effect on his proud heart (Ex. ix. 1—7).

(vi) Accordingly Moses and Aaron were commanded to take *handfuls of ashes of the furnace,* and *sprinkle* them upwards *towards heaven,* and on their so doing, *Boils* and *Blisters,* and other eruptive disorders, broke forth upon man and upon beast. Even the royal magicians suffered so terribly from this the *sixth* plague,

---

[1] The exact meaning of the Hebrew word is here also unknown: 1. Some, as the English Version, understand it to denote *swarms of flies,* but see Margin at Ex. viii. 21 ; 2. Others, as the LXX., take it to be the *dog-fly;* 3. Others, the *beetle.*

[2] Stanley's *Lectures,* p. 119.   Smith's *Bibl. Dict.* II. 885.

that they *could not stand before Moses*, but the heart
of their master was still hardened, nor would he yield
to the will of God (Ex. ix. 8—12).

(vii) With still greater solemnity, therefore, the
coming of the *Seventh* Plague was announced to him,
and he was warned to send his servants and gather
together such of his cattle as were grazing in the fields,
if he would not have them utterly destroyed by a terrible *Storm of thunder, lightning, and hail*[1]. By some,
who heard the warning, it was heeded in time, by others
it was utterly disregarded. But it was too surely fulfilled. Moses stretched forth his rod toward heaven,
and on the fair garden of Egypt, with its green meadows
and fields of corn and barley and maize, the storm burst
forth with unwonted fury. *The Lord thundered out of
heaven, and the Highest gave His thunder* (Ps. xviii.
13). *The fire ran along upon the ground*, the hail
rattled, and smote *the vines and fig-trees* (Ps. cv. 33), and
every herb of the field, and every tree of the field, the
barley then *in the ear*, and the flax then *bolled* or risen
in the stalk, as also the cattle and herdmen that had not
been removed to any place of shelter. Alarmed beyond
measure at this unexampled tempest, Pharaoh begged
Moses to intercede for him, owned this time that he had
sinned, that the Lord was righteous, that he and his
people were wicked, and promised to do all that was
required of him. But, as before, when the fury of the
elements was hushed he refused to abide by his word
(Ex. ix. 13—35).

(viii) And now for the *eighth* time the release of
the people was demanded, and the monarch was told
that, in the event of refusal, the country, already grievously devastated, should be given up to the awful ra-

---

[1] Hail and thunderstorms are by no means of rare occurrence in Egypt, but by the concurrent testimony of all
travellers mild and harmless in their effects.

vages of the *Locusts*, which, in numbers, *such as neither his fathers nor his fathers' fathers had seen*, should swarm in the palace and the hut, covering the face of the ground, and eating up whatever herb or tree had escaped the fury of the late storm. This announcement filled the Egyptians, already suffering severely, with uttermost alarm. *Let the people go*, they cried to their king, *that they may serve the Lord their God : knowest thou not yet that Egypt is destroyed?* Even Pharaoh was fain to lend an ear to this remonstrance. Summoning Moses and Aaron, he informed them that he was ready to allow such as were *men* amongst the Israelites to depart and serve their God, but their wives and children must remain as a guarantee for their return. The servants, however, of Jehovah, were not empowered to make this concession, and the plague began. A strong east wind blew continuously and brought the locusts, which in dense swarms covered the face of the land, so that it was darkened and became a desolate wilderness, without a leaf upon the trees or a blade of grass in the fields[1]. The obduracy of the monarch now broke down, and was followed by a brief repentance, which lasted no longer than the west wind which swept away the locusts ; for once more, in the face of an utterly devastated country and a murmuring people, he refused to hearken to the word of the Lord (Ex. x. 1—20).

(ix) Without the pre-announcements, therefore, which had preceded the infliction of the other plagues, the *ninth* now appeared in the shape of *Darkness*[2] so dense *that it might be felt*, which for three days enve-

[1] For a wonderfully vivid description of the ravages of the locust see Joel ii. 1—11.

[2] The horrors of the Egyptian Samoom or *Chamsîn*, which is regarded by some as the basis of this Plague, has been described by many travellers. See Robinson's *Bib. Res.* I. 207. Kurtz, II. 287. Smith's *Bib. Dict.* II. 888.

loped the entire land, save only the favoured country of Goshen. During this period the light of the sun was obscured, an awful and preternatural gloom shrouded the land, so that the Egyptians neither could see one another nor rise from their place. At the end of the three days Pharaoh once more capitulated ; all the Israelites, young and old, might depart, the flocks and herds alone must remain. These conditions, however, were rejected by Moses, and he was dismissed from the palace with the warning to take heed that he saw the face of Pharaoh no more, for *on the day that he saw his face, he should surely die* (Ex. x. 21—29).

CHAPTER III

THE LAST PLAGUE--THE PASSOVER— THE EXODUS.

Exod. xi.—xv.

HITHERTO the elements of nature had each in their turn been commissioned to fight against Pharaoh. In all the preceding plagues there had been human intervention. The rod or the hand of Moses had summoned from the sacred river, or the fertile soil, or the rainless air, or the desert sands of Arabia, the ministers of punishment, and wrought *signs and wonders in the land of Ham*, and had proved that the God he served was no mere national god, but was Lord over earth and air and water, over cattle and man, over tree and herb. But none of the elements of nature were to bring on Pharaoh God's *last sore judgment. At midnight*, said Jehovah, *will I go out into the midst of Egypt, and all the firstborn in the land of Egypt shall die, from the firstborn of Pharaoh that sitteth upon his throne, even unto the firstborn of the maid-servant that is behind the mill, and all the firstborn of beasts;*

I will execute judgment against all the gods or princes (Ex. xiii. 12 *Marg.*) *of Egypt, I am Jehovah.*

Before, however, this last great blow was struck, involving the firstborn of the highest and the lowest in one common fate, certain important preliminaries were to be enacted. It was now the Hebrew month of Nisan or Abib, the *month of green ears.* On the fourteenth day of this month it was announced that the last sore judgment would be inflicted. But on the tenth day of this month, a month to be to the Israelites henceforth the *beginning of months,* the first month of their sacred year, the father of every household was to select a lamb or kid, without blemish, a male of the first year. It was to be kept till the fourteenth day, and then slain just before the evening twilight (Ex. xii. 1—6). A portion of the blood was to be sprinkled with a bunch of hyssop on the two side-posts and the upper door-post of the houses of the Israelites, and on the selfsame night the lamb, roast with fire, whole, not a bone being broken, was to be eaten with unleavened bread and bitter herbs. Of this meal each household was to partake, with their loins girded, their shoes on their feet, their staves in their hands, in haste like persons in a hurry to depart. Of the flesh of the lamb nothing was to be allowed to remain until the morning, and all remnants were to be burnt with fire. And at midnight, while they were partaking of this mysterious meal, the Lord, they were told, would *pass through the land of Egypt,* and smite all the firstborn, both of man and beast, but when He saw the blood sprinkled on the houses of the Israelites, He would *pass over* them, and the plague should not be upon them to their destruction (Ex. xii. 7—12).

Such was the ordinance of the PASSOVER, a Memorial-Feast to be celebrated, not on that night only, but throughout all future generations. and to be kept for a period of seven days, during which leavened bread was neither to be eaten nor found in any of the houses of the Israelites. On receiving from Moses the Lord's commands respecting this Feast, the elders of Israel, partakers with him of a like faith in the certainty of the events about to be enacted (Heb. xi. 28), *bowed their heads and worshipped.* On the tenth day of Nisan, the Month of Redemption, each household selected a lamb or kid, kept it till the fourteenth day, slew it, sprinkled the blood upon the side-posts and the upper door-post of their houses, and at midnight were eating of it with the prescribed ceremonies, when suddenly the last and most awful of all the Ten Plagues began. The Lord smote all the firstborn in the land of Egypt, from the firstborn of the captive that was in the dungeon unto the firstborn of the mighty Pharaoh himself, and all the firstborn of cattle. In the darkness of that awful night the monarch rose up, he and all his servants, and all the Egyptians, and a loud frantic cry arose throughout the land, for there was not a house where there was not one dead. Terrified and confounded the stubborn king could no longer resist the power of Jehovah. He implored Moses and Aaron, as an act of kindness, to depart with the utmost speed. And not only he, but all his people joined in the petition, and pressed upon the Israelites jewels of silver and jewels of gold, earrings, signet-rings, necklaces, and festal apparel. Thus furnished by the Egyptians themselves with costly ornaments befitting the great day of their deliverance[1], the whole host of the Israelites, numbering 600,000 men capable of bearing arms, besides women and children and a mixed multitude from the lower orders of the

[1] Moses had already *before* the tenth day of Nisan (Ex. xi. 1—3) notified to the elders (xii. 21) what was to be done respecting the Departure, and, therefore, ample preparations had doubtless been made.

Egyptians, went forth from RAMESES, and in the darkness and cool of the night pursued their way (Ex. xii.
37, 38).

The nearest route to Canaan would have been the
usual caravan route, which runs in a north-easterly
direction along the coast of the Mediterranean, and
would not have occupied more than a few days. But
it would have brought the host into collision with the
warlike and powerful nation of the Philistines, and for
such an encounter they were as yet totally unfit. From
RAMESES, therefore, which was probably on the eastern
skirts of the Delta in the *Wady Tumeilat*, they proceeded in a southerly course, and after a day's journey
halted for the first time at SUCCOTH (Ex. xii. 37), the
place of *booths*, "formed by the luxuriant foliage of
tamarisk, sycamore, and palm" at the verge of the cultivated land of Egypt. The next day's halt was at
Etham in the edge of the wilderness (Ex. xiii. 20). At
this point the Lord Himself in an outward and visible
form assumed the direction of their march, appearing
by day in a Pillar of Cloud, and by night in a Pillar of
Fire. Such a miraculous intervention was indeed needed
to confirm the faith of the host, for instead of being
conducted round the northern extremity of the Red
Sea, so as to escape with all speed beyond reach of
their Egyptian oppressors, they were commanded to
turn and encamp before Pihahiroth (*the place of sedge*),
between Migdol (a frontier *Watchtower*) and the
western side of the Red Sea over against Baal-
zephon. Here they had scarcely encamped, when lifting up their eyes the Israelites discerned the terrible
horses and chariots of Pharaoh pursuing after them.
Astonished that the people had not made good their
flight into Asia, and deeming them entangled in the
land and shut in by the wilderness, the monarch had
directed all his forces to give chase to the fugitives.

7

In wild alarm the Israelites cried out to Moses, and already complained of their deliverance from the bondage of Egypt. But the faith of their leader was not shaken. He bade the trembling, panic-stricken host stand still and *see the salvation of the Lord.*

They had not long to wait. For at this moment the Angel of God, who went before the host of Israel in the Pillar of Cloud and Fire, stationed himself behind them so as to deepen the gloom in which the Egyptians were advancing, and afford light and encouragement to the Israelites. Simultaneously, Moses advanced towards the Red Sea, either at the present fords of Suez, or at some point higher up, and stretched over it his rod. Thereupon a strong East wind began to blow, the waters were divided, the bottom of the sea was exposed, and amidst walls of water standing up on either side of them on their right hand and on their left, the caravan of the Israelites defiled in long procession. All night the wondrous passage continued, and as the morning broke they had safely landed on the further shore. Meanwhile their foes, determined to prevent the second escape of their prey, had rushed on amidst the pitchy darkness that surrounded them into the same awful pass. But, at the morning watch, when they had reached the midst of the sea, the Lord looked upon them from the Pillar of Fire and of the Cloud, and troubled their hosts, and caused their heavy chariot-wheels to sink in the sand, so that *they drave them heavily.* In wild confusion they shouted to one another to turn back, but it was too late. Again the hand of Moses was uplifted, and straightway the waters, till now congealed from their lowest depths (Ex. xv. 8), began to break and give way, and the sea *to return to his strength.* All efforts to escape were fruitless, fast and furious the sea swept on, the engulphing waves closed over them, horse and chariot and horseman *sank like lead in the mighty waters.* Then from the Israelitish leader, and the host which had stood still and seen the deliverance Jehovah had wrought for them, there burst forth a noble song of praise and thanksgiving, while Miriam his sister, and her women, accompanied them with timbrels and dances. Together they sang the praises of Him who *had triumphed gloriously, who had cast Pharaoh's chariots and his host into the sea, and drowned his chosen captains in the waves, whose right hand become glorious in power had dashed in pieces the enemy, who had blown with His wind, and gathered the waters with the blast of His nostrils, and in His mercy led forth the people which He had redeemed.* (Ex. xv. 1—19. Comp. Ps. lxxvii. 16—19.)

Thus, at length, the word of the Most High, which He spake to the patriarch Abraham at least 400 years before, was fulfilled. The seed of the Patriarch had grown into a great nation; they had been strangers in a land that was not theirs; they had suffered cruel affliction and degradation; but the oppressing nation had been judged, and *with much substance* the oppressed had come forth. The jewels of silver and gold and the festal apparel, which their late tyrants had forced upon them, well became this their national birthday. Once slaves, they were now free; once a degraded tribe, they were now an independent people. They had left behind them Egypt with its grinding tyranny, and its memories of years of suffering. They had been *baptized unto Moses in the cloud and in the sea* (1 Cor. x. 2), their faces were set towards a Promised Land, their hopes fastened on a glorious Future.

CHAPTER IV

THE JOURNEY FROM THE RED SEA
TO REPHIDIM.

EXOD. XV.—XIX. B. C. 1491.

AND now the ransomed people commenced their
journey. Skirting the eastern shore of the Red
Sea, they "entered" the wilderness of Shur (or Etham,
Num. xxxiii. 8), on the western base of the high table-
land which forms the northern portion of the peninsula
of Sinai[1]. A three days' march brought them to a well,
probably *Ain Howâra*, plentifully supplied, indeed,

[1] The triangular peninsula of Sinai, bounded on the west
by the Gulf of Suez, and on the east by the Gulf of Akaba,
consists of three main divisions. (i) The northern part,
the desert of Et-Tîh, or "the Wanderings," is a high table-
land of limestone, of which the *western* portion is called in
Scripture *the wilderness of* SHUR (Ex. xvi. 22), and the *eastern*,
the wilderness of PARAN. (ii) To this succeeds a range
called *Jebel-et-Tîh*, which extends in a curved direction from
the upper end of the Gulf of Suez to that of the Gulf of
Akaba, and skirts the sea for some distance on either side.
(iii) South of this ridge, and separated from it by "a narrow plain or belt of sand" is the great triangular mass
of red granite mountains called the Tôr (*rock*), the approach
to which from its three sides is through rugged passes leading
upwards to the cliffs and mountains, " beginning in a gradual,
but terminating usually in a very steep ascent—almost a
staircase of rock." Of this mountain-mass the chief heights
are (*a*) on the N.W. *Jebel-Serbâl*, overlooking *Wady Feirân*
= Rephidim; (*b*) in the centre, *Jebel Katherin* (5705 ft.) and
Jebel Mousa (7560 ft.); (*c*) on the S. *Um Shômer* (8850 ft.).
On which summit the Law was given is uncertain, but not
improbably it was the majestic height of *Ras Sasâfeh* at
the N.W. end of Jebel Mousa, which overlooks the plain of
Er-Raheh. The country between the *Jebel-et-Tîh* and the
Gulf of Suez is called in Scripture the wilderness of ETHAM
(Num. xxxiii. 8); that between the Gulf and the western base
of the Tôr *the wilderness of* SIN (Num. xxxiii. 11, 12) =
the N. portion of the present *plain of El-Kâa*, which must be

with water, but so bitter that they could not drink of it, whence they called it Marah (*"bitterness"*). This was the first test of their faith in their Invisible Leader, and they proved unequal to it. They murmured against Moses, saying, *What shall we drink?* In his distress Moses turned to the Lord, who bade him cast a tree into the waters, and they were straightway sweetened. Leaving Marah they reached ELIM (Wâdy *Ghurundel,* or Wâdy *Useit*), where were twelve wells of refreshing water, and three-score and ten palmtrees. Here they probably staid some days, and then passing between vast cliffs, probably at the mouth of the *Wâdy Tayibeh,* again came in sight of the deep blue waters of the Red Sea (Num. xxxiii. 10), where they encamped, and were able for the last time to discern the shadowy line of Egypt, the land of bondage. Leaving the sea-shore on the fifteenth day of the second month, they entered the shadeless desert of Sin (Ex. xvi. 1). By this time the supply of bread they had brought with them from Egypt was consumed, and the people burst forth into loud murmurings against Moses and Aaron. *Would God,* they cried, *we had died by the hand of the Lord in the land of Egypt, when we sat by the fleshpots, and did eat bread to the full.* Thereupon Moses was commissioned to assure them of speedy relief, and that very evening dense flocks of quails, immense numbers of which are found in Arabia Petræa and the adjoining countries, covered the ground around their encampment (Ex. xvi. 13). Moreover the next morning, when *the dew had gone up, behold! there lay on the face of the wilderness a small round thing, as small as the hoar frost, white, like coriander seed, the taste of which was like wafers made with honey.* On seeing this

carefully distinguished from *the wilderness of* ZIN (Num. xx. 1; xxxiii. 36), a desert tract between the Dead Sea and the Gulf of Akaba, now *the Arabah.*

curious substance, and not knowing its origin or properties, the Israelites exclaimed Man-hu, "*What is it?*" whence the substance hitherto unknown received the name of MANNA (Ex. xvi. 14—36).

Two conditions were annexed to the enjoyment of this extraordinary and unlooked-for blessing. The people were instructed to gather only a sufficient quantity for the wants of a single day, an omer (about five pints) each man, and they were to leave none of it until the morning. Some of them, however, infringed both these conditions, and in both instances found cause to regret their conduct. Some took the trouble to gather more than the prescribed quantity, and found that in spite of their exertions *he that gathered much had nothing over, and he that gathered little had no lack.* Others *did* leave some of it until the morning, but they too found themselves disappointed, for it was in a state of decomposition and utterly unfit for food. On the sixth day, however, each man was surprised to find himself able to gather twice the usual quantity. This circumstance Moses explained to them. The seventh day was to be observed as a holy SABBATH (*rest*) unto the Lord, on that day no manna would be found lying on the ground, but on the sixth day they were to gather twice the usual quantity to make provision for the deficiency on the Sabbath. This command, however, was not universally obeyed. Some went out to gather on the Sabbath, but returned empty-handed. Thus the institution of the Day of Rest was presented as one of peculiar significance, and a preparation was made for the more precise legislation respecting it to be afterwards promulgated. In memory of this miraculous supply of the people's needs, Moses directed that an omer of the Manna should be put aside in a vessel as a memorial to all future generations (Ex. xvi. 32—34; John vi. 31, 32; 1 Cor. x. 3; Heb. ix. 4).

After a halt of a week in the wilderness of Sin, and also at two intermediate stations, Dophkah and Alush (Num. xxxiii. 12—14), the positions of which are unknown, the Israelites reached Rephidim ("*places of Rest*"), most probably the *Wâdy Feirân*, and "the finest valley in the whole peninsula." Two circumstances distinguished their encampment in this valley. In consequence of a second failure of water the murmurings of the people against their leader reached such a pitch, that they showed signs of a readiness even to stone him with stones. Again, however, the Lord interposed, and mercifully directed Moses to strike a rock in Horeb, *i.e.* one of the outer hills in the Sinaitic group, whereupon a copious stream flowed forth, and refreshed the thirsty host. In memory of the murmuring of the people, Moses named the spot Massah ("*temptation*"), and Meribah ("*strife*") (Ex. xvii. 7).

The other circumstance which rendered memorable the encampment at this spot was of a different nature. One of the main streams of population occupying at this time the Sinaitic Peninsula, was the powerful tribe of Amalek. Their settlements extended from the northern part of the peninsula, even to the borders of Palestine. They were descended from Esau, and were governed by a chief, who bore the title, by some deemed hereditary, of Agag, the "*Burner*" or "*Destroyer.*" (Comp. Num. xxiv. 7; 1 Sam. xv. 8, 9.) Regarding the encampment of the Israelites in the rich and fertile valley of Rephidim with no friendly feelings, they mustered their forces, and treacherously falling upon their exhausted rear, *smote the hindmost of them and the feeble amongst them, when they were faint and weary* (Deut. xxv. 17—19). To repel this attack Moses directed a young man, whose name is here for the first time mentioned, Joshua, or as he was now called Hoshea (*salvation*), the son of Nun, of the tribe of

Ephraim, to select a body of men, and go forth to meet
Amalek in the valley. Meanwhile he himself ascended
the hill, whence, probably, the refreshing streams had
issued, with the rod of God in his hand, and accompanied by Aaron and Hur. There within sight of the
battle in the valley below, he stood and stretched forth
his hands in supplication to heaven. So long as his
hands remained thus uplifted, the Israelites made good
their superiority over the foe, but as often as from wea-
riness his hands drooped Amalek prevailed. For a long
time the contest seemed undecided. At length Aaron
and Hur, seeing Moses wearied with his exertions, took
a stone and placed it under him, and stayed up his
hands in the attitude of supplication, till the sun went
down, by which time Amalek had sustained a total defeat, and been smitten with the edge of the sword. This
victory and the circumstances leading to it were too
important to be forgotten. On the summit of the hill,
where he had stood in the attitude of prayer, Moses
erected an altar, which he called JEHOVAH-NISSI (*the
Lord is my Banner*), and, by the Divine direction,
inscribed in a book the account of Amalek's attack, and
rehearsed it in the ears of Joshua. Their treacherous
conduct had placed them under the same ban as the
nations of Canaan, and the Lord *would utterly put out
the remembrance of Amalek from under heaven* (Ex.
xvii. 14; 1 Sam. xv. 2, 3; 2 Sam. viii. 12).

Not long afterwards, JETHRO, the father-in-law of
Moses, having heard all that the Lord had done for his
kinsman, and of the wonderful deliverance of the Israelites from Egypt, left his tents among the Midianites
and came to meet him, with his daughter Zipporah, and
her two sons Gershom and Eliezer. After mutual salutation, the two passed into the tent, and Moses recounted to his father-in-law the marvels of the Exodus, the
travail of the people by the way, and their late deliver-

ance from the sword of Amalek. Jethro rejoiced at the
recital, bestowed upon the Israelites his solemn blessing, and offered sacrifices to Jehovah, to which and the
thanksgiving-feast that followed, Aaron the future high-
priest, and all the elders of Israel were invited. On the
morrow, perceiving Moses occupied from morning until
evening with the administration of justice and the settlement of disputes among the people, Jethro ventured to
remonstrate with him on the risk he incurred by undertaking unaided so heavy a burden. He suggested that
judges, rulers, and elders, *able men, such as feared
God, and hated covetousness*, should be appointed, who
should at stated seasons see justice done between man
and man, and reserve only the weightier matters for the
attention of Moses himself. His wise advice was adopted, and men were duly appointed to preside over every
ten, every fifty, every hundred, and every thousand of
the people, and thus equalize the burden hitherto sustained by Moses alone (Ex. xviii. 1—27).

CHAPTER V

SINAI AND THE GIVING OF THE LAW.

Exod. xix. xx.   B. C. 1491.

AT length the halt at Rephidim came to an end. In
the third month (Ex. xix. 1), the Israelites once
more set out in a southerly direction, and after ascending winding valleys and rugged passes and staircases of
lofty rocks rising one above the other in long succession,
reached a level plain (probably *Er-Raheh*)[1], in front of
which "towered the massive cliffs of Sinai," rising "like
a huge altar in front of the whole congregation." Here
in a spot where they could find water and pasture for

[1] See note, p. 100.

their flocks and herds, they pitched their tents *before the Mount* (Ex. xix. 2). The natural aspect of everything around them was of a character calculated to exert a most solemnising influence upon their feelings. They had reached a kind of "natural sanctuary, not made with hands," which for magnificence and grandeur far exceeded any of those massive Egyptian temples, on which their eyes had rested by the green valley of the Nile. Far removed from the stir and confusion of earthly things[1], amidst a scene of desolate grandeur and a silence unbroken even by the sound of waters or the trickling of rills down the mountain gorges[2], they experienced everything that the natural influence of scenery and association could effect towards fitting their minds for the great and sublime transactions now about to be enacted between them and the Almighty. They were about to receive direct communication from the Lord of all the earth, and to learn why *with an outstretched arm, and signs and great wonders,* they had been delivered from the bondage of Egypt, and thus led forth into the wilderness.

By way of preparation for the great scene, Moses left the congregation encamped on the plain, and proceeded up the winding steep ascent of Sinai. On reaching the summit, the Lord called unto him, and made known His intention of renewing the patriarchal Covenant, which, though it might seem to have been forgotten during the weary years of bondage in Egypt, had never been disannulled (Gal. iii. 17), and was now to be solemnly republished. Like all Covenants, it contained a stipulation and a promise. If Israel would obey the Voice of Him, who had delivered them from

[1] "If I were to make a model of the end of the world, it would be from the valley of the convent of Mount Sinai." Quoted in Stanley, *S. and P.* 43, *n.*

[2] Stanley, *S. and P.* 14; *Lectures*, p. 140.

Egypt, and *borne them on eagles' wings, and brought them to Himself* (Ex. xix. 4), if they would submit themselves to His laws, and keep His commandments, then, *though all the earth was His,* yet should they be *a peculiar treasure unto Him above all people.* Jehovah "would enter into a special relation towards them, He would undertake the duties and claim the privileges of sovereignty," while they should be unto Him *a kingdom of priests, and a holy nation.* It was not a single and peculiar order that was to be elevated to the high position of a member of the priest-kingdom, as was the case in Egypt. Every Israelite was to sustain this relation, and in the midst of a world given up to idolatry, was called to preserve the knowledge of the one true God, and exhibit to the nations the spectacle of a people walking in the ways of Holiness, Righteousness, and Truth. The conditions of this Covenant Moses made known to the Elders and people of Israel; he laid before them *all the words which the Lord commanded Him,* and when they had voluntarily agreed to obey them, he returned with their reply to the Lord, and was told of the intention of Jehovah to come unto him *in a thick cloud, that the people might hear him, and believe him for ever* (Ex. xix. 9).

Three days, therefore, were now devoted to preparatory and ceremonial ablutions, during which the people were commanded to abstain from all sensual and worldly enjoyments. Then bounds were set round the mountain on which a God of Holiness was about to appear, lest any of the people should ascend or even touch it. Of any infringement of this prohibition death was denounced as the certain penalty, and that not inflicted in the usual way, lest the executioners should themselves be polluted, but from a distance with stones and arrows (Ex. xix. 12, 13; Heb. xii. 20). At length the morning of the third day dawned, and the awful

silence of the mountain-sanctuary was broken by peals
of thunder, which echoed and re-echoed amidst the
rocky gorges, while flashes of lightning lit up the peaks
of Sinai, and revealed by their contrast the pitchy darkness and the thick cloud which had settled upon the
mountain-top. Presently the Voice *as of a Trumpet*
(comp. Rev. i. 10, iv. 1), sounded exceeding loud, audible even above the crash of the thunder, so that
every soul in the camp trembled. This was the signal
God had made known to Moses, who straightway led
forth the people out of the camp *to meet with God,
and they stood at the nether part of the mount,* which
appeared *altogether on a smoke, like the smoke of a
furnace,* enshrouding a mysterious flame in which the
Lord descended (Ex. xix. 18). Again the Trumpet
pealed with a long-continued blast, and *waxed louder
and louder, and Moses spake, and God answered him
by a voice,* summoning him to meet Him on the top
of Sinai. Arrived there, he was commanded again to
warn the people, and even the priests, against drawing
too near, or breaking through the bounds that had been
set about the mount for the purpose of indulging any
profane gaze, and so incurring the inevitable penalty of
death (Ex. xix. 21). Moses therefore returned to the
awestruck crowd on the plain below, and renewed the
solemn warning. Then *from out of the midst of the
fire, and the cloud, and the thick darkness, with a
great voice* (Deut. v. 22), JEHOVAH Himself spake to
the assembled host *face to face,* and proclaimed the
Ten fundamental Words of the law of the Covenant.
Not as the Lord of the universe, or the Creator of
all things, did the Most High now reveal Himself to
the people, but as their Redeemer, who had *brought
them out of the land of Egypt, and from the house
of bondage* (Ex. xx. 2). (I) *Beside Him,* therefore, they
were to have *no other god;* (II) *of Him* they were to

make no *representation*, or construct any *graven image*, or any *likeness* in the form of anything either in the heaven above or the earth beneath, or the waters under the earth; (III) for His *Name* they were to entertain the deepest reverence, nor profane it by taking it in vain; (IV) His *Day*, the seventh Day, *the Day of rest*, they were ever to observe; six days they might labour, and do all their work, but on the seventh day, the Sabbath of the Lord their God, no work might be done by the head of the family, or his son, or his daughter, his manservant, or his maidservant, his cattle, or the stranger sojourning within his gates. Such was the duty of the Israelite towards God. But now also the Almighty proclaimed man's duty towards his neighbour. He enjoined and connected with a special promise of temporal prosperity (V) *filial Reverence for Parents*, and forbade (VI) *Murder*, (VII) *Adultery*, (VIII) *Theft*, (IX) *False Witness*, and (X) *Covetousness* (Ex. xx. 1—17).

These were the Ten Words, the fundamentals of the Divine Law, under which the Israelites were henceforth called to live, and which they were to accept as the charter of their constitution. But so great was their terror, when they heard God thus speaking to them *face to face*, that they fled, and standing afar off implored Moses to intercede with the Almighty that they might no more hear His voice, lest they should die. *Go thou near*, said they, *and hear all that the Lord our God shall say, and speak thou unto us all that the Lord our God shall speak unto thee, and we will hear it and do it* (Deut. v. 27). Their request found favour in the sight of Jehovah, and Moses was now solemnly appointed as the Mediator between the Israelites and God. At the same time, the Lord intimated that He would raise up a still greater PROPHET than Moses, from the midst of the Israelites, yet like unto him, *that He would put His words in His mouth, and He should speak unto them all that He commanded* (Deut. xviii. 13—19). Accordingly in his capacity of Mediator, Moses now returned up the mountain, and ascended into the thick darkness that still abode upon it for the purpose of receiving the further commands of Jehovah. After remaining there for some time, he came back to the people. They had on their part already agreed to enter into covenant with God. But it was necessary that this Covenant should now be solemnly ratified by them, its provisions read in their hearing, and formally accepted as the basis of their constitution. Accordingly Moses first wrote all the words that Jehovah had spoken in a book, probably a papyrus-roll, and then, having built an altar at the foot of the mount and set up twelve pillars, he caused calves and goats to be slain as burnt-offerings and peace-offerings by the hands of certain selected youths. In the ears of the assembled people he next read every word of the Law, and when these conditions of the Covenant had been formally accepted by them, he took the blood of the victims already slain, together with water, scarlet wool, and hyssop (Heb. ix. 19—21), sprinkled one half of the blood on the altar, and the roll containing the Covenant-conditions, and the other half on the people, saying as he did so, *Behold the blood of the Covenant which the Lord hath made with you concerning all these words.*

But one portion only of the ceremony was complete. The victims had yielded up their life. The blood, the source of life, had been sprinkled on the altar and accepted by Jehovah. It was now necessary that the sacrificers should join in the Covenant-feast. To celebrate this, Moses, accompanied by Aaron, Nadab and Abihu, and seventy elders, as representatives of the people, ascended to a level spot near the summit of Sinai. There they saw the glory of the God of Israel, under whose feet there was, as it were, *a paved work*

*of a sapphire-stone, and the body of heaven in its
clearness.* But instead of suffering any harm from such
close proximity to the majesty of the Supreme, they
ate and drank in His presence of the Covenant-feast,
and thereby were assured of His mercy and loving-
kindness (Ex. xxiv. 9—11).

CHAPTER VI

MOSES IN THE MOUNT—THE CONSTRUCTION OF THE CALF.

Exod. xxiv.—xxxiv.   B. C. 1491.

THUS the Covenant was formally ratified, and the
nation solemnly devoted itself to the service of the
God of Israel. Further revelations, however, awaited
Moses, and after committing the charge of the people
to Aaron and Hur (Ex. xxiv. 14), he again went up into
the mount accompanied only by Joshua, his minister
and attendant. After an interval of six days the voice
of God summoned him to ascend alone yet higher into
the midst of the cloud that still overhung the mount,
and for forty days and forty nights he there remained
in mysterious converse with Jehovah. During this
period the Lord showed him in vision a representation
of the sanctuary (Heb. viii. 5), which He required
should be the solemn place of meeting between Him
and the people, and gave him the necessary instructions
for its erection (Ex. xxv.—xxviii.), together with full
particulars respecting the order of its services and
ritual (Ex. xxix. xxx.), as also the names of the two
men who were to be employed in building it, viz. BE-
ZALEEL of the tribe of Judah, and AHOLIAB of the
tribe of Dan (Ex. xxxi. 1—11). At the same time
Moses received two tables of stone, on which the Ten
Commandments had been written by the finger of God.
While, however, the Israelitish leader had been

engaged in solemn converse with the Supreme, a far different scene had been going on in the plain below. His prolonged absence had filled the Israelites with doubt and perplexity. When the glory of the Lord descended upon Sinai, they had, indeed, felt the mountain quake, they had heard the thunder roar, they had seen the lightning flash, but of JEHOVAH Himself they had beheld no form or similitude. Now to believe in One who did not, like the gods of every other nation round about, reveal Himself under any palpable figure, was not easy for men who had so long lived amidst the fascinations of the idolatrous rites of Pagan Egypt. As weeks therefore passed away, and still no sign appeared of the return of their leader, the people began to lose their trust in Him whom they had promised to obey. They wished to break up their long encampment; but who would go before them, and guide them in the way? Yearning therefore for some visible representative of Jehovah, and possibly yielding to the suggestions of some of the Egyptians amongst *the mixed multitude* in the camp, they gathered themselves together before Aaron, with the petition that he *would make them gods to go before them,* for as for Moses, who had brought them up out of the land of Egypt, they knew not what was become of him. Unable to stem the popular clamour, and taking refuge in an unworthy expediency, Aaron bade them bring him the golden earrings of their wives, their sons, and their daughters, and of these he fashioned a calf, probably according to the well-known form of the Egyptian Apis or Mnevis, whose worship the people must often have witnessed during their sojourn in the Nile Valley. Then building an altar he proclaimed a three days' festival to Jehovah. Accordingly, with the earliest dawn of the following day, the people arose, and offered burnt-offerings and peace-offerings before the image, exclaiming, *These be thy gods, O Israel, which brought thee out of the land of Egypt,* and concluded the ceremony with one of those licentious orgies, accompanied by song and dance, which were so common amongst heathen nations (Ex. xxxii. 4; 1 Cor. x. 7).

It was while they were in the very act of celebrating this idolatrous festival that Moses, accompanied by Joshua, returned from the presence of the nation's invisible King. He had already received Divine intimation of the apostasy of the people, and in his capacity of Mediator had already interceded in their behalf. Now with the two tables of the Law in his hands he descended the Mount. To the ear of his companion the noise of the host, as it ascended upwards from the valley below, sounded *like the noise of war in the camp.* But Moses knew otherwise. *It is not the noise of them that shout for the mastery,* he replied, *neither is it the voice of them that cry for being overcome, but the noise of them that sing do I hear.* Then as he drew near the camp, and beheld with his own eyes the heathenish orgies that were going on, his feelings overmastered him; his anger waxed hot, and he cast the Tables out of his hands, and brake them beneath the Mount. Next advancing towards the senseless image, he seized it, burnt it with fire, reduced it to powder[1], strewed the ashes on the neighbouring brook of Horeb, and compelled the people to drink thereof. Then after sternly rebuking his brother for conniving at so heinous a sin, he stationed himself at the entrance of the camp, and bade all, who still remained faithful to Jehovah, gird on their swords, and without regard to family tie or private friendship, slay the offenders from gate to gate with the edge of the sword. It was a severe but necessary test of the fidelity of the people, and the sons

[1] Probably, if it was a laminated figure, he destroyed the wooden portion of it with fire, reduced the gold to dust, and then strewed it upon the water. Kurtz, III. 162.

of Levi were found faithful. With a zeal very dissimilar from that which had animated their forefather at Shechem (Gen. xxxiv. 25, 26), instead of siding with Aaron, though their tribal leader, they arose and slew about 3000 of the offenders, thus effacing the blot on the memory of their tribe, and qualifying themselves for high functions in the sanctuary (Ex. xxxii. 25—29).

In order to make an atonement for the people's sin, Moses, on the next day, re-ascended the mount, and solemnly interceded with the Almighty on their behalf. Standing *in the gap* (Ps. cvi. 23) between a justly offended God and an erring nation, he offered, if no other way of forgiveness was possible, freely to surrender his own life, and to suffer the blotting out of his own name from God's Book. Eventually his intercession prevailed. The Almighty promised that the nation should not be cut off, and that He would send His Angel before them, who should lead them into the land promised to their forefathers. But further punishment certainly awaited them ; in the day of His visitation, He would visit their sin upon them, an earnest of which they speedily experienced in the shape of plagues (Ex. xxxii. 35), with which *the Lord plagued the people*, because of their sin in *turning His glory into the similitude of a calf that eateth hay* (Ps. cvi. 20).

The announcement of Moses that their journey into the Promised Land was not to be suspended, but that Jehovah would not go up in their midst, was received by the people with much lamentation (Ex. xxxiii. 4). Their sorrow was accepted as a sign of repentance, and Moses caused his own tent to be pitched at a long distance without the camp, and named it the *Tent, or Tabernacle of Meeting* (Ex. xxxiii. 7). Then, accompanied only by Joshua, he passed through the long line of the people's tents, at the doors of which they stood and watched him, and, as he entered his own, the Cloudy Pillar, which hitherto had rested on the top of

Sinai, descended, and stood before it, and amidst the joyful reverence of the watching host, the Lord con- versed with Moses, *face to face, as a man speaketh untò his friend* (Ex. xxxiii. 11). The descent of the Cloudy Pillar, and its position at the entrance of the tent of Israel's leader, though at a distance from the people, was a sign that his intercession had prevailed. In spite of their recent sin, Jehovah had not *forgotten to be gracious*, He would fulfil His promise, and the nation should be led into the land assured to Abraham, Isaac, and Jacob, and every one, who sought the Lord, might draw nigh, and consult Him through His servant Moses in the appointed place of meeting.

Emboldened by this measure of success, Moses ex- pressed a desire, since he was the ordained leader of the people, and had found grace in the sight of God, that he might be permitted to behold the essential Glory of Him, with whom he was privileged to speak face to face (Ex. xxxiii. 13). He asked for more than he, or any other finite creature, could endure. The Face—the essential Majesty—of Jehovah no man could see and live. But if he ascended the mount on the morrow, and took precautions that no man or beast appeared in sight, and brought with him two fresh tables of stone hewn out of the rock, the Lord promised that he should see so much of His Glory as mortal eye could bear. Accordingly on the morrow with two fresh-hewn tables he ascended, and awaited the mysterious revelation. Every precaution had been taken; no man was allowed to be seen throughout all the mount, no flock or herd was suffered to feed before it (Ex. xxxiv. 3). Alone, unattended even by the faithful Joshua, the accepted mediator between the people and their invisible King stood in a cleft of the rock. And while he stood " co- vered with Jehovah's hand," the Lord passed by and proclaimed, *The Lord, the Lord God, merciful and gracious, long-suffering and abundant in goodness*

*and truth, keeping mercy for thousands, forgiving
iniquity, transgression, and sin, and that will by no
means clear the guilty, visiting the iniquity of the
fathers upon the children, and upon the children's
children, unto the third and fourth generation.* As
Moses listened to this proclamation of the incommuni-
cable attributes of the Most High—" Justice and Mercy,
Truth and Love"—like Elijah after him in a cleft of the
same jagged rocks (1 K. xix. 9—13), he bowed his head
towards the earth and worshipped, and interceded for a
more complete renewal of the broken covenant between
Jehovah and His people. His prayer was heard. The Covenant was once more renewed, and for a second period
of forty days and forty nights Moses remained in the
Divine Presence, and received fresh instructions respecting the moral and ceremonial laws of the Theocracy.

At the close of this period, with the two fresh
Tables, inscribed with the Ten Words, he again returned to the people. On this occasion, he retained
more permanent marks of the awful converse he had
been permitted to hold. Aaron and the elders of the
people were afraid to approach him, for *the skin of
his face shone* with a celestial radiance, and the reflection of Jehovah's glory gilded his brow. The lawgiver
himself, not aware of the change that had come over
his features, called unto them, and at length emboldened to approach, they heard at his mouth all the commands of God. But the unearthly splendour was not
permanent. Lest, therefore, the people should behold
the fading away of this visible credential of his interview with the Supreme, Moses was in the habit of
placing a veil upon his face whenever he departed from
them (Comp. 2 Cor. iii. 13)[1], but removed it as often as
he was permitted to behold the presence of the Lord,
and receive fresh renewals of the celestial radiance.

[1] See the LXX. Version of Exod. xxxiv. 30—35, and
Alford's and Wordsworth's Notes on 2 Cor. iii. 13.

BOOK IV

THE MOSAIC WORSHIP AND POLITY.

CHAPTER I

THE TABERNACLE.

EXOD. XXXVI.—XL. B. C. 1490.

THE encampment of the Israelites before Sinai continued for more than a year (Num. i. 1). At this point, then, it will be convenient to group together and consider the most important of those ordinances which they now received, and the chief features of the constitution under which they were called to live.

The purpose for which the Jewish nation was raised up was of the most momentous character. In the midst of surrounding idolatry and moral degeneracy, they were called to preserve intact the doctrine of *the Unity of God*, to be the guardians of *His gracious promises of Redemption*, and to exhibit to the world *holiness* (See Rom. ix. 4, 5).

The doctrine of the Divine Unity was the kernel of the Mosaic law, and as such was defended by the sternest and most rigorous enactments. The Israelites were forbidden even to mention the names of the gods of the Canaanite nations (Ex. xxiii. 13): they were commanded to burn or destroy their images, their altars, their sacred groves (Ex. xxiii. 24; xxxiv. 13); they were to deem accursed the precious metals of which their idols were composed (Deut. vii. 25), and on no pretence whatever were they to conclude any treaty or make any marriage with them (Deut. vii. 2, 3). Relapse into idolatry was to be regarded as the greatest crime, and whether committed by a city or an individual was to be punished with unrelenting severity. In the latter case, death by stoning was the inevitable penalty; in the former, all the inhabitants were to be put to the sword, the whole spoil was to be collected into a heap and burnt, and a solemn curse was to be pronounced against any one who attempted to rebuild it (Deut. xiii. 6—18). No less vigorous were the enactments against the construction of any representation of the true God under any form or similitude, whether of man or animal, of bird or fish or star.

But while all idolatrous forms of worship were thus rigorously forbidden, the Almighty condescended to make known to His people the way in which He was willing to receive their adoration. Stooping to the infirmities of a nation just delivered from degrading bondage, He took them by the hand, and provided for the wants of their religious nature in a way marvellously adapted to their native genius and character, as also to their previous habits and modes of thought.

And first, that the Israelites might have a visible assurance of the Divine presence in their midst, a sanctuary was to be erected, not according to any model suggested by the people themselves, but according to a Divine pattern shown to Moses in the Mount (Ex. xxv. 9; Heb. viii. 5). The Patriarchs had their pillars of stone (Gen. xxviii. 18, 19), or the shade of the consecrated grove (Gen. xxi. 33). The Egyptian had his huge colossal temples, built of vast granite blocks, or hewn out of the solid rock. Not such was to be the sanctuary of Jehovah amongst a people journeying through a wilderness to a Promised Land. As the nomad chief had his tent in the midst of his tribe, so Jehovah, as the

Head of the Hebrew pilgrim-nation, ordained that a Tent or *Tabernacle* should be erected for Him, where He might *meet and speak unto* His people, and *they might draw nigh to Him. I will sanctify*, said God, *the Tabernacle of meeting,......there will I meet with ......and will dwell among the children of Israel, and will be their God, and they shall know that I am the Lord their God* (Ex. xxix. 42—46 ; xxx. 6, 36).

In the erection of this Pavilion-Temple every member of the nation was invited to take a part, and to contribute either the gold and jewels of which the Egyptians had been spoiled, or the arts which, as we have seen, many of the Israelites had learnt from them. While, therefore, the superintendence of the work was entrusted to two skilful artificers, Bezaleel of the tribe of Judah, and Aholiab of the tribe of Dan (Ex. xxxi. 2, 6 ; xxxv. 34), many of the congregation contributed offerings of gold and silver and brass, of blue and red and crimson, of fine linen, and goat-skins, and ram-skins dyed red. Others were despatched in different directions throughout the fertile valley where they were encamped, to fell the Shittah or Acacia tree, which grew abundantly in the neighbourhood of Sinai, and was exactly adapted by its durability and lightness for the construction of a moveable tent, and while the workmen prepared it for its different purposes, the women employed themselves diligently in weaving and spinning blue and crimson hangings, thus consecrating the arts which they had learnt, while serving as bond-slaves in the houses of the princes of Egypt (Ex. xxxv. 20—35).

(A) The Area, or Court, within which the Tabernacle stood, was an oblong square, 100 cubits[1] in length by 50 in breadth, formed by curtains of fine linen

---

[1] The ordinary cubit was = 18¼ English inches ; there was a shorter one = 15 inches ; the Babylonian cubit was = 21 inches.

5 cubits in height, hanging from pillars of wood with capitals overlaid with silver and furnished with sockets of brass. These pillars, 20 on each longer side and 10 on each shorter, were held together by means of silver rods attached by silver hooks, and were fastened into the ground by means of pegs of brass. The entrance[1] was from the east, so as to catch the rays of the rising sun. Here the curtains extended only 15 cubits from each corner, and the intervening space with its 4 pillars formed the entrance, and was overhung with curtains of fine twined linen, of the richest and most brilliant colours, blue and purple and scarlet.

In a line with the Entrance and the Tabernacle itself stood (*a*) The Altar of Burnt-sacrifice, and (*b*) The Great Laver for purification.

(*a*) *The Altar of Burnt-offering*[2] (called in Malachi i. 7, 12, *the table of the Lord*) was in form a square, 5 cubits long, 5 broad, and 3 high, and was constructed of hollow boards of acacia-wood overlaid with brass (Ex. xxvii. 4, 5). So long as the Tabernacle was stationed in any one place, these were probably filled with earth, which thus formed the upper side or surface, on which the sacrifices were offered. Each corner of the altar was furnished with horns of acacia-wood overlaid with brass ; to these the victims were fastened, and on them their blood was sprinkled at the consecration of the priests, and the sacrifice of the sin-offering (Ps. cxviii. 27 ;

---

[1] It seems probable that the Tabernacle did not stand in the centre of the area, but 20 cubits from N., S., and W., so that there was a square of 50 cubits in front, where the sacrifices were offered, and the worshippers assembled.

[2] The position of the altar of Burnt-offering was very striking. It was the first object that confronted the worshipper on his entrance. The High-priest could not go into the sanctuary to burn incense before the Lord without taking live coals from this altar, nor could he enter and perform his holy functions without being himself sprinkled with the blood of the victims slain thereon. See Fairbairn's *Typology,* II. 282.

Ex. xxix. 12; Levit. iv. 7, 18, 25). From each side projected a horizontal ledge, to the outer edge of which was
attached a perpendicular grating of brass, resting like the
Altar upon the ground, for the purpose of catching any
portions of the sacrifice or the fuel that might fall. The
ledge, on which the priests officiated, was approached
by a slope of earth, for the Law forbade the construction of steps leading up to the altar (Ex. xx. 26). The
implements used in the sacrifices, such as pans and
shovels for collecting and removing the ashes, basins for
receiving the blood, fleshhooks for turning the pieces of
flesh, were all of brass (Ex. xxvii. 3; see 1 Sam. ii. 13,
14).

(*b*) *The great Laver for purification* stood between
the Altar of Burnt-offering and the Tabernacle. It was
made of the brass from the metal mirrors belonging to
the women who served at the door of the Tabernacle
(Ex. xxxviii. 8), and was probably of a circular form
standing on a basis or foot. In it the flesh of the victims
was washed, as also the hands and feet of the priests, before they performed any holy function (Ex. xxx. 18—21).

(B) The TABERNACLE itself was entered, at its
eastern side, through a magnificent curtain, 10 cubits in
width, supported on five pillars (Ex. xxvi.). Its dimensions inside were 30 cubits in length, 10 in breadth, and
10 in height. It was formed of planks of acacia-wood
overlaid with gold, fixed into the ground by means of
two tenons, each fitting into a socket of silver, re-
sembling the sharp end of a spear. At the top they
were united by bars of acacia-wood, 5 bars to each
piece, passing through golden rings. The roof was
formed of several sets of curtains; the innermost,
10 in number, formed of fine twined linen of various
colours, and adorned with cherubic figures of curious
workmanship; next to these were 11 curtains of goats'
hair; then one of rams' skins with the wool on dyed

red; and lastly, another of badgers', or, more probably, seals' skins[1].

The Tabernacle consisted of two portions, (*a*) The Holy Place, and (*b*) The Holy of Holies (Ex. xxvi. 33, 34: and comp. Heb. ix. 2, 3).

(*a*) *The Holy Place*, 20 cubits in length and 10 in height and width, was divided from the *Holy of Holies* by a veil of the most costly materials and the most splendid colours. Without any opening to admit the light from above, it was illumined only by a *Golden Lamp* or *Candlestick*, with *seven* lights, fed with pure olive oil, kept burning day and night, and trimmed each morning by a priest with golden snuffers, who carried away the snuff in golden dishes. From the base, on which the lamp rested, rose a shaft dividing itself on either side into three branches, so that it had seven arms, each adorned with calyxes of almond flowers, apples, and buds of pomegranates or lilies (Ex. xxv. 31; xxxvii. 17—25; Heb. ix. 2).

Opposite the Golden Lamp was the *Table of Shew-bread* (Ex. xxv. 23—29), made of acacia-wood, overlaid with gold, 2 cubits in length, 1 in breadth, and $1\frac{1}{2}$ in height, and standing on 4 feet. It had a border to prevent the loaves from falling off, and was furnished with rings and staves for removal. Belonging to it were cups or spoons for incense, bowls for wine, dishes for bringing and removing the loaves, all of gold. These loaves, called also *bread of the face*, being set *before the face of the Lord* (Levit. xxiv. 5—9), were twelve in number, according to the number of the tribes. Baked of the finest meal, flat and thin, they were placed every Sabbath on the Table in 2 rows, 6 in each, and sprinkled

---

[1] Seals were numerous on the shores of the Sinaitic peninsula. Pliny mentions the use of the skins of seals as a covering for tents, and as a protection from lightning. The exact meaning, however, of the Hebrew word *tachash* is very uncertain. See Smith's *Bib. Dict.* III. 21; article *Badger*.

with incense, and accompanied with libations of wine in
the golden bowls. Here they remained till the next
Sabbath, when they were taken away and replaced by
twelve fresh loaves, and eaten by the priests[1] in the
Holy Place, out of which they might not be carried, the
frankincense having been burnt as an oblation on the
Altar of Sacrifice.

Between the Table of Shewbread and the Golden
Lamp and immediately before[2] the veil separating the
Holy Place from the Holy of Holies was the *Golden
Altar of Incense* (Ex. xxx. 1—11). Made of acacia-wood,
in shape a square, 1 cubit in length and breadth and 2 in
height, and ornamented round the middle with a golden
wreath, it was furnished, like the Altar of Burnt-offering, with horns, rings, and staves; but unlike it was
wholly overlaid with *gold*. On it incense, carefully prepared of four different ingredients (Ex. xxx. 34—38), was
placed by the officiating priest morning and evening,
with live coals taken from the Altar of Burnt-offering,
that the smoke of the incense might perpetually ascend
before the Lord. Once a year its horns were sprinkled
with the blood of the sin-offering of the Atonement, and
on no other occasion, except when a sin-offering was
presented for the High-priest or the congregation.

(*b*) *The Holy of Holies*, separated, as we have just
said, from the Holy Place by a costly veil supported on
a screen of 4 pillars, formed *a perfect cube* of 10 cubits in length, breadth, and height. While the Holy
Place, though never penetrated by the daylight, was

---

[1] Comp. Matt. xii. 4; Mark ii. 26; Heb. ix. 2; and, for
the importance of the Shewbread, the words of Abijah
(2 Chron. xiii. 11).

[2] In Heb. ix. 4, it is mentioned among the objects within
the *second veil*, and in 1 Kings vi. 22 is said to belong to the
Oracle or *Holy of Holies*. Possibly, from its position and
great typical importance, it was considered to belong to the
"second Tabernacle."

illumined by the splendid Golden Lamp, the Holy of Holies was left *in utter darkness*, symbolical of Him whom *no man hath seen, nor can see* (1 Tim. vi. 16). Within this most sacred enclosure neither priests nor people as a body, but the High-Priest only, and that but once a year, ever entered. Here stood nothing but the ARK *of the Covenant* (Ex. xxv. 10—16). This was an oblong chest of acacia-wood overlaid with the purest gold within and without, $2\frac{1}{2}$ cubits in length, $1\frac{1}{2}$ in breadth, $1\frac{1}{2}$ in height. It stood on 4 small feet, which were provided with 4 golden rings, through which staves of acacia-wood overlaid with gold were passed, and which when once inserted were never to be removed. Within it were placed[1] the two stone tables, on both sides of which the Decalogue had been inscribed. Round the top ran a crown or wreath of pure gold, and upon it was the *Mercy-Seat*, of the same dimensions as the Ark, made not of wood overlaid with gold, but entirely of pure gold. At either end of the Mercy-Seat rose two golden Cherubim, with outspread wings and faces turned towards each other, and eyes bent downwards, as though desirous *to look into* its mysteries (1 Pet. i. 12). Neither their size nor their form are distinctly described. By some they are thought to have been handed down by patriarchal tradition from those which were placed in Paradise (Gen. iii. 24); by others to have resembled Egyptian models; while Josephus (*Ant.* iii. vi. 5) declares that they resembled no figures known to men, and that in his day their form was utterly lost. In Ezekiel (i. 5—13) we find them likened to compound figures with the head of a man, an ox, a lion, and an eagle, with four wings, two serving for flight, two to cover the body, and straight feet inflexible at the knee. It is not improbable that they re-

---

[1] From Heb. xi. 4 it appears that the *pot of manna* and *Aaron's rod that budded* were also laid up before the Ark.

presented the manifold powers of nature—created life
in its highest form—their overshadowing wings meeting
as in perfect harmony, their eyes cast downwards towards the Divine Law, over which seemingly so rigid
and unbending was the compassion of ONE *forgiving
iniquity, transgression and sin*[1].

NOTE.

HISTORY OF THE TABERNACLE.

SUCH was the Pavilion-Temple which Moses constructed
according to the pattern shown him in the Mount. The chief
facts connected with its history are as follows.

i. During the wanderings in the wilderness it was the
one place, where Jehovah "met His people," and where from
the ineffable glory above the mercy-seat He revealed His
Will. There the Spirit came upon the 70 elders and they
prophesied (Num. xi. 24, 25); thither Moses and Aaron were
summoned on all important occasions, as on that of the
rebellion of Miriam (Num. xii. 4), of the unfaithfulness of the
spies (xiv. 10), of the rebellion of Korah (xvi. 19), of the sin
of Meribah (xx. 6): there on the death of Moses his successor
was solemnly appointed (Deut. xxxi. 14).

ii. During the conquest of Canaan it was, probably,
moved from place to place, wherever the host of Israel was
encamped.

iii. Afterwards it was brought to *Shiloh* (Josh. ix. 27;
xviii. 1; xix. 51), on account, doubtless, of its secluded and
central position, and as being within the territory of the
powerful tribe of Ephraim, to which Joshua belonged, and
here it remained during the entire period of the Judges (comp.
Josh. xix. 51; xxii. 12; Judg. xxi. 21).

iv. But in the time of Eli, the licentiousness of his sons
stained the sanctity of Shiloh, and degraded the Tabernacle
almost to the level of a heathen temple (1 Sam. ii. 22),
while the capture of the ark by the Philistines (1 Sam. iv. 22)
still further dimmed its glories, and Samuel himself sacrificed
at other places, Mizpeh (1 Sam. vii. 9), Ramah (ix. 12; x. 3),
Gilgal (x. 8; xi. 15).

v. After this it was for some time settled at *Nob* (1 Sam.

[1] Hardwick's *Religions of Egypt*, p. 114.

xx. 1—6), and thither also misfortune followed it: Saul murdered the priests (1 Sam. xxii. 11—19), and Abiathar fled with the sacred ephod to David (xxiii. 6).

vi. In the time of David and Solomon we find it at *Gibeon* (1 Chron. xvi. 39; xxi. 29), but the ark was now removed to Kirjath-jearim, and afterwards, on the capture of Jerusalem, to that city, where a new Tabernacle was constructed to receive it (1 Sam. vi. 17; 1 Chron. xv. 1). Its glory now waned more and more, it became connected with the worship of the high-places (1 Kings iii. 4), retained only the old altar of burnt-offering (1 Chron. xxi. 29), and eventually it seems to have been either taken down, or left to be forgotten and *"vanish away*[1].*"*

CHAPTER II

THE PRIESTS.

Ex. xxviii. xxix. Lev. viii. ix. Num. iii. iv.

PRIOR to the Mosaic period, as has been already noticed[2], the head of each family and the firstborn appear to have exercised all kinds of government, ecclesiastical as well as civil, being both kings and priests in their own houses.

At the departure, however, from Egypt, it was declared that all the firstborn were specially sanctified to God in token of the mercy shown to them there (Ex. xiii. 2), and when Moses received the Divine commands concerning the construction of the Tabernacle, it was ordered that from the children of Israel Aaron and his sons should be specially selected *to minister in the priests' office* (Ex. xxviii. 1). Subsequently, when the whole tribe of Levi displayed such signal zeal on the occasion of the construction of the golden calf (Ex. xxxii. 26), that tribe was separated for the service of the sanctuary, and accepted in the place of the firstborn,

---

[1] See Art. *Tabernacle* in Smith's *Bib. Dict.*
[2] See above, p. 75.

as the royal guard to wait on Israel's King (Num. i. 47—54; iii. 5—13).

But though the whole tribe was set apart for these important purposes, a strictly prescribed order regulated its particular functions to each branch, of which there were three, (*a*) The Levites, (*b*) The Priests, (*c*) The High-Priest.

(*a*)   *The Levites* entered on their duties at the age of 30 (Num. iv. 23, 30, 35), and were consecrated, not as the priests, by anointing and investiture, but by a ceremony of washing accompanied by sacrifices, after which the elders laid their hands upon them, and Aaron presented them *as a wave-offering before the Lord*, in token that they were offered to the Lord by the congregation for the service of the sanctuary, and handed over by Him to the Priests[1]. Thus occupying a middle place between the people, who were all ideally *a kingdom of priests*, and the higher sacerdotal orders, they might approach nearer to the Tabernacle than the other tribes, but they might not offer sacrifice, nor burn incense, nor handle the holy vessels of the Sanctuary, till they were concealed from view (Num. iv. 15).

The Levites, then, were *the assistants of the priests,* and consisted of three families or sections, the sons of Gershon, Kohath, and Merari.

i.   The *Kohathites* held the first rank, as being the family to which Aaron belonged. It was their duty, on the removal of the Tabernacle, to bear all the sacred vessels, including the Ark itself, but not before the priests had concealed them from the profane gaze with a dark blue pall (Num. iii. 31; iv. 6, 9, 15; Deut. xxxi. 25).

ii.   The *Gershonites* were charged with the removal of the curtains, veils, and tent-hangings (Num. iv. 22—26).

---

[1] Kurtz, *Sacrificial Worship of the Old Testament,* 341.

iii. To the *Merarites* was entrusted the heavier portion of the Tabernacle furniture, such as the boards, pillars, and bars, and therefore with the Gershonites they were permitted to use the oxen and waggons contributed by the congregation, while the Kohathites were only suffered to remove the sacred vessels on their shoulders (Num. vii. 1—9). With this arrangement agreed their position in the encampment in the wilderness. While the place of honour on the east was occupied by the sons of Aaron, the Kohathites were on the south, the Gershonites on the west, the Merarites on the north.

In place of territorial possessions, the Levites received the tithe of the produce of land and cattle, of which they again gave one-tenth to the priests (Num. xviii. 24—26). At the close of the wanderings they would need a more fixed abode, and 48 cities with suburbs of pasture-land for their flocks and herds were assigned them. Of these the Levites had 35; Kohath 10; Gershon 13; Merari 12; while the remaining 13, including the six *Cities of Refuge*, were assigned to the Priests.

It was also designed that at the settlement of the nation in the Land of Promise their functions should be not only diffused as widely as possible, but should include others besides those of merely assisting the priests. They were to take the place of the old *household priests*, to share in all festivals and rejoicings (Deut. xii. 19; xiv. 26, 27; xxvi. 11), to preserve and transcribe the law (Deut. xvii. 9—12), and to read it publicly at the Feast of Tabernacles every seventh year (Deut. xxxi. 9—13).

(*b*) The *Priests* were consecrated to their office with far more imposing ceremonies than the Levites. After laying aside their old garments, they washed their bodies with pure water, were anointed with the

holy oil, and then arrayed in their new vestments (Ex.
xxix. 4—7). Themselves *compassed about with infirmity*, they needed to *offer up sacrifice first for their
own sins* before they could intercede for others (Heb.
v. 2 ; vii. 27). On the head therefore of a bullock they
solemnly laid their hands, and thus symbolically transferred to it the guilt that clung to themselves ; then
in token of their entire devotion to their solemn calling, a ram was slain as a burnt-offering, and its blood
sprinkled on the altar (Ex. xxix. 10—18; Lev. viii. 18,
19). Another ram was next slain as a peace-offering,
and some of its blood was smeared on the tip of the
right ear, the thumb of the right hand, the great toe
of the right foot, in token of their intention to devote
every member to the service of Jehovah; and finally,
as they were not only to intercede for the guilt of
the people, but to offer their praises and thanksgiving,
sacrificial cakes of unleavened bread with portions of
the sacrifice were placed in their hands, and these they
waved before the Lord (Ex. xxix. 19—24).

The vestments they wore during their ministrations
consisted of fine linen drawers, and over these a closely-
fitting tunic or cassock, white, woven whole in one piece
and broidered, reaching to the feet. This was confined
round the waist by a girdle wrought with needle-work,
exhibiting the three sacred colours, blue, purple, and
scarlet, intermingled with white. Upon their heads
they wore a linen tiara in the form of the calyx of a
flower. In all their ministrations they seem to have
been bare-footed.

Certain qualifications were essential before they
could enter on the discharge of their duties. As the
victim was required to be without blemish, so also was
the sacrificer, and in Levit. xxi. 17—21 the defects are
enumerated, which excluded from the priestly office.
During their period of ministration they might drink

9

neither wine nor strong drink (Levit. x. 9); except in
the case of the nearest relatives they might make no
mourning for the dead (Levit. xxi. 1—5); or shave their
heads, or, like the priests of heathen nations, "*make
cuttings in their flesh*," or otherwise mutilate themselves (Levit. xix. 28; 1 Kings xviii. 28). They were
permitted to marry, but might not ally themselves with
one of an alien race, or an unchaste woman, or one
who had been divorced, or the widow of any one but a
priest (Lev. xxi. 7, 14).

Their duties were to keep the fire ever burning on
the altar of burnt-offering both day and night (Levit.
vi. 12); to trim and feed with oil the golden lamp (Ex.
xxvii. 20, 21); to offer morning and evening the regulated
sacrifices at the door of the Tabernacle (Ex. xxix. 38—
44); to lay the fresh shewbread on the table every
seventh day (Lev. xxiv. 8); to blow the silver trumpets
and proclaim all solemn days (Num. x. 1—10); to ex-
amine the lepers and pronounce whether they were
clean or unclean (Lev. xiii.); to act as judges and ex-
positors of the law, and teach the people the statutes
of the Lord (Lev. x. 11; Deut. xxxiii. 10).

A distinct provision was made for their support,
and consisted of (i) one-tenth of the tithes of the whole
produce of the country paid to the Levites (Num. xviii.
21, 26); (ii) the loaves of shewbread (Levit. xxiv. 9);
(iii) the firstfruits of oil, wine, and corn (Num. xviii. 12);
(iv) the redemption-money for the firstborn of man or
beast, five shekels a head, and also for everything devoted
(Num. xviii. 14, 15); (v) the perquisites of the sacrifices,
the flesh of the burnt-offerings, peace-offerings, and
trespass-offerings, and especially the heave-shoulder and
the wave-breast (Num. xviii. 8—14; Levit. x. 12—15);
(vi) a fixed portion of the spoils taken in war (Num.
xxxi. 25—47).

(*c*) The office of *High-priest* was conferred first

on Aaron, then on his son Eleazar[1] and his descendants. At some period before the time of Eli, the succession passed to the line of Ithamar, and there continued till the time of Solomon, in whose reign it reverted to the line of Eleazar (1 Sam. ii. 35 ; 1 Kings ii. 35).

The same ceremonies accompanied the consecration of the High-priest as that of the priests, save that the anointing, which in the latter appears to have been confined to the sprinkling of their garments with the sacred oil, was more copious in his case, and the oil was poured upon his head (Lev. viii. 12 ; Ps. cxxxiii. 2).

The vestments of the High-priest were far more rich and splendid than those of the priests. Like the latter he wore the linen drawers, but in place of the closely-fitting tunic he wore *the robe of the Ephod,* which was all blue, of woven work, without sleeves, reaching down to the feet, and drawn over the head through an opening, which was fringed with a border of woven work to prevent its rending. The skirt of this robe was set with a trimming of pomegranates of the three sacred colours, blue, crimson, and purple, with a golden bell between each pomegranate, designed to give forth a tinkling sound as he went in and out of the holy place. Immediately above this robe was *the Ephod* itself, a short cloak consisting of two parts, one covering the back, and the other the breast and upper part of the body, wrought with colours and gold. The two halves were united on the shoulder with two onyx stones, on each of which were engraved the names of six of the tribes. It was gathered round the waist by a curious *girdle* of fine twined linen, adorned with gold, blue, purple, and scarlet. Just above the girdle, and

---

[1] NADAB and ABIHU, his two elder sons, having been suddenly struck dead for presuming to burn incense with common or *strange* fire (Levit. x. 1—11).

attached to the Ephod by rings and ribbons of blue, was the *Breast-plate*, or the *Breast-plate of Judgment*. This, like the Ephod, was of cunning work, a square of a span breadth, formed double so as to make a bag, set with 12 precious stones, in 4 rows, each engraved with the name of one of the tribes. Within the Breast-plate was the *Urim and the Thummim* (*Light* and *Perfection*, Ex. xxviii. 15—30). Not a word in Scripture explains the meaning of these mysterious objects, but they were certainly employed in some way now unknown for ascertaining the Divine will (comp. 1 Sam. xxviii. 6 ; Judg. i. 1 ; xx. 18 ; 1 Sam. xiv. 3, 18 ; xxiii. 9 ; 2 Sam. xxi. 1). Some identify them with the twelve stones inscribed with the names of the twelve tribes, and suppose that "the illumination, simultaneous or successive, of the letters" guided the High-priest to the answer ; others think that within the Breast-plate was a stone or a plate of gold inscribed with the name of Jehovah, and that by means of this he was enabled to discern the Divine Voice, as it proceeded from the glories of the Shechinah.

Like the other members of the order, the High-priest wore on his head a tiara, but attached to this by a blue ribbon was a gold plate, on which was engraved *Holiness to the Lord* (Ex. xxviii. 36—39 ; xxxix. 30).

Some of the functions of the High-priest were peculiar. (i) To him alone it appertained to enter the Holy of Holies on one day in the year, the day of Atonement, to sprinkle the blood of the sin-offering on the mercy-seat, and burn incense within the veil (Lev. xvi.). On this occasion he did not wear his full pontifical dress, but was arrayed entirely in fine white linen (Lev. xvi. 4, 32), a custom which afterwards seems to have undergone some change. (ii) To him alone it belonged to consult the Divine Oracle (Num. xxvii. 21), and preside over the Court of Judgment (Deut. xvii. 9).

(iii) Even greater purity and blamelessness was required
of him than of the other priests ; he could marry none
but a virgin in the first freshness of her youth (Lev.
xxi. 13), and as illegitimacy was an absolute bar to the
office, the importance attached to genealogies was
great, and in these the name of the mother as well as
father was registered.

The office lasted for life, but does not seem to have
had any peculiar emoluments attached to it over and
above those enjoyed by the Priests.

CHAPTER III

THE SACRIFICES AND OFFERINGS.

Ex. xxix. xxx. Lev. i.—vi. Num. xv.

THE rite of sacrifice so universal in the ancient
world came down to the Israelites from the earliest times, from the days of their forefathers Abraham,
Isaac, and Jacob, and the generations that lived before
the Flood, and was regulated by Moses with the utmost
precision.

One rule applied to all sacrifices. They could only
be offered on the *Great Brazen Altar of the Tabernacle.* To offer them on high places, or spots selected
by the caprice of the worshipper was expressly forbidden (Lev. xvii. 4 ; Deut. xii. 13, 14), though this
rule appears to have been subsequently relaxed in the
case of the prophets (1 Sam. xiii. 8—14 ; xvi. 1—5 ;
1 Kings xviii. 21—40).

Perhaps the simplest classification of sacrifices is
that which arranges them under the heads of (I) Those
offered without, and (II) Those offered with Blood.

I.   *Unbloody sacrifices* will include (*a*) *First-fruits
and Tithes,* (*b*) *Meat- and Drink-offerings,* (*c*) *Incense.*

(*a*) *First-fruits and Tithes* were presented by every Israelite to the priests in token of gratitude and humble thankfulness to Jehovah, and consisted of the produce of the land either in its natural state, as grain, fruit, grapes, wool, or prepared for human use, as meal, oil, new wine (Ex. xxiii. 19; Num. xviii. 12; Deut. xviii. 4). To the Levites also was paid the tenth part of all produce of the land and of cattle (Lev. xxvii. 30—33; Num. xviii. 21—24).

(*b*) *Meat- and Drink-offerings* generally accompanied each other. The Meat-offering was composed of fine flour seasoned with salt, and mingled with frankincense and oil, but without leaven. A portion of the flour and oil the priest placed upon the altar, together with all the frankincense, and there burnt them, the rest of the flour and oil becoming his own perquisite. Sometimes cakes of fine flour were offered with oil and salt, but without leaven or honey (Lev. ii. and vi. 14—23). A Drink-offering consisted of wine, which was poured at the foot of the altar; the quantity varying according to the victim, being for a lamb or kid a quarter of a *hin* (= 1 gallon, 2 pints); for a ram one-third, for a bullock one-half (Num. xv. 5, 7, 10; xxviii. 14). By these offerings, as by those of tithes and first-fruits, the Israelite acknowledged the undeserved bounty of Jehovah, and dedicated to Him the best of His gifts, *flour* the staff of life, *wine* the symbol of strengthening and refreshing, *oil* the symbol of richness. (Comp. Ps. civ. 15.)

The Meat-offering might be presented,

Either (1) by itself as a free-will offering, as in the instance of (i) *the twelve unleavened cakes on the Table of Shew-bread,* (ii) *the sheaf of the first-fruits of barley on the second day of the Passover,* (iii) *the two wheaten loaves at Pentecost,*

Or (2) together with the Burnt- and Thank-offering,

but *not* with the Sin- or Trespass-offering ; as (I) of *public* sacrifices, with (i) the daily morning and evening sacrifice, (ii) the Sabbath-offering, (iii) the offering at the new moon, (iv) on the great day of Atonement; (II) of *private* sacrifices, at (i) the consecration of priests and Levites, (ii) the cleansing of the leper, (iii) the termination of the Nazarite vow.

(*c*) *Incense*, the last example of an unbloody offering, accompanied every proper meat-offering, but was also offered daily on the golden altar in the Holy Place, and on the great day of Atonement was burnt in the Holy of Holies by the High-priest before the Ark. The greatest pains were taken in its preparation. It was compounded by the "art of the apothecary" of four ingredients beaten small[1], stacte, onycha, galbanum, and pure frankincense (Ex. xxx. 34—36), nor could any other kind be offered (Ex. xxx. 9). Desecration of this incense by using it for common purposes was to be punished with death (Ex. xxx. 38).

II. In reference to the second class of sacrifices, in which the life of a victim was taken and its blood poured upon the Altar, it is to be observed that these were limited to the *herd, the flock, and all clean birds.*

---

[1] (i) *Stacte* (Heb. *drops*), probably the gum from the storax tree, a plant about twelve feet high, like the quince; (ii) *Onycha,* the name of the covering of a shell-fish, met with in the Red Sea, yielding a scent not pleasant in itself, but giving strength and continuance to other perfumes; (iii) *Galbanum,* resin from a shrub growing on the Syrian mountains, with a strong and disagreeable odour, but when mixed with other perfumes, increasing their sweetness; (iv) *Frankincense,* the highly prized resin of a small shrub, about ten feet high, growing in Arabia (Is. lx. 6 ; Jer. vi. 20), especially Saba and India. Successive incisions were made in the bark of the tree, the first yielded the purest and whitest kind, the succeeding incisions yielding the same, but spotted with yellow. For the comparison of prayer to incense, see Ps. cxli. 1, 2 ; Rev. v. 8; viii. 3, 4.

All wild and unclean beasts were strictly excluded. The Israelite was to select only those animals which were *most nearly connected with man*, and of these, again, such as were *most meek, innocent, pure, and valuable*, such as oxen, sheep, goats, pigeons, and turtle-doves[1]. The selected victim was required to be perfect of its kind and without blemish, not less than eight days old, and usually a year. If it was blind, or broken, or maimed, or had any defect, as a wen or scab, it could not be offered (Lev. xxii. 20—27 ; Deut. xv. 21, 22 ; xvii. 1).

Such being the conditions respecting the victim, the offerer was required first to purify himself by ablutions, and then to bring the victim to the door of the Tabernacle, *i. e.* to the *Great Brazen Altar of Burnt-offering* in the court. There, whatever might be the precise kind of offering, he was to lay his hand on its head in token of surrender, dedication, and substitution, and then to slay it *himself* (Lev. i. 5). He had now performed his part, all the rest devolved upon the priest. He began by receiving the blood of the animal in a vessel, and then sprinkled it in different ways upon the Brazen Altar (Lev. iv. 6, 7, 25 ; v. 9), or, as we shall see, in some cases, on the Golden Altar of Incense, and, on one day in the year, on the Mercy-seat in the Holy of Holies. He then performed other ceremonies, which varied according to the nature of the

---

[1] The animals offered by the Greeks and Romans were generally of the domestic kind, but also included pigs, dogs, horses, and sometimes even fish, which are mentioned as pleasing to certain gods. The Hebrew sacrificial system, therefore, which rejected all animals caught in the chase, as stags, gazelles, antelopes, could never have contemplated such a sacrifice as that of the Roman emperors, who not unfrequently slaughtered for their hecatombs a hundred lions, and as many eagles. See Hengstenberg, *On the Sacrifices of Holy Script.* p. 377 ; Kurtz, p. 59 ; Michaelis' *Laws of Moses*, III. 95.

sacrifice. *But uniformly it was required* (*a*) of the *offerer*, (i) to bring his victim to the altar, (ii) to lay his hand upon it, and (iii) to slay it; (*b*) of the *priest*, (i) to receive the blood in a vessel, and (ii) to sprinkle it upon the altar.

Of the bloody sacrifices the chief were (*a*) BURNT-OFFERINGS, (*b*) PEACE-OFFERINGS, (*c*) SIN- AND TRESPASS-OFFERINGS.

(*a*) In the case of the *Burnt-offering*, any kind of animal fit for sacrifice might be offered, but the victim was always required to be a male, and to be accompanied by a meat-offering. After presentation at the great altar, imposition of the hands of the sacrificer, and slaughtering, the priest sprinkled the blood upon the altar round about (Lev. i. 5, 11). The victim was then flayed, washed with water, and cut in pieces, and the parts thus divided were laid on the altar upon the wood, and entirely consumed by fire.

The *burning by fire* was the chief point in this class of offering, and "marked it as an expression of perpetual obligation to complete, sanctified, self-surrender to Jehovah[1]." Hence it was not presented, like the sin- and trespass-offerings, upon the commission of any particular sin, nor like the peace-offerings upon the acceptance of any special Divine mercies; it embodied the *general idea* of sacrifice, and in a sense represented the whole sacrificial institute. Every morning and evening, therefore, a lamb was sacrificed with its usual meat- and drink-offering as a burnt-offering on behalf of the whole covenant people, and the evening victim was to be so slowly consumed that it might last till the morning, an expressive symbol of that continual self-dedication to God, which is the duty of man[2] (Ex. xxix. 38—44; Lev. vi. 9—13).

[1] Kurtz's *Sacrificial Worship*, p. 250.
[2] The chief public burnt-offerings were presented at

(*b*) Of *Peace-offerings* there were three kinds, representing various emotions of the offerer, the *thank-offering*, the *freewill gift*, and the *vow* (Lev. iii. 1—17; vii. 11—21, 28—36).

The nature of the offering was left to the sacrificer; it might be taken from the herd or from the flock, might be male or female, but not birds (Lev. iii. 1). Like the burnt-offering it was always accompanied by a meat-offering, which consisted of unleavened cakes mingled with oil, and leavened bread (Lev. vii. 12, 13).

The ritual of the Peace-offering was up to a certain point the same as that of the Burnt-offering. The sacrificer brought his victim to the Brazen Altar, laid his hands upon it and slew it, while the priest sprinkled the blood upon the altar; but after this there was a distinction. The victim was divided, and the priest laid upon the altar the fat of the kidneys, and the "lobe" or flap of the liver, and in the case of a sheep the fat tail, and burnt them with fire. He then separated the right shoulder and breast, and waved them before the Lord, and they became his portion which he was to eat *in a clean place* with his family and friends. The remaining portions of the victim were then restored to the sacrificer, who the same day feasted thereon, together with his whole family and his friends (Lev. vii. 15—21; xix. 6; xxii. 30).

(i) the daily morning and evening service; (ii) on the Sabbath, which was double that of every day, with a double meat- and drink-offering (Num. xxviii. 9, 10); (iii) at the New Moon, the three great Festivals, the great Day of Atonement, and the Feast of Trumpets (Num. xxviii. 11). Private burnt-offerings were appointed (i) for the consecration of the priests (Ex. xxix. 15); (ii) the purification of women (Lev. xii. 6—8); (iii) the cleansing of the leper (Lev. xiv. 10); (iv) removal of any ceremonial uncleanness (Lev. xv. 15, 30); (v) any accidental breach, and the conclusion of the Nazarite vow (Num. vi. 10, 14; and comp. Acts xxi. 26).

This *Sacrificial Feast* was peculiar to the *Peace-offerings*, and indicated that the atonement was complete, that the sin was covered and cancelled which had separated the offerer from Jehovah, who now welcomed him to His table, and in this meal gave him a pledge of reconciliation. "To an Oriental mind two ideas were inseparably united in the notion of a meal; on the one hand, that of fellowship and friendship existing among the participators themselves, and also between them and the provider of the meal; and on the other hand, that of joy and gladness, so that even the highest and purest joy, viz. blessedness in the kingdom of heaven is described under the figure of a meal[1]" (Ps. xxiii. 5; xxxvi. 8; Matt. viii. 11; xxii. 2—13; Lk. xiv. 16). As the *total consumption by fire* on the altar was the culminating point in the burnt-offering, so this *sacrificial feast* was that of the peace-offering, which, therefore, whenever presented with other offerings, was invariably the *last*[2]. (Comp. Ex. xxiv. 5, 11; xxix. 1—32).

(*c*) The *Sin-* and *Trespass-offerings* were peculiar to the Mosaic Law, which was *added on account of transgression* (Gal. iii. 19), and deepened the knowledge and conviction of sin (Rom. vii. 7, &c.).

(*a*) The *Sin-offering* consisted of *one animal only,*

[1] Bähr's *Symbolik* quoted in Kurtz's *Sacrif. Worship*, p. 163.
[2] From this circumstance also arises the fact that Peace-offerings were offered on the most magnificent scale at seasons of great solemnity and rejoicing; *e.g.* at the inauguration of the Covenant (Ex. xxiv. 5); the consecration of Aaron and the Tabernacle (Lev. ix. 18); the solemn reading of the Law on Ebal and Gerizim (Josh. viii. 31); at the accession of Saul (1 Sam. xi. 15); at the introduction of the Ark by David into Mt. Zion (2 Sam. vi. 17); at the dedication of the Temple by Solomon (1 Kin. viii. 63; ix. 25); at the great Passover of Hezekiah (2 Chron. xxx. 22); while on two occasions only do we find them connected with national sorrow (Judg. xx. 26; 2 Sam. xxiv. 25).

and was not accompanied by a meat-offering. The
victim if offered for the whole covenant people was *a
kid of the goats* (Lev. xvi. 5, 9, 15; Num. xxviii. 15, 22,
30); for the priests and Levites at their consecration *a
young bullock* (Ex. xxix. 11; Numb. viii. 8 ff.); for the
High-priest on the great day of Atonement *a young
bullock* (Lev. xvi. 3, 6, 11); for the purification of women after childbirth *a young pigeon or turtle-dove*
(Lev. xii. 6, 8; comp. Lk. ii. 22, 24); for the cleansing
of a leper or a leprous house *a yearling ewe;* or, in a
case of poverty, *a bird for the leper and two for the
house* (Lev. xiv. 13, 22—49); for an inadvertent transgression of some prohibition, (*a*) on the part of the
whole congregation or the High-priest, *a young bullock*,
(*b*) a prince, *a he-goat*, (*c*) a common man, *a yearling
ewe* or *kid* (Lev. iv. 1—35).

The Ritual of the Sin-offering deserves attention.
The offerer brought the victim to the great altar, laid
his hand upon it with a confession of the sin and a
prayer for its expiation, and then slew it. The priest
then dipped his finger in the blood, and in the case of
a prince or individual, sprinkled it seven times on the
horns of the Brazen Altar (Lev. iv. 7, 18, 30, 34); in
that of the High-priest and congregation seven times
on the veil before the Ark, and seven times on the
horns of the Golden Altar of Incense (Lev. iv. 6, 17, 25);
on the great day of Atonement, the High-priest himself sprinkled it seven times on and before the Mercy-
seat, and then seven times streaked with it the horns
of the Altar of Incense (Lev. xvi. 14, 15, 19); the rest of
the blood was poured on the ground before the Brazen
Altar. After the sprinkling, the same portions were
burnt on the altar, as in the case of the peace-offerings,
and in ordinary cases the rest of the victim was eaten
by the priest in the court of the Tabernacle with only
the males of his family; but any vessels in which the

flesh had been boiled were required, if earthenware, to be broken; if metal, to be carefully scoured (Lev. vi. 24—30). But in the case of the more important Sin-offerings, where the blood was sprinkled within the Holy Place, or the Holy of Holies, the entire carcase, except the altar-pieces, with the hide, entrails, &c., was conveyed to a clean place without the camp, and there burnt with fire (Lev. iv. 11, 12, 21; xvi. 27).

Except when offered for the whole people, or the priests and Levites at their consecration, Sin-offerings were presented as an atonement for sins of *culpable weakness and ignorance, negligence and frailty,* repented of by the unpunished offender, who was thus restored to his place in the commonwealth. They could not be offered for *presumptuous,* or *deliberate* and *unrepented* sins, such as wilful murder or adultery, for which the punishment of death was appointed (Num. xv. 30, 31; Deut. xvii. 12; and comp. Heb. x. 26).

(*b*) The *Trespass-* or *Debt-offering,* on the other hand, though closely connected with the Sin-offering and sometimes offered with it, as in the case of the leper (Lev. xiv. 12), was always offered for some *special act* of sin, and was regarded in the light of reparation to the Lord for a wrong done to Him. Hence it was presented for sins "in which the offence given, or the debt incurred by the misdeed, admitted of some sort of recompence, which could be actually estimated[1]."

The following cases will illustrate the occasions on which a trespass-offering could be presented. A leper, on the occasion of his cleansing, owed a debt-offering to Jehovah, for the time of his exclusion from the camp; the Nazarite for a temporary suspension of his vow by touching a dead body (Num. vi. 12); a man, who had inadvertently appropriated or made away

---

[1] See Kurtz's *Sacrificial Worship,* p. 192; Fairbairn's *Typology,* II. 348; Browne's *Hebrew Antiquities,* 114, 115.

with anything consecrated to the Lord (Lev. v. 15, 16), or unwittingly violated a Divine prohibition (Lev. v. 17, 18), or denied a trust or any damage sustained by the thing entrusted, or denied having found some lost article of property, or sworn falsely in such a matter (Lev. vi. 2 ff.). In these cases, whether the wrong done was in a matter of property or to the Lord, the damage was made good with an overplus, generally a fifth of the value, while the trespass-offering itself was the substitute for the damages due to the Lord, and assessed by the priest. The victim was, as in the case of the sin-offering, *one animal only*, and always a ram.

CHAPTER IV

HOLY TIMES AND SEASONS.

Exod. xx.   Levit. xxiii. xxv.   Deut. xv. xvi.

THE Holy Times and Seasons of the Israelites may be arranged under three heads.

I.   Those that were connected with the *Seventh Day of Rest*, such as (*a*) the *Weekly Sabbath*, (*b*) the *Month-Sabbath* or *New Moon*, (*c*) the *Year-Sabbath*. (*d*) the *Year of Jubilee.*

II.   The *Day of Atonement.*

III.   The *Great Historical Festivals;* (*a*) The *Passover*, (*b*) The *Feast of Pentecost* or *Weeks*, (*c*) The *Feast of Tabernacles.*

I.   Those connected with the *seventh Day of Rest.*

(*a*)   The observance of the weekly Sabbath, or day of Rest, is not improbably thought to have been known to the Israelites before the giving of the Law (Ex. xvi. 22, 23), as, indeed, the words of the Fourth Commandment, "*Remember* the Sabbath-day to keep it holy," seem to imply (Ex. xx. 8—11, comp. Gen. ii. 1—3). The observance of this day was appointed for *a perpetual covenant*, as *a sign between God and the children of Israel for ever* (Ex. xxxi. 16, 17). It was to be shared by the whole people with the stranger; and, to complete the picture of tranquillity, with the animals. Bodily labour was strictly prohibited: it was unlawful to kindle a fire for cooking food (Ex. xxxv. 3; Num. xv. 32), or to go out of the camp to gather manna (Ex. xvi. 22—30). Wilful desecration of the day was punished by stoning (Ex. xxxi. 14; Num. xv. 35).

In the Tabernacle-service the daily burnt-offering was doubled (Num. xxviii. 9), the shew-bread was renewed (Lev. xxiv. 8), and the priestly course for the week commenced their duties.

The Sabbath was not regarded as a fast, but a day for rest from worldly occupation and holy joy; it was ordained by God *for man* and the furtherance of his truest and highest interests (Mk. ii. 27, 28). "The thought of HIM, who is raised above all change, and who after the completion of the works of Creation rejoiced that everything was very good; this coupled with the cessation from work was to lead man up to the contemplation of his own origin from God. As the bodily refreshment restored his physical energies, so should the consciousness of union with the Almighty and the Eternal restore the true life to the soul[1]."

(*b*) *The Month-Sabbath*, or *New Moon Festival*, was ushered in by blowing with the silver trumpets, and by the sacrifice of eleven victims in addition to the daily

---

[1] Von Gerlach, *On the Pentateuch.* After the return from the Captivity the observance of the Sabbath was fenced about by a multitude of petty prohibitions. Not only was marketing prohibited (Neh. x. 31; xiii. 15—19), but travelling beyond a Sabbath-day's journey, i.e. 2000 paces or about 6 furlongs, bearing arms even in time of war (1 Macc. ii. 36), plucking ears of corn, healing the sick, carrying a bed (comp. Matt. xii. 10; Mk. iii. 2; Lk. vi. 7; Jn. ix. 14, 16).

offering (Num. x. 10; xxviii. 11, &c.). Business and trade were in later times suspended (Amos viii. 5), sacrificial feasts were held (1 Sam. xx. 5—24), and the people resorted to the prophets for religious instruction (2 Kings iv. 23).

The New Moon of the *seventh* month (*Tisri*, October), being the commencement of the civil year, was observed with still greater solemnity. It was one of the seven[1] days of Holy Convocation. Not merely were the trumpets blown at the time of offering the sacrifices, but it was a day *for the blowing of trumpets* (Num. xxix. 1—6), whence its name the *Feast of Trumpets*. In addition to the daily sacrifices, and the eleven victims offered on the first day of each month, nine other victims were offered as burnt-offerings with a kid for a sin-offering[2].

(*c*) During the *Seventh* or *Sabbatical year* the land was to lie fallow, and *enjoy her Sabbaths* (Ex. xxiii. 10, 11; Lev. xxv. 2—7; Deut. xv.). No tillage or cultivation of any sort was to be practised, and the spontaneous produce of the fields, instead of being reaped, was to be freely gleaned by the poor, the stranger, and even the cattle. By this rest the land, like man, was to do

---

[1] Of these there were two at the Passover, one at Pentecost, one at the feast of Trumpets, one on the Day of Atonement, and two at the feast of Tabernacles.

[2] The tendency of the Eastern nations to worship the Moon was inveterate. In Egypt this luminary, under the name of Isis, was one of the only two deities which commanded the reverence of all the Egyptians (Herodotus, II. 42, 47); in Syria she was worshipped under the name of Ashtaroth Karnaim, the *horned Astarte;* in Babylonia under the name of Sin, and called *Lord of the Month.* We see, therefore, how necessary it was that the Israelites should have, besides a penal prohibition, some positive preservative against such worship, and by the blast of the sacred trumpets and the additional sacrifices be taught to pay honour to the Eternal One, the Creator and Sustainer of all things, who *appointed the moon for seasons* (Ps. civ. 19).

homage to its Lord and Creator, and the poorest were to share without stint in those spontaneous blessings which by His will it brings forth, and the Israelite, who every seventh day acknowledged God's claim on his time, thus acknowledged also His claim upon his land. In Deut. xv. we find that the seventh year was also to be one of release for debtors. In spite of the threatenings in Lev. xxvi. the Sabbatical year, as appears from 2 Chron. xxxvi. 20, 21, was greatly neglected; after the return from the Captivity its observance revived (see 1 Macc. vi. 49)[1].

(*d*) *The Year of Jubilee.* At the end of seven times seven years, that is, forty-nine entire years, the fiftieth was observed as the year of *Jubilee,* a word of uncertain meaning. It was proclaimed by the sound of trumpets on the tenth day of the seventh month, Tisri, the Day of Atonement. During this year the soil was to lie fallow, as in the Sabbatical year, but in addition to this, all land that had been alienated was to return to those to whom it had been allotted at the original distribution, and all bondmen of Hebrew blood were to be liberated (Lev. xxv. 8—16, 23—35; xxvii. 16—25). " As the weekly Sabbath and the Sabbatical year was intended to restore thorough rest to man and to the

---

[1] Both Alexander and Julius Cæsar exempted the Jews from tribute during it. Comp. Joseph. *Ant.* xiv. 10, § 6. See article *Sabbatical Year,* in Smith's *Bib. Dict.* At first sight, it is there observed, the provisions of this enactment seem impracticable. But it is to be remembered (i) that the land would actually derive much benefit from lying fallow at a time when the rotation of crops was unknown; (ii) in no year was the owner allowed to reap the whole harvest (Lev. xix. 9; xxiii. 22); and the remainder would in the fertile soil of Palestine resow itself and produce a considerable result; (iii) the vines and olives would naturally yield their fruit; (iv) owners of land were expected to lay in provision during previous years (Lev. xxv. 20—22).

land, so the year of *Jubilee* was designed to raise the whole people, in respect to their rights and possessions, from the changeableness of outward circumstances to the unchangeableness of the Divine appointment; to prevent the inordinate accumulation of wealth in the hands of a few; to relieve those whom misfortune or fault had reduced to poverty; to restore that equality in outward circumstances which was instituted on the first settlement of the land by Joshua; and to vindicate the right of each Israelite to his part in the Covenant, which God had made with his fathers respecting the Land of Promise[1]."

II. *The Day of Atonement* was observed on the tenth day of the seventh month, Tisri, as the great day of national humiliation, and for the expiation of the sins both of the priests and the people. This was the highest, the most perfect, the most comprehensive of all the acts of expiation, and not only took place but once in the entire year, but was performed by the High-priest alone, and that not in the Holy Place but the Holy of Holies.

Its celebration is prescribed in Lev. xvi.; xxiii. 26—32; Num. xxix. 7—11. The day was to be regarded as a *high Sabbath*, a day of *holy Convocation,* on which the Israelites, under pain of extirpation, were expected to *afflict their souls* with fasting and mourning. (Comp. Lev. xvi. 29, 31 with Acts xxvii. 9.) The ritual was as follows. The High-priest having bathed, arrayed himself not in his gorgeous robes, but in the white linen garments common to himself and the rest of the priesthood. As a sacrifice for himself and the priests he brought a bullock for a Sin-offering, and a ram for a Burnt-offering, which he had purchased at his own cost; as a sacrifice for the people two he-goats for a Sin-offer-

---

[1] Von Gerlach, *On the Pentateuch.*

ing, and a ram for a Burnt-offering, which were purchased out of the public treasury. The two he-goats he
then brought to the Door of the Tabernacle, *i. e.* to the
Brazen Altar, and there having presented them before
the Lord, cast. two lots upon them, one inscribed *for
Jehovah*, the other for *Azazel*[1]. This done, as the head
of a priesthood itself *compassed with infirmity* (Heb.
v. 2), he first proceeded to make atonement for his own
order. Accordingly he slew the bullock, and taking a
censer filled with live coals from the Altar of Burnt-
offering and two handfuls of Incense, he passed with
these through the Holy Place onwards behind the veil
into the Holy of Holies, and there threw the incense
upon the coals so that the fragrant cloud might envelope
the Mercy-Seat. Then returning to the Brazen Altar
and taking some of the blood of the bullock in a vessel
he once more passed into the Holy of Holies, and
sprinkled it seven times before the Mercy-Seat, the
seat of the glory of Jehovah. Having thus made expiation for himself and his own order, he slew the goat
upon which the lot *for Jehovah* had fallen as a Sin-
offering for the people, and sprinkled its blood as he
had done that of the bullock. Then on his return from
the Holy of Holies he purified the Holy Place, now
solitary and deserted, by sprinkling the blood of both
victims seven times on the horns of the Golden Altar of

[1] This most difficult word is variously explained, as a
designation (i) of the *goat* itself, and = *the goat sent away*, or
let loose, the *scape-goat ;* (ii) of the *place* to which it was sent,
and = *desert places*, or the name of a mountain near Sinai ;
(iii) of a *personal being* to whom the goat was sent, and = *the
apostate, the unclean*, an evil demon, or the devil himself ;
(iv) of the lot cast upon it, = for *complete sending away*, or
removal of sin. Of these explanations, No. i. has in its
favour the most ancient authorities ; No. ii. the largest
majority of the latest commentators, who compare Isai.
xiii. 22 ; xxxiv. 14 ; Lev. xvii. 7 ; Matt. xii. 43 ; Lk. viii. 27 ;
Rev. xviii. 2.

Incense, and, as some think, on those of the Altar of Burnt-offering.

The purification of the Tabernacle completed, he came forth and laid both his hands upon the goat, on which the lot *for Azazel* had fallen, solemnly confessed over it the sins of the people, and then gave it to a man chosen for the purpose to be led away into the wilderness, *into a place not inhabited*, and there let loose. This done, he once more entered the Tabernacle, bathed, and having arrayed himself in his gorgeous robes, offered the two rams as a burnt-offering, one for himself, the other for the people, and at the same time placed upon the altar the fat of the two sin-offerings[1]. While these were consuming, the remains of the victims were conveyed outside the camp, nor could they who were deputed for this office, or the man who had led away the scape-goat, return into the camp till they had purified themselves and their clothes with water.

The distinction between this solemnity and others is very striking. It took place but once a year, five days before the joyous Feast of Tabernacles, which testified to the nation's gratitude for the preservation of *the seasonable fruits of the earth.* In it the High-priest alone officiated. Clad not in his gorgeous robes, but in the simple, pure white robes common to him and the rest of the priesthood, he made expiation for himself, his order, and the people,—an atonement for the sins of the whole year. On this day, and this day only, he entered within the Veil, and sprinkled the blood before the Mercy-Seat seven times. On this day, and this day only, the idea of the remission of sin found its highest expression in the sacrifice of one goat as a sin-offering to Jehovah, and the solemn confession of the sins of the whole people over another, and its dismissal laden with

[1] And, according to Num. xxix. 7—11, other sacrifices with the usual meat-offering.

its awful typical burden into a far distant and separated land, *a land not inhabited*, lying, as it were, under the curse of Jehovah. This solemnity contained the exact antidote to the sombre and often cruel rites of heathenism. The lots were cast over both the goats, both were presented to Jehovah at the Door of the Tabernacle, at *His* command the Scape-Goat carried away the burden of the people's sins into an unknown desert land, *He* sanctified the people, and accepted the atonement for the High-priest, the priestly order, and the entire nation, and the purification of the Place where He had condescended to meet the Israelites. In the Epistle to the Hebrews (ix., x.) we have the key to the expressive imagery of this Great Day in the Jewish year. The fact that once in the year the High-priest could enter within the Veil, intimated that under a system of provisional and typical ordinances the way *into the Holiest of all was not as yet made manifest.* But when the true High-priest, even Jesus Christ, offered Himself unto death on the Altar of His Cross for the sins of the whole world, the Veil of the Temple *was rent in twain from the top to the bottom* (Matt. xxvii. 51 ; Mark xv. 38). He died, He rose again, and, clad not in the resplendent robes of that Divine Nature He had before the world, but in the garb of our human nature, He ascended into the Heavenly Sanctuary, the antitype of the Jewish Sanctuary on earth, and there pleads, and will for ever plead, the merits of His blood before the throne of God.

CHAPTER V

THE GREAT FESTIVALS.

Exod. xxiii. 14—17; Lev. xxiii. 1—22; Num. xxviii. 16—31;
Deut. xvi. 1—16.

THE great Historical Festivals, at which all males amongst the Israelites were required to appear before the Lord, were, as has been said already, (i) *The Passover;* (ii) *The Feast of Weeks* or *Pentecost;* (iii) *The Feast of Tabernacles.*

(i) *The Passover.* The original institution of this Festival has been already noticed. The directions for its yearly celebration are given in Ex. xxiii. 14—17; Lev. xxiii. 5—8 ; Num. xxviii. 16—25; Deut. xvi. 1—8.

As in Egypt, so now, on the 10th day of *Nisan* or *Abib*, corresponding to the close of March or the beginning of April, each Paschal company, which might not exceed twenty or be less than ten, was to select a lamb or kid, a male of the first year, and keep it till the 14th day. If pronounced by the priests to be free from blemish, it was to be slain *between the evenings*, in the Court of the Tabernacle, and its blood poured round the Altar of Burnt-offering. It was then, after being flayed, to be taken to the house where the Paschal Company intended to assemble, to be roasted with fire, whole and entire without the breaking of a single bone, and to be eaten with unleavened bread and bitter herbs.

The Festival lasted from the 14th to the 21st of Nisan, and during this period nothing but unleavened bread might be eaten, and all leaven was to be carefully removed from the house before the 14th. The daily sacrifices for the nation consisted of (i) a *Burnt-Offering* of two bullocks, one ram, seven yearling lambs, accompanied by the usual meat-offering, and (ii) one goat for a *Sin-Offering.* Thank-offerings, called by the Jews

Chagigah, might also be offered by individuals during the Festival, especially on the 15th, the first day of Holy Convocation. (Comp. Lev. vii. 29—34; 2 Ch. xxx. 22—44; xxxv. 7.)

On the 16th the first ripe sheaf of barley was to be brought into the sanctuary, and there waved by the priest before the Lord, and at the same time a yearling lamb was offered with a meat- and drink-offering (see Lev. xxiii. 9—14). Till this sheaf had thus been waved, and this offering presented, no produce of the now ripening harvest, whether bread or parched corn, or green ears, might be eaten (Josh. v. 11, 12)[1].

[1] The Passover was eminently an Historical Festival. Year after year, from generation to generation, it was to recall, as in "a living drama," the great facts of the national deliverance, the awful night when there was not a house in Egypt where there was not one dead, when the Destroying Angel passed over the houses of the Israelites, and the people were delivered, not by their own might or by their own strength, but by the uplifted hand of Jehovah. It was the nation's annual Birth-day Feast, the Festival of Redemption. Its chief features were (i) the offering of a *single victim* for each Paschal company; (ii) the *Paschal Meal* with which the Festival began; (iii) the eating of *unleavened bread* during the whole time it lasted.

No other Festival was so full of typical meaning, or pointed so clearly *to good things to come* (Heb. x. 1). (i) It was a Feast of Redemption foreshadowing a future and greater Redemption (Gal. iv. 4, 5); (ii) The Victim, a lamb *without blemish and without spot*, was a striking type of the *Lamb of God that taketh away the sin of the world* (Jn. i. 29; 1 Cor. v. 7; 1 Pet. i. 19); (iii) Slain not by the priest but by the head of the Paschal company, its blood shed and sprinkled on the Altar, roasted whole without the breaking of a bone, it symbolized Him who was put to death by the people (Acts ii. 23), whose Blood during a Paschal Festival was shed on the Altar of His Cross, whose side the soldier pierced, but brake not His legs (Jn. xix. 32—36); (iv) Eaten at the sacrificial meal (peculiar to the peace-offering) with bitter herbs and unleavened bread (the symbol of purity) it pointed to that one Oblation of Himself once offered, whereby Christ has made us at peace with God (Eph. ii. 14, 15), in which whosoever

(ii) At the end of seven complete weeks from the 16th of Nisan, the second day of unleavened bread, commenced *the* Feast of Weeks (Ex. xxxiv. 22; Deut. xvi. 10), or of *Harvest* (Ex. xxiii. 16), or of *First-fruits* (Numb. xxviii. 26), or of *Pentecost* (Acts ii. 1), from the Greek word for the *fiftieth* day.

The passages bearing on it will be found in Ex. xxiii. 16; Lev. xxiii. 15—22; Num. xxviii. 26—31; Deut. xvi. 9—12.

The Festival lasted but one day, which was kept with a holy Convocation. Its distinguishing feature was the offering of *two leavened loaves,* made from the new corn of the now completed harvest, which together with two lambs as a thank-offering were waved before the Lord. The especial sacrifices in addition to the daily offering were one young bullock, two rams, and seven yearling lambs as a *Burnt-offering* with the usual meat- and drink-offering, and a goat for a *Sin-offering;* but thank-offerings might, as at the Passover, be made at pleasure by individuals.

The character of the Festival was pre-eminently an expression of gratitude for the harvest, which commenced with the offering of the first sheaf of ripe barley at the Passover, and ended with that of the two loaves now presented and made of the newly-ripened wheat. In its festive joy the man-servant and maid-servant, the stranger, the fatherless and the widow were to share with the freeborn Israelite, who was to be reminded of the bondage in Egypt, and his obligation to keep the Law[1] (Deut. xvi. 12).

truly believes must walk in repentance, and sincerity and truth (1 Cor. v. 7, 8); (v) It was at a Paschal Supper that its Antitype the Christian Eucharist was instituted by our Lord. (Matt. xxvi. 17; Mark xiv. 12.)

[1] Though nowhere mentioned in Scripture, the later Jews saw in this Festival a commemoration of the giving of the Law on Mount Sinai, which is made out from Ex. xix. to

(iii)   The Feast of *Tabernacles* or of *Ingathering*
(Ex. xxxiv. 22) was so called as being (i) a feast of
thanksgiving for the completion of the ingathering of
fruits and of the vintage, and (ii) as commemorating the
dwelling of the Israelites in tents during their wanderings in the wilderness (Lev. xxiii. 43).

The chief passages relating to it are Ex. xxiii. 16;
Lev. xxiii. 34—43; Num. xxix. 13—39; Deut. xvi.
13—15; and compare with these Neh. viii.

It was celebrated in the autumn on the 15th of the
seventh month Tisri, and lasted seven days, of which
the first and last were days of Holy Convocation. It
was the most joyous of all the Festivals.   During it the
Israelites were commanded to live in tents or booths of
green boughs of the olive, palm, pine, myrtle, and other
trees with thick foliage (Neh. viii. 15, 16).   The burnt-
offerings were more numerous at this Feast than any
other, including, besides the sacrifice on each day of 2
rams, 14 lambs, and a kid for a sin-offering, that of 70
bullocks, 13 on the first day, 12 on the second, and so
on to the seventh, when 7 bullocks only were offered.
If the Festival fell in a Sabbatical year, portions of
the Law, chiefly Deuteronomy, were read each day
in public (Deut. xxxi. 10—12; Neh. viii. 18).   The
most remarkable celebrations of this Feast were (i)
at the dedication of Solomon's Temple (1 Kings viii.

have taken place on the fiftieth day after the departure from
Egypt, and may possibly be hinted at in Deut. xvi. 12.   Certainly Christians in the early ages of the Church observed the
coincidence between the bestowal of the Holy Spirit on the
Apostles at Pentecost (Acts ii. 1), and the giving of the Law
on the same day.   "It may have been on this account that
Pentecost was the last Jewish Festival (as far as we know)
which St Paul was anxious to observe (Acts xx. 16; 1 Cor.
xvi. 8), and that *Whitsunday* came to be the first annual Festival instituted in the Christian Church."—Art. *Pentecost* in
Smith's *Bib. Dict.*

2, 65); (ii) after the Captivity (Ezra iii. 4; Neh. viii. 17)[1].

Later festivals were (i) the Feast of Purim, or *Lots*, instituted by Mordecai to commemorate the defeat of Haman's machinations against the Jews (Esth. iii. 7—15; ix. 24—26). It began on the 14th day of the 12th month Adar, and lasted two days. (ii) The Feast of Dedication, to commemorate the cleansing of the Temple after its defilement by Antiochus Epiphanes (Dan. xi. 31). Established by Judas Maccabæus, it was kept on the 25th of the winter month Chisleu, *December* (Jn. x. 22), and lasted eight days, being distinguished by the offering of many sacrifices, a general illumination (hence its name the *Feast of Lights*), and other rejoicings.

In Scripture, dates are often fixed by a reference to the seasons or productions (Num. xiii. 20; 2 Sam. xxi. 9). The following Table, therefore, is here given, in which the civil and sacred months, their *approximate* English equivalents, the various annual feasts, and the chief features of the seasons are combined. It is assumed that *Abib* or *Nisan* answers to April. (See Article *Month* in Smith's *Bib. Dict.* and Angus's *Bible Handbook*, p. 270.)

---

[1] Other customs are alluded to in the New Testament in connexion with this Feast. (*a*) On the evening of the first day the Court of the Women at the Temple was illuminated with golden candelabra (Jn. viii. 12), accompanied by the chanting of eleven Psalms, cxx—cxxxi, and the same joyous ceremony was renewed on each of the seven days. (*b*) Every day, at the time of morning sacrifice, the Israelites in festive attire, and bearing branches in their hands, repaired to the Temple, and the priest having drawn water in a golden vessel from the fountain of Siloam, advanced to the Brazen Altar amidst the sound of trumpets, and poured it into a vessel on the western side furnished with small openings at the bottom, and wine into a similar vessel at the eastern side; whence by pipes it was conveyed to the Kidron (comp. Jn. vii. 37—39 with Isai. xii. 3).

CALENDAR.

Year.		Month.	English Month (nearly.)	Festivals.	Seasons and Productions.
Sacred. i.	Civil. 7	ABIB or NISAN (green ears) Days 30. Exod. xii. 2.	April.	14. The PASSOVER. 16. First-fruits of barley - harvest presented.	Fall of the *latter* or *spring* rain. (Deut. xi. 14.) Floods (Josh. iii. 14). Barley ripe at Jericho. Wheat partly in the ear.
ii.	8	ZIF (blossom) Days 29. 1 Kings vi. 1.	May.	14. *Second Passover* for those who could not keep the first. Num. ix. 10, 11.	Barley harvest general (Ruth i. 22). Wheat ripens.
iii.	9	SIVAN. Days 30. Esth. viii. 9.	June.	6. PENTECOST or Feast of WEEKS.	Wheat harvest. Summer begins. No rain from April to Sept. (1 Sam. xii. 17).
iv.	10	THAMMUZ. Days 29. Zec. viii. 19.	July.		Heat increases.
v.	11	AB. Days 30. Esth. vii. 9.	Aug.		The streams dry up. Heat intense. Vintage (Lev. xxvi. 5).
vi.	12	ELUL. Days 29. Neh. vi. 15.	Sept.		Heat still intense (2 Kin. iv. 18—20). Grape harvest general (Num. xiii. 23).
vii.	1	TISRI or ETHANIM. Days 30. 1 Kin. viii. 2. 2 Chr. v. 3.	Oct.	1. Feast of *Trumpets.* 10. Day of ATONEMENT. 15. Feast of TABERNACLES. First-fruits of wine and oil (Lev. xxiii. 39).	Former or *early* rains begin (Joel ii. 23). Ploughing and sowing begin.
viii.	2	BUL (rain). Days 29. 1 Kin. vi. 38.	Nov.		Rain continues. Wheat and barley sown. Vintage in N. Palestine.
ix.	3	CHISLEU. Days 30. Neh. i. 1.	Dec.	25. Feast of *Dedication.* (1 Macc. iv. 52—59).	Winter begins. Snow on the mountains.
x.	4	THEBETH. Days 29. Est. ii. 16.	Jan.		Coldest month. Hail, snow (Josh. x. 11).
xi.	5	SHEBAT. Days 30. Zech. i. 7.	Feb.		Weather gradually becomes warmer.
xii.	6	ADAR. Days 29. Esth. iii. 7. Esth. ix. 27.	March.	14, 15. Feast of *Purim.*	Thunder and hail frequent. Almond-tree blossoms.

(Margin labels: HARVEST, HOT SEASON, SEED TIME, WINTER, COLD SEASON)

Note.

Laws of Purity.

Not altogether unconnected with these regulations respecting Holy Times and Seasons were other enactments of the Mosaic code, having for their object the enforcement of ideas of purity and holiness. *Ye shall be holy unto Me*, was the Divine command; *for I the Lord thy God am holy, and have severed you from other people that ye should be Mine* (Lev. xix. 2 ; xx. 7). Many of these regulations were, doubtless, laws of health, tending to regulate diet, enforce cleanliness, and guard against many prevalent disorders. But over and above this, they had a higher object, and formed part of the moral discipline of the elect nation.

They regard (i) things unclean to eat; (ii) things unclean to touch ; (iii) unclean matters or conditions [1].

i. *Things unclean to eat.* The prohibitions respecting food follow directly the laws concerning sacrifice. Portions of many sacrifices, as we have seen, might be eaten. From this eating the Law passes on to food generally, the nature of which has "commonly no little influence on the refinement and manners of a people." Concerning vegetable eating, no rules are laid down. In respect to animal food, the laws are clear and precise. (i) Of *quadrupeds*, the clean were such as *both parted the hoof and chewed the cud*, all others were unclean. All animals, therefore, used in sacrifice might be eaten, as also the numerous species of deer and gazelles (Deut. xiv. 5), but none of the *carnivora*, or such animals as the camel, coney, hare, or pig. (ii) Of *birds* also, all that were offered in sacrifice might be eaten, such as doves, pigeons, and also quails, but all birds of prey, and nearly all the water-fowl, were unclean. (iii) Of *Fish*, those only were clean that had both fins and scales. (iv) All *Reptiles* and *Insects* were unclean, except locusts, and such as had four legs for walking and two for springing (Lev. xi. 21, 22 ; comp. Matt. iii. 4). But the Israelite was also strictly forbidden to eat anything that died of itself (Ex. xxii. 31), or was torn by beasts, emphatically the blood of any animal (Gen. ix. 4 ; Lev. iii. 17; xvii. 10, 12 ; Comp. 1 Sam. xiv. 32, 33).

(ii) *Things unclean to touch.* An Israelite incurred defilement who touched or handled (i) the dead body of any animal, whether clean or unclean (Lev. xi. 24—28), (ii) the body, bones, or grave of a dead man (Num. xix. 11, 13, 16).

[1] Browne's *Hebrew Antiquities.*

The latter was deemed a defilement calling for special purification. The person was unclean seven days. For his cleansing a young red heifer was slain outside the camp or town, in
the presence of one of the priests. Some of the blood the
priest was then to sprinkle seven times in the direction of the
Sanctuary, to burn the entire carcase, and cast into the fire
cedar-wood, scarlet wool, and hyssop. The ashes were then
collected, and laid up in a clean place, and a portion mixed with
water was to be sprinkled on whatever had been defiled, man,
or place, or vessel. This ceremony was to be repeated twice,
on the third and on the seventh day. On the latter day the
person defiled washed his clothes, bathed, and was clean at
even. But still stricter regulations were enforced when a
priest or a Nazarite had become defiled (Num. xix. 1—22).

(iii) *Unclean matters or conditions.* Many are enumerated,
but we need speak of only one, the disease of Leprosy.
This fearful malady, indigenous in Egypt and Asia Minor,
disfiguring the whole person, and making it horrible to the
beholder, was called by the Jews *the Stroke,* and even by the
Greeks the *first-born son of Death*[1]. It made itself apparent
by a white swelling on the skin, especially on the face, turning the skin white (Ex. iv. 6), and the hair white or yellow
(Lev. xiii. 3, 10, 30), and producing other disfigurements.
The person affected with it was instantly to repair to the
priests (Lev. xiii. 2, 9), whose duty it was to make a minute
examination, and pronounce whether it was a case of "true
leprosy." If so, the sufferer was pronounced *utterly unclean,*
and forthwith assumed the awful badges of his sad condition. He rent his clothes, bared his head, put a covering
on his upper lip (Lev. xiii. 45), as though he was mourning
for the dead (Ezek xxiv. 17, 22), and wherever he went cried
out, *Unclean! unclean!* An exile from his home, his family,
his friends (Num. v. 2), he was bound to reside without the
camp or city in a separate house by himself, or in the society of others similarly afflicted (Lev. xiii. 46; 2 Kings
xv. 5; 2 Kings vii. 3; Lk. xvii. 12). No Israelite ever pretended to effect a cure of this awful malady. The priest
could pronounce upon the symptoms, shut out the sufferer
from the congregation, but he had no power to heal. If,
however, the symptoms abated, and there were any signs of
a cure, the sufferer again went to the priest, who carefully
ascertained whether this was the case. If so, a peculiar ceremony celebrated the healing. It consisted of two stages,

[1] Æschylus, *Choeph.* 271.

(i) Two birds were taken, one killed by the priest over running water, the other dipped, together with cedar-wood, scarlet wool, and hyssop, in its blood, and suffered to fly away into the open air. The priest then sprinkled the leper with the blood seven times, and pronounced him clean. (ii) But before he could return to the society of his fellowmen, he must wash his clothes, shave off all his hair, bathe, and then present himself at the Sanctuary with a he-lamb as a *Trespass-offering*, an ewe lamb as a *Sin-offering*, and a he-lamb as a *Burnt-offering* with its usual meat-offering. In cases of poverty two doves or pigeons might be presented in place of the two latter offerings, but the he-lamb as a *Trespass-offering* was indispensable. This was first slain, and its blood smeared by the priest on the leper's right ear, the thumb of his right hand, and the great toe of his right foot. Consecrated oil was then similarly applied, and poured on his head, and the other sacrifices offered, at the conclusion of which atonement was deemed to have been made, and the Leper was clean (Lev. xiv. 49—53).

The regulations respecting this fearful malady were no mere sanitary regulations, for it was not catching from one person to another (comp. 2 Kings v. 1; viii. 4), and the ordinances respecting it did not apply to the stranger and the sojourner. "From the whole host of maladies and diseases which had broken in upon man's body, God selected this, the sickness of sicknesses, that He might thereby testify against that out of which it and all other sicknesses grew, against Sin, as not from Him, and as grievous in His sight[1]." It was the outward and visible sign of the innermost spiritual corruption, a meet emblem in its small beginnings, its gradual spread, its internal disfigurement, its dissolution little by little of the whole body, of that which corrupts, degrades, and defiles man's inner nature, and renders him unmeet to enter the Presence of a Pure and Holy God.

(iv) Among the *Vows* known before the time of Moses (and which, as a general rule, were discouraged by him, comp. Deut. xxiii. 21—23) was that of the *Nazarite*. The person making this vow was bound, usually for a certain term, to abstain from wine or strong drink, from grapes or anything made from the vine, from cutting the hair of his head, or approaching a corpse, even that of his nearest relative (Num. vi. 2—7). If he accidentally touched a corpse, he was obliged on the seventh day to cut off his hair, and begin his vow

---

[1] Archbp. Trench *On the Miracles*, pp. 210—214.

afresh on the next day, after presenting to the priest two turtle-doves, or two young pigeons, one for a sin, and the other for a burnt-offering, and a lamb as a trespass-offering. At the expiration of his vow, he brought to the Tabernacle a burnt-, sin-, and thank-offering (Lev. vii. 12, 13) with a meat- and drink-offering (Num. vi. 15), had the left shoulder of the thank-offering waved upon his hands by the priest (Num. vi. 19, 20), and cutting off his hair burnt it in the fire on the altar. Of Nazarites for life three are mentioned in Scripture, *Samson* (the only one actually called a Nazarite, Judg. xiii. 5), *Samuel* (1 Sam. i. 11), *John the Baptist* (Lk. i. 15).

CHAPTER VI
CIVIL AND MORAL LAWS.
Exod. XXI.—XXIII. Deut. XIX.—XXIV.

HITHERTO we have been concerned with those portions of the Mosaic Law, which instructed the Israelite in his duty towards God, and the mode in which He was to be worshipped. We will now turn to the chief of those which instructed him in his duty as (i) *a member of a family*, and (ii) *of a nation.*

(i) The FAMILY RELATIONS include (1) *The mutual duties of Parents and Children*, (2) *of Husband and Wife*, (3) *of Master and Servant.*

(1) *The duties of Parents and Children.* Reverence for parents is enjoined in the Decalogue as the first duty next after those appertaining to God Himself. *Honour thy father and mother* is the first and the only commandment to which a promise of long life and continuance in the Promised Land is definitely attached (Ex. xx. 12; Eph. vi. 2), and to smite or revile father or mother is made a capital offence (Ex. xxi. 15, 17; Lev. xix. 3; xx. 9). In the Patriarchal times, as we have already seen[1], the authority of the father over

---
[1] See above, p. 74.

his children was very great. His blessing conferred
special benefits, his curse special injury (Gen. ix. 25, 27 ;
xxvii. 27—40; xlviii. 15, 20; xlix.). His authority was
of great moment, not only in the marriage of sons (Gen.
xxiv. 3), but of daughters, though in the latter case the
consent of the brothers, or at least of the elder brother,
was deemed important (Gen. xxiv. 50, 51; xxxiv. 11). But
the Mosaic Law did not invest the father with the same
boundless power as the Greek or Roman Law[1]. He
could not inflict death irresponsibly. The incorrigible
son, whom he could not restrain from flagrant crimes,
he might bring before the elders of the city, who, having
obtained the concurrence of *both* parents, might sentence him to be stoned to death. But in the execution
of the judgment the whole congregation were required
to take part, in order to promote a more general ab-
horrence of the sin (Deut. xxi. 18—21). The father
could not disinherit his sons; to the firstborn he must
give two portions, and equal shares to the rest; but in
case of extreme indigence he might sell his children,
especially his daughters, into servitude, or surrender
them to creditors as a pledge (Ex. 21. 7).

(2) *The Relations of Husband and Wife.* The institution of marriage was jealously guarded by the
Mosaic Law. Adultery ranked next to murder, and the
punishment for both parties was death by stoning (Lev.
xviii. 20; xx. 10; Deut. xxii. 22). In deference to the
universal custom of Oriental nations, and the example
of the Patriarchs, polygamy was *allowed*, though by no
means *encouraged*, and though frequently practised by
the kings of Israel, was rare in private life (1 Sam. i. 2).
The right of divorce was conceded (Deut. xxiv. 1—4) on
account of *the hardness of the hearts* of the people
(Matt. xix. 8), but a woman once divorced and marry-

---

[1] Milman's *History of the Jews*, I. 171.

ing again might not return to her first husband, either
on the death of, or when put away by, the second. The
Mosaic Law sanctioned a custom of the Patriarchal age
(Gen. xxxviii. 8), which made it necessary that if a man
died childless, his wife should be taken in marriage by
his surviving brother, and it was further ordained that
the firstborn son by such a marriage should succeed in
the name of his brother, that it be not put out in Israel
(Deut. xxv. 5, &c.). The rigour, however, of the old
custom was relaxed. If the brother had children of his
own alive, he was exempt; and if he declared in open
court his unwillingness to enter into the marriage, the
duty devolved on the next relation of the deceased husband. (See Ruth iv. 5—11.)

(3) *The Relation of Master and Servant.* Slavery
existed amongst the Israelites as amongst all other Eastern nations. Slaves could be acquired in four ways. (1)
They might be taken in war (Num. xxxi. 11, 35; Deut.
xx. 14); (2) they might be purchased of parents or former
owners or merchants in time of peace (Gen. xvii. 23;
Lev. xxv. 44, 45); (3) they might have sold themselves
in satisfaction for a debt (Lev xxv. 39—43; 2 Kings iv.
1); (4) they might be the children of slaves born in
their master's house. But while slavery was thus recognised as an institution, it was the aim of the Mosaic
Law to mitigate its evils as much as possible. Thus,
not only does it open with a number of precepts relating to slaves (Ex. xxi. 2—6), but it ever pronounced
them to be equal before God as regarded their spiritual
relation, and freely admitted them to all religious privileges, circumcision (Gen. xvii. 10—14; Ex. xii. 44), the
rest of the Sabbath (Ex. xx. 10), the festivals (Ex. xii. 44),
and gave them an interest in all the sacrifices offered
by the family (Deut. xvi. 11, 14).

In regard, again, to civil rights, the Hebrew slave
was never looked upon as a mere *thing* or *chattel.* A

11

master could not chastise a slave to death without being
punished (Ex. xxi. 20, 21), and if he inflicted bodily mutilation, the slave, whether male or female, might claim
to be free (Ex. xxi. 26, 27). In the seventh year of his
service the Hebrew slave might take up his freedom,
leaving, however, his wife given him by his master
during service and her children (Ex. xxi. 3, 4); if he
declined to avail himself of this privilege, his master
might take him before the elders, bore his ear with an
awl to the door, and then he was his servant for ever,
i. e. till the year of Jubilee (Ex. xxi. 5, 6; Deut. xv. 16,
17). Moreover, as the Israelites when delivered from
Egyptian bondage had not gone forth empty, so the
Hebrew bondslave at his release (which took effect in
the Jubilee year, even though he had not served his full
time) was to be furnished liberally out of the flock, the
floor, and the winepress (Deut. xv. 13, 14). Besides
bondslaves we also find *hired servants* among the Hebrews. They were to be treated kindly, and their wages
duly paid (Lev. xix. 13; Deut. xxiv. 14, 15). Strangers
also within the gates, whether runaway slaves or exiles
from their own land, who would naturally be in extreme
want, were to be treated with great kindness, for the
Israelite himself was a *stranger in the land of Egypt*
(Ex. xxii. 21; xxiii. 9). Together with the poor generally, whether Hebrews or heathens, they were to have
the free enjoyment of the gleaning of the field and the
garden (Lev. xix. 9, 10; xxiii. 22; Deut. xxiv. 19—21), of
the spontaneous produce of the Sabbatical year (Lev.
xxv. 5, 6), of the sacrificial and tithe-feasts (Deut. xiv.
28, 29), and their share at joyous family festivals, such
as marriages, circumcision, the weaning of children.

(ii) The Laws affecting the Israelite in his civil
capacity may be arranged in three groups, according as
they regarded the sanctity of (1) *Life,* (2) *Character,*
and (3) *Property.*

(1) *Life.* The Laws protecting the life and person
include those against (*a*) *premeditated murder*, and
(*b*) *unintentional manslaughter*.

(*a*) *Premeditated murder.* The wilful shedder of
man's blood met with no compassion from the Mosaic
Code. The original law at Sinai (Ex. xxi. 12—14) and
the subsequent repetition of it (Deut. xix. 11—13) made
death the inevitable penalty of murder, even as it had
been in the days of Noah (Gen. ix. 6). The murderer
was regarded as accursed; for him the horns of the
altar were to be no refuge; he was to be dragged from
them by force to suffer his doom, nor could rank or
wealth exempt him from it, for it was expressly provided that on no pretext whatever should any ransom
be taken (Num. xxxv. 31, 32). Nor was his person only
regarded as accursed, but so long as he remained un-
discovered, even the land was looked upon as polluted.
If no efforts could detect the murderer, the elders of the
nearest town were to take a heifer, and bring it down
to a *rough valley, neither eared nor sown*, and there
strike off its head. They were then to wash their hands
over it, and in the presence of the Levites pronounce
the following words; *Our hands have not shed this
blood, neither have our eyes seen it. Be merciful, O
Lord, unto Thy people, whom Thou hast redeemed, and
lay not innocent blood to Thy people of Israel's charge.*
Thus atonement was to be made (Deut. xxi. 1—9).

(*b*) *Unintentional homicide.* Prior to the Mosaic
age, the duty of avenging blood devolved upon the next
of kin, who was called the Goel or *Avenger*, and together with his office inherited the property of the
deceased. Sometimes a whole family took upon them
this duty (2 Sam. xiv. 7). Amongst the other nations, as
the Arab tribes of the present day, "any bloodshed
whatever, whether wilful or accidental, laid the homicide open to the *duteous* revenge of the relatives and

11—2

family of the slain person, who again in their turn were then similarly watched and hunted by the opposite party, until a family war of extermination had legally settled itself from generation to generation, without the least prospect of a peaceful termination." It was the aim of the Mosaic Law, without abolishing this long established custom, to mitigate its evils as far as possible. Accordingly it was directed that, on the arrival of the people in the Promised Land, six *Cities of Refuge* should be set apart, to which the homicide might fly, if not overtaken by the *Avenger*. Of these, three were to be on either side of the Jordan, almost equally remote from each other, and the roads leading to them were to be kept in a state of perfect repair (Ex. xxi. 13; Num. xxxv. 11; Deut. xix. 3). They were to be chosen out of the priestly and Levitical cities, as likely to be inhabited by the most intelligent portion of the community. On reaching one of them, the case of the homicide was to be examined by the elders; if they pronounced him guilty he was to be delivered up to the Avenger; if innocent, an abode was to be provided him in the city, where he was to remain till the death of the high-priest, but if found at any time by the Avenger beyond the limit of protection, 2000 cubits, he was liable to be put to death. On the demise of the high-priest he might return to the city of his possession (Num. xxxv. 25, 28)[1].

(2) The sacredness of a *man's character* was en-

---

[1] The same respect for the sacredness of human life marked other regulations. If an ox gored a man to death, it was to be killed, and if its owner, conscious of its ferocity, did not keep it in, he was also liable to death, but in this case a compensation was allowed to be assessed by the Avenger (Ex. xxi. 29—32). For other offences, such as cutting, maiming, wounding, assault, the *lex talionis, an eye for an eye, and a tooth for a tooth,* was enforced, and, in certain cases, compensation for loss of time, and the expenses of the cure (Ex. xxi. 24, &c.; Lev. xxiv. 19, 20; Deut. xix. 21).

forced by the commandment in the Decalogue forbidding *false witness*, and by laws prohibiting calumny, hatred, partiality in judgment for rich or poor (Ex. xxiii. 1—3; Lev. xix. 16—18). No exact penalty was enforced, but it was enjoined that in case of false witness the parties should be brought before the priests and judges, and if after diligent inquisition the charge was established, then should be done unto the slanderer as he had thought to have done unto his brother, that so the evil might be put away (Deut. xix. 19—21).

(3) *Property* was carefully guarded in the Mosaic Law, which forbade not only stealing, the act, but coveting, the intention.

(*a*) *Direct theft* was punished by restitution. If the stolen goods were found in the hands of the thief, he was to restore twofold; if before his detection he had applied them to his own use, he was to restore five oxen for an ox, four sheep for a sheep (Comp. 2 Sam. xii. 6); but a still heavier fine was exacted if he had not only sold, but killed and injured. If unable to pay the fine, he was to be sold into slavery to a Hebrew master, and serve him till he could pay (Ex. xxii. 1—4). A night-thief might be resisted even to death (Ex. xxii. 2). Man-stealing or kidnapping was a capital offence (Ex. xxi. 16). The crime of removing a neighbour's landmark was severely reprobated (Deut. xix. 14; xxvii. 17).

(*b*) *Indirect injury through carelessness or other causes.* This included injury done to property entrusted to another for safe keeping. If it was stolen and the thief detected, he was to repay double; if he could not be found, the trustee, on being declared guilty of negligence by the judges, was to restore twofold. Compensation was also exacted, where property was injured through a pit being left open, through cattle straying amongst other cattle or trespassing on another's land, or through fire spreading to standing corn (Ex. xxi. 33—36; xxii. 5, 6). Straying or suffering beasts, even if the property of an enemy, were to be brought back or relieved (Ex. xxiii. 4, 5).

Land. All land was to be regarded as belonging to God, and the holders as His tenants. At the conquest of Palestine each tribe was to have its allotment, and each family its portion, and these were to remain for ever inalienable (Num. xxvii. 1—11; xxxvi.; comp. 1 Kings xxi. 3; 2 Kings ix. 25, 26). All sold land, therefore, was to return to its original owners at the Jubilee, but might be redeemed by the owner or his representative at any period before then (Lev. xxv. 13—16, 23—28).

Laws of debt. An Israelite who had fallen into debt from any cause, might (i) sell himself as a slave to one of his own nation, with the right of resuming his freedom after six years, and at the Jubilee recovering his inheritance, (ii) claim a timely loan (Deut. xv. 1—11), but no usury might be taken from an Israelite (Ex. xxii. 25—27; Deut. xxiii. 19, 20). Thus pledges would become frequent, but they might not be cruelly or ruinously exacted. The handmill, a necessity in every family, might not be pledged (Deut. xxiv. 6); the cloak must be restored before nightfall when it became essential (Ex. xxii. 26, 27; Deut. xxiv. 12, 13); the lender was not to go into the house of his debtor to claim his pledge, or seize any article he chose; he was to stand abroad, and the pledge was to be brought out to him (Deut. xxiv. 10, 11).

BOOK V

FROM THE DEPARTURE FROM SINAI TO THE DEATH OF MOSES.

CHAPTER I

KADESH-BARNEA AND THE MISSION OF THE SPIES.

NUMB. X.—XIV. B. C. 1490.

THE period of the encampment of the Israelites at Sinai had now occupied upwards of a year. The Covenant had been concluded, the Law had been given, the Tabernacle had been erected, the priests had been consecrated, and Jehovah dwelt in the midst of His chosen people. It was now time to think of marching onwards towards Canaan. As, however, the occupation of that country must of necessity be preceded by its conquest, an organization of the Israelitish forces was the first duty. Accordingly, a census was taken of all who were fit for war, or about twenty years old, and the result gave a total of 603,550 fighting men (Num. i. 46), to whom if we add the Levites, the women, and the children, we may conclude that the host numbered altogether between two and three millions. The first anniversary of the Passover was then duly celebrated and on the twentieth day of the second month in the second year, the Pillar of Cloud moved from off the Tabernacle, and this signal for departure having been given, the order of the march was marshalled.

First, borne by the Kohathites, went the Ark of the Covenant, the lid of which was the throne of Jehovah, and was overspread by the Cloudy Pillar (Num. x. 33). Then followed the tribe of Judah, the most numerous and the strongest of all the tribes, supported by Issachar and Zebulun, under the standard of a "Lion," the ensign of Judah. Then followed the sons of Gershon and Merari, bearing the external portions of the Tabernacle, the coverings and hangings, the boards, the pillars, and the sockets. They were succeeded by the tribe of Reuben, flanked by Gad and Simeon, marching under the common standard of Reuben, a "Man's Head." Next came the rest of the Kohathites, bearing the sacred vessels of the Sanctuary. Then the tribe of Ephraim, flanked by Benjamin and Manasseh, under the standard of Ephraim, the figure of an "Ox;" and the long procession closed with the tribe of Dan, between Naphtali and Asher, with the standard of Dan, an "Eagle with a Serpent in its talons."

These arrangements having been made, the Silver Trumpets sounded, the silence of the desert was broken by the shout, *Rise up, Lord, and let Thine enemies be scattered, and let them that hate Thee flee before Thee* (Num. x. 35; comp. Ps. lxviii. 1, 2), and the march began. At this time there was present in the camp HOBAB, by some supposed to have been the father-in-law, by others the brother-in-law of Moses. The Israelitish leader knew how invaluable would be the experience of one so well acquainted with every track and pass in the terrible wilderness they were now about to traverse, and he earnestly entreated him to continue with them, and share the goodness which the Lord would show to Israel (Num. x. 29). There seems little doubt that Hobab consented to accompany the people, and to be to them *instead of eyes* amidst the dangers of the inhospitable desert[1].

In the course of three days the host entered on the sandy plain which parts the mountain-mass of Sinai from the table-land of the Tîh[2]. Having for more than a year enjoyed the pleasant encampment before the Mount of God, they no sooner entered on this arid tract, than they gave vent to their feelings of discontent. During the journey from the Red Sea to Sinai God had borne with similar manifestations of their weakness. But now that they had been brought into nearer and more visible relations with Him, having the Sanctuary in their midst, the Ark preceding them, and the Manna dropping upon them from day to day, their murmurings could not be thus passed over, but brought down instant rebuke and punishment. On this occasion the Divine displeasure was marked by the outbreak of a fire on the extreme outskirts of the encampment, which inflicted considerable damage, and was only removed by the intercession of Moses, who called the spot TABERAH, or *the burning* (Num. xi. 1—3).

But this judgment had scarcely been removed when the same spirit of discontent broke out afresh. The *mixed multitude*, which had accompanied them from Egypt, and soon afterwards the Israelites themselves, began to complain of the Manna, *this light food*, as they called it, and lamented the loss of the fish, the cucumbers, the melons, the leeks, and other vegetables, they had enjoyed in the fertile valley of the Nile. So loud and general were their complainings, that Moses despaired of accomplishing the purport of his mission, and poured out his soul in prayer to God, begging for some

---

[1] For subsequent traces of the descendants of Hobab in connection with the Israelites, see Judg. i. 16; iv. 11; 1 Chron. ii. 55; 2 Kings x. 15; Jer. xxxv. 2. See Blunt's *Coincidences*, Pt. I. xxii.

[2] See above, p. 100, note.

relief from the burden of daily anxiety which weighed him down. In mercy towards His despairing servant, the Lord bade him select seventy elders, and bring them to the door of the Tabernacle, and promised to take of the spirit that was upon him and bestow a portion on them, that they might share with him the weight of responsibility. He also promised that on the morrow flesh, such as the people had pined after, should be given them, and that not for one day only but for a whole month, until it became even more loathsome to them than the celestial food they had so lately despised. In obedience to this command, the seventy elders were brought before the Tabernacle, and the Lord bestowed upon them a portion of the spirit that was upon the Israelitish leader, and *they prophesied, and did not cease.* Two of their number, Eldad and Medad, though selected for this high office, either from accident or some other cause, did not accompany the rest to the appointed place, and though they remained in the camp, and at a distance from the Cloudy Pillar, became inspired with the same spirit. This striking incident was announced to Moses by Joshua, who, jealous for his master's honour, thought that such prophesying ought to be prohibited. But Moses thought otherwise. *Enviest thou for my sake?* he replied; *would God that all the Lord's people were prophets, and that the Lord would put His Spirit upon them* (Num. xi. 24—30. Comp. Mk. ix. 38; Lk. ix. 49).

Shortly afterwards the second promise of the Lord was also fulfilled. A strong wind brought up a prodigious number of quails from the sea in the proximity of the Gulf of Akaba, which covered the ground to the extent of a day's journey on either side of the camp. For two days and a night the people were busily occupied in collecting, and spreading the birds abroad, probably for the purpose of drying them. So they *did eat and were filled;* for *God gave them of their own desire, they were not estranged from their lust* (Ps. lxxviii. 29, 30). But while the meat was still *between their teeth,* His *wrath fell upon them,* and He smote them with a severe plague, *and slew the mightiest of them, even the chosen ones of Israel* (Ps. lxxviii. 31), and the spot where they were buried was named KIBROTH HATTAAVAH, the *graves of lust.*

From this ill-omened encampment the host proceeded in a north-easterly direction to *Hazeroth,* which is thought to have been the modern *Ain-el-Huderah,* and to have consisted of the unenclosed semi-permanent villages, in which the Bedouins are found to congregate[1]. Here a still severer trial awaited Moses. There arrived in the camp a Cushite or Ethiopian woman (Num. xii. 1) whom he had married, and who is identified by some with Zipporah, while others believe her to have been an Egyptian whom he had espoused previous to his flight from that country. Hitherto the position of Miriam had been one of great influence in the camp, and second only to that of Moses and Aaron (Comp. Micah vi. 4). To her the arrival of the stranger was most unwelcome, and she feared she would now be deposed from her high position as a "mother in Israel." Having, therefore, induced Aaron to share her views, she openly turned against Moses and maintained that he was not the sole expositor of Jehovah's will, that she and Aaron were of equal authority with him (Num. xii. 1—4).

With his wonted self-control Moses was content to endure these reproaches in silence. But the Lord interposed to defend the honour of His servant. The Pillar of Cloud suddenly appeared before the Tabernacle, and thither Aaron and Miriam were summoned together with Moses himself. There in words of stern

[1] See Robinson, II. 175; Stanley, *S. and P.* 81, 82; Article *Hazer* in Smith's *Bib. Dict.*

rebuke the Lord denounced their hard speeches against
His chosen servant. Very different was his position
from that of an ordinary prophet, to whom the Divine
will might be made known by vision or dream. *My
servant Moses*, said Jehovah, *is faithful in all my
house. With him will I speak mouth to mouth, even
apparently and not in dark speeches, and the similitude of the Lord shall he behold; wherefore, then,
were ye not afraid to speak against my servant Moses?*
With this vindication of the true position of the Hebrew leader the Cloud removed, and Aaron looked on
Miriam, and behold! she had become leprous, *as white
as snow*. Thereupon Moses interceded for her, and the
Lord promised that the judgment should not be permanent, but as unclean she must remain without the
camp for seven days, during which period the host remained at Hazeroth (Num. xii. 4—16).

The days of her purification being ended, the Israelites resumed their march, and striking northwards
across the plateau of the Tîh, probably after several
intermediate encampments, reached KADESH or KA-
DESH-BARNEA (Num. xxxiii. 36). This spot, whether
identified with the spring of *Ain-Kŭdes*, or with *Ain-
esh-Shehabeh* south of *Jebel-el-Mŭkhrah*, or with *Ain-
el-Weibeh* in the *Arabah*[1], was at the very gates of
the Promised Land. It required but a strenuous and
persevering effort to reach the final goal of their long
journey. This effort Moses exhorted them to make
(Deut. i. 20, 21), bidding them not be afraid, but go
up boldly and possess the land, which the Lord God
of their fathers had given them. On this the people
proposed (Deut. i. 22) that spies should first be sent
to ascertain the best route, and what cities ought first
to be attacked. Moses consented to this proposal, and
with the Divine concurrence selected twelve princes,

---

[1] See Article *Kadesh* in *Bib. Dict.* See Map.

one from each tribe, whom he exhorted to make a
thorough search throughout the length and breadth of
the land, and ascertain its character, its products, and
its inhabitants (Deut. i. 23 ; Num. xiii. 1—20).

One of the select twelve was HOSHEA, the valiant
attendant of Moses, whose name was now changed to
JEHOSHUA or JOSHUA (*God the Saviour*), a title which
well became the future leader of the Israelitish hosts.
It was now *the time of the first ripe grapes* (Num. xiii.
20), or the month of September[1]. Setting out from the
wilderness of Paran, the spies traversed the land as far
north as Rehob on the way to Hamath, in the valley
of the Orontes, which divides the ranges of Lebanon
and Anti-Lebanon. Then they *ascended by the south*[2],
and came to Hebron, where dwelt Ahiman, Sheshai, and
Talmai, the gigantic sons of Anak. In a valley opening
on this city, celebrated even now for its vineyards, they
plucked pomegranates, and figs, and a bunch with one
cluster of grapes of such enormous size that it required
to be carried on a staff between two men, whence the
valley was named ESHCOL, or the *Valley of the Cluster*.
With these proofs of the fertility of the land, after an
absence of forty days, the spies returned and presented
themselves in the camp at Kadesh before the host assembled to hear their report.

The productiveness of the promised land, they said,
was sufficiently attested by the fruits they had brought
back. It was, indeed, *a good land, and flowed with
milk and honey*. But the people, it could not be denied, were strong, and of great stature, and among them
were the sons of Anak, before whom they themselves
appeared as grasshoppers (Num. xiii. 33). They were
proceeding to enumerate the chief tribes whom they
had encountered, when Caleb, the Kenezite, of the tribe

[1] See Calendar, p. 155.
[2] See above, p. 30, and note 1.

of Judah, one of their number, anxious to dispel the feelings of despondency with which their report was received, broke in with the advice that the people should make an immediate attack, and promised them speedy and certain success. But, save the valiant Joshua, he found no other to support his brave counsels; the rest of the spies dwelt only on the dangers of the expedition, and their despondency found but too faithful an echo in the hearts of the people, who burst forth into lamentation, openly murmured against Moses and Aaron for having brought them thither, and even proposed to appoint a captain to lead them back into Egypt. In vain Joshua and Caleb tried to calm the tumult, and to check the mutiny. The host would listen to nothing, and even threatened to stone them to death. But at this moment the Glory of Jehovah appeared before the Tabernacle in the sight of the whole people. Terrible though most just was His wrath at this signal proof of faithlessness, in spite of all the signs and wonders He had wrought in their midst. He threatened to destroy them utterly with pestilence, and make of Moses a nation greater and mightier than they. But, as before on Sinai, so now that unselfish leader stood heroically in the gap. He pleaded earnestly with the justly offended Jehovah; he represented the joy the rejection of the people would cause to the Egyptians and the nations of Canaan, who had all heard of *the mighty Hand and the stretched out Arm*, which had guided them through the wilderness. Finally, he appealed to the Name which the Lord Himself had proclaimed on the top of Sinai[1], *the Lord God, merciful and gracious, longsuffering, and abundant in goodness and truth*, and implored the forgiveness of the people (Num. xiv. 11—19).

His prayer was heard. The Almighty assured him that the nation, as a nation, should be preserved, their

[1] See above, pp. 115, 116.

name should not be utterly blotted out. But, save Joshua and Caleb, not one of that generation, which in spite of the wonders they had seen in Egypt and in the wilderness had refused to trust in God, should enter into the promised Land. For them, all hope of entry was cut off; every one, from twenty years old and upwards, should die; their carcases should lie bleaching in the wilderness (1 Cor. x. 5), while their children, whom they had deemed a certain prey to the Canaanites, should atone for their faithlessness by wandering forty years, a year for each day the spies had been engaged in searching out the land (Num. xiv. 33, 34). As an earnest of this judgment, the ten spies, who by their faithless despondency had been the primary cause of the mutiny, were struck with instant death, and the command was given to the rest of the host to *return into the wilderness by the way of the Red Sea.* This announcement was received by the people with universal lamentation, and on the morrow they rose up, and in spite of the earnest exhortations of Moses (Deut. i. 42, 43), and the ominous circumstance that the Cloud had not removed from the Tabernacle, made a wild rush up the steep and difficult pass, probably *es-Sufah*, leading into the uplands of Southern Palestine, where they encountered the A'morites (Deut. i. 44), the *highlanders* of the mountains, and their old enemies the Amalekites (Num. xiv. 45), by whom they were driven back, routed and discomfited as far as Hormah (Num. xiv. 20—45).

CHAPTER II

THE WANDERINGS. DEATH OF MIRIAM AND AARON.

Numb. xv.—xxi. B. C. 1490—1451.

AFTER this signal defeat it was clear that the sentence pronounced upon the existing generation was irrevocable, and the host remained for a considerable time at Kadesh (Deut. i. 46). During this period a formidable conspiracy broke out against the authority of Moses and Aaron. In their natural state of mortification at recent events, the people were now more than ever likely to lend a ready ear to those who whispered that under the auspices of any other than their present leaders, they might escape from their humiliating doom, and reach the goal of their hopes. Such fatal advisers soon appeared in the persons of KORAH, a Kohathite, of the tribe of Levi, and DATHAN, ABIRAM, and ON, of the tribe of Reuben. The former, jealous probably of the sacerdotal pre-eminence of the line of Amram, and the latter loth to see their tribe deprived of their ancestor's right of primogeniture, conspired, it is thought, "to place Korah at the head of a priesthood chosen by popular election, and possibly to restore the tribe of Reuben to the rights of the firstborn, of which it had been deprived[1]."

Successful in gaining over to their views 250 princes of the people, they rose up against Moses and Aaron, and publicly charged them with *taking too much upon themselves*, and usurping functions which ought to have been shared by the congregation at large, who were all, every one of them, *holy unto the Lord.* On hearing these charges Moses resolved to refer the matter to the Divine decision, and bade Korah and his company assemble on the morrow with lighted censers before the Tabernacle. A similar summons was addressed to the Reubenite leaders, but they flatly refused to attend at the place of meeting, and charged Moses with having disappointed the hopes of the people, and being anxious only to make himself a prince over them. Curiosity, however, induced them to stand at the doors of their

---

[1] Kurtz, *History of the Old Covenant*, p. 293. See Blunt's *Coincidences*, Pt. I. 75—79.

tents in full view of the Tabernacle, where Korah and his associates stood with lighted censers awaiting the Divine decision (Num. xvi. 1—16).

Before long the Glory of the Lord appeared, and Moses was instructed to command that a clear space should be kept round the tents of Korah, Dathan, and Abiram, and that the people should be careful to touch nothing belonging to them, lest they should be consumed in their sin. Then the servant of Jehovah offered to submit his claims to an awful and infallible test. If the ringleaders in this rebellion *died the common death of all men, or were visited after the visitation of all men, then the Lord had not sent him;* but if a new and terrible fate befell them, and *the earth opened her mouth, and swallowed them up,* then it would be known that they had provoked the Lord. His words had hardly been uttered, when this awful catastrophe took place. The earth clave asunder, and swallowed up Korah, Dathan, and Abiram, with everything belonging to them, and at the same time a fire burst forth and consumed the 250 men, who had presumed to offer incense at the Sanctuary. Thus this great conspiracy was signally punished, and as a memorial of the occurrence, Eleazar the son of Aaron was directed to take the brazen censers of the offenders, and therewith to make plates for the altar of burnt-sacrifice.

In spite, however, of this terrible proof of the Divine displeasure, the very next day saw the people again murmuring against Moses and Aaron, complaining that they had slain *the people of Jehovah,* and threatening to break out into a fresh and general mutiny. Thereupon the Glory of Jehovah once more overshadowed the Tabernacle, and a plague broke out amongst the host. But at the exhortation of Moses, Aaron took a lighted censer from off the altar, and standing between the living and the dead, made an atonement for the people,

12

but not before 14,700 men had by their deaths paid the penalty for their murmuring and insubordination. Thus the divinely-ordained priesthood of Aaron averted, while that assumed by Korah only brought destruction upon the host. But in order that the Aaronic priesthood might be still further attested, and that for all future generations, another sign was vouchsafed. Moses was directed to receive from the Prince of each tribe an almond rod with the name of the tribe inscribed thereon, and to lay these rods before the Ark in the Holy of Holies, that on the morrow it might be proved incontestably which tribe had been selected to perform the priestly functions. Moses obeyed, and on the morrow, when the rods were removed, behold! that of Levi, on which the name of Aaron had been inscribed, instead of being dry like the rest, *had brought forth buds, and bloomed blossoms, and yielded almonds.* Thus to the confusion of all other pretenders, the claims of this branch of the tribe of Levi were confirmed in a way that could not be gainsaid, and the Mystic Rod was directed to be laid up before the Ark, as a testimony against all future pretenders, and a pledge of the Divine choice (Num. xvii. 1—11; Heb. ix. 4).

From Kadesh the host now *took their journey into the wilderness by the way of the Red Sea* (Deut. ii. 1), and for thirty-eight years continued to wander in the deserts of Paran. This long period of punishment and humiliation is shrouded by the sacred historian in profound obscurity. It is probable that Kadesh was for some time a sort of head-quarters, whence the great mass of the people were scattered far and wide in smaller or larger groups over the peninsula, while afterwards encampments were made at different spots, wherever Moses and the Tabernacle were settled (Num. xxxiii. 19—36). From a comparison of the four passages[1] of

---

[1] See Kurtz's *History of the Old Covenant*, III. 310.

Holy Scripture which alone throw any light upon this dark period of Israel's history, Deut. viii. 2—6 ; Josh. v. 4—9; Ezek. xx. 10—26; Amos v. 25, 26, we infer that it was a period of "training and temptation, of humiliation and blessing, of natural wants and supernatural existence;" that the rite of circumcision was neglected, and the annual celebration of the Passover not kept up, while the Sabbath also was not strictly observed[1] (Josh. v. 5; Ezek. xx. 13). Meanwhile, according to the sentence pronounced upon them, all the men of that generation from twenty years old and upwards died, save Moses and his brother, and the two faithful spies Joshua and Caleb.

At the close, however, of this period, the host once more assembled at Kadesh. Moses was now far advanced in years, and his second approach to the very threshold of the Promised Land was saddened by two events of a peculiarly mournful character. First, Miriam his sister, and companion of his childhood, died, and was buried at Kadesh (Num. xx. 1). But, however afflicted he may have been at her loss, the conduct of the people, whom he led, must have grieved him still more. For, again, on a failure of water, the new generation proved faithless, and brake forth into murmurings and complainings as violent as their forefathers at Rephidim. For the second time the ill-omened words of disaffection sounded in his ears, and roused in him and his brother feelings of greater irritation than they had ever displayed before. On appealing to the Lord, they were commanded to assemble the people before the Rock facing the encampment, and it was promised that it should bring forth water in obedience to their word. Thereupon the Brothers gathered the people together

---

[1] A recurrence also to idolatry was not uncommon, and especially the worship of the heavenly bodies. (Comp. Ezek. xx. 16, with Amos v. 25—29, and Acts vii. 42, 43.)

before the Rock, but instead of appealing to *it*, Moses
began to speak *unadvisedly* (Ps. cvi. 32, 33) *to them*,
saying, *Hear now, ye rebels! must we fetch you water
out of this rock?* Then, instead of doing as he had
been instructed, he lifted up his hand, and with the rod
struck the Rock, not once, but twice, on which the refreshing streams indeed flowed forth abundantly, and
supplied the wants of the people and their cattle, but
the fidelity and self-control of the Brothers, of the Prophet and the Priest, had alike failed, neither had they
sanctified Jehovah in the eyes of the host. (Comp. Num.
xxvii. 14; Deut. xxxiii. 51.) For this sin, whatever may
have been its precise heinousness, the Almighty pronounced on both the Brothers the sentence of exclusion
from the Promised Land. Into it they were never to
enter, or realise with the people they had led the
hopes and anticipations of so many long and weary
years.

But though thus excluded from the goal of his long
pilgrimage, there was on the part of Moses no diminution of the zeal he had ever displayed in behalf of the
people. Always preferring their welfare to his own, he
was ready to lead them *towards*, if he was not to lead
them *into* the Promised Land, and as a preliminary he
sent ambassadors to the Edomites and Moabites, requesting a free passage through their territory. But
though his messengers recounted the various proofs of
Divine protection which had accompanied the journey-
ings of the people, and promised to keep to the highway, and injure neither the fields, the vineyards, nor
the wells, but pay for any water they might use, they
met with a direct refusal. Edom not only forbad them
a passage through his territory, but posted a strong force
to guard all the approaches into it. Thereupon, in obedience to the Divine command, the Israelites abstained
from any retaliation against the descendants of Esau,

and the latter did not openly venture to attack them. But an Amorite tribe inhabiting the southern highlands of Palestine, under the command of their chief Arad, fell upon them, and took some of them prisoners. This roused the spirit of the people; they attacked their foes, and utterly destroyed them and their cities, naming the spot in memory of the incident Hormah, or *utter Destruction* (Num. xxi. 1—4).

Thus debarred from what would have been the natural route towards the country east of the Jordan, nothing remained but to march southward down the Arabah towards the eastern arm of the Red Sea, and then take a long and wearisome circuit round the territory of the Edomites. Accordingly they set out, and reached Mount Hor[1], at the edge of the land of Edom (Num. xxxiii. 37), and the highest and most conspicuous of the whole range of its sandstone mountains, overshadowing the mysterious city of Sela, or Petra, *the Rock*. Here it was intimated to Moses that another of the few remaining links which connected him with the generation that had come forth from Egypt must be taken from him. He had already laid Miriam in her desert-grave at Kadesh; now he was told that on the craggy top of Hor he must leave his brother, the high-priest Aaron, who in accordance with his recent sentence must die for his sin at the Waters of Strife. For the last time, therefore, the Brothers repaired to the Tabernacle, where Aaron was arrayed in his priestly robes, and then, accompanied by Eleazar his son, the three ascended the toilsome height in the sight of the mournful and watching host. Arrived at the summit Moses stripped his brother of his priestly garments, and put them on Eleazar, and there, in full view of the desert, the scene of his long pilgrimage, and just in sight of the utmost borders of the

---

[1] Even now called *Jebel Nebi-Haroûn*, the "Mount of the prophet Aaron." Robinson, *Bib. Res.* II. 125.

Land of Promise, on the first day of the fifth month, in the 123rd year of his age, the great High-priest was gathered to his fathers. Then Moses and Eleazar reverently interred him in his rocky tomb, and descended from the mount, and Eleazar ministered " that evening in the familiar garments of him, whom the people would see no more" (Num. xx. 22—29)[1].

Thirty days were spent in mourning for Aaron, and then the host continued their march down the Arabah, and after encamping at Ezion-geber at the eastern head of the Red Sea, entered on the sandy, shadeless waste, which stretched eastward from the mountains of Edom far on to the Persian Gulf, and was even more terrible than the desert they had left. This and the thought of the long circuit that awaited them so wrought upon the spirit of the people, that they again broke out into bitterest complaints against their leader, their tedious march, and their food. The region they were now traversing abounded in *fiery* or deadly serpents[2], of which the Lord sent many among the people, and much people of Israel died. But on the manifestation of a spirit of repentance, Moses, by the Divine command, made a Brazen Serpent, and fixed it upon a pole in the sight of

---

[1] Drew's *Scripture Lands*, p. 84.

[2] "The snakes against which the Brazen Serpent was originally raised as a protection, were peculiar to the eastern portion of the Sinaitic desert. There and nowhere else, and in no other moment of their history, could this symbol have originated."—Stanley, *Lectures*, 182. "The sand on the shore (of the Gulf of *Akaba*) showed traces of snakes on every hand. They had crowded there in various directions. Some of the marks appeared to have been made by animals which could not have been less than two inches in diameter. My guide told me that snakes were very common in these regions, and that the fishermen were very much afraid of them, and put out their fires at night before going to sleep, because the light was known to attract them."—Burckhardt's *Travels*, II. 814, quoted in Kurtz, *History of the Old Covenant*, III. 343.

the congregation, and all who looked thereon were healed. The symbol of this wonderful deliverance was long preserved, and was regarded with veneration as late as the days of Hezekiah (2 Kings xviii. 4), by whom it was destroyed. The occurrence is also memorable as having suggested one of the most sacred similitudes of the New Testament, for in His well-known conversation with Nicodemus, the Saviour likened to the uplifting of this serpent by Moses His own uplifting upon the Cross, *that whosoever believeth on Him should not perish, but have eternal life* (John iii. 14, 15).

After this incident the Israelites resumed their march, and pressing forward in a northerly direction, skirted the eastern frontier of Edom, and eventually encamped near the willow-shaded brook or valley of Zered[1], which ran into the Dead Sea near its south-east corner, and formed the southern boundary of Moab. Hence they advanced towards the rushing stream of the Arnon (*swift, noisy*), "dashing through a deep defile of sandstone rocks," the first river they had seen since they left the Nile. Crossing one of its fords, an incident commemorated in an ancient song (Num. xxi. 14, 15; Deut. ii. 24), they reached a spot which they called by a name sufficient of itself to indicate that their weary wanderings were at an end, and that they were approaching a cultivated land. Needing water, the princes and nobles, at the command of Moses, dug in the ground with their staves till they reached a cool refreshing spring. In memory of this grateful discovery they called the spot BEER-ELIM[2], *the well of the Heroes*, and

---

[1] Comp. Deut. ii. 13, 18; Isai. xv. 7; Amos vi. 14.

[2] "The *well* of the Hebrew and the Arab is carefully distinguished from the *spring*. The *spring* (*ain*) is the bright, open source—the *eye* of the landscape, such as bubbles up among the crags of Sinai, or rushes forth in a copious stream from En-gedi or from Jericho. But the *well* (*beer*) is the

celebrated their thanksgiving in a burst of sacred poetry (Num. xxi. 17, 18). They were now encamped on "the vast range of forest and pasture on the east of the Jordan."

CHAPTER III

CONQUEST OF THE EAST OF JORDAN—BALAAM AND BALAK

Num. xxi.—xxiv. B. C. 1451.

THE country north of the present encampment of the Israelites from the Arnon to the Jabbok was at this time possessed by the Amorites. We have already met with this tribe on the western side of the Jordan (Gen. xiv. 7, 13; xiii. 18; Num. xiii. 29[1]). Tempted by the rich pasture lands east of this river a colony of them appears to have crossed, and having driven the Moabites with great slaughter and the loss of many captives from the country south of the Jabbok (Num. xxi. 26—29), to have made the wide chasm of the Arnon henceforth the boundary between them.

The Amorite king at this time was SIHON, and his capital was Heshbon, twenty miles east of the Jordan, on the parallel of the northern end of the Dead Sea. Thither the Israelitish leader sent messengers requesting a peaceful passage through his territory, and promising the same respect for his land and possessions, which had already been proposed to the Edomites. But

deep hole bored far under the rocky surface by the art of man. ......Such wells were the scenes of the earliest contentions of the shepherd-patriarchs with the inhabitants of the land; the places of meeting with the women who came to draw water, ...the natural halting-places of great caravans, or wayfaring men, as when Moses gathered together the people to the well of Moab, which the princes dug with their sceptered staves."—Stanley, *S. and P.* 147.

[1] See p. 32, note.

their request was rudely rejected. Sihon would not allow them even to pass through his borders, but assembled his forces, and prepared for battle. The Israelites did not decline the engagement, which took place at Jahaz, probably a short distance south of Heshbon, and resulted in the total defeat of the Amorites; Sihon himself, his sons, and all his people were smitten with the sword, his walled towns Ar and Heshbon, Nophah and Medeba were captured, and his numerous flocks and herds fell into the hands of the victors, who thus became masters of the entire country between the Arnon and the Jabbok (Num. xxi. 27—30).

Apparently about the same time that Sihon had expelled the Moabites from the rich territory south of the Jabbok, another Amorite chief seized the country extending from that river to the foot of Hermon, and known as the land of Bashan. His name was OG, one of the last of the giant-race of Rephaim. He ruled over sixty cities, and his stronghold was a remarkable oval district, about 22 miles from north to south by 14 from west to east, called by the Hebrews *Argob*, or the *stony*, afterwards by the Greeks *Trachonitis*, and now *Lejah*. This extraordinary region has been described as "an ocean of basaltic rocks and boulders, tossed about in the wildest confusion, and intermingled with fissures and crevices in every direction, and yet in spite of its ungainly and forbidding features thickly studded even now with deserted cities and villages, in all of which the dwellings are solidly built and of remote antiquity[1]." On a rocky promontory south-west of this marvellous region, "without water, without access, save over rocks and through defiles almost impracticable[2],"

[1] Porter's *Syria and Damascus*, II. 220; *Handbook*, II. 506; Article *Argob, Dictionary of the Bible*, p. 42.
[2] Article *Edrei*, Smith's *Bib. Dict.* "Ibrahim Pasha, flushed with victory, and maddened by the obstinacy of a

was the city of Edrei (*strength*). Here, "as if in the
Thermopylæ of his kingdom," the giant king of Bashan
and all his people resolved to encounter the advancing
hosts of the Israelites, led, it seems probable, by two
eminent chiefs of the tribe of Manasseh, Jair and Nobah.
(Comp. Num. xxxii. 41, 42; Deut. iii. 14.) Like the
Amorite chief of Heshbon, Og could not withstand the
valour of the Israelites. He was utterly routed, and
*his threescore cities fenced with high walls, gates and
bars*, besides *unwalled towns a great many*, fell into
their hands. A trophy of this victory, long preserved by
the children of Ammon in the city of Rabbath, was the
huge iron bedstead[1] of the Amorite king, nine cubits
long, by four wide; and long afterwards the subjugation
of *Sihon king of the Amorites*, and *Og the king of
Bashan, great kings, famous kings, mighty kings*, was
deemed worthy of being ranked with the tokens and
wonders wrought in the land of Egypt, and the overthrow of Pharaoh in the Red Sea (Ps. cxxxv. 10—12;
cxxxvi. 15—21).

After these two decisive engagements, which made
them masters of the entire country east of the Jordan,
from the wide chasm of the Arnon to the foot of the snow-
capped Hermon, the Israelites encamped in the plains of
Shittim, or *the Meadow of the Acacias*, amidst "the long

handful of Druzes, attempted to follow them into the *Lejah*,
but scarcely a soldier who entered it returned. Every rock
concealed an enemy. From inaccessible nooks death was
dealt out; and thousands of the bravest of the Egyptian
troops left their bones amid the defiles of the Lejah. The
Turks were still less successful in 1852."—Porter's *Handbook*,
p. 504.

[1] Probably one of the common flat beds used at times
on the housetops in Eastern countries, and made of bars of
iron instead of the usual palm-sticks, Kitto's *Bib. Illustrations*, II. 210. Others, however, suppose it was a "sarcopha-
gus of black basalt."—Smith's *Bib. Dict.* Stanley's *Lectures
on Jewish History*, p. 216.

belt of acacia-groves, which, on its eastern as well as its western side, line the upper terraces of the Jordan over against Jericho[1]." South of the Arnon was the little corner of territory occupied by Moab, who viewed with no little alarm the successes of the Israelites against such *mighty kings* as Sihon and Og. *This people*, said BALAK the king of Moab to the elders of Midian, *lick up all that are round about us, as the ox licketh up the grass of the field.* Sensible of the uselessness of attacking a nation so manifestly under the protection of an Invisible Power, the two confederate tribes resolved before falling upon them to place them under an awful curse, which might have the effect of paralysing their arms[2]. At this time no man was supposed to have greater power in this way than a famous Prophet named BALAAM, the son of Beor. He lived far away from the present encampment of the Israelites at Pethor, beyond the Euphrates, in Aram among *the mountains of the East*, but his fame had spread across the Assyrian desert even to the shores of the Dead Sea. His gifts he exercised as a Prophet of the same God, who had wrought so many miracles in behalf of the Israelites. If, therefore, he could be persuaded to lay upon them his powerful ban, their further success the Moabites thought might be checked, and the children of Lot might not only recover the land of which they had been deprived by the Amorites, but possibly add to them the

[1] Stanley, *S. and P.* p. 298. Porter's *Handbook*, I. 198.

[2] "Even at the present day the pagan Orientals, in their wars, have always their magicians with them to curse their enemies, and to mutter incantations for their ruin. In our own war with the Burmese, the generals of the nation had several magicians with them, who were much engaged in cursing our troops; but as they did not succeed, a number of witches were brought for the same purpose."—Kitto's *Bible Illust.* II. 214, where he also quotes such a formula of imprecation from Macrobius. Comp. also Butler's *Sermon on the Character of Balaam.* Blunt's *Script. Coincidences,* Pt. I. xxiv.

fertile territory the Israelites had so lately won from Sihon and Og.

Accordingly, elders both of Moab and Midian, with the rewards of divination in their hands, were despatched eastward across the Assyrian desert to intreat the aid of the powerful Prophet. On reaching their destination and announcing the purport of their errand, Balaam, uncertain of the lawfulness of complying with it, requested them to lodge there that night, while he ascertained the will of Jehovah. The answer he obtained was unfavourable. *Thou shalt not go with them;* said God, *thou shalt not curse the people: for they are blessed.* On the morrow, therefore, he sent the messengers away, bidding them announce to their master that Jehovah forbade his accompanying them.

Undeterred by this failure, and possibly informed by his messengers that the Prophet *himself* did not seem unwilling to come, the king of Moab sent a second embassy consisting of princes *more and more honourable than the last,* to inform him that he would advance him to very great honour, and do whatever he commanded, if only he would come. Again, therefore. the toilsome Syrian desert was traversed, and the messengers preferred their request. But again they seemed to have come in vain. *If Balak would give me his house full of silver and gold,* said the Prophet, *I cannot go beyond the word of the Lord to do less or more.* But instead of at once sending the messengers away, he bade them lodge with him that night, while he consulted the Lord a second time. On this occasion the word of the Lord came to him, and bade him go, but authorized him to speak nothing more and nothing less than the very words that should be put into his mouth. Balaam accordingly set out on his journey, but he was not to accomplish it without receiving another and a more terrible warning against it and its object. As he rode upon his ass, the *Angel of the Lord* stood in the way, with his sword drawn in his hand.   As if in derision of his claims to be a powerful Seer, the beast alone discerned the celestial Adversary, and started aside out of the way into a field.   On this, Balaam smote it, and turned it into a path running through some vineyards. But again the Angel confronted the wilful Prophet, and the frightened ass in its efforts to avoid him crushed his foot against the wall.   Therefore Balaam struck it a second time, and now, as if in still deeper derision of one, who claimed to be able to reveal to kings and princes the will of the Invisible, the dumb beast, in the accents of a man *forbad the madness of the Prophet* (2 Pet. ii. 16).   On this, Balaam's eyes were at length opened, and as he bowed himself down before the Angel, he was sternly rebuked for his wilfulness, and proposed to turn back rather than displease the Lord. But since his mind was wholly bent on that course, he was a second time bidden to proceed, but a second time also warned against uttering any other words than those which a Divine Power should put into his mouth.

The journey was now resumed, and at length the watchmen of Balak announced to their master that the mighty Prophet was approaching.   Therefore Balak went forth to meet him, and after a brief rebuke of his delay, conducted his visitor to Kirjath-Huzoth, *the Town of Streets,* a place in the furthest borders of his kingdom, and possibly of sacred or oracular reputation[1], where he entertained him at a great feast.   On the next day he conducted him to the high places dedicated to Baal (Num. xxii. 41) that rose above the encampment of the Israelites, whence he might gain a view of the utmost part of the people he had desired him to curse.   There by the Prophet's direction the king erected seven altars, and on each they offered together a bullock and a ram,

[1] Article *Kirjath-huzoth,* in Smith's *Bib. Dict.*

and while Balak with his attendant princes stood by his burnt-offering, Balaam went forth to *a high place* (Num. xxiii. 3) to learn the Divine will. *And God met Balaam, and put a word in his mouth,* and returning to the expectant king, he declared that it was impossible for him to curse Jacob and defy Israel, that he could not *curse him whom God had not cursed, or defy him whom Jehovah had not defied.*

On hearing this response so entirely opposite to what he had expected, Balak was highly incensed, but thinking a change of view might have a different influence on the Prophet's spirit, he brought him to Zophim[1], a *cultivated field of the Watchmen* high up on the range of Pisgah. Again the altars were built, and the victims slain; again the king stood by his burnt-sacrifice, and again Balaam went forth *to meet the Lord.* But still the answer was unfavourable. The steam of sacrifice could not bend the will of Jehovah; *He was not a man that He should lie,* or repent of His fixed purpose; what He had said He would do, what He had spoken He would perform; *in Jacob He had not beheld iniquity, neither had He seen perverseness in Israel; He had brought them out of Egypt,* and neither augury nor divination could prevail against them.

More incensed than before, the king of Moab burst forth into bitter complaints against the Prophet, and though the latter reminded him that he could speak nothing but the word of Jehovah, yet he determined from one more point to show him the people, that peradventure he might thence effect the potent curse. He led him up, therefore, to a peak, where stood the sanctuary of Peor (Num. xxiii. 28), looking toward Jeshimon or *the waste,* "probably the dreary barren waste of the hills lying immediately on the east of the Dead Sea." There the seven altars were for the third time

[1] Porter's *Handbook,* p. 300.

built, and the victims for the third time slain. But
Balaam was now convinced that Jehovah was pleased
only to bless the people. Without resorting, therefore,
any more to useless divinations, he lifted up his eyes,
and looked down upon the tribes encamped in the
acacia groves below him, with their *goodly tents spread
out like the valleys,* or watercourses of the mountains,
like the hanging gardens beside his own great river
Euphrates, as *lign-aloes which the Lord had planted,
as cedar trees beside the waters* (Num. xxiv. 6). And
as he stood, "with tranced yet open gaze" he saw the
Vision of the Almighty, and "in outline dim and vast"
beheld the future of the "desert-wearied tribes" that
lay encamped before him "in sight of Canaan[1]." He
beheld them *pouring water from their buckets, their
seed in many waters, their king higher than any Amalekite Agag* ruling in the Arabian wilderness south of
where he stood. He knew that God had *brought them
forth out of Egypt,* and that their *strength was like
that of the unicorn.* He foresaw them *couched as a lion,
and lying down as a great lion, eating up the nations
their enemies, breaking their bones, and piercing them
through with the arrows* of their archers. *Blessed was
he that blessed them, and cursed was he that cursed
them* (Num. xxiv. 1—9).

Balak's vexation was now increased tenfold. Smiting
his hands together he upbraided the Prophet for his
deceit, and in place of advancing him, as he had intended, to high honour, bade him flee for his life to his
native land. Nor was the other loath to go. But before he went, for he felt himself still moved by the prophetic spirit, he would *advertise* the king of what
this mysterious people *would do to his people in the
latter days* (Num. xxiv. 14). Again, therefore, he took

[1] Keble's *Christian Year,* 2nd Sunday after Easter;
Stanley's *S. and P.* p. 299.

up his parable, *and saw, but not now,—he beheld but
not nigh, a Star,* bright as any that spangled the
Eastern sky, *coming out of Jacob, and a sceptre
rising out of Israel, smiting through the princes of
Moab*[1], *and destroying* all their wild warriors *the sons
of tumult*[2]. One by one he saw "the giant forms of
empires on their way to ruin;" Edom and Seir becoming
a possession for their enemies; Amalek, then *the first
of the nations, in his latter end perishing for ever;*
the Kenites, then *strong in their dwelling-place, and
putting their nest in the* neighbouring *rocks* of En-gedi
wasted and made a prey; nay even Israel *carried away
captive by Asshur.* And yet once more he saw woe in
store even for Asshur, even for his own native land.
Far in the distant future he saw *ships* coming *from
Chittim,* the island of Cyprus, *to afflict Asshur and to
afflict Eber,* till the proud kingdoms of the Eastern
world, and he who should *afflict* them *perished for
ever*[3]. And then the Vision closed. The "true Prophetic light died away," and the king of Moab, baffled
and disappointed, returned to his people.

CHAPTER IV

WAR WITH THE MIDIANITES—DEATH OF MOSES.

Numb. xxv.—xxxii.   Deut. xxxii.   B. C. 1451.

BUT though his tongue had pronounced eloquent
blessings upon the people he found he could not

[1] Num. xxiv. 17 *Margin.*
[2] Article *Sheth* in Smith's *Bib. Dict.*
[3] For the version here adopted, and on this early prophecy
of the future rise of the power of Greece and of Europe, see
Dr Pusey's *Lectures on the Prophet Daniel,* pp. 58, 59

curse, Balaam's heart was filled with malice against them. Dismissed by the king of Moab without the promised honours and rewards, he lingered amongst the neighbouring Midianites, and with the keen hatred of his now hardened heart counselled them to join the children of Moab in seducing the Israelites from their allegiance to Jehovah. The festival of Baal-Peor was at hand, and was celebrated with all the unbridled licentiousness of a heathen orgy. If the Israelites could be persuaded to join in it, they might, he suggested, become "as other men," and the Invisible protection now vouchsafed would be withdrawn (Num. xxxi. 16). His artful suggestion was adopted. The festival was celebrated, and the Israelites fell into the snare. They joined themselves to Baal-Peor, took part in the hideous rites, and defiled themselves before the Lord. Thus they brought upon themselves a curse far more real than any that the divinations of Balaam could have effected. Had such apostasy gone unpunished, the Strength of Israel would indeed have ceased, and the counsels of the wily Prophet would have been successful. The crisis required severe and exemplary visitation. A plague broke out which swept off upwards of 24,000, and the princes of the tribes, at the command of Moses, slew the guilty with unsparing vigour, and hanged them up before the Lord. On this occasion PHINEHAS, the son of Eleazar, and grandson of Aaron, particularly distinguished himself by his righteous zeal, which was accepted as an atonement for the people, and rewarded not only by the cessation of the pestilence, but with a promise that the priesthood should remain in his family for ever.

But a terrible vengeance was denounced against the crafty Midianites, and after a second numbering of the people by Moses and Eleazar, a Sacred War was proclaimed. A thousand warriors from each tribe, led

13

not by Joshua, but by Phinehas, and accompanied by
the Ark, went forth to execute the task of righteous
retribution. The silver trumpets sounded the signal
for the onset, and the Midianites were utterly routed.
Five of their chiefs, Evi and Rekem, Zur and Hur and
Reba, as also all their males, were put to death; their
cities were burnt; their goodly castles fired; their women and children taken captive; nor did the crafty
prophet escape; *he received the wages of his unright-
eousness*, and perished by the sword (Num. xxxi. 8;
2 Pet. ii. 15).

The country east of the Jordan, which the Israelites
had now wrested from Sihon and Og, was to a great
extent a long table-land of undulating downs famed
for its rich pasturage[1], and clothed with luxuriant vegetation.   It was the forest-land, the pasture-land of
Palestine, *a place for cattle* (Num. xxxii. 1). Of the
tribes of Israel, as we have already noticed[2], Reuben
and Gad were eminently pastoral, *they had a very great
multitude of cattle* (Num. xxxii. 1). On the conclusion,
therefore, of the Sacred War against the Midianites,
they approached Moses and the elders of Israel with
the petition that they might be allowed to settle down
in a region so peculiarly suited to their requirements.
This request seemed to the Israelitish leader to savour
of a desire to shrink from the arduous work which lay
before the nation, and as likely to discourage the people
from crossing over and attempting the conquest of the
rugged western country, and he reproached them for
their apparent selfishness and indifference to the welfare of their brethren. But the two tribes protested
their perfect sympathy with the great national cause;
they were ready to send the flower of their troops

---

[1] Stanley, *S. and P.* p. 324. " It is still the favourite tract
of the Bedouin shepherds."
[2] See above, p. 78.

across the river, and only wished for the present *to build sheepfolds for their cattle, and cities for their little ones*, whither they might return on the conquest of the western country. This promise was deemed sufficient, and Moses distributed between them the lately conquered territory, assigning to Reuben and Gad the kingdom of Sihon from the Arnon to the Jabbok[1], and intrusting to the half of the warlike tribe of Manasseh, whose warriors had taken so prominent a part in the conquest of the east of Jordan (Num. xxxii. 39; Deut. iii. 13—15), the inaccessible heights and impassible ravines of Bashan, and the almost impregnable tract of Argob[2], the chief stronghold of the giant Og.

Meanwhile it had been once and again intimated to the Israelitish leader that the day drew near, when he must be gathered unto his fathers. Under the special direction, therefore, of Jehovah, he now occupied himself with giving final and specific instructions respecting the future government of the nation. Joshua "his minister" was solemnly appointed to be his successor; the boundaries of the Promised Land were definitely marked out (Num. xxxiv.); its cities with their suburbs, including six "cities of refuge" for the unwitting manslayer, were assigned to the tribe of Levi (Num. xxxv), and other necessary regulations were made.

For an ordinary leader this would have been enough. But the recent sad occurrences in the matter of Baal-Peor had only too surely reminded Moses of the fickle tendencies of the nation, and none knew better than himself the awful consequences of national apostasy. For the last time, therefore, he assembled the people together and delivered to them his final counsels. Com-

---

[1] "And the eastern side of the Jordan valley up to the lake of Chinnereth, or Gennesareth" (Num. xxxii. 34—38), Article *Gad* in *Bib. Dictionary*.

[2] Article *Manasseh* in Smith's *Bib. Dict.;* Stanley, *S. and P.* p. 327.

mencing with a retrospect of the past forty years, he reminded them of the *goodness and faithfulness* which had always followed them, in spite of their mur-, murings and discontent, and the victories they had been enabled to achieve (Deut. i—iv. 43). He recapitulated the Law given on Mount Sinai, with such additions or modifications as his own enlarged experience suggested (Deut. v. i—xxvi. 19), and appointed a day, on which, at the conclusion of the conquest, its blessings and curses were to be ratified by the nation with the most imposing and solemn ceremonies (Deut. xxvii.). He then, for the last time, enlarged on the exalted vocation of the nation, and the blessings which would assuredly accompany obedience to the Divine laws, *in the city and the field, in their basket and their store, in their going out and their coming in*, and dwelt with no less earnestness on the terrible punishments which would follow apostasy and transgression, "in furnishing images for which the whole realm of nature was exhausted, and which nothing excepting the real horrors of the Jewish history, the misery of their sieges, the cruelty, the contempt, the oppressions, which for ages this scattered, despised, and detested nation have endured, can approach[1]" (Deut. xxviii—xxx).

But oral delivery was not deemed sufficient. He, therefore, wrote out the Law, with its blessings and its curses, and gave it to the priests, charging them to place it beside the Ark in the Holy of Holies, and to read it, in the hearing of all the people, once every seven years, at the Feast of Tabernacles (Deut. xxxi. 9, 26). Then turning to Joshua, whom he had already nominated as his successor, he bade him *Be strong and of a good courage*, assuring him that Jehovah would be with him, and would make all he did to prosper. But as if to deepen the gloomy forebodings past experience

[1] Milman's *History of the Jews*, p. 211.

must have suggested, the Lord Himself not only announced in the clearest terms the future apostasy of the people (Deut. xxxi. 16—18), but directed Moses to compose a Song, which the people were to learn and teach their children, as a testimony against themselves in the days to come, when they should have turned unto other gods, and served them, and provoked the Lord, and broken His covenant (Deut. xxxi. 18, 21; xxxii. 1—43). Having composed this Song of Witness[1], and pronounced his last solemn blessing, not like Jacob upon twelve men gathered round his deathbed, but on a mighty nation, on *the ten thousands of Ephraim, and the thousands of Manasseh*, the aged Prophet, *whose eye was not dim nor his natural force abated*, was warned that his hour was come. From the plains of Moab he went up the mountain of Nebo, to the highest point in the long eastern range over against Jericho, and there He who called him to his high mission at the Burning Bush showed him that land, which had been so long sworn to the sons of Abraham, Isaac, and Jacob. Eastward and westward, southward and northward, he surveyed that goodly Land; he saw it all with his eyes though he was not to set his foot thereon. "Beneath him lay the tents of Israel ready for the march; and 'over against' them, distinctly visible in its grove of palm-trees, the stately Jericho, key of the Land of Promise. Beyond was spread out the whole range of the mountains of Palestine, in its fourfold masses; 'all Gilead' with Hermon and Lebanon in the east and north; the hills of Galilee, overhanging the lake of Gennesareth; the wide opening where lay the plain of Esdraelon, the future battle-field of the nations; the rounded summits of Ebal and Gerizim;

---

[1] On the expressive figure of *the Rock*, as applied to God six times in this Song, xxxii. 4, 15, 18, 30, 31, 37, see Stanley, *Lectures*, 198.

immediately in front of him the hills of Judæa, and,
amidst them, seen distinctly through the rents in their
rocky walls, Bethlehem on its narrow ridge, and the
invincible fortress of Jebus[1]." Such was his Pisgah-
view, and then all was over. The great Prophet had
served his day and his generation, he had reached his
120th year, and his work was ended. There, *in the
land of Moab*, he died, and He whom he had served
faithfully in all His house, buried him in a valley or
ravine in the land of Moab, over against the idol-sanc-
tuary of Beth-Peor (Deut. xxxiv. 6), but *no man know-
eth of his sepulchre unto this day.*

Note.

Three points in reference to Moses deserve attention:
(i) His work, (ii) His character, (iii) His office. (i) *His work.*
"The Hebrew lawgiver was a man who, considered merely in
an historical light, without any reference to his Divine inspi-
ration, has exercised a more extensive and permanent influence
over the destinies of his own nation and mankind at large,
than any other individual recorded in the annals of the world.
...To his own nation he was chieftain, historian, poet, lawgiver. He was more than all these, he was the founder of
their civil existence. Other founders of republics and distinguished legislators have been, like Numa, already at the
head of a settled and organized community; or have been
voluntarily invested with authority, like Lycurgus and Solon,
by a people suffering the inconvenience of anarchy. Moses
had first to form his own people, to lead them out of captivity, to train them for forty years in the desert, and bestow
on them a country of their own, before he could create his commonwealth." (ii) *His character.* "The word *meekness* (Num.
xii. 3) which is used in Scripture in reference to his personal
character 'represents what we should now designate by the
word *disinterested.*' All that is told of him indicates a with-
drawal of himself, a preference of the cause of his own nation
to his own interests, which makes him the most complete example of Jewish patriotism." He joins his countrymen in
their degrading servitude (Ex. ii. 11 ; v. 4) ; he forgets him-

[1] Stanley's *Lectures on Jewish History,* pp. 199, 200 ;
Comp. also *S. and P.* p. 301.

self to avenge their wrongs (Ex. iv. 13). He wishes that not he only, but all the nation were gifted alike: *Enviest thou for my sake?* (Num. xi. 29.) When the offer is made that the people should be destroyed, and that he should be made a great nation (Ex. xxxii. 10), he prays that they may be forgiven—*if not, blot me, I pray thee, out of Thy book which Thou hast written* (Ex. xxxii. 32). Even when excluded from realizing the hopes of a lifetime, his zeal for his people suffers no diminution. (iii) *His office.* While other prophets saw Jehovah only in visions and dreams, Moses spake with Him *mouth to mouth*, and was entrusted *with the whole household of God* (Heb. iii. 2, 5). He was at once Deliverer, Lawgiver, Priest, Teacher, Leader, and Judge. His prophetic gift controlled, pervaded, inspired, and regulated all these functions, and he was thus an eminent type of a still greater PROPHET (Deut. xviii. 15, 18) to be raised up to Israel *from among their brethren,* (i) as a Redeemer of his people; (ii) as a Mediator between them and God; (iii) as a Teacher and Lawgiver; (iv) as receiving the fullest communications from God; (v) as the Revealer of a new name of God; (vi) as the founder of a new religious society. See Milman's *History of the Jews,* I. 214; Article *Moses,* in Smith's *Bib. Dict.*; Kurtz's *History of the Old Covenant,* III, 478; Davison *On Prophecy,* pp. 110—112.

BOOK VI

JOSHUA AND THE CONQUEST OF WESTERN PALESTINE.

CHAPTER I

THE PASSAGE OF THE JORDAN AND FALL OF JERICHO.

Josh. i.—vi. B. C. 1451.

JOSHUA, the son of Nun, of the powerful tribe of Ephraim, had, as we have seen, been already selected as the successor of Moses, and the leader of the Israelitish forces. When, therefore, the thirty days of mourning for that eminent servant of God were ended (Deut. xxxiv. 8), he was encouraged by the Lord to undertake the task of conquest, which now devolved upon him, and was assured of complete success, if careful to observe the commandments of the Law. Accordingly preparations were made for the enterprise without delay; provisions for three days were issued to the host, and the tribes of Reuben, Gad, and Manasseh, already located on the eastern side of the Jordan, were reminded of their promise to accompany their brethren, and share the perils and hardships of the campaign.

The general distribution of the nations now inhabiting western Palestine has been already described[1]. Along the valley of the Jordan, and a large portion of the plain of Esdraelon, as also the sea-coast, dwelt the

[1] See p. 32, note.

THE HOLY LAND

divided among

THE TWELVE TRIBES.

The six Cities of Refuge, as ...HEBRON
The Levitical Towns as ....Libnah
Those in Benjamin, Judah and Simeon,
were allotted to the Priests

Statute Miles
10   0   10

London : Macmillan & Co. L^{td}

Stanford's Geographical Establish^t

Numerical reference
to
Places in Benjamin

1   Mizpeh
2   Gibeon
3   Anathoth
4   Ramah
5   Geba
6   Michmash
7   Chephirah
8   Gibeah (of Saul)

CANAANITES proper or *Lowlanders;* the JEBUSITES held the strong fortress of Jebus (*Jerusalem*); the HITTITES Hebron and its vicinity; between the HITTITES and the Dead Sea were the powerful and warlike AMORITES or *Highlanders;* the HIVITES occupied the country about Gibeon and under Mount Hermon; the PERIZZITES the high plains under the range of Carmel; while in the extreme north dwelt a powerful chief, who bore the hereditary name of JABIN, or *the wise.* His fortress was at Hazor, somewhere on the high ground overlooking the waters of Merom, a strong and fortified position, and the principal city of that portion of the land.

The first step to any complete subjugation of the country was the capture of the important city of Jericho, situated immediately opposite the camp of Joshua in a vast grove of noble palm-trees, nearly three miles broad, and eight miles long, which "must have recalled to the few survivors of the old generation of the Israelites the magnificent palm-groves of Egypt, such as may now be seen stretching along the shores of the Nile at Memphis[1]." It was a fenced city, enclosed by walls of considerable breadth, was the residence of a king, and not only contained sheep and oxen, but abounded in silver and gold, and vessels of brass and iron (Josh. vi. 24). From its position it was the key of Western Palestine, and "commanded the two main passes into the Central Mountains."

The first act of Joshua, therefore, was to send two spies to reconnoitre this important place. Setting out from Shittim, or the *meadows of Acacia,* and crossing the Jordan, they effected their entrance into the house

[1] Stanley, *S. and P.* p. 307; *Lectures,* p. 235. Its modern name is *Erîha,* or, as it is more commonly pronounced, *Rîha,* "a degenerate shoot, both in name and character, of the ancient Jericho." One single solitary palm now timidly rears its head where once stood the renowned "City of Palm-trees," Deut. xxxiv. 3; Judg. i. 16; Rob. *Bib. Res.* I. 552.

202 THE PASSAGE OF THE JORDAN [Book VI.

of a woman named Rahab on the city wall. Their arrival was not unobserved, and was reported to the king of Jericho. He sent to Rahab's house, and demanded their surrender, but she had already concealed her visitors among the flax-stalks spread out to dry on the flat roof of her house, and when the king's messengers arrived, she informed them that the two men had departed, and advised a speedy pursuit. Misled by this information, the officers of the king went after them in all haste, while she came up to the spies upon the roof, and related what had occurred. The townsfolk, she said, had heard of the marvellous passage of the Red Sea, and of the defeat of the great Amorite chiefs on the east of Jordan, and despaired of offering any effectual resistance to a nation thus visibly protected by a God powerful *in heaven above, and in earth beneath* (Josh. ii. 11). These fears she herself shared, and now offered to assist them (Heb. xi. 31, Jas. ii. 25) in escaping, by letting them down by a cord from her window, that they might fly to the "jagged range of the white limestone mountains[1]" behind the city, and conceal themselves for three days till their pursuers were returned. As a requital for this kindness she implored them at the capture of the city, which she regarded as certain, to spare her life, and the lives of her father and mother, and all her relatives. To this the spies assented, and having agreed that the scarlet cord should be bound in the window whence they effected their escape, to mark out the house to their comrades, and be a pledge of its security, suffered themselves to be lowered down, and in the course of three days, after hiding in the mountains, once more crossed the Jordan, and announced to Joshua the despondency of the people of Jericho.

Early therefore the next morning the Hebrew leader

---

[1] Stanley, *S. and P.* p. 307. Comp. 2 Kings ii. 7.

broke up the encampment on the upper terraces of Shittim, and descended to the lower banks of the Jordan, where three days were spent in ceremonial purifications, and in preparing for the passage of the river. The Ark was to lead the way borne by the priests, and the people were to follow at a distance of 2000 cubits, or nearly a mile, and were assured that the feet of the priests should no sooner rest in the river, than the waters from the south would be cut off from the waters that came down from above, and would stand on a heap, thus at once affording a passage, and a pledge of future and complete victory over all the nations of Canaan (Josh. iii. 1—13).

It was now the time of harvest, which ripens three weeks earlier in the plain of Jericho than in other parts of Palestine; and the Jordan, at this point three quarters of a mile wide, had overflowed all its banks[1]. On the 10th of Nisan, the sacred month, and therefore four days before the Feast of the Passover, the signal for the passage was given. The priests advanced bearing the Ark, and presently reached the brim or "broken edge" of Jordan (Josh. iii. 15). But no sooner were their feet dipped in the water, than far up the river, *in Adam, the city which is beside Zaretan*, that is, about thirty miles from the place where the Israelites were encamped, the waters which rushed down from above *stood and rose up upon a heap*, while those that came down towards the Salt Sea *failed, and were cut off* (Josh. iii. 16). Thus from north to south the waters were *driven backwards* (Ps. cxiv. 3), and the dry river-bed was exposed to view. Into it the priests descended bearing the Ark, and there they stood firm and motionless, as if on dry ground. Meanwhile, below the spot where they stood, the host, probably at various points, *hasted and passed over* (Josh. iv. 10), led by the

---

[1] See the *Calendar*, p. 155.

tribes of Reuben and Gad, and the half-tribe of Manasseh, whose vanguard amounted to 40,000 men (Josh. iv. 12). When at length from the deep bed of the river all had ascended to the desert plains on the further side, Joshua gave the signal to the priests to come out of the river. Preceded by twelve chiefs of the tribes with twelve huge stones taken from the bed of the Jordan, which were set up as a memorial on the upper bank of the Jordan valley, they moved from the spot where they had stood so long, and no sooner had they reached the other side than the waters rushed back to their accustomed channel, and the river overflowed its banks as before (Josh. iv. 18).

Intelligence of this marvellous event reached the ears not only of the Amorite mountain-chiefs, but also of the Canaanite lowlanders on the sea-coast, and filled them with the utmost alarm, *their heart melted, neither was there spirit in them any more.* No attack, therefore, was made upon the Israelites, who were left in quiet possession of their advanced post on the western side of Jordan. Here the rite of circumcision, so long neglected during their desert wanderings, was performed, and in memory of this removal of the reproach of their uncircumcised state, the rising ground of their encampment was called Gilgal, *rolling away* (Josh. v. 9). They were now also in a condition to keep the Passover, which was duly celebrated on the 14th day of the month at even *on the plains of Jericho*, and the unleavened cakes prescribed for this Festival were made of the old corn of the land, and not of the manna, which on the next day entirely ceased, and thus proved that their desert life was really over (Josh. v. 10—12).

The capture of Jericho was the next step to be taken, and while Joshua was, in all probability, deeply meditating thereon, there appeared to him *a Man with*

his sword drawn in his hand, who in answer to the
enquiries of the Israelite leader declared himself to be
the *Prince of the army of Jehovah*[1]. In deep reverence Joshua fell on his face to the ground, and was
bidden to loose his shoes from off his feet, *for the place
on which he stood was holy ground.* Instructions were
then given him respecting the method of the city's
capture. To mark in the strongest manner the singu-
larity of the campaign, to distinguish it from anything
that had been known before, the great frontier fortress
of the Jordan valley was to fall in a way above all others
calculated to show that *the Lord fought for Israel.*
Once a day for six days the host, preceded by the
sacred Ark and seven priests each blowing a trumpet
of ram's horn, was to march in procession round the
city. On the seventh day the circuit was to be made
seven times, at the conclusion of which the priests were
to sound a long blast with the rams' horns. This was
to be the signal for a general shout, on which Joshua
was assured that the walls of Jericho would fall down
flat, and the host would be enabled to advance every
man straight before him into the doomed city. Once
within it, the Israelites were to consider every thing save
the house and family of Rahab as devoted to Jehovah.
Man and woman, young and old, ox and sheep, were to
be given up to wholesale destruction, and the city itself
was to be burnt with fire, and all that was therein, save
the vessels of gold and silver, of brass and iron, which
were to be consecrated to the service of Jehovah.

Accordingly, early the following morning, the strange
advance was ordered. First went a select body of armed
men (Josh. vi. 9), then followed the priests blowing with
the trumpets, next the Ark, and lastly the vanguard.

---

[1] By some the Captain of the Lord's Host is supposed to
have been a created being, by others an uncreated Angel, the
Son of God.

Save the blast of the trumpets, there was no war cry of the troops, no sound even of human voice. Once a day for six days the strange procession passed round the city. What the swords of the Israelites could effect had already been proved in fierce conflicts with Sihon and Og, but now they hung unused in their sheaths. At early dawn on the seventh day the same procession went forth, and compassed the city not once but seven times. The last circuit complete, the priests sounded a long continued blast, and on a given signal from Joshua, the *great shout* of the entire army rose to heaven. Immediately the walls of Jericho fell down flat, and the host advanced straight into it, and captured it. In the house of Rahab her father and mother and other relatives were gathered together as had been agreed, and having been identified by the spies, were led forth to a place of safety without the camp of Israel. The rest of the inhabitants without exception were slain with the edge of the sword; the city was burnt, and everything was consumed save the vessels of gold and silver, of brass and iron. And not only was the proud "City of Palm-trees" thus utterly destroyed, but Joshua imprecated a solemn curse on any one who attempted to rebuild it, he should lay the foundation *thereof in his firstborn, and in his youngest son should he set up the gates of it*[1] (Josh. vi. 26). Thus the first step in the conquest was brought to a successful end, and the most important town in the Jordan valley, the key of western Palestine, was in the hands of the Israelites.

[1] Never again did Jericho become a *fortified city*: as a *town*, it was assigned to the tribe of Benjamin (Josh. xviii. 21), and as such was inhabited (Judg. iii. 13; 2 Sam. x. 5); but not till the time of Ahab was the attempt made by the Bethelite Hiel (1 Kings xvi. 34), to make it once more a fortified city. In his case the curse of Joshua was fulfilled: his eldest son Abiram died at its foundation, and his youngest, Segub, when the gates were set up.

CHAPTER II

CONQUEST OF THE SOUTHERN AND CENTRAL MOUNTAINS.

JOSH. VII.—XI.   B. C. 1451.

THE passes into the central hills being thus secured, Joshua without delay sent men to reconnoitre the position of Ai, a royal city, strongly posted beside Beth-aven, on the east side of Bethel, "at the head of the ravines running up from the valley of the Jordan." The spies reported it as easy of capture, and suggested that two or three thousand men would be amply sufficient for the undertaking. Acting on their advice Joshua dispatched the suggested number, who advanced boldly up the ravine, but only to meet with an unexpected and disastrous repulse. The men of Ai, strong in their high position, chased them down the "steep descent" from the gates, and slew about thirty-six men.

This unlooked-for reverse excited the profoundest despondency in the Israelitish camp. Joshua and the elders, with dust upon their heads, lay till eventide upon the ground before the Ark, which had so lately been led triumphantly round Jericho, anticipated nothing less than a general attack of the collected Canaanites, emboldened by the discomfiture of the people. From this dejection they were roused by the Voice of the Captain of the Lord's Host informing them that the Israelites themselves were the cause of this defeat; they had not kept themselves from *the accursed thing* in the devoted city of Jericho, but had taken and concealed a portion of the spoil, nor till atonement was made for this sin, could they expect any further success to attend their arms.

On the morrow, therefore, all Israel was assembled by their tribes, and an appeal was made to the sacred

Lot to discover the offender. The tribe of Judah having been taken, its clans, families, and households were successively led forth, and at length the transgressor was found in the person of ACHAN, the son of Carmi. Adjured by Joshua to make a full confession, he owned that from the spoils of Jericho he had secretly set aside a richly ornamented Babylonish or Assyrian robe[1], 200 shekels of silver, and a solid wedge of gold weighing 50 shekels, and had hidden them in the ground under his tent. Thither messengers were sent, and there the stolen property was found, and spread before the assembled host. Achan was then taken to a valley south or south-west of Jericho, and there stoned to death, together with his sons, his daughters, and all his family; their remains together with his tent, the stolen property, and all his possessions were then burnt with fire, while a great mound of stones was set up over the scene of the execution, and the valley was henceforth known as that of Achor (*trouble*).

The host was now in a position to resume the attack upon Ai. Selecting[2] 30,000 men from his forces, Joshua set out from Gilgal, and on reaching the neighbourhood of the city detached 5,000 men to place themselves during the night in ambush behind it. Meanwhile he himself, with the rest of his army, took up his position on an eminence near the north side of the town. Early the following morning he descended into the valley, and the king of Ai no sooner detected them than he advanced with all his forces to the encounter. Thereupon the Israelites feigned a retreat, and were hotly pursued

[1] Probably a stiff embroidered robe, made in the loom with the needle and of several colours. See Layard's *Nineveh*, II. 319, quoted by Kitto, *Bib. Illustrations*, II. 204. This seems to indicate the existence of a trade between Canaan and Mesopotamia.

[2] See Keil's *Commentary on Joshua*, p. 208. And for the situation of Ai, Smith's *Bib. Dict.*, Article *Ai*.

by their foes towards the desert of the Jordan[1], while at the signal of Joshua's uplifted spear the ambuscade rushed into Ai and set it on fire. The smoke of their city ascending up to heaven was the first announcement to the inhabitants of the success of the stratagem practised by the Israelites. Attacked before and behind they were utterly routed, and their whole population, numbering 12,000, were put to the sword. The city itself was sacked and burnt, and its king having been taken prisoner was hanged upon a tree till sunset, when the body was taken down, and a huge heap of stones was piled up over his grave.

After this signal victory the Israelitish leader determined to take advantage of the terror which the success of his arms had inspired in the hearts of the Canaanites, and carry out the command of Moses[2] touching the ratification of the Law with imposing and solemn ceremonies, on the mountains Ebal and Gerizim (Deut. xxvii.). From Ai, to the north of which the host had already advanced, Ebal was about 20 miles distant. Thither accordingly the host repaired; an altar of unhewn stones was erected, and burnt-offerings and peace-offerings were sacrificed to Jehovah. The stones were then plastered with lime, and the words of the Law, probably the Ten Commandments, or the Blessings and Cursings contained in Deut. xxvii. inscribed thereon[3]. Half of the assembled tribes then ascended the summit of Ebal, the other half that of Gerizim. In the intermediate valley[4]

---

[1] Stanley's *S. and P.* p. 203.

[2] See above, p. 196.

[3] "Such writing was common in ancient times: I have seen numerous specimens of it certainly *more than two thousand years old*, and still as distinct as when they were first inscribed on the plaster." Thomson's *Land and the Book*, p. 471, Mill's *Modern Samaritans*.

[4] The acoustic properties of this valley are interesting, the more so that several times they are incidentally brought to

14

stood the priests and Levites with the Ark, surrounded
by the elders, officers, and judges, with Joshua at their
head.   Of the blessings and cursings of the Law each
was then read aloud by the Levites, and as they read,
to each curse the six tribes on Ebal responded with a
unanimous loud *Amen*, and to each blessing the assembled thousands on Gerizim similarly testified their acquiescence[1].

On their return from this solemn ratification of the
Covenant the Israelites assembled at Gilgal[2].   Here
they were met by an embassy from GIBEON, now *El-
Jib*.   It was a royal city, situated exactly "opposite
the opening of the pass of Ai," inhabited by the commercial Hivites, and was at this time the head of a small
group of confederate cities, *Chephirah, Beeroth*, and
Kirjath-jearim (Josh. ix. 17).   Alarmed by the successes of Joshua, the Canaanite kings of the hills, the
valleys, and the sea-coast had mustered their forces for
a general attack upon him.   In this the Gibeonites had

our notice in Holy Writ (comp. Josh. viii. 33; Judg. ix. 7).
It is impossible to conceive a spot more admirably adapted
for Joshua's purpose than this one, in the very centre of the
newly acquired land, nor one which could more exactly fulfil all
the required conditions...A single voice might be heard by
many thousands, shut in and conveyed up and down by the
enclosing hills.   In the early morning we could not only see
from Gerizim a man driving his ass down a path on Mount Ebal,
but could hear every word he uttered as he urged it on; and in
order to test the matter more certainly, on a subsequent occasion two of our party *stationed themselves on opposite sides of
the valley, and with perfect ease recited the commandments anti-
phonally.*" Tristram's *Land of Israel*, pp. 149, 150.

[1] It was probably on this occasion that the Egyptian
coffin containing the embalmed body of their great ancestor
was laid by the two tribes of the house of Joseph in the
parcel of ground near Shechem, *which Jacob bought of the
sons of Hamor* (Gen. xxxiii. 19; l. 25).

[2] Or another place of the same name now called *Jilgilia*,
situated near Bethel in the direct route from Shechem to Ai.

resolved to take no part, but determined if possible to make a league with the Israelites. For this purpose they sent ambassadors arrayed in old and tattered garments and clouted shoes, carrying old sacks upon their asses, dry and mouldy bread, and goat-skin bottles patched and shrivelled, the better to keep up the appearance of being toil-worn travellers from a far country (Josh. ix. 3—13).

Completely deceived by this wily embassage, without waiting to take counsel of the Lord, Joshua and the princes concluded a covenant with them, and solemnly swore that they would spare their lives. Within three days, however, they arrived in the midst of their cities, and ascertained that instead of being very far off, they were their near neighbours. Loud was the murmuring of the people against their chiefs, when they saw how they had been duped. But the latter nobly determined to abide by their oaths, and in place of putting the Gibeonites to death reduced them to the condition of bondmen, and made them *hewers of wood and drawers of water* for the congregation, and for the altar of the Lord[1].

Meanwhile news of the capitulation of Gibeon having reached the ears of the southern kings, they resolved to attack the recreant city, and five powerful chiefs, the king of JEBUS, the king of HEBRON or KIRJATH-ARBA, the king of JARMUTH, the king of LACHISH, the king of EGLON, marched against it, and commenced a regular siege. In their alarm the Gibeonites sent an urgent message to Joshua at Gilgal, bidding him *slack not his hand*, but come to their aid with the utmost speed, and deliver them from their powerful foes. Perceiving that

---

[1] They became "slaves of the Sanctuary,"=Deo donati. Comp. Ezra viii. 20; 1 Chron. ix. 2; Num. viii. 16, 19. On the subsequent breaking of this compact by Saul, see 2 Sam. xxi. 1—5.

not a moment was to be lost, Joshua instantly arrayed all his forces, and by a forced march suddenly burst upon the Amorite kings, as they lay encamped before the city. Unable to offer any effectual resistance to this utterly unexpected attack, they were helpless before the Hebrew leader, and *the Lord who fought for Israel*. Numbers were slaughtered at Gibeon itself, numbers fled along the rocky ascent leading to Upper Beth-horon (*the house of Caves*), about four miles distant. Hence, however, they were chased by the triumphant Israelites along the rough descent leading to Lower Beth-horon, and thence to Azekah and Makkedah, when a terrific storm burst forth; *the Lord thundered out of heaven* and *cast down great hailstones* upon the flying Canaanites, *so that they were more which died with the hailstones than they whom the children of Israel slew with the sword* (Josh. x. 11). Standing on the summit of Upper Beth-horon[1], Joshua watched the foe flying in helpless confusion towards the western lowlands. The Lord had already delivered them into his hands, and time only was needed to render the rout complete and enable his forces to *avenge themselves* on their enemies. But the day was far advanced, and he feared the Canaanites might yet make good their escape. *In the sight*, then, *of all Israel*, he cried, *Sun, stand thou still upon Gibeon, and thou, Moon, in the valley of Ajalon* (*the place of deer* or *gazelles*). And the Lord, who fought for Israel, hearkened to the voice of His servant: *the sun stood still, and the moon stayed*, and in the lengthened afternoon the pursuit was continued without pause or rest. Arrived at Makkedah, some-

---

[1] In this same locality Judas Maccabæus won his first great victory over the forces of Syria (1 Macc. iii. 16—24), and later the Roman army under Cestius Gallus was totally cut up by the insurgent Jews (Joseph. *B. J.* ii. 19, 8, 9). See Stanley's *S. and P.* p. 212; Smith's *Bib. Dict.*, Article *Beth-horon*.

where in the Shephelah or maritime plain, the five
kings hid themselves in a well-known cave[1] shaded by
trees. But thither also the tide of battle brought the
triumphant Joshua, who bade his followers only pause *to
roll great stones to the mouth of the cave, and set men
by it for to keep them.* Longer he would not tarry ;
intent upon the pursuit he urged his forces to smite the
hindmost of their foes, and prevent their escaping into
their cities. His words were obeyed, nor till they had
made an end of slaying the Canaanites with a great
slaughter did the pursuers return to Makkedah. Here
a camp was formed, and the mouth of the cave having
been opened, the five kings were dragged forth in the
sight of Joshua and all the men of Israel. As they lay
prostrate upon the ground, the Israelite leader bade
the captains of the men of war put their feet on their
necks, and then smote them, and slew them, and hanged them upon five trees, until the evening. Then, as
the sun went down upon that memorable day, like
which was *no day before or after it,* they were taken
down, and flung into the cave where they had vainly
tried to conceal themselves, great stones were once
more rolled to its mouth, and the royal sepulchre was
closed (Josh. x. 16—27).

Such was the issue of the eventful battle of
Beth-horon. It sealed the fate of every important city
of southern Palestine. One after another, Makkedah
and Libnah, Lachish and Eglon, Hebron and Debir fell
before the victorious Israelites. From one captured city
they passed on to another conquering and to conquer,
till they had smitten *all the country of the hills and of
the south, and of the vale, and of the springs* from
Kadesh-Barnea in the southern desert to the central
plain of Esdraelon (Josh. x. 41).

[1] See Keil *on Joshua,* p. 219 ; and Article *Makkedah* in
Smith's *Bib. Dictionary.*

CHAPTER III

BATTLE OF MEROM AND DIVISION OF THE LAND.

Josh. xi.—xxi.   B. C. 1450—1444.

INTELLIGENCE of the decisive battle of Beth-horon before long reached the ears of that powerful chief in northern Palestine, who has been already mentioned, JABIN, *the Wise,* whose capital Hazor was the principal fortress in that part of the country. Determined to make a last effort to defeat the Israelites he rallied round his standard[1] not only the chiefs in his own immediate neighbourhood, but from the plains south of the sea of Galilee, or, as it was then called, *the sea of Chinnereth,* from the valley of the Jordan, the maritime plain of Dor, and the as yet unconquered fortress of Jebus.

Again encouraged by the Lord with the promise of a decisive victory, Joshua did not shrink from encountering this formidable confederacy. Setting forth on a forced march, he burst upon the combined armies of the northern chiefs, as they were encamped by the waters of Merom. As before, his attack was irresistible. The Lord delivered the vast hosts of the foe into the hands of Israel, who smote them with great slaughter, and chased them as far as the friendly city of great Zidon on the west, and the valley of Mizpeh on the east. This was the first occasion on which the Israelites encountered the horses and iron chariots of the Canaanites. According to the special command of their leader (Josh. xi. 6), they cut the ham-strings of their horses, so as to render them unfit for further use, and burnt the chariots

---

[1] " As the British chiefs were driven to the Land's End before the advance of the Saxon, so at this Land's End of Palestine the kings were gathered for this last struggle." *S. and P.* p. 391.

with fire. Hazor, the stronghold of Jabin, was captured and burnt, its king and all its inhabitants were put to the sword, the flocks and herds only being reserved as spoil for the people.

The battle of Merom was the last of Joshua's recorded engagements, but a long war, considered to have lasted nearly seven years, now occupied his energies, during which he proved his fidelity to the instructions given by the great Lawgiver of the nation. *As the Lord commanded Moses His servant, so did Moses command Joshua, and so did Joshua,* till by the time he had completed his campaigns, six nations and thirty-one kings had swelled the roll of his triumphs (Josh. xi. 18 —23; xii. 24).

At length, when he was old and stricken in years, he was commanded to divide the conquered territory among the nine tribes and the half tribe of Manasseh.

The mode adopted was twofold.

1. In some cases individual chiefs claimed particular spots on the score of their own prowess, or putting themselves at the head of armed predatory expeditions conquered certain portions with the sword. The chief instance of this was afforded by the aged compeer of Joshua, CALEB the son of Jephunneh, who now won distinction and renown for his own tribe of Judah. Forty-five years had elapsed since as one of the twelve spies in company with Joshua he had come down the *Valley of the Cluster* to Hebron, the fortress of the giant Arba, where they gathered the enormous bunch of Syrian grapes. On that memorable day Moses had rewarded his eminent faithfulness by promising him the *land whereon his feet had trod as an inheritance for himself and his children for ever* (Num. xiv. 23, 24; Josh. xiv. 9). This winding *Valley,* then, *of the Cluster,* this *mountain* (Josh. xiv. 12) on which rose the stronghold of the Anakims, was the portion Caleb desired for

himself, and hence with the Divine aid he vowed to drive forth its gigantic possessors, and take it for his own.

Joshua willingly granted his request, and the great warrior of the tribe of Judah went up against the city of Arba, and drove out the sons of Anak, Sheshai, Ahiman, and Talmai. Thence he proceeded southward to DEBIR or Kirjath-sephir[1], *the City of Books*, probably a sacred oracular place, and promised to give to its successful assailant his daughter Achsah in marriage. Thereupon OTHNIEL his nephew, or according to others his younger brother, attacked and took the fortress, and won the promised prize. On the way to Othniel's house, Achsah dismounted from the ass on which she rode, and begged her father to give her some "better heritage than the dry and thirsty frontier of the desert." Below the spot on which rose the newly captured fortress was a bubbling rivulet, falling into a rich valley. *Thou hast given me,* said she, *a south land, give me also the bubbling rills,* and he gave her *the upper and lower bubblings,* and thus Hebron and Debir with the rich valley below became the inheritance of the great warrior of Judah, and was long after known by his name (1 Sam. xxv. 3; xxx. 14).

2. But the more general mode of dividing the conquered land, in accordance with the Divine instructions, was by casting lots before the Tabernacle at Shiloh[2], in the presence of Joshua, the High-priest, and the elders of the nation. As the distribution of the tribes of REUBEN, GAD, and the half-tribe of MANASSEH on the

---

[1] See Keil *on Joshua,* x. 39. The etymology, however, is not certain. It was also called Kirjath-sannah, *city of palms* (Josh. xv. 49). See Wilton's *Negeb,* 212 *n.*

[2] The position of *Shiloh* is very definitely described in Judg. xxi. 19, as *on the north side of Bethel, on the east side of the highway that goeth up from Bethel to Shechem, and on the south of Lebonah.* Exactly in the position here indicated. Dr Robinson found a ruin called *Seilûn.* "We

east of the Jordan has been already described, we may confine ourselves to those on the western side, under the threefold division of (*a*) *The South*, (*b*) *the Centre*, (*c*) *the North*.

(*a*) *The South.*

i. The most southerly frontier was assigned first to Judah but afterwards to SIMEON (Josh. xix. 9), and is often called in Scripture *the South* (Josh. x. 40; Judg. i. 9). Like Reuben on the east of Jordan, Simeon was destined to have little influence on the subsequent history, to be *divided in Jacob and scattered in Israel* (Gen. xlix. 5—7), and to be constantly exposed to the attacks of the Amalekites and other nomadic tribes on its frontier (comp. 1 Chron. iv. 39—43).

ii. Next to Simeon on the North was the territory of the lion tribe of JUDAH, comprising the undulating pasture country of the South, the fertile lowland of the West, the hill fortresses of the centre, and the wild desert bordering on the Dead Sea. Part of his inheritance was fertile, and covered with corn-fields and vineyards (Gen. xlix. 11), part was a wild country, "the lair of savage beasts," where amidst caverns, ravines and mountains, Judah, true to the description in the blessing of Jacob, could *stoop down and couch as a lion*, guarding the southern frontier of the Promised Land.

iii. North-east of Judah was the warlike little tribe (Ps. lxviii. 27; 1 Sam. ix. 21) of BENJAMIN, famous for its archers (2 Sam. i. 22), slingers (Judg. xx. 16), and left-handed

were," he says, "on the east of the great road between Bethel and Shechem, and in passing on towards the latter place we came, after half-an-hour, to the village of Lebonah, now *El-Lubban*." *Bib. Res.* II. 269. "The selection of the site for the Tabernacle belongs to this period, and could belong to no other. The place of the sanctuary was naturally fixed by the place of the Ark. This was, in the first instance, at Gilgal. But as the conquerors advanced into the interior, a more central situation became necessary. This was found in a spot unmarked by any natural features of strength or beauty, or by any ancient recollections, recommended only by its comparative seclusion, near the central thoroughfare of Palestine, yet not actually upon it." Stanley, *Lectures on Jewish History*, p. 278.

warriors (Judg. iii. 15; xx. 16). Its territory was small, being hardly larger than the county of Middlesex, but its position was of great importance. Containing numerous rounded hills[1], which presented favourable sites for strong fortresses, it commanded the chief passes leading down from the central hills to the Jordan on the one side, and the plains of Philistia on the other. In this broken and hilly country the tribe became warlike and indomitable, *ravening as a wolf* (Gen. xlix. 27).

iv. Compressed into the narrow space between the north-western hills of Judah and the Mediterranean was the tribe of DAN, containing within the 14 miles from Joppa to Ekron one of the most fertile tracts in the land, the corn-field and garden of southern Palestine. But for this rich prize it had to contend first with the Amorites (Judg. i. 34), and afterwards with the Philistines (Judg. xiv. &c.), and eventually, as we shall see, was obliged to seek a new home in the North (Judg. xviii. 27—29).

(b) *The Centre.*

The central portion of the Holy Land, the *Samaria* of after ages, was assigned to the two brother tribes of the *house of Joseph*, EPHRAIM and MANASSEH. Of this territory, which may be roughly estimated at 55 miles from E. to W., and 70 from N. to S., and which was about equal in extent to the counties of Norfolk and Suffolk combined[2], (i) the more southerly portion was assigned to Joshua's own tribe of EPHRAIM. It extended as far south as Ramah and Bethel within a few miles of Jerusalem, and was rich in fountains and streamlets, in "wide plains in the hearts of mountains, and continued tracts of vegetation," in corn-fields and orchards, *the precious things of the earth and the fulness thereof*, which the Lawgiver invoked on *the ten thousands of Ephraim* (Deut. xxxiii. 13—17), and of whose father Jacob had said that he should be *a fruitful bough, a fruitful bough by a well* (Gen. xlix. 22). (ii) And as the duty of guarding the northern outposts on the east of Jordan had been assigned to one half of the tribe of MANASSEH, so to the remaining half on the west was assigned the duty of defending the passes into the great plain of Jezreel. Its territory

---

[1] Gibeon, Gibeah, Geba and Gaba, all mean *hill;* Ramah and Ramathaim, *eminence;* Mizpah, *a watch-tower.*
[2] Article *Ephraim* in Smith's *Bib. Dict.*

stretched westwards to the Mediterranean and the slopes of Carmel, but did not quite reach the Jordan on the East.

(c) *The North.*

The northern portion of the Holy Land, the *Galilee* of after times, extending from the range of Carmel to the mountains of Lebanon, was assigned to four tribes "allied by birth, and companions on the desert march," ISSACHAR, ZEBULUN, ASHER, and NAPHTALI.

i. The territory of ISSACHAR lay above that of Manasseh, and exactly consisted of the plain of Esdraelon (the Greek form of the Hebrew *Jezreel, = the seed-plot of God*). The luxuriance of this plain,—the battle-field of Palestine[1]—is the theme of every traveller. The soil yielded corn and figs, wine and oil (1 Chr. xii. 40), the stately palm waved over the villages, and the very weeds to this day testify to its extra-ordinary fertility. Here Issachar rejoiced in his *tents* (Deut. xxxiii. 18, 19), couched down as the strong he-ass (Gen. xlix. 14, 15) used for burden and field-work, and seeing that *rest was good, and the land that it was pleasant, bowed his shoulder to bear, and became a servant to the tribute*, which various marauders, Canaanites (Judg. iv. 3, 7), Midianites, Amalek-ites (Judg. vi. 3, 4), Philistines (1 Sam. xxix. 1; xxxi. 7—10) exacted, bursting through his frontier open both on the east and west, and tempted by his luxuriant crops[2].

ii. Immediately north of Issachar was the allotment of ZEBULUN, extending from the *Sea of Chinnereth*[3] (afterwards *the Lake of Gennesareth*) on the east, towards the Mediterra-nean on the west. Besides the fertile plain near the fisheries of the lake, this tribe possessed the *goings out* (Deut. xxxiii. 18), the outlet of the plain of Akka, where it could *suck of the abundance of the seas*.

iii. The land of NAPHTALI stretched from the Sea of Chinnereth to the valley which separates the ranges of Lebanon and Anti-Lebanon, and was one of the most densely

---

[1] It has been compared to the plain of Stirling, situated in like manner at the opening of the Scottish Highlands, and in like manner the scene of almost all the decisive battles of Scottish history. Stanley's *S. and P.* p. 337 *n.*

[2] Porter's *Handbook of Syria and Palestine*, II. 352.

[3] By some derived from Cinnoor (κινύρα, *cithara*, a "harp"), as if in allusion to the oval shape of the lake.

wooded districts of the country; its forests surpassed even those of Carmel, and the land has been described as a "natural park of oaks and terebinths." Its soil also was rich and fertile, *full with the blessing of the Lord* (Deut. xxxiii. 23).

iv. To the West of Naphtali and resting on the sea-shore was the lot of the tribe of ASHER. It was an important position, including the creeks and harbours (Judg. v. 17, 18) on the coast, and commanding all approaches to Palestine from the sea on the north. Its soil was pre-eminently fertile, and well fulfilled the blessings of Jacob and Moses. Here Asher could dip his foot in the *oil* of his luxuriant olive-groves (Deut. xxxiii. 24), fatten on the *bread*, the fruit of his rich plains, and the *royal dainties* (Gen. xlix. 20), the produce of his vineyards and pastures, while *for* or *under his shoes* (Deut. xxxiii. 25) was the *iron* ore of Lebanon, and the *brass*, or copper, of the neighbouring Phœnician settlements [1].

One tribe alone received no share in this allotment. Like Simeon, but in a different sense, the tribe of LEVI was to be *divided in Jacob and scattered in Israel* (Gen. xlix. 7). Devoted to the service of the sanctuary and sacrificial and other ministrations, this tribe depended for its maintenance on the tithes of the produce of land and cattle (Num. xviii.) ; but besides this, from each tribe, four cities and their suburban pastures, or forty-eight in all, were set apart for it, and amongst these were included the *six cities of Refuge*, three on each side of the Jordan,

On the West.	On the East.
1. *Kedesh* in Naphtali.	4. *Golan* in Bashan.
2. *Shechem* in Mt Ephraim.	5. *Ramoth-Gilead* in Gad.
3. *Hebron* in Judah.	6. *Bezer* in Reuben.

The division of the Promised Land being thus concluded, and his own inheritance having been assigned to him at Timnath-serah in Mount Ephraim, where he built a city and settled amongst the people he had led so prudently, Joshua summoned the tribes of Reuben, Gad, and the half tribe of Manasseh, and having commended them for their bravery and fidelity, gave them

[1] Porter's *Handbook of Syria and Palestine*, II. 363; Pusey's *Lectures on Daniel*, p. 294.

his blessing, and bade them return to their own settlements beyond the Jordan (Josh. xxii. 1—6).

Accordingly these tribes departed. But while yet on the western side of the river they set up a great Altar, not indeed for burnt-offering or for sacrifice, which could only be presented at the Brazen Altar of the Tabernacle at Shiloh (Lev. xvii. 8, 9; Deut. xii. 4—29), but as a standing witness to all generations, that though parted by that river, they were not sundered in religion or national interests from their western brethren. No sooner, however, was the erection of this altar announced to the other tribes, than they assembled at Shiloh, and made war upon their brethren, whom they deemed guilty of apostasy. But first, they prudently resolved to send an embassy, with Phinehas and ten princes at its head, to try the effect of a friendly expostulation. Phinehas accordingly set out and laid before them the complaint of their brethren. What trespass, he asked, was this of which they were guilty in building this altar? Had they forgotten the judgments the nation had incurred by their sin in the matter of Baal-Peor, or the trouble the nation suffered in consequence of the trespass of Achan? What, then, did they mean by this turning away from following the Lord, and exposing the whole people to His deserved wrath?

Startled at this suspicion of faithlessness, the two tribes and a half reiterated the most solemn protestations of their innocence. The Altar they had erected was not intended for any sacrificial purposes whatsoever. It was simply an Altar of Memorial, a Testimony to future generations that they had the same part and lot in the interests of the nation as their brethren on the west of Jordan. Even the zealous Phinehas could not but be satisfied with this explanation. It was no apostasy or rebellion, but at the worst an error in judgment. And the embassy returned with the joyful intelligence

that there were no grounds for a quarrel or an appeal
to arms, while the two tribes and a half, having named
the altar ED, or a Witness, continued their journey to
their eastern homes, where they settled down in the territories assigned them by Moses.

And now at length the land had rest. The tribes
east and west of Jordan established themselves in *the
lands of the heathen, and inherited the labour of the
people* (Ps. cv. 44). Before long Joshua, already stricken
in age, became aware that the day was at hand when
he must go the way of all the earth. Summoning,
therefore, the tribes of Israel, with their elders, their
judges, and their officers to Shechem, a spot consecrated by the remains of Joseph (Josh. xxiv. 33), and
the national acceptance of the blessings and cursings of
the law (Josh. viii. 30—35), he for the last time exhorted the nation to faithfulness to Jehovah. He reviewed
their history from the day that their fathers dwelt on
the other side of the Euphrates in the old time until now,
when the Lord had given them cities which they builded
not, vineyards and oliveyards which they planted not.
The call of Abraham, the descent of Jacob into Egypt,
the wonders of the Exodus, the desert wanderings, the
conquest of the Amorites on the east of Jordan, of the
Canaanites on this, all these great events in their history were reviewed, and then the aged Chief solemnly
bade them choose whom they would serve, Jehovah
who had done so great things for them, or the gods of
their fathers and of the nations in whose land they
dwelt. Thereupon the people solemnly renewed the
Covenant they had before made on the same spot, and
as an abiding memorial of their promise Joshua set up
a Stone Pillar under a sacred oak of Abraham and
Jacob[1], and wrote out the words of the Covenant in the

---

[1] Keil *on Josh.* xxiv. 26—28.

Book of the Law of God (Josh. xxiv. 26). This done, he bade every man depart unto his inheritance, and shortly afterwards, at the age of 110, this devout, blameless, fearless warrior died, and was buried in the border of his inheritance in Timnath-serah[1] (Josh. xxiv. 30).

[1] Holy Scripture itself suggests (Heb. iv. 8) the consideration of Joshua as a type of Christ. The following amongst many other typical resemblances may be pointed out: (1) the name common to both; (2) Joshua brings the people of God into the land of Promise, and divides it among the tribes; Jesus brings His people into the presence of God, and assigns to them their mansions; (3) as Joshua succeeded Moses and completed his work, so the Gospel of Christ succeeded the Law, announced One by whom all that believe are justified from all things from which we could not be justified by the Law of Moses (Acts xiii. 39). See Article *Joshua* in Smith's *Dictionary;* Pearson *on the Creed*, Art. II.

BOOK VII.

PERIOD OF THE JUDGES.

CHAPTER I

EVENTS SUBSEQUENT TO THE DEATH OF JOSHUA.

Judg. i. P. C. circ. 1425.

THE position of the Israelites at the death of Joshua was eminently favourable. A nation of freemen, entrusted at Sinai with the "Oracles of God," they were now in possession of the Promised Land. Though their late leader had not appointed any successor to those extraordinary functions he had retained throughout his life, a complete form of government had always obtained amongst them ever since they became a nation in Egypt. This was mainly kept up by the chiefs of the several tribes, the heads of the great families or clans, and the heads of houses. (Comp. Josh. viii. 33; xxiii. 2; xxiv. 1.) God Himself was their King, and in a sensible and living presence manifested Himself at the Tabernacle now set up at Shiloh, and revealed His will through the mediation of the High-priest.

But though their position was one of great privileges and blessings, it was none the less one of trial and probation. The purposes for which the Vine of Israel had been called out of Egypt (Ps. lxxx. 8) and planted in this goodly land could not be fulfilled without trouble and exertion.

There were enemies without and within their newly-acquired territory, ready at the first opportunity to attempt its recovery from their hands. If they were secure from their old oppressors the Egyptians, yet on the south and south-east the Midianites and Amalekites were only too likely to attack a people, whose late victories must have been a continual source of jealousy; while on the north-east were formidable chiefs, who might, as in the days of their forefather Abraham[1], sweep down upon the country beyond the Jordan, and grievously harass the eastern tribes. Moreover, extensive as the conquests of Joshua had been, they had not achieved nor were they intended to achieve the entire extirpation of the Canaanites. The conquered population retained large tracts and important positions in the very heart of the country. The Philistines retained the fertile plain of the Shephelah in the southwest; the almost impregnable fortress of Jebus still remained unconquered on the very border of Judah; well nigh the entire sea-coast from Dor to Sidon was in the hands of the Phœnicians; the strong towns of Bethshean, of Taanach, and Megiddo were still held by the Canaanites in the fertile plain of Jezreel; while on the north still lingered formidable remnants of the great confederacy under Jabin. These nations had *not been driven out hastily*, but had been left to test and prove the fidelity of the generation that *had not known the wars of Canaan* (Judg. ii. 22), and the duty of subjugating them had been solemnly enforced by Joshua in his last address to the assembled tribes (Josh. xxiii. 5—10).

Accordingly we find that all the days of the elders that outlived Joshua, the nation did not forget its vocation, but carried on the work to which it had been called (Judg. ii. 7).

[1] See above, p. 35.

1.   Thus *Judah*, whose conquest of Hebron and its vicinity has been already related, in alliance with the neighbouring tribe of Simeon, attacked Bezek, slew 10,000 of its Canaanite and Perizzite inhabitants, and captured its ferocious king Adoni-bezek, whose cruel mutilation of seventy vassal princes gives us an insight into the character of the native chiefs, whom Israel was commissioned to expel (Judg. i. 6, 7). As he had done to others, so Judah did to him. They *cut off his thumbs and his great toes*, and carried him captive to Jerusalem, *i. e.* to the Lower City, which was taken, and set on fire. But the Upper City resisted all their efforts, as afterwards those of the tribe of Benjamin (Judg. i. 21[1]). They were more successful, however, in other places, and reduced numerous cities of the Canaanites in the central mountains, the southern desert, and the low country of the west (Judg. i. 17, 18).

2.   The powerful house of *Joseph* was not behind-hand in following the example of the lion-tribe of Judah. They sent spies to descry the town of Luz, who seeing a man coming from thence, seized him, but consented to spare his life and that of his family on condition that he shewed them the entrance, on ascertaining which, they smote the place with the edge of the sword. Thus in addition to Shechem, the house of Joseph became possessed of another spot consecrated by the most sacred associations, even the town, near which was the stone Pillar their father Jacob had set up on his way to Padan-Aram, and called the place Beth-el, *the House of God* (Judg. i. 22—26). But they were not similarly successful in expelling the Canaanites from Gezer near lower Beth-horon (Judg. i. 29), or from their strongholds in the plain of Jezreel, Taanach, Megiddo, and Beth-shean. Instead of utterly driving them out, they put

---

[1] Such is the explanation of Josephus, *Ant.* v. ii. § 2, who adds that the siege lasted some time.

them under tribute, as also the Amorites, who succeeded in thrusting the children of Dan from the fertile lowland of the sea-coast into the mountains, to be themselves dispossessed in turn by the Philistines (Judg. i. 34, 35).

3. Similar declensions from the strict line of duty marked the conduct of other tribes. *Zebulun* contented itself with merely imposing tribute on the nations within its borders ; *Asher* made no attempt to expel the powerful Phœnicians on the sea-coast from Accho to Zidon, or from their more inland settlements; and *Naphtali* spared the inhabitants of the fenced cities of Beth-shemesh and Beth-anath (Judg. i. 30—33). This neglect of an obvious duty soon led to worse results. Contrary to the express commands of the Law, and the repeated exhortations of Moses and Joshua, the Israelites began to make leagues with the heathen nations. Leagues with nations led to marriages with individuals, and these to their natural consequences. Their new relatives invited the Israelites to their idolatrous festivals, where the consecrated licentiousness gratified their sensual appetites, and before long there *arose a generation, which knew not the Lord, nor yet the works which He had done for Israel* (Judg. ii. 10). Forgetting Him who had done so great things for them, they bowed themselves to strange gods, and practised the worst abominations, even sacrificing their sons and their daughters to Baal and Ashtaroth (Ps. cvi. 37, 38 ; Judg. ii. 13).

This gradual spread of idolatry, and as a natural consequence, of moral and social degeneracy, is strikingly illustrated by two incidents recorded in the last five chapters of the Book of Judges, which seem to have been inserted for this very purpose as a kind of appendix to that Book[1].

[1] See the marginal date at Judges, chap. xvii. It is to be observed that (i) Dan was not yet settled, Judg. xviii. 1 ; (ii) Phinehas, the grandson of Aaron, was living (Judg. xx. 28),

CHAPTER II.

MICAH AND THE DANITES, THE TRIBAL WAR.

Judg. xvii.—xxi.   B. C. circ. 1406.

THERE was living about twenty years after the death of Joshua in Mount Ephraim in central Palestine a man named MICAH, whose mother one day lost 1100 shekels of silver. So terrible was the curse she imprecated on the thief, that her son in alarm confessed that he had abstracted the money. Instead of reproaching him, his mother thereupon informed him that she had dedicated this sum, probably the savings of a lifetime[1], to the Lord, to make a graven and a molten image. Upon this Micah restored the money to his mother, who sent 200 shekels to a founder for the purpose of fashioning the idol. When made, it was set up in Micah's house, and he consecrated one of his sons as priest, and arrayed him in a sacred vestment, probably made in imitation of the ephod of the High-priest. Not satisfied, however, with the ministrations of his son, on the arrival of a young Levite of Bethlehem in Judæa, travelling, probably, in search of employment as a teacher of the Law, he persuaded him also to become his priest, and agreed to give him 10 shekels of silver a-year, suitable sacerdotal vestments, and his living. On these terms the Levite was content to dwell with him, became his priest, and *was unto him as one of his sons.*

Soon after this it happened that the tribe of Dan being still hard pressed by the Amorites[2], and desirous of an addition to their territory, sent five spies from two towns in the low country to discover a new and

as also the grandson of Moses; (iii) the iniquity of Gibeah is mentioned, Hos. x. 9, as the first open sin of Israel in Canaan. See Angus' *Bible Handbook,* 460 n.

[1] Kitto's *Bibl. Illus.* II. 447.   [2] See above, p. 218.

advantageous settlement. The spies set out, and on
their way came to Mount Ephraim, where they obtained
a lodging in the house of Micah. Recognizing the voice of
the young Levite, they enquired the cause of his presence
there, and on ascertaining the position he held, begged
him to ask counsel of Jehovah as to the success of their
expedition. The Levite did so, and the answer was
propitious. Thereupon the spies resumed their journey,
and tracking the Jordan to its source beyond the waters
of Merom, came to an eminence on which rose the town
of Laish (*Tell el-Kâdy*), a colony from Sidon, whose inhabitants, "separated from their mother-city[1] by the
huge mass of Lebanon and half of Anti-Lebanon,"
dwelt quiet and secure (Judg. xviii. 7) in the enjoyment
of the warm climate and exquisite scenery, and tilling
the fertile soil irrigated by many streams.

The spies marked the spot, and on their return bade
their brethren arise, and take possession of a place
*where there was no want of anything that is in the
earth* (Judg. xviii. 10). Upon this, six hundred Danites
from Zorah and Eshtaol girded on their weapons of war,
and went up and encamped at a spot behind Kirjath-
jearim, which though it belonged to Judah, they named
Mahaneh-Dan, or *the Camp of Dan*. Thence they ascended into the mountain-range of Ephraim, and like
the spies before them, drew near the house of Micah.
Informed that here there was an ephod and teraphim,
a graven image and a molten image, the six hundred
warriors took their stand by the gateway leading into

[1] Mr Thomson compares it with the soil of the lower portion of the Mississippi; "even now the region produces large
crops of wheat, barley, maize, sesame, rice, and other plants,
with very little labour...while horses, cattle, and sheep fatten
on the rich pastures, and large herds of black buffaloes luxu-
riate in the streams and in the deep mire of the marshes."
Thomson's *Land and the Book*, p. 214; Robinson, *Bib. Res.*
III. 396; Blunt's *Coincidences*, Pt. II. 108—110.

the court, and engaged the Levite in conversation, while the spies ascended into the sanctuary, and stole away the images with the sacerdotal vestments. On re-appearing, the Levite tried to expostulate, but was speedily bidden to hold his peace, and without much difficulty suffered himself to be persuaded that it would be better to accompany them, and instead of being a priest unto one man, to become a priest *unto a tribe and a family in Israel* (Judg. xviii. 19). With such secrecy was their departure effected, that the Danites had got a good way from the house of Micah, before the latter became aware of the grievous wrong he had sus-tained. Gathering together the inhabitants of the houses, which had gradually clustered round his idolatrous sanc-tuary, he pursued after the roving warriors. But it was in vain that he gave vent to his grief and rage. The spoilers only mocked him, and bade him take care he did not lose his life as well as his gods; consequently he was fain to return to his rifled sanctuary, while the six hundred held on their way northward.

Reaching the source of the Jordan far up in the north-ern mountains, they found the town of Laish just as the spies had described it. Far from its mother-city, the care-less colony had no deliverer in its hour of peril. Without warning the spoilers burst upon it, scaled its walls, set it on fire, and massacred its inhabitants, men, women and children without mercy. They afterwards rebuilt it, called it *Dan after the name of Dan their father*, and there set up the images they had taken from Micah. There too the young Levite, who, it seems, was no unimportant personage, but no other than Jonathan, the son of Ger-shom, the son of the great lawgiver Moses[1], ministered

[1] In the English version the reading is *the son of Manas-seh* (Judg. xviii. 30), a name probably substituted out of re-spect for the great Lawgiver, whose name is preserved in several Hebrew MSS. and the Vulgate. See Articles *Micah, Jonathan, Manasseh,* and *Laish* in Smith's *Bib. Dict.*

at this new sanctuary, and his descendants remained till
the Captivity (Judg. xviii. 14—31).

If any proof were wanting of the association of religious with moral declension at this period, it is supplied
by the biography of another Levite, which is also given
in these concluding chapters of the Book of Judges.

2. This Levite, who, like the other, dwelt on the
edge of Mount Ephraim, took him a concubine out of
Bethlehem-Judah, who proved faithless, and returned
to her father's house. On this her husband went in
quest of her, and was received by her father with true
Eastern hospitality. As the fifth day declined after his
arrival, resisting the importunities of his father-in-law
who would have had him stay longer, he rose up to
return, and as night fell drew near the town of Jebus,
which still remained in the hands of its Canaanite inhabitants. Rejecting the advice of his servant to lodge
there during the night, he pressed on, and it was already
dark when he reached Gibeah in Benjamin.

As he was sitting in the streets of the town awaiting
an offer of shelter, an old man approached coming from
his work in the fields. His home, too, was in Mount
Ephraim, but he was sojourning at Gibeah, and taking
compassion on the homeless condition of the Levite he
brought him into his house, and gave him a lodging for
the night. As they sat at meat, certain of the lowest
inhabitants of the place set upon the house, and treated
the Levite's concubine with such violence, that in the
morning when he arose he found her lying dead before
the door. Enraged at this savage act he took her home,
and there with his knife divided her together with her
bones into twelve pieces, and sent them among the
twelve tribes. This ferocious summons to vengeance
roused all Israel as one man (Judg. xx. 1). Even the
tribes beyond the Jordan assembled with the rest of
their brethren, and 400,000 warriors met at Mizpeh in

Benjamin, a fortified eminence a little to the north of
Jebus, and listened to the Levite while he recounted
the dark tale of outrage (Judg. xx. 2—6).

The recital excited still greater indignation, and all
the people *knit together as one man* bound themselves
by a solemn vow never to return to their homes till
they had taken deep vengeance on the inhabitants of
Gibeah for the disgrace they had brought upon Israel.
Messengers were accordingly sent through the territory
of Benjamin demanding their surrender. This the Benjamites absolutely refused, and making the cause of
Gibeah their own, prepared to encounter the men of
Israel with all their forces, amounting to 26,000, together
with the 700 warriors of Gibeah, chosen men, left-handed, every one of whom *could sling stones at an hair
breadth, and not miss* (Judg. xx. 16).

In this juncture, instead of consulting the Divine
Will whether they should embark in this war at all, the
indignant tribes having already decided on the campaign
only sought to know who should take the lead. Judah
was the tribe indicated by the Divine response, and in
the engagement that ensued, the Israelites were defeated with a loss of upwards of 22,000 men. On the
day following they renewed the attack, but only to sustain a second reverse and a loss of 18,000 of their best
troops. In the greatest distress at this double defeat,
the eleven tribes assembled at Bethel, fasted the whole
day until the evening, and offered burnt-offerings and
peace-offerings before the Lord. Then Phinehas, who
had led the sacred war against the Midianites, enquired
whether a third engagement should be hazarded, and in
reply was bidden to go up, for this time the Lord would
deliver Benjamin into their hand (Judg. xx. 28).

Thereupon it was resolved to repeat the tactics so
successful at Ai. An ambuscade was planted behind
Gibeah, and on the descent of the Benjamites a flight

was feigned to draw them from the town towards a spot, where the road divided into two paths, the one leading to Bethel, the other to Gibeah-in-the-Field, probably the modern *Jeba*. Unconscious of their danger the Benjamites suffered themselves to be decoyed from the town, and slew about 30 of their foes. Meanwhile the ambuscade arose, and bursting on the defenceless town, put the inhabitants to the sword. A great pillar of flame and smoke signalled to the rest of the army the success of the stratagem, and the Benjamites at last awakened to their danger fled eastward to the desert region bordering on the Jordan valley. But their foes now turned, and inclosing them round about (Judg. xx. 43), trode them down, and slew 25,000.

From this indiscriminate massacre only 600 of the Benjamites effected their escape to the cliff of Rimmon, an inaccessible natural fortress situated about 7 miles north-east of Gibeah, and overhanging the wild region bordering on the Jordan. Here they entrenched themselves for a space of four months, while the eleven tribes not content with firing and ravaging every town in the territory of Benjamin, bound themselves by a vow to abstain from all intermarriage with them. Regret, however, for the almost entire extinction of a tribe in Israel subsequently softened their hearts, and by a curious stratagem characteristic of this troubled period, when there *was no king in Israel,* and *every man did that which was right in his own eyes* (Judg. xxi. 25), they enquired whether any city had failed to take part in the late tribal war. Thereupon it was discovered that Jabesh-gilead, a city on the east of the Jordan, had sent no forces to aid their brethren. Thither, therefore, 12,000 men were despatched, with instructions utterly to destroy the recreant city and massacre every man and married woman. This ruthless order was executed to the letter, and the entire population was put to the

sword, save 400 virgins, who were given in marriage to
the remnant of Benjamin. These not sufficing for wives,
the Benjamites took advantage of a yearly festival at
the sanctuary of Shiloh, when the daughters of the place
assembled to take part in the sacred dances, and concealing themselves in the neighbouring vineyards, burst
forth upon the unsuspecting maidens and carried off
each one a wife for himself, with whom they returned,
repaired their towns, and dwelt in them (Judg. xxi.
23—25).

CHAPTER III

OTHNIEL AND EHUD, DEBORAH AND BARAK.

Judg. ii.—v.   B. C. circ. 1406—1296.

THE two incidents just recorded are illustrations of
the turbulence and disorder of the period which
followed the death of Joshua and of the elders that outlived Joshua. Forgetful of their vocation, the Chosen
People intermingled with the heathen Canaanites, conformed to their rites and customs, and so forfeited the
protection and blessing of their Invisible King. He therefore *delivered them into the hands of spoilers that spoiled them, He sold them to their enemies round about...
and they were greatly distressed* (Judg. ii. 14, 15).

But on the first manifestation of repentance, *He regarded their affliction, He heard their cry* (Ps. cvi. 44,
45), and raised up *Deliverers*, who saved them from
their enemies. The Hebrew word used to denote these
Deliverers, these Saviours of their country, *Shofet,
Shophetim*[1], and which we have translated *Judge*, is
much the same as the *Suffes, Suffetes* of the Carthaginians at the time of the Punic wars. Raised up on
extraordinary occasions, like the Dictators in the history

[1] Comp. Livy, xxx. 7; xxviii. 37; in xxxiii. 46, xxxiv.
61 they are called *judices*. Stanley's *Lectures,* p. 292.

of Rome, they delivered the nation from some pressing danger, and their power and authority generally terminated with the crisis which had called them forth. Higher than the princes of the tribes, vested with extraordinary powers for the emergency, their office was not hereditary, though we shall see it finally tending in more than one instance towards fixedness and perpetuity, and in the person of Eli united with that of the Highpriest (Judg. x. 3, 4; xii. 8—14; 1 Sam. viii. 1—3).

Invasion from the North-east. Othniel.

The crisis, which called forth the first of these Deliverers, was the invasion of the country by *Chushan-rishathaim*, king of Mesopotamia. From the seat of his dominion between the Euphrates and the Tigris he extended his conquests so far southward, that the Israelites suffered grievously from his oppressions for a space of 8 years. At the close of this period, OTHNIEL, whose valour in attacking Kirjath-sepher and marriage with the daughter of the famous Caleb have been lately recorded [1], went out against him and defeated him, and restored rest to the land for 40 years (Judg. iii. 8—11).

Invasion from the South-east. Ehud.

On his death, the people again fell into idolatry, and the Moabites under EGLON, aided by their old allies the Ammonites and Amalekites, crossed the Jordan and seized the ruined site of Jericho. From this vantage ground, Eglon was enabled to extend his dominion at least over the tribe of Benjamin, from which, if not from other tribes, he exacted annual tribute for a space of 18 years. This was brought to him at Jericho, where he would seem to have constructed a palace. On one occasion, EHUD, the son of Gera, a Benjamite, was selected to command the party deputed to carry this proof of subjection. Having executed his commission, he accom-

[1] See above, p. 216.

panied his men as far back as the *quarries,* or rather
the *graven images* at Gilgal (Judg. iii. 19, *margin*),
possibly the idol-temples, with which the Moabites had
profaned the associations of that sacred spot. Thence
he turned back, and on pretence of having a message
from God to deliver to him, obtained a private interview
with Eglon, as he sat in his *summer parlour,* or "parlour of cooling" (Judg. iii. 20, *margin*), probably on the
roof of his house, where he might catch the cool breezes
that tempered the tropical heat of the Jordan valley.
On entering, Ehud repeated the purport of his errand,
and Eglon bade the attendants instantly withdraw. Then
as he rose from his seat to meet his visitor, Ehud, who
was left-handed like many of his tribe, drew a long two-
edged dagger, which he had made[1] and hidden under
his mantle upon his right thigh (Judg. iii. 16), and stabbed
him with such force as to leave the weapon in his body.
Without lingering a moment, he then shut and locked
the doors of the chamber, and fled "through the porch
or gallery that ran round the roof[2]," and passing beyond
Gilgal, made for the wooded, shaggy, hills of Seirath,
in the mountains of Ephraim. There he blew a horn,
and roused the Israelites, who rushed down the hills
and followed him in the direction of Jericho. Meanwhile the attendants had opened the door of Eglon's
chamber, and beheld the corpse lying on the floor.
Panicstricken at this unexpected death of their leader,
and still more by the sudden rising of the Israelites, the
Moabites fled towards the fords of the Jordan. But the
Israelites had been beforehand with them, and suffering
none to cross, slew upwards of 10,000 men.

Rest was now restored at least to the tribe of Benjamin for 80 years, but in the south-west the Philistines,
encouraged probably by the success of the Moabites,

---

[1] See Blunt's *Coincidences,* Pt. II. v. 114—117.
[2] Stanley's *Lectures on Jewish History,* p. 317.

made an inroad, and reduced the Israelites to great straits (Judg. v. 6). But SHAMGAR, the son of Anath, was raised up to be a deliverer. Armed with nothing but a long iron-spiked ox-goad[1], he made a sudden and desperate assault upon the Philistines, and slew 600 of them, thus obtaining a temporary respite for his people (Judg. iii. 31).

Invasion from the North. Deborah and Barak.

But a more terrible invasion was in store for the nation, which again on the death of Ehud relapsed into idolatry (Judg. iv. 1). This time the oppressor came from the north, where under a second JABIN, the Canaanites, whom Joshua had defeated in his memorable victory at the waters of Merom, had recovered a portion of their former strength. With his vast hosts, and his 900 chariots of iron commanded by SISERA his captain, who resided at *Harosheth of the Gentiles*[2], he overran the country of the neighbouring tribes, Asher, Naphtali and Zebulun.

Such was the general prostration and terror that, as had already been the case in the days of Shamgar, *the*

---

[1] "The ploughman still carries his goad—a weapon apparently more fitted for the hand of the soldier than the peaceful husbandman. The one I saw was of the 'oak of Bashan,' and measured upwards of 10 feet in length. At one end was an iron spear, and at the other a piece of the same metal flattened. One can well understand how a warrior might use such a weapon with effect in the battle-field." Porter's *Syria and Damascus*, II. 35. Comp. Homer, *Il.* VI. 135.

[2] Identified by Thomson with *Harothieh*, the Arabic form of the Hebrew Harosheth, an enormous double mound about 8 miles from Megiddo, exactly in the line of the retreat of the Canaanites, at the entrance of the pass to Esdraelon from the plain of Acre. "It was," he writes, "probably called Harosheth *of the Gentiles,* or *nations,* because it belonged to those Gentiles of Acre and the neighbouring plains whom we know from Judg. i. 31 the Hebrews could not subdue." *The Land and the Book,* p. 437.

highways were unoccupied, and the travellers stole
from place to place by *crooked, tortuous by-paths*
(Judg. v. 6). Village life ceased in Israel, and the
peasantry, abandoning the cultivation of the ground,
retired for refuge to the walled towns. But even
here they were not secure. There was *war in the
gates,* the place usually devoted to the administration
of justice, and even *in the places of drawing water the
noise of the archers* could be heard twanging their terrible bows (Judg. v. 8, 11). No resistance could be offered, for according to a common policy (1 Sam. xiii. 19—22)
there had been a general disarmament of the people, and
*not a spear or shield was to be seen among forty thou-
sand in Israel* (Judg. v. 8). The spirit of the nation was
completely crushed, and the second Jabin and Sisera
his captain carried on unchecked for upwards of 20
years those measures, whereby they reduced the Israelites to a condition of degrading servitude (Judg. iv. 3).

At length, however, a Deliverer appeared. Under a
solitary palm-tree in the mountain-range of Ephraim
between Ramah and Bethel, lived a prophetess named
DEBORAH, who was or had been the wife of Lapidoth.
In the failure of all other leaders she was now regarded
by the oppressed people with the utmost reverence,
and *they went up to her for judgment* (Judg. iv. 5).
Like Joan of Arc in after times, her whole soul was
fired with indignation at the sufferings endured by her
people, and at length from Kadesh-naphtali, a City of
Refuge, not far from Jabin's capital (Josh. xx. 7; xxi.
32), and therefore peculiarly animated with hostility to
the oppressor, she summoned BARAK[1] (*lightning*) the
son of Abinoam. On the strength of a Divine commission, she then enjoined him to gather 10,000 men from
his own and the neighbouring tribe of Zebulun to the

[1] Compare the family name of Hannibal, Barca = fulmen
belli. See *Barak* in Smith's *Bib. Dict.;* Joseph. *Ant.* v. 5, § 2.

green summit of Tabor[1], and promised to draw to the
river Kishon in the plain of Esdraelon the great captain
of Jabin's army with his chariots and his host, and there
deliver them into his hand. Barak declined to undertake the arduous enterprise, unless the Prophetess promised to accompany him. To this she assented, but
distinctly warned him that the expedition would not be
for his honour ; as he was thus willing to lean upon a
woman's aid, so into the hands of a woman would the
Lord deliver the leader of his enemy's forces.

Leaving her seat of judgment, Deborah then accompanied Barak to Kedesh, and he employed himself in
rousing his own tribe of Naphtali and that of Zebulun
to join in the insurrection. Having at length gathered
10,000 men around his standard he marched, still attended by the Prophetess, to the high places of Tabor.
There he was joined by portions of other tribes, whom
the influence of Deborah had roused to take part in the
great struggle, consisting of the princes of Issachar, a
body of Ephraimites, and detachments from Benjamin
and north-eastern Manasseh (Judg. v. 14, 15). Other
tribes, however, came not thus zealously *to the help of
the Lord against the mighty.* Of the two maritime
tribes, Dan on the south clung to his ships in the port of
Joppa, and Asher forgat the perils of his fellows in the
creeks and harbours of his Phœnician allies (Judg. v. 17).
The name of Judah is not even mentioned among the
patriot forces. Amongst the tribes across the Jordan
great was the debate as to the course to be pursued.
Reuben preferred to *abide secure among his sheepfolds*[2],

---

[1] Probably = *height*, "rising abruptly to a height of about
1000 ft. from the north-eastern arm of the plain of Esdraelon,
and standing entirely insulated, except on the W., where a
narrow ridge connects it with the hills of Nazareth." See
Robinson, *Bib. Res.* II. 352.

[2] See above, pp. 78, 194.

and to *listen to the bleating of his flocks,* and Gad to *linger beyond Jordan* in his grassy uplands (Judg. v. 17). But amidst the wavering of many hearts, Zebulun and Naphtali remained firm, and prepared *to jeopardize their lives unto the death* on the high places of Tabor (Judg. v. 18).

Meanwhile certain of the Kenites[1], who had separated from the rest of their tribe in the hill country of Judah (Judg. i. 16), and now dwelt under the oaks of Zaanaim[2] near Kedesh, informed Sisera of the sudden movement of Barak towards Tabor (Judg. iv. 11, 12). Thereupon, without delay he gathered all his forces, and encamped on the level plain of Esdraelon, between the friendly towns of Taanach and Megiddo[3], where he was also joined by other Canaanite chiefs anxious to quell the sudden insurrection (Judg. v. 3, 19).

At length the heroic Deborah gave the encouraging command to Barak, *Up, for this is the day in which the Lord hath delivered Sisera into thine hand.* Probably long before it was light[4] the camp of Barak's little army was struck, and the patriot tribes rapidly descending the winding mountain-path fell upon the hosts of Sisera and threw them into wild confusion. As they fled in utter dismay along the plain, not only the troops of Barak, but *the stars in their courses* (Judg. v. 20), the elements of heaven, began to fight against

---

[1] See above, p. 169, note 1.

[2] Or the "Oak of the Unloading of Tents," Stanley's *Lectures,* p. 326. "The black tents of the Turkman and Kurds, strangers like the Kenites, may still be seen pitched among the oaks and terebinths that encompass the little plain of Kedesh ; proving that after the lapse of more than 3000 years the state of society in the country is but little changed." Porter's *Handbook of Syria and Palestine,* II. 444. For the forests of Naphtali, see above, p. 219.

[3] See above, p. 226.

[4] Thomson, *Land and the Book,* p. 435.

the Canaanites. A furious storm of rain and hail[1]
gathered from the east, and bursting right in their
faces, rendered useless the bows of their archers[2], and
swelled into a mighty torrent the rivulets, springs, and
spongy marshes near Megiddo. Before long *the ancient
torrent* of the *Kishon* (*twisted* or *winding*) rose in its
bed, and the plain became an impassable morass[3]. The
chariots of Sisera were now utterly useless. The hoofs
of the horses vainly plunging in the tenacious mud and
swollen streams *were broken by means of their prans-
ings* (Judg. v. 22). The torrent of the Kishon, now
rushing fast and furious, *swept them away,* and the
strength of the Canaanites *was trodden down.* Stuck
fast, entangled, overwhelmed they could not stand for
a moment before the avenging Barak, and not a man
made good his escape to the city of their great leader,
Harosheth of the Gentiles, before their pursuers had
smitten them with the edge of the sword (Judg.
iv. 16).

Meantime, while his mother and her attendants were
vainly awaiting the return of his triumphal chariot

---

[1] Josephus, *Ant.* v. 5, § 4. See Thomson, p. 436.

[2] "As in like case in the battle of Cressy." Stanley's
Lectures, p. 324.

[3] " I have seen this stream swollen and rapid, after heavy
rains, when the winter torrents of Galilee and Carmel flow
into it; then it is a river 'with waters to swim in, a river
that cannot be passed over;' and I can well imagine the hosts
of Sisera, his chariots and horses, struggling there." *Domestic
Life in Palestine,* pp. 111, 112. " When largely swollen during
the great rains of winter it is *spongy* enough—much easier to
find than to get over—I once crossed through the lower part of
Esdraelon...and had no little trouble with its *bottomless mire*
and *tangled grass.*" Thomson, *L. and B.,* p. 435 ; and Compare Van de Velde, 1. p. 289. Some of the results of this
battle were nearly reproduced in the battle of Mount Tabor,
April 16, 1799, when many of the fugitive Turks were drowned in the Kishon. See Smith's *Bib. Dict.,* Article *Kishon.*

(Judg. v. 28), Sisera himself fled away on foot to the
friendly tribe of Heber the Kenite beneath the oaks of
Zaanaim, where he hoped for safety from his remorseless
pursuers.   After a while he drew near the tent of Jael,
Heber's wife, and chieftainess of the tribe.   She herself
had descried him approaching, and went forth to meet
him.   *Turn in, my lord,* said she, *turn in to me, fear
not.*   And he turned in, and she covered him with a
rug or blanket (Judg. iv. 18).   Spent and weary,
before he lay down, he asked for a little water to drink;
but she gave him something better than water.   She
opened the skin bottle of milk, such as always stands by
Arab tents, she brought forth butter, or " thick curdled
milk " in a *lordly dish*[1], or the bowl used for illustrious
strangers, and covered him again with the rug.

Thus doubly assured of hospitality Sisera bade her
deny his presence if any enquired after him, and then
laid him down and slept.   But as she stood at the tent-
door, other thoughts than those of kindness towards the
slumbering chief came over Jael.   At length taking one
of the wooden sharp-pointed tent-nails in one hand and
a mallet in the other, she went softly unto him, and
smote him with such force that the nail entered into his
temples, and fastened his head to the ground, *for he
was fast asleep and weary, and so he died.*   Meanwhile
the pursuing Barak drew near.   Him too Jael went
forth to meet, and taking him within, showed him his
terrible foe, the captain of the nine hundred iron chariots, lying dead upon the ground, with the nail driven
through his temples.

Thus on that day, as the Prophetess had said, God
delivered Sisera into the hand of a woman.   Together
she and Barak returned from the battle-field, and
chanted responsively a sublime Triumphal Hymn, cele-

---

[1] See Thomson, *The Land and the Book,* p. 441.

brating the recent victory over the northern Canaanites,
which now secured to the land rest for 40 years (Judg.
v.).

CHAPTER IV

INVASION OF THE MIDIANITES. GIDEON.

Judg. vi.—viii.   B.C. circ. 1256—1249.

AS so often before, the effects of this last great deliverance were but transitory.   Again the Israelites
relapsed into idolatry, and in consecrated groves practised all the abominations that disgraced the worship of
Baal.   The national punishment they thus drew down
upon themselves was more severe than anything they
had yet endured.   Since the sacred war led by Phinehas
against the Midianites[1] (Num. xxxi. 1—13), that people
had recovered much of their ancient strength, and now
in concert with the Amalekites, and *the children of the
East* (Judg. vi. 3), or the Arabian tribes beyond the
Jordan, they determined to invade the territory of Israel.
Led by two superior chiefs, having the title of king,
Zebah and Zalmunna, and two inferior chiefs, Oreb
and Zeeb (*the Raven and the Wolf*), they poured into
the country with their herds, their flocks, and their
camels, like locusts for multitude, and gradually overran
it from the plain of Jezreel down the valley of the
Jordan, and southward as far as Gaza in the fertile
Lowlands of the west.   Here they established themselves,
destroyed the crops[2], and for a period of seven years

---

[1] See above, p. 194.

[2] "In precisely the same manner do the Bedawîn Arabs,
these modern Midianites, come up the Wady of Jezreel and
Wady Sherrar, *after the people have sown*, and destroy the increase of the earth ; and not only destroy the increase of the
field, but commit wholesale murder, as these did upon the
brethren of Gideon at Tabor...Both these valleys are now
swarming with these *children of the East*, come over Jordan

16—2

reduced the Israelites to the greatest straits, so that they left the plains, and fled for refuge to dens or catacombs, which they cut out of the rocky mountains, to inaccessible strongholds, and the limestone caves with which Palestine abounds[1] (Judg. vi. 2).

As so often before, the Deliverer came from the quarter most exposed to the ravages of the invaders. At Ophrah, in the hills of western Manasseh, not far from Shechem, and overlooking the plain of Jezreel, the head-quarters of the Midianitish host, lived a high-born Abi-ezrite, a descendant of one of the princely families of Manasseh (Josh. xvii. 2 ; Num. xxvi. 30), named JOASH. The invasion had brought not only impoverishment but dire bereavement into his home. In a skirmish near the heights of Tabor the Midianite kings, Zebah and Zalmunna, had slain all his noble sons save one, GIDEON (Judg. viii. 18, 19).

On one occasion, as Gideon was threshing wheat, not in the open summer threshing-floor, but by the winepress[2] near his native Ophrah, to hide it from the Midianites, an Angel appeared and saluted him with the words, *The Lord is with thee, thou mighty man of valour.* In reply Gideon contrasted the present degraded condition of the nation with the glorious days when Jehovah brought them out of Egypt, and com-

---

to consume the land." Thomson, *The Land and the Book,* p. 448 ; *Domestic Life in Palestine,* pp. 178, 179. "This is one of the chief causes of the present poverty of the country."

[1] Stanley, *S. and P.* p. 151 ; Smith's *Dict.,* Article *Caves.*

[2] "The summer threshing-floors are in the open country, and on an elevated position, to catch the wind when winnowing the grain, and of course they would be altogether unsafe at such a time, while the vineyards are hid away in the wadies and out on the wooded hills, and thus adapted for concealment. Indeed, I myself have seen grain thus concealed in this same country, during the lawless days of civil war." Thomson, *The Land and the Book,* p. 448.

plained that He had now deserted them, nor was there
any hope of deliverance. Thereupon the Angel informed
him that *he* was the destined Saviour of his people, that
the Lord would be with him, and that he should *smite
the Midianites as one man* (Judg. vi. 16). Unable to believe that such a mission could be designed for himself,
Gideon requested a sign to assure him that the Speaker
was a messenger of Jehovah, and by direction of the
Angel made ready a kid, and cakes of unleavened
bread, and presented them under the oak. The Angel
then bade him lay the flesh and unleavened cakes upon
the rock and pour the broth over them, and when he
had done so touched them with a rod he bore in his
hand. Instantly there rose up fire from the rock, and
consumed the offering, in the midst of which the Angel
suddenly disappeared. The fact that he had thus been
permitted to converse face to face with Deity filled
Gideon with alarm, but the Lord reassured him, and he
built an altar there which he called Jehovah-Shalom,
or, the *Lord send Peace*, in memory of the salutation
of the Angel (Judg. vi. 24).

i. Thus solemnly called to be the Deliverer of his
countrymen, Gideon was first commissioned to testify
against the idolatrous practices which had caused the
present national degradation. The Lord appeared to
him in a dream, and bade him throw down an altar
which his father had erected in honour of Baal, and cut
down a grove he had set up, and then to build in an
orderly manner an altar to Jehovah on the rock where
his meat-offering had been accepted, and sacrifice
thereon his father's second bullock of seven years old.
With the assistance of his servants, Gideon during the
night-time executed this commission, and on the morrow
the townspeople were surprised to find that both altar
and grove had disappeared. Enquiry led to the detection of the offender, and Joash was bidden to bring

forth his son that he might be put to death for the sacrilege of which he had been guilty. But Joash replied with much irony that he was truly guilty of impiety who believed that Baal could not defend himself. *Will ye take upon yourselves,* said he, *to plead Baal's cause? let him plead for himself.* A new name, which Gideon henceforth bore, Jerub-Baal, or the *Tryer of Baal,* attested the national acquiescence in the wisdom of his father's reply (Judg. vi. 32).

ii. Tried and not found wanting in moral courage, Gideon was now directed to carry out the second part of his commission. Blowing a trumpet he first gathered around him his own clan of Abi-ezer, and then sending messengers throughout Manasseh, Asher, Zebulun, and Naphtali[1], invited the aid of these tribes against the common enemy. With characteristic caution, however, he requested a further sign from Jehovah before actually entering upon his arduous task. A double sign was vouchsafed to him. A fleece of wool, first dripping with dew while all the soil around was hot and dry, then dry while all the soil around was damp, convinced him that the Lord would indeed deliver Israel by his hand.

By this time upwards of 32,000 of his countrymen had gathered around him, and with this force he encamped on the slope of Gilboa, near the spring of Jezreel, henceforth known as the *Spring of* Harod or *Trembling,* overlooking the plain of Jezreel covered

---

[1] " It is worthy of remark that the men of Issachar are not mentioned, and we can from this point readily imagine the reason. The people of Issachar lived here on this great plain (Esdraelon), and were, of course, altogether surrounded by and at the mercy of the Midianites, as these villages of Sulan, Shûtta, Zer'in, &c., now are in the power of these Bedawîn. They therefore *could not* join the army of Gideon." Thomson, *The Land and the Book,* p. 449 ; Stanley's *Lectures,* p. 344.

with the tents of the Midianites. But the host was too
many and too great for God to give victory thereby. If
they were successful with their present numbers they
might vaunt that their own hand had saved them. Proclamation was, therefore, made that from the *Spring of
Trembling* all who were afraid to persevere in their
arduous enterprise might return to their homes. Of
this permission 22,000 at once availed themselves and
went their way. But another trial was to test the qualifications of the rest. By Divine command Gideon took
the remaining 10,000 of his forces to the spring, and
watched them as they asswaged their thirst. While all
the rest bowed down upon their knees, three hundred
*putting their hand to their mouth, lapped of the water
with their tongues as a dog lappeth* (Judg. vii. 5, 6).

These three hundred Gideon set by themselves, the
rest he sent away. Night now drew on, and with his
little band, like the same famous number at Thermopylæ, he was left alone on the brow of the steep mountain which overlooks the vale of Jezreel, where Midian
and Amalek and all the children of the east lay along
like locusts for multitude, their camels gaily caparisoned,
numerous as the sand on the seashore (Judg. vii. 12).
To confirm the faith of Gideon in this great crisis, God
now bade him, attended by Phurah his armourbearer,
drop down from the height where he was, and go to the
host of his enemy. Accordingly the two crept down
cautiously from rock to rock[1] in the still night to the
outskirts of the Midianitish tents, where Gideon overheard a man tell his fellow how he had dreamt a dream,
and lo ! a cake of common[1] *barley bread tumbled into
the host of Midian, and came unto a tent, and smote
it that it fell, and overturned it, that the tent lay
along.* To this recital the other replied, showing the

---

[1] Thomson, *The Land and the Book,* p. 449.

reputation Gideon had gained even amongst his foes, *This is nothing else save the sword of Gideon the son of Joash, a man of Israel: into his hands hath God delivered Midian, and all the host* (Judg. vii. 13, 14).

The Listener heard the dream and the interpretation, and straightway knew what he was to do. Returning up the mountain to his faithful three hun¬ dred, he divided them into three companies, and gave to every man a horn, an earthen pitcher, and a fire-brand or torch[1] (Judg. vii. 16, *margin*) to put therein. Then bidding them follow him, and do exactly as they saw him do, in the beginning of the middle watch he again stole down towards the outskirts of the tents of the Midianites, while the three companies following silently took their places every man round about the slumbering camp. Then Gideon and his company suddenly blew their horns, and at this signal 300 horns blew, 300 pitchers crashed, 300 torches blazed, and the always terrible war-cry of the Israelites, *The Sword of Jehovah and of Gideon*[2], rent the midnight air. In a moment the Midianites and Amalekites were roused, and thrown into inextricable confusion and alarm. Amidst the blazing of so many torches, the crashing of so many pitchers, and the blast of so many trumpets all on different sides, they imagined themselves attacked by an enormous force. Filled with uncontrollable terror,

[1] The *Zabit* or *Agha* of the police at Cairo carries with him at night "a torch which burns soon after it is lighted, without a flame, excepting when it is waved through the air, when it suddenly blazes forth: it therefore answers the same purpose as our dark lantern. *The burning end* is sometimes concealed in a small pot or jar, or covered with something else, where not required to give light." Lane's *Modern Egyptians*, I. ch. iv. ; Smith's *Bib. Dict.*

[2] For similar stratagems, see Liv. xxii. 16; Sall. *de Bell. Jug.* ch. 99.

they turned their swords against one another, and then
rushed with one accord down the steep descent towards
the Jordan eastward, to Beth-Shittah, *the House of the
Acacia,* and Abel-Meholah, *the Meadow of the Dance,*
hotly pursued not only by the three hundred, but
some of the forces of Naphtali, Asher, and Manasseh,
now convinced amidst the returning light of day
that Gideon had indeed achieved a great victory
(Judg. vii. 23).

The Midianites hoped to reach the fords of Beth-
barah immediately under the highlands of Ephraim.
But Gideon had already sent messengers thither, and
the Ephraimites were not slow to seize the fords and
intercept the flying foe, but not before a considerable
body had already crossed with the two kings, Zebah
and Zalmunna. But they were in time to capture the
two inferior chiefs, Oreb and Zeeb, the one at a sharp
cliff, the other at a winepress, where they slew them,
and cutting off their heads hurried after Gideon, who
with his three hundred was already on the other side of
the Jordan, *faint yet pursuing.* Annoyed, now the
victory was won, that they had not been summoned to
join in the battle, the haughty Ephraimites chode with
him, and manifested great resentment. With rare self-
restraint the victorious Leader asked what after all he
had done in comparison with them. Pointing to the
bloody heads of the princes they had slain, he enquired
whether the *grapes* Ephraim had already *gleaned* were
not better than the entire *vintage* of his little clan of
Abi-ezer. This soft answer turned away the wrath of
the offended tribe, and the chase was renewed (Judg.
viii. 1—3).

Two places on the track of the pursuit refused to
befriend Gideon. The men of Succoth[1] on the east of

___
[1] See p. 55.

Jordan, near the ford of the torrent Jabbok, and of
Penuel further up the mountains, declined to supply his
nearly exhausted troops with bread, and mocked at
him, when he said he was chasing the kings of Midian.
Halting only to threaten them with vengeance on his
return, he hurried on after the enemy. The victorious
Israelites had already slain 120,000, but 15,000 with
the two kings had reached Karkor, far from any towns
in the open desert-wastes east of the Jordan. Here
they thought themselves secure, but Gideon ascending
from the valley of the Jordan burst upon them, put
them to a complete rout, and at last captured the two
kings, Zebah and Zalmunna.

Then in triumph the conqueror returned down the
long defiles leading to the Jordan, followed by his cavalcade of captives mounted on their gaily decked camels
(Judg. viii. 21). As he passed Penuel he razed to the
ground its lofty watchtower, and slew the men of the
city. Reaching Succoth he obtained from a young man
of the place a description of its 77 head-men, and showed
them the captive kings, and then "with the thorny
branches of the neighbouring acacia-groves" he beat
them to death. Then pushing westwards he reached
his native Ophrah. There turning to the captive kings[1]
and at length revealing the secret of this long pursuit,
he enquired what manner of men they were whom they
had murdered on the green slopes of Tabor. *As thou
art, so were they*, was the reply, *each one resembled the
children of a king*. The remembrance of his brethren,
the sons of his own mother, filled the warrior with
wrath. Had they shown mercy to them, he would have
spared his prisoners, but now that could not be. Summoning, therefore, his firstborn Jether, he bade him
draw his sword and slay them. But the boy quailed

---

[1] See Article *Zebah*, in Smith's *Bib. Dict.*; Josephus, *Ant.*
v. 6, § 5.

before those mighty kings, and at their request Gideon
himself took the sword and slew them, and gathered up
the golden chains and crescent-shaped collars and trap-
pings of their camels (Judg. viii. 18—21).

The immediate effect upon the nation of this deliverance was greater than that of any other.   Not only
had the country quietness for 40 years (Judg. viii. 28),
not only did Gideon's Altar, and the Spring of Trembling, and the rock Oreb (or the *Raven's Crag*), and
the winepress of Zeeb remain standing monuments of
this great day, when God *made like a wheel*[1], and drove
over the uplands of Gilead *as stubble before the wind*
(Ps. lxxxiii. 13, 14), like clouds of chaff blown from the
summer threshing-floors, the proud people which had
said, *Let us take to ourselves the pastures of God in
possession* (Ps. lxxxiii. 12), but for the first time the
Israelites offered hereditary royal dignity to the great
conqueror.   *Rule thou over us,* said they, *both thou,
and thy son, and thy son's sons also.*   Gideon had the
rare self-control to decline the flattering request.   *I
will not rule over you,* said he, *neither shall my son
rule over you; Jehovah shall rule over you.*   One request only and a strange one did he make of the grateful tribes, that they would give him the golden ear-
rings and other ornaments they had taken from the

---

[1] Rendered in Isai. xvii. 13 a *"rolling* thing." Probably the allusion is to the wild artichoke which "in growing
throws out numerous branches of equal size and length in all
directions, forming a sort of sphere or globe, a foot or more
in diameter.   When ripe and dry in autumn, these branches
become light and dry as a feather, the parent stem breaks off
at the ground, and the wind carries these vegetable globes
whithersoever it pleaseth....The Arabs derive one of their
many forms of cursing from this plant ; 'May you be whirled
like the 'akkûb (wild artichoke), before the wind, until you
are caught in the thorns, or plunged into the sea.'"   Thomson, *Land and the Book*, p. 564.

conquered foe. Willingly into his cloak the people flung the ornaments, jewels, and chains from the camels' necks to the weight of 1700 shekels, and with these Gideon made an ephod, and put it in his native Ophrah, and all *Israel went a whoring after it,* which thing became a snare unto Gideon and to his house. Though he declined the royal dignity, he was addicted to a royal failing. He multiplied wives and begat 70 sons, and after living to a good old age descended in peace to the tomb of his father Joash in Ophrah of the Abi-ezrites[1] (Judg. viii. 32).

CHAPTER V

ABIMELECH AND JEPHTHAH.

JUDG. IX.--XII.　B. C. circ. 1249—1188.

AFTER the death of Gideon, Jehovah, whose minister he had been for the deliverance of the people, was again forgotten by the Israelites. Forgetting Gideon, forgetting Him who had sent Gideon, they made Baal-Berith, *Baal of the Covenant,* their god, and set up his sanctuary even in Shechem, though hallowed by the memories of the patriarchs[2] and the solemn ratification of the Law[3].

Meanwhile Gideon's 70 sons appear to have exercised authority over some portion of the country. One of them, whose name was ABIMELECH, the son of a slave a Canaanite native of Shechem, after consultation with his mother's brethren and her relatives (Judg. ix. 1), suggested that in place of the divided authority of his numerous brothers, he, *their bone and their flesh* (Judg. ix. 2), should be vested with the supreme authority.

---

[1] For subsequent mention of this deliverance, see 1 Sam. xii. 11; Ps. lxxxiii. 11; Isai. ix. 4, x. 26; Heb. xi. 32.
[2] See above, pp. 31, 55.　　　[3] See above, p. 209.

The spirit of clanship was strong. *He is our brother,* whispered the family to the Shechemites, who at length fell in with the scheme, and lent Abimelech seventy pieces of silver from the sanctuary of Baal-Berith.

With the money he hired a body of men, and going to his father's house at Ophrah, murdered all his brethren, save JOTHAM the youngest, who managed to escape. He was now left alone, and was solemnly anointed king by the men of Shechem, who thus formally signified their revolt from the Hebrew commonwealth. Tidings of what was going on reached the ears of Jotham. Emerging from his hiding-place, he stationed himself on one of the rocky inaccessible spurs of Mount Gerizim[1], and taking up his parable from the variegated foliage of the valley below and the neighbouring forest, bade the men of Shechem listen while he addressed to them the earliest Parable, that of the Bramble-King. *Once, he said, the Trees went forth to anoint a king over them. The Olive, the Vine, the Fig were each asked to accept the royal dignity, but each declined;*

[1] "Several lofty precipices of Gerizim literally overhang the city, any one of which would answer Jotham's purpose. Nor would it be difficult to be heard, as everybody knows who has listened to the *public crier* of villages on Lebanon. In the stillness of the evening, after the people have returned home from their distant fields, he ascends the mountain-side above the place, or to the roof of some prominent house, and then *lifts up his voice and cries* as Jotham did. Indeed, the people in these mountainous countries are able, from long practice, so to pitch their voices as to be heard distinctly at distances almost incredible. They talk with persons across enormous wadies, and give the most minute directions, which are perfectly understood; and in doing this they seem to speak very little louder than their usual tone of conversation. Jotham, therefore, might easily be heard by the greater part of the inhabitants of Shechem...The very trees which most abound at Nablous (Shechem) are the olive, the fig, the vine, and the bramble." Thomson, *The Land and the Book,* p. 474; Stanley's *Lectures,* p. 350; Tristram, p. 150.

the Olive could not leave his fatness, or the Fig-tree his sweetness, or the Vine the juice of his grapes. Recourse *was then had to the Bramble, which not only accepted the proffered honour, but bade the other trees put their trust in its shadow, and threatened, if they did not, that fire should come forth from it and devour even the cedars of Lebanon.* Jotham then reminded the Shechemites of the services his father had rendered to the nation, and rebuked them for their gross ingratitude to his family. If they thought they had done well in electing Abimelech, the Bramble-King, he bade them rejoice in him ; if not, he hoped a fire might come forth from the king, in whose shadow they had placed their trust, and destroy him and all who had joined in electing him. With these words the speaker fled.

In a short time his words were fulfilled. For three years Abimelech maintained his supremacy, residing himself at Arumah (Judg. ix. 41), not far from Shechem, while that place was entrusted to Zebul, his viceroy. During the joyous season of the vintage[1] (Judg. ix. 27) Gaal the son of Ebed, a leader of a body of freebooters tried to persuade the people of Shechem to transfer their allegiance from Abimelech, who was but half a kinsman, to the Hivite tribe of Hamor. Intelligence of this movement reached the ears of Zebul, who without delay sent word to Abimelech, bidding him levy his forces and surprise the plotters in the city. After a desperate battle Abimelech captured the place, put the entire population to the sword, and sowed the ruins of the city with salt (Judg. ix. 45). A remnant, however, of the insurgents took refuge in the temple of Baal-Berith. Thither Abimelech pursued them at the head of his followers, whom he commanded on their way to cut down boughs from the trees on the wooded emi-

[1] See Calendar, p. 155.

nence of Zalmon (Ps. lxviii. 14) close to the city. These he piled against the hold, set them on fire, and suffocated and burnt the refugees. From Shechem he repaired to Thebez[1] (*Túbas*) and speedily captured the town; but again the inhabitants took refuge in one of its strong towers, and there held out. Forcing his way up to it, Abimelech was about to repeat the stratagem he had found so successful at Shechem (Judg. ix. 52), when a woman flung a fragment of millstone at his head[2]. Unwilling to die thus ingloriously, he bade his armourbearer thrust him through with his sword, and so expired.

Other judges now succeeded, of whom TOLA, of the tribe of Issachar, governed Israel for a space of 23 years at Shamir in Mount Ephraim (Judg. x. 1, 2); he was succeeded by JAIR of Gilead, who during 22 years shared his almost regal honours with his thirty sons (Judg. x. 3, 4).

Invasion of the Ammonites; Jephthah.

But recent judgments had not the effect of restraining the people from apostasy. To the worship of Baal and Astarte they now added that of the gods of Syria, of Zidon, of Moab and Ammon, as also of the Philistines. The national punishment they thus drew down upon themselves came from two quarters. On the south-west and along the fertile borders of the Shephelah the Philistines rose and reduced a portion of the country to subjection, while the tribes on the east of Jordan fell a

---

[1] "Situated 13 Roman miles from Shechem, on the road to Scythopolis. There it still is; its name—*Tubâs*—hardly changed; the village on a rising ground to the left of the road, a thriving, compact, and strong-looking place, surrounded by immense woods of olives." See Robinson, *Bib. Res.* III. p. 305; Smith's *Bib. Dict.*, Article *Thebez*.

[2] See 2 Sam. xi. 21.

prey to the Ammonites, and for 18 years endured the humiliation of irksome oppression. Nor were they the only sufferers, for the Ammonites crossed the Jordan and carried on their ravages even in the territories of Judah, Benjamin, and Ephraim (Judg. x. 6—9). So terrible was the oppression they now endured, that at length the Israelites were roused to a deep repentance; finding it in vain to cry unto their false gods in the day of tribulation, they put them away, and besought Jehovah if only this once to stretch forth His hand and deliver them. *Grieved for the misery of Israel* (Judg. x. 16), the Lord raised up a deliverer in the person of JEPHTHAH, a base-born native of Gilead. Driven forth from his father's house by his legitimate sons, Jephthah had fled into the land of Tob, somewhere on the east of Gilead, where putting himself at the head of brave but lawless men, he lived the life of a freebooter, making incursions from time to time into the territories of neighbouring tribes, and living on the proceeds of the spoil (Judg. xi. 1—3).

Determined to throw off the Ammonitish yoke, the tribes on the east of Jordan now turned to Jephthah, and promised him the chieftaincy, if he would undertake to lead them against the enemy. Jephthah consented, and it was formally agreed that, in the event of success, he should retain the supreme command. His first step was to send an embassy to the Ammonites urging the right of the Israelites to the land of Gilead. This being unsuccessful, he prepared for open war, and traversing Gilead and Manasseh collected warriors from such places as acknowledged his authority. But before entering on the campaign, in imitation probably of heathen customs, and especially of the Ammonites (2 Kin. iii. 27), he solemnly vowed to offer as a burnt-offering to Jehovah whatever should first come forth from his house to meet him on his return from

battle. The engagement took place in the forests of
Gilead, and the Ammonites were utterly routed. Twenty
cities, from Aroer on the Arnon to Minnith and Abel
Keramim (*the Meadow of the Vineyards*), fell into the
hands of the conqueror (Judg. xi. 33).

But his rash and heathenish vow cast a deep shadow
on his triumphal return. As he drew near his home in
Mizpeh (*the Watch-tower*) of Gilead, his daughter and
only child came forth to meet him with timbrels and
with dances. When the father saw her he rent his
clothes, and with the utmost grief made known to her
his vow, from which he declared he could not go back.
But the noble maiden did not decline the awful sacrifice
demanded of her. All she requested was that for two
months she might be allowed to wander with her companions among the mountain-gorges of her native Gilead,
and bewail her virginity. At the expiration of this
period she returned to her father, and Jephthah without referring the matter to the High-priest, or remembering the strict commands of the law on this subject[1],
his spirit clouded with gloomy superstition, *did with
her according to his vow that he had vowed* (Judg. xi.
39). The memory of this awful sacrifice was kept up by
a yearly festival, lasting four days, during which the
daughters of Israel went up into the mountains of Gilead
to praise and lament the death of their heroic sister.

Jephthah, however, was not long suffered either to
enjoy his triumph, or lament the fatal vow which had
stained it. Like Gideon before him, he had to encounter
the complaints of the proud and jealous tribe of Ephraim for not summoning them to share the glories of
the late victory. In vindication of their absurd claims,
they even threatened to burn his house over his head,
and invaded the territory of the Gileadites, whom they

---

[1] Lev. xviii. 21; Deut. xii. 31.

taunted with being *fugitives of Ephraim among the Ephraimites and Manassites.* A second tribal war ensued, in which the men of Ephraim were thoroughly worsted. Rushing routed to the fords of the Jordan, they found them already in possession of Jephthah's forces, who allowed none to cross that failed to pronounce the word *Shibboleth*[1]. Upwards of 42,000 revealed their Ephraimite origin by substituting the simple *s* for *sh,* and were massacred. The supreme authority, for which he had covenanted, Jephthah only lived to enjoy for 6 years, when he died, and was buried in one of the cities of his native land (Judg. xii. 1—7).

After him other and obscurer judges rose to display the growing tendency towards hereditary monarchy. Thus IBZAN of Bethlehem in Zebulun judged, at least north-western Israel, for 7 years, and conferred a portion of his dignity on his 30 sons and 30 daughters; ELON of the same tribe ruled for 10 years; and after him ABDON, of Pirathon in the land of Ephraim, about 6 miles from Shechem, exercised the supremacy for 8 years, and was succeeded in a portion of his almost regal honours by his numerous children (Judg. xii. 8—14).

CHAPTER VI

INVASION FROM THE SOUTH-WEST.   SAMSON.

JUDG. XIII.—XVI.   B. C. 1161–1120.

MEANWHILE the Philistines[2] on the south-west had not only established themselves in the She-

---

[1] Signifying 1st *an ear of corn,* and 2ndly *a stream or flood.*

[2] The PHILISTINES, a race of "strangers," appear to have made three immigrations into the fertile south-western Lowland of Palestine, just as there were different immigrations of Saxons and Danes into England. (i) The *first* came from the

phelah, or Low Country, but now commenced that long
and deadly hostility to the Israelites, which lasted from
this time through the reigns of Saul and David, and
was not finally terminated till the time of Hezekiah
(2 Kings xviii. 8). Their oppressions naturally pressed
most heavily on the little tribe of Dan, already hard
pushed by the Amorites. From this tribe, then, the
Deliverer came. But unlike others who had been called
to the same office, he was specially set apart for it even
before his birth.

On the high hill of Zorah overlooking the fertile lowlands of Philistia lived a Danite named Manoah. To his
wife, who as yet had no child, it was announced by an
Angel that she was about to become the mother of a son,
whom she was to devote as a Nazarite[1] unto God from
his birth; no razor was ever to come upon his head;
wine and strong drink he was never to touch; and he
should *commence* the deliverance of Israel from the
Philistines (Judg. xiii. 5). These words were announced
to Manoah by his wife, and a second appearance of the

Casluhim (Gen. x. 14); (ii) the *second* and chief from the
Caphtorim (Deut ii. 23; Jer. xlvii. 4; Am. ix. 7), either from
some part of Egypt, or of Asia Minor and its adjacent
islands, probably Crete; (iii) the *third* from the *Cherethim*
(1 Sam. xxx. 14). The earliest immigrants having expelled
the *Avim* (Deut. ii. 23) had in the time of Abraham and
Isaac established a kingdom, the capital of which was at
Gerar, and possessed a standing army (Gen. xxi. 22; xxvi.
26). After the Exodus, Gerar disappears from history, and
the power of Philistia is concentrated in five new towns,
Gaza, Ashdod, Ashkelon, Gath, Ekron, each raised on its slight
eminence above the maritime plain, each possessing its dependent or "daughter towns" and villages (Josh. xv. 45—
47; 1 Ch. xviii. 1), and each having its own king or prince,
who all consulted and acted as one. "The third immigration
of the *Cherethim* would account for the sudden increase of
the strength of the Philistines at this period." See Pusey,
Comment. on Amos ix. 7.

[1] See above, pp. 158, 159.

Angel was vouchsafed to assure both parents of the certainty of these events, which was further confirmed, as in the case of Gideon, by the disappearance of the Angel in the flames which consumed the Danite's meat-offering (Judg. xiii. 20).

In process of time the child was born, and was named SAMSON, either *the sunlight*, or *the strong*. As he grew, he became distinguished for supernatural strength, and from time to time in Mahanah-Dan, the camp of the famous Six Hundred of his tribe[1], was moved to perform those exploits which made him the terror of the Philistines. His first action, however, when come to man's estate, did not display that hostility to the national enemy which his parents would naturally have expected. At Timnath, then in the occupation of the Philistines, he saw one of the daughters of the place, whom he was resolved to marry. Very unwillingly did his father and mother give their consent, and went down from Zorah with their wayward son "through wild rocky gorges" to the vineyards of Timnath, situated, as was often the case, far from the village to which they belonged, and amidst rough wadies and wild cliffs[2]. In one of these Samson encountered a young lion, and, though he had nothing in his hand, rent it *as he would have rent a kid*. Thinking little of the circumstance, he did not mention it to his father and mother, but went with them to Timnath, and talked with the woman, and she pleased him well. On his second descent through the same wild rocky pass, he turned aside to see the carcase of the lion, and discovered amongst the bones a swarm of bees. A portion of the honey he took himself, and gave a portion to his parents, saying nothing of his exploit, or the place whence he had ob-

---

[1] See above, p. 229.
[2] Thomson, *The Land and the Book*, p. 566.

tained the honey. The wedding festival was celebrated
at Timnath, and lasted several days, on one of which
the bridegroom put forth a riddle to his thirty Philistine
"companions," promising thirty sheets and thirty changes
of garments to any that guessed it, but demanding the
same of them if within the days of the feast they failed
to discover it. The young men accepted the challenge,
and Samson put forth his riddle, saying,

> *Out of the eater came forth meat,*
> *Out of the strong came forth sweetness.*

For three days the Philistine youths tried to unravel
it, and failed. Then they beset Samson's wife, and
threatened to burn her and her father's house, if she
did not ascertain for them the interpretation. During
the remaining days, therefore, she implored of Samson
with tears the revelation of the secret. At first he was
proof against her entreaties, but on the last day of the
feast he told her, and she revealed it to the thirty
Philistines, who came to him in the evening and said,

> *What is sweeter than honey?*
> *What is stronger than a lion?*

*If ye had not ploughed with my heifer, ye had not
found out my riddle* was the giant's brief reply, and
going down to Ashkelon, one of the five cities of the
lords of the Philistines, on the extreme southern edge
of the Mediterranean Sea, he slew thirty men and of the
spoil brought the stipulated reward.

Then in great wrath he returned to Zorah. But
when wheat-harvest came round, his passion for the
woman was somewhat rekindled, and he resolved to
present her with a kid, and now learnt from her father
for the first time, that, probably during his absence at
Ashkelon, thinking he utterly hated her, he had bestowed her upon another. Thereupon Samson, being enraged, resolved to wreak his vengeance on the Philistines, and catching, probably in pitfalls and snares, 300

foxes, he fastened them tail to tail with lighted fire-brands in the midst, and sent them into their cornfields, olive-yards, and vine-yards. Terrible was the mischief thus inflicted in a country, which even now, "in the summer months, is one sea of dead-ripe grain, dry as tinder[1]." At length the Philistines ascertained who was the author of this destructive conflagration, and went to the house of his late wife, and burnt her and her father to death. Thereupon Samson avenged himself by inflicting upon them a great slaughter, and went and took up his abode on the lofty cliff of Etam, probably not very far from Bethlehem. Thither the Philistines pursued him, and demanded his surrender of the men of Judah. So utterly lost to all feelings of honour, so degraded from its former high estate was this tribe, that 3000 men actually scaled the rocky cliff, and brought Samson bound with two new cords to his enemies. On his approach, the Philistines raised a mighty shout. But at the moment supernatural strength was given to the captive. He burst his bonds as though they had been cords of flax burnt in the fire, and seizing the jawbone of an ass, and aided probably by the now inspirited Israelites, slew a thousand of the Philistines. In memory of this exploit, he named the place Ramath-Lehi (*the casting away of the jawbone*). Sore athirst after his exertions, he feared that from sheer exhaustion he might fall once more into the hands of his foes, but from a hollow place in Lehi God caused water to issue, and his spirit reviving he called the spot En-hakkore (*the Spring of the crier*) (Judg. xv. 16—19).

Samson is next found at Gaza (*the strong*), which though allotted to and conquered by Judah (Josh. xv.

[1] Thomson, *The Land and the Book*, p. 552. "So great is the dread of fire in harvest-time, that the Arabs punish with death any one who sets fire to a wheat-field, even though done by accident." *Ibid.* p. 553.

47; Judg. i. 18) had fallen into the hands of the Philistines, who now encompassed the gate of the city, intending to capture him in the morning. But at midnight he arose, and taking the doors of the gate and the two posts, carried them, bar and all, to the top of the hill before Hebron. After this, he fell in love with Delilah, a Philistine courtesan, of the valley of Sorek, apparently near Gaza. This last amour led to his capture and death. For the enormous reward of 1100 pieces of silver from each lord, equivalent to 5500 shekels, the five lords of the Philistines persuaded her to undertake the task of discovering the secret of his great strength. Three times she importuned him to reveal the mystery, but he succeeded in putting her off with wiles. Green withes, new ropes, the binding of his seven clustering locks to the web, all these expedients were powerless to detain him prisoner, and he escaped with ease from the hands of the Philistines. The fourth time, however, she succeeded, and he told her all his heart, revealing the secret of his Nazarite vow. Accordingly, while he was asleep upon her knees, she caused the seven locks to be shaved off, and when he awoke the giant found that his strength had departed from him. The watching Philistines sprang into the chamber, took him, bored out his eyes, and brought him bound with brazen fetters to Gaza, where they made him grind in the prison-house (Judg. xvi. 21).

Then a day was fixed for a solemn festival in honour of Dagon, their national deity, half man and half fish[1], to whom the deliverance of the nation from their dreaded foe was ascribed. In the midst of the feast,

---

[1] "The five cities of the Philistines divided, as it were, their idolatry between them; Ashdod being the chief seat of the worship of *Dagon;* Ashkelon of *Derceto;* Ekron of *Baalzebub;* Gaza of the god *Marna* ('nature')." Pusey, *Comment. on Amos* i. 8.

Samson was brought in to make sport for his unfeeling captors. The temple, where the festival was held, situated probably on a sloping hill, was full of men and women, and even on the roof upwards of 3000 were packed together. The blinded giant was led in by a lad, and at his own request was suffered to feel the pillars on which the temple stood. Standing there, he prayed that his old strength might for this once be restored to him, and that he might be enabled to wreak a complete revenge on his unfeeling enemies. Taking hold of the pillars with both hands, and praying that he might die with the Philistines, he bowed himself with all his might, and the temple walls fell in, and crushed the lords of the Philistines and the assembled crowd. Samson's body was extricated from the ruins, and in sad procession was borne by his brethren and kinsmen " up the steep ascent to his native hills," and laid between Zorah and Eshtaol in the burial-place of Manoah his father (Judg. xvi. 31).

As Judge, Samson's supremacy had lasted twenty years. The words of the Angel to his parents had declared that *he should begin to deliver Israel out of the hand of the Philistines,* and in truth his work was only begun. Its completeness was marred chiefly by himself. " His acts were dictated mainly by caprice and the impulse of the moment; he frittered away the great powers which had been bestowed upon him, and forgot the Divine call which he had received. Still these incomplete results may in some measure be fairly ascribed to the character of his countrymen; they always permitted him to stand unaided and alone, and even surrendered him to the enemy[1]." The work that he *began* needed a very different man to *complete* it, the spirit of the people needed renewal, and an internal reformation was essential.

[1] Kurtz's *Sacred History,* p. 171.

Before recounting the means whereby this was brought about, the Sacred Narrative presents us with a little history, which strikingly illustrates the repose and peacefulness which characterized some of the calmer intervals in the disturbed period of the Judges. From Bethlehem-Judah there went forth during a season of famine[1] two Ephrathites of the place, ELIMELECH and NAOMI, with their sons MAHLON and CHILION, to seek a home across the Jordan in the land of Moab. Here Elimelech died, and his two sons married two of the daughters of Moab, ORPAH and RUTH.

After a period of about ten years his sons also died, and Naomi hearing that the famine had ceased in the land of Israel, prepared to return to her native town accompanied by her daughter-in-law Ruth, whom no entreaties could induce to remain amongst her own people. It was the beginning of barley-harvest[2] when they returned, and Ruth went to glean near Bethlehem in the fields of Boaz, a man of wealth and a kinsman of Elimelech. The appearance and the story of the beautiful stranger, which he learnt from the townspeople, attracted the attention of Boaz to the Moabitess, and he permitted her not only to glean in his fields, but to share with his labourers the provisions supplied them. By the advice of her mother-in-law, Ruth afterwards claimed kinship with the wealthy Boaz, and he was not slow to acknowledge it. A nearer kinsman, however, was first asked to discharge these duties, which included not only the redemption of the land that had belonged to Elimelech, but also the taking of Ruth in marriage *to raise up the name of the dead upon his inheritance* (Deut. xxv. 5—10). On his declining to perform the latter duty, Boaz redeemed the land in

---

[1] Some think during the judgeship of Ehud, others during that of Gideon. Kurtz, p. 164.

[2] See Calendar, p. 155.

the presence of ten elders of Bethlehem and the assembled people, and married Ruth, by whom he became
the father of Obed, the grandfather of King David[1].

A more pleasing picture of Hebrew country life can
hardly be imagined than the story of "the gleaner
Ruth," illustrating, as it does, "the friendly relations between the good Boaz and his reapers, the Jewish land-
system, the method of transferring property from one
person to another, the working of the Mosaic Law for
the relief of distressed and ruined families, but above
all handing down the unselfishness, the brave love, the
unshaken trustfulness of her, who though not of the
chosen Race was, like the Canaanitess Tamar (Gen.
xxxviii. 29; Matt. i. 3) and the Canaanitess Rahab (Matt.
i. 5), privileged to become the ancestress of David, and
so of "great David's greater Son" (Ruth iv. 18—22).

[1] For David's subsequent connection with Moab, see
below, p. 303.

BOOK VIII

FROM THE TIME OF SAMUEL TO THE ACCESSION OF DAVID.

CHAPTER I

ELI AND SAMUEL.

1 Sam. i.—iv. B. C. circ. 1171—1141.

DURING the twenty years that Samson judged
Israel, the High-priesthood, diverted for reasons
not revealed from the line of Eleazar to the younger
line of Ithamar (1 Chron. vi. 4—15; xxiv. 4), had been
filled by ELI, who henceforth appears to have discharged
the united duties of High-priest and Judge. The Tabernacle with the Ark was now at Shiloh, where a town
had rapidly grown up. Inside the gateway leading
up to it was a "seat" or "throne" (1 Sam. i. 9; iv. 13),
on which Eli used to sit, and thence survey the worshippers as they came up on high days to the Festivals.

Year by year, as he sat there, he would see amongst
the pilgrims coming up to the Feast of Tabernacles the
family of ELKANAH, a man of Ramathaim-Zophim[1] in

---

[1] The situation of Ramathaim = *double eminence*, is uncertain. "But the place long pointed out as Samuel's tomb,
and therefore the site of his birth, 1 Sam. xxv. 1, is the height,
most conspicuous of all in the neighbourhood of Jerusalem,
immediately above the town of Gibeon, known to the Cru-
saders as 'Montjoye,' being the spot from whence they first
saw Jerusalem, now called *Neby Samwil*, 'the Prophet Samuel.'" Smith's *Bib. Dict.*, Article *Ramah*, No. 2.

Mount Ephraim. Though a Levite in the line of Kohath (1 Chron. vi. 27—34), he affords one of the few instances of polygamy in the ranks of the lower orders. By his wife Peninnah he had several children ; by Hannah, his favourite wife, he had none, which was to her a source of much trouble, and brought down upon her many taunts from her rival. On one occasion, as Eli sat on his throne at the gate, he was led more particularly to notice one of this little family group. At the close of the sacrificial Feast, unable any longer to endure the mockery of her rival and her own bitterness of heart, Hannah remained long in silent prayer at the Sanctuary. The High-priest saw her lips move, but heard no sound of her voice, as she prayed. Thinking that she had indulged to excess at the feast, he rebuked her, and bade her put away her wine from her. Then Hannah told him of her secret grief, and the aged priest, convinced of his error, quickly made amends by bestowing upon her his blessing, and expressing a hope that the God of Israel might grant the petition she had preferred (1 Sam. i. 17).

The story of the wife of Manoah was, probably, not unknown to Hannah, and she too prayed that if the Lord would grant her a man-child, she would devote him as a Nazarite to His service all the days of his life. Her prayer was heard. Before the Feast of Tabernacles came round again, she had become the mother of a son, to whom she gave the appropriate name of Samuel *"the Asked* or *Heard of God."* When he was weaned, she brought him to Shiloh, with three bullocks, an ephah of flour, and a skin bottle of wine, and having poured forth her thankfulness in an inspired hymn, presented the boy to Eli, as the child for whom she had prayed, and whom she now wished to return to the Lord (1 Sam. ii. 1—11).

In striking contrast with the simplicity and innocence of the young child, who henceforth waited upon Eli, the two sons of that pontiff, HOPHNI and PHINEHAS were *sons of Belial, they knew not the Lord.* By their rapacity and lust they had filled all Israel with loathing and indignation, so that *men abhorred the offering of the Lord.* But Eli *restrained them not,* and, as years went on, their wickedness seemed only to increase in spite of his expostulations. It was a dark day in Israel, and their conduct gives us a terrible glimpse into the fallen condition of the chosen people (1 Sam. ii. 12—21).

Before long the first warning came to Eli. A *man of God* stood before him, and after reminding him of the high honour God had conferred upon him, when He chose him to be His priest, sternly rebuked him for honouring his sons above their Maker, and announced that instead of the office remaining in his family, its high functions should be transferred to another and more faithful line. And not only did he thus denounce distant punishment but an immediate and speedy pledge of it in the death on one day of both his sons (1 Sam. ii. 27—36).

But this warning produced no effect. Eli was old and greyheaded. However fitted he might have been once for the task of ruling his family, that day was gone by now. A second warning, therefore, of coming doom was now given him, not by the mouth of any stranger, but of the child, whom Hannah had left in the Tabernacle at Shiloh *a loan unto the Lord.* Clad in a white linen ephod, and the little mantle[1] reaching to the feet, which his mother brought him from year to year, his long flowing hair betokening his Nazarite vow, Samuel ministered before Eli. The degraded state of the priesthood in the hands of Hophni and Phinehas had made intimations of the Divine Will rare and precious in those days, *there was no open vision.* But the Lord found a way to intimate the coming doom of Eli's house.

[1] See Smith's *Bib. Dict.,* Article *Mantle.*

One night, when the aged priest had lain down to rest in one of the chambers hard by the Tabernacle, which was illumined only by the light of the seven-branched Golden Candlestick, in the early morning, before it was yet light, a Voice called Samuel and awoke him from his slumber. Thinking Eli had called him, he went to him, and enquired the cause. But Eli had not spoken, and bade him lie down again. He did so, and again the Voice pronounced his name. Once more he ran to the bed-side of the High-priest, who as before denied that he had called him, and told him to return to his bed. A third time the Voice pronounced his name, and then Eli perceived that the Lord had called the child, and bade him, if he heard it again, reply, *Speak, Lord, for thy servant heareth.* Samuel returned to his bed, and when the Voice called to him for the fourth time, answered as the aged priest had bidden him, and heard the purport of the mysterious call. *The Lord was about to do a thing in Israel, at which both the ears of him that heard it should tingle. Eli's sons had made themselves vile, and he had not restrained them. For this iniquity his house was now to be judged and neither sacrifice nor offering could make atonement; when the Lord began, He would also make an end.*

Until the sun was up, Samuel lay still, and forbore to tell Eli what he had heard. But the High-priest, whose conscience, doubtless, only too surely whispered what it was, bade him hide nothing from him. And then the old man, whose eyes were dim that he could not see, listened, while the child told him every whit. Death awaited his sons, beggary and desolation his family. *It is the Lord*, was his brief reply, *let Him do what seemeth Him good*, and in the course of time the warning was fulfilled. As Samuel grew, the Lord began to reveal Himself more and more to him. The influence of Eli, already weakened, now dwindled from day to day.

He "decreased" and Samuel "increased," and the Lord
was with him, and *let none of his words fall to the
ground,* so that all Israel, from Dan even to Beersheba,
knew that he was established to be a Prophet, a revealer
of the Divine Will (1 Sam. iii. 19—21).

Meanwhile the strength of the Philistines had recovered from the wounds it had received from the
champion of Dan. Advancing their forces to Aphek,
no great distance from the fortress of Jebus, they attacked the Israelites, and inflicted on them a loss of
4,000 men. Alarmed at this reverse, the Israelites resolved to fetch the Ark and take it into battle, that
it might save them out of the hands of their enemies.
The sacred symbol was thereupon removed from the
curtains that enclosed it, and the two sons of Eli accompanied it to the field. *A great shout, so that the earth
rang again,* greeted its arrival in the Israelite camp,
and the Philistines alarmed at the proximity of the
*mighty Gods, that smote the Egyptians with all the
plagues,* resolved to sell their lives dear, rather than
become subject to their enemies. Again, therefore, the
battle was joined, and Israel sustained a still more disastrous defeat. Upwards of 30,000 were slain, amongst
whom were Eli's sons, and worse than all, the *Ark of
God was taken* (1 Sam. iv. 11).

On his elevated "seat" by the wayside Eli sat to receive any tidings from the battle-field, his heart trembling for the sacred Symbol of which he was the guar-
dian. As the day closed, a young man of the tribe of
Benjamin came running into the town of Shiloh. His
clothes were rent, his hair sprinkled with dust. A wail
of lamentation arose from the people, who no sooner saw
him thus attired, than they knew how the day had gone.
Eli heard the noise of the tumult, and enquired the
cause. *I am he that came out of the army, and I fled
to-day out of the army,* said the young man. *And what*

is there done, my son? enquired the pontiff. *Israel is fled before the Philistines,* was the reply, *and there hath been also a great slaughter among the people— and thy two sons, also, Hophni and Phinehas are dead—and the Ark of God is taken.* No sooner did the last part of his terrible tidings fall from his mouth, than the aged priest fell *from his seat backwards, and his neck brake, and he died.* Ninety-eight summers had passed over his head, and forty years he had judged Israel, and now his doom was come. But still another death was to mark that dreadful day. The wife of Phinehas was near to be delivered of her second child. The news reached her that her husband and her father-in-law were dead, that Israel had been defeated, that the Ark had been taken. She bowed her head, the pangs of childbirth came upon her, a son was born, and the women that stood by tried to cheer her fainting spirits. But in vain. *The Ark of God was taken,* that was all her mind could realize. With her last breath she gave the child a name that should be a memorial of that fearful day. *Call him* Ichabod, she said, *The glory is departed from Israel* [1] (1 Sam. iv. 12—22).

CHAPTER II

SAMUEL'S JUDGESHIP.

1 Sam. v.—viii. B. C. 1141—1095.

MEANWHILE the Ark was carried by the Philistines in triumph to Ashdod[2], one of their five confederate cities, and placed in the Temple of Dagon. But

---

[1] According to some, it was now that Shiloh was destroyed. See Ps. lxxviii. 60 sq., and Jer. vii. 12.

[2] "Ashdod, as well as Ekron, have their name from their strength ; Ashdod = *the mighty,* like Valentia ; Ekron = *the firm-rooted.*" Pusey, *Comment. on Amos* i. 8.

there its sanctity was remarkably vindicated, for on the morrow that idol was found lying on its face upon the ground. In vain did its votaries set it up in its place again. The next day saw it a second time laid prostrate, and not only fallen, but broken, without head or hands. Moreover while a plague of mice destroyed their crops, "emerods," *i.e.* hemorrhoids or piles, tormented their bodies. In great consternation they, thereupon, removed the Ark to Gath, but there, too, the same plague broke out, and when they were on the point of removing it to Ekron, the inhabitants of that city interfered, and declared they would not admit it within their walls.

The advice of the priests and diviners was then asked, and they suggested that the sacred Coffer should be placed in a new cart drawn by two milch kine, which had never been yoked, and with a trespass-offering of five golden mice and five golden emerods be sent back to the Israelites. If the kine of their own accord took the road to Beth-shemesh, (*house of the Sun*)[1], under the hills of Dan, and close to the Philistine lowlands, then it would be certain that their misfortunes were due to the hostility of the Gods of the Israelites, otherwise it might be concluded that some chance had smitten them.

The plan was adopted. The Ark was placed in the new cart, together with the coffer containing the trespass-offerings, and the kine took the high-road from Ekron to Beth-shemesh, without turning to the right hand or the left. It was the time of wheat-harvest, and the people of the town were busy gathering in their corn, when lifting up their eyes they with joy beheld the Ark, which they had not seen for seven months (1 Sam. vi. 1). The kine, meanwhile, stopped not till they

[1] A name which suggests an early worship of the Sun there. In Josh. xix. 41, it is called *Ir-shemesh*. It is now called *'Ain es-Shems*, about 2 miles from the great Philistine plain, and 7 from Ekron. Thomson, *Land and Book*, p. 535.

had reached the field of Joshua, an inhabitant of the place, where there was a great stone. Beth-shemesh being a suburb-city, and allotted to the priests (Josh. xxi. 16 ; 1 Chr. vi. 59), the Levites residing there took down the Ark and the coffer, placed them on the great stone, then clave the wood of the cart, and offered up the kine as a burnt-offering to Jehovah, at the close of which ceremony, the five lords of the Philistines, who had joined the procession, returned to their own country (1 Sam. vi. 10—16).

But even this joyous day was not to pass by without a great calamity. Not content with offering sacrifices, the people of Beth-shemesh approached the Ark, and though even the priests were not allowed to touch it, removed the lid, to do which some force must have been used, and looked into it, for which profanity a considerable number were stricken with instant death. Messengers were, therefore, dispatched to Kirjath-jearim (*the fields of the wood*, see Ps. cxxxii. 6), and thither through the hills the Ark was sent, and placed in the house of the Levite Abinadab, whose son Eleazar was consecrated to keep it, and there it remained until the time of David (1 Sam. vii. 1).

Meanwhile Samuel, of whom we have not heard since he denounced the doom of the house of Ithamar, was growing up an acknowledged Prophet of the Lord. In this sad crisis of the nation's history he now came forward and convening an assembly at Mizpeh, probably the *Watch-tower* of Benjamin, solemnly expostulated with the Israelites on their idolatrous practices. With fasting and public confession they acknowledged the righteousness of the late judgments. Water was poured upon the ground, and the people entered into a covenant to abandon the worship of Baal and Ashtaroth. From this day Samuel's career as Judge began, and was inaugurated by a great victory over the Philistines, who hearing that the Israelites were recovering from their former depression, once more gathered together at Mizpeh, prepared to give them battle. At this crisis, Samuel taking a lamb offered it as a whole burnt-offering for the nation's sins, and was thus piously employed when the Philistines made their onslaught. But at this moment a terrific thunder-storm burst forth, accompanied, according to Josephus, by an earthquake. Seized with a sudden panic, the Philistines fled in disorder, and were pursued with great slaughter by the victorious Israelites as far as Beth-car (*the house of lambs*), a height to the west of Mizpeh. On the very spot, where twenty years before the Philistines had gained their most signal triumph, Samuel now set up a huge stone to commemorate his victory, and named it Ebenezer, *the Stone of Help* (1 Sam. vii. 12).

The subsequent effects of this success were still more apparent. Not only did the Philistines receive a decided check, but the Amorites also, the scourge of the little tribe of Dan, made peace with Israel, and all the cities in the Philistine territory, which had been taken from the Israelites, from Ekron to Gath, were restored. Samuel's office as Judge was now confirmed. Ramah, his birth-place, was his residence, and here he erected an altar to the Lord, and thence from year to year went forth in solemn circuit to the old sanctuaries, Bethel, Gilgal, and Mizpeh, combining with the duties of a Judge the functions also of a Seer or Prophet, and with all the weight of an Oracle advising in any of the troubles of national or domestic life (1 Sam. ix. 11, 18, 19). As years passed on, and he waxed old, his sons JOEL and ABIAH, like those of Jair and Abdon before him, shared a portion of his judicial functions, and administered justice in the more southerly portions of the country. But they did not walk in their father's footsteps. He who, when a child, had denounced the terrible

doom on Eli for the wickedness of his sons, lived to see
his own sons turning aside after lucre, exacting excessive usury, and perverting judgment (1 Sam. viii. 3).

A new and more advanced period in the history of
the nation was at hand, and the supremacy of the
Judges was about to close. Samuel, who came like
Numa after Romulus, did not fail to prepare the people
for the new epoch. At Ramah, at Bethel, at Mizpeh, at
Gilgal[1] he gathered together *Schools of the Prophets,*
and was the great reformer of the prophetical order, a
work of such importance that he is even classed with
Moses, the great Lawgiver of the nation. (Comp. Ps.
xcix. 6; Acts iii. 24; xiii. 20.) The title, indeed, of "prophet" has occurred already more than once, and is applied to Abraham (Gen. xx. 7), to Moses (Deut. xviii.
15—18), to Aaron (Ex. vii. 1), to Miriam (Ex. xv. 20), to
the seventy elders (Num. xi. 24—30), to Deborah[2] (Judg.
iv. 4). But these were isolated cases. It was the work
of Samuel to give permanence and effectiveness to the
prophetical functions.

Promising youths were gathered by him into Schools
or Colleges of Prophets, where they lived together
in a society or community, under a head or leading prophet, whom they called their *Father* (Comp. 1 Sam. x.
12; xix. 20), or *Master* (2 K. ii. 3), while they were
termed his *sons.* Here they employed themselves in
studying the Law of Moses; practised the composition
of sacred poetry; and became skilled in sacred music,
the psaltery, harp, tabret, pipe, and cymbals (1 Sam. x.
5; 2 K. iii. 15; 1 Ch. xxv. 1, 6). They also preserved
and copied historical records, and "gathered up the
traditions of their own and former times." Their call-

---

[1] For subsequent notices of such schools at Bethel and
Jericho see 2 Kings ii. 3, 5; at Gilgal, iv. 38; vi. 1; on Mount
Carmel, 1 Kings xviii. 30—42; 2 Kings ii. 25; iv. 25.
[2] See also Judg. vi. 8; 1 Sam. ii. 27.

ing was not merely, sometimes not at all, to predict future events. They were to be forth-speakers for God, to commune with God, to speak of God, to teach His truth, to declare His will, and that not only in words, but sometimes in action. Studying the Law of Moses, and the records of God's past dealings with their nation, they were to see the earnest of His presence for rebuke or consolation in the present. Their vocation required of them to preach morality and spiritual religion, to denounce oppression and covetousness, injustice and profligacy, cruelty and idolatry. And while called to reveal God's will in each successive crisis of the nation's history, they were also specially raised up to fix the eye of their countrymen on the future, to keep alive the belief in God's promises of Redemption, and to foretell the incarnation of Him, in whom all nations were to be blessed. If they often typified Him, whose appearance they announced and whose Spirit dwelt in them, in His humiliation, being despised and rejected by the generation in which they lived, yet from time to time they typified Him also in His exaltation, for the Lord, whose messengers they were, stood by them, frequently confirmed their word by miracles, and punished those who injured them[1].

The subsequent position of the Prophetical order at momentous periods of the national history is strikingly illustrated by the conduct of its Reformer and Organizer now. The misconduct of Samuel's sons produced dissatisfaction and a cry for change. Samuel himself was stricken in age. He had been a man of peace. One military success and one only had distinguished his Judgeship. On the west the ever-restless Philistines gave signs of recovery from their late defeat (1 Sam. x. 5), while beyond the Jordan Nahash the Ammonite threatened the cities of the tribes of Reuben, Gad, and Manasseh (1 Sam. xii. 12) There was no known general in Is-

[1] See Kurtz's *Sacred History*, p. 176.

rael qualified by his position or powers to take the command of the nation's armies, and lead them to battle. The fixed form of kingly government, which the people saw enjoyed by all the nations around, which they had themselves partially adopted under Gideon and Abimelech, under Jair and Abdon, and to which events appeared to have been rapidly tending, was not yet realized.

At this juncture, then, the elders and accredited heads of the nation repaired to Ramah, and on the ground of Samuel's advanced age, the misconduct of his sons, and, as we gather from an incidental remark of Samuel himself afterwards, an apprehended invasion by the Ammonites, they requested that the form of government might be changed, that a king might rule over them, like the nations round about (1 Sam. viii. 5).

This demand was a shock to Samuel's feelings, and *the thing displeased him.* He knew well the abuses such a form of government was too likely to entail. But he did not reject the petition of the nation. He was a true mediator between the old order that was changing and the new order, to which it was destined to give place. He prayed to the Lord for advice and direction in this great crisis, and his prayer was heard. Though he had been rightly displeased with the people's request, though they had done worse than rejecting him and had rejected their invisible Ruler, he was directed to hearken to their voice, but he was not to leave them without warning. He was to *shew them the manner of the king that should reign over them* (1 Sam. viii. 9).

Accordingly Samuel convened an assembly, and faithfully described the Oriental court and ceremonial, which the election of a king would inevitably entail ; how he would at his own pleasure take their sons and appoint them to command his chariots and his horses, would set them to ear his ground and reap his harvest, and fashion his chariots and instruments of war ; how he would take their daughters to be his confectioners, his cooks, and his bakers ; how their property would cease to be their own, and their fields, their oliveyards and vineyards, their flocks and herds, their menservants and maidservants would be required to be at his disposal. Under this despotism he warned them that a day would come when they would cry unto the Lord, but He would not hear them (1 Sam. viii. 10—18).

His words, however, fell on unheeding ears. The pomp and ceremonial of a court had too many attractions for the nation ; without a king to judge them and fight their battles, they affected to feel isolated and degraded in the eyes of neighbouring peoples, and a king they were resolved to have. This answer of the elders Samuel carried back to the Lord, who again bade him hearken to their voice, and promised the fulfilment of their wishes, with which assurance they were dismissed to their several cities [1] (1 Sam. viii. 22).

CHAPTER III

ELECTION OF THE FIRST KING.

1 Sam. ix. B. C. 1095.

THE elders of Israel had not long to wait for the king they so earnestly desired. Shortly after Samuel's return to Ramah he received Divine intimation

[1] It is to be remembered that God had promised to Abraham that *kings* should come from him (Gen. xvii. 6) ; Jacob had prophesied that the *Sceptre* should not depart from Judah till Shiloh came (Gen. xlix. 10); and Moses had distinctly anticipated, nay, provided for the election of a king by laying down specific directions concerning the kingdom (Deut. xvii. 14—20). The elders, therefore, of Israel might well have inferred that it was the Divine intention ultimately to give the nation a monarchical constitution, and consequently that it was their duty patiently to await the development of the Divine counsels. See Kurtz's *Sacred History,* p. 177.

that on the morrow one would be sent him, whom he was to anoint to be *captain over the Lord's people.* Accordingly the next day, as he was on his way to the high place to give his benediction at a sacrificial feast, he met two wayfaring men. One was a man of Benjamin, Saul the son of Kish, of a noble and handsome mien and gigantic stature, from his shoulders and upward higher than any of the people ; the other was his servant. In quest of the asses of Saul's father, which had strayed, the two had been traversing without success the central region of Palestine, and now guided by certain maidens of Ramah, whom they had met at the entrance of the place going out to draw water, they had resolved to ask the advice of Samuel.

The Prophet had already noticed the tall handsome stranger, and as he drew near the Divine Voice assured him that he was the destined Ruler of His people (1 Sam. ix. 15, 16). When, therefore, Saul enquired for the Seer's house, Samuel not only declared that he was the person he sought, but revealed his mysterious acquaintance with the secret of his three days' journey, and bade him lay aside all further anxiety, for the asses were found. Then, turning to Saul, he added in yet more mysterious words, *On whom is the desire of Israel? Is it not on thee, and on all thy father's house?* Marvelling at the import of this significant question addressed to one who belonged to *the smallest of the tribes of Israel,* and whose family was *the least of all the families of Benjamin* (1 Sam. ix. 21), Saul followed the Prophet to the high place, where with his servant he was made to sit in the chiefest place among the thirty guests assembled at the sacrificial feast, and to partake of a special portion which had been reserved for him.

Thence he returned to the town, and in the evening held further conversation with Samuel on the house-top of his dwelling. Next morning at daybreak Samuel roused his guest, and accompanied him some little, way to the end of the town. There the servant was bidden to pass on, and the two being left alone the Prophet taking a phial of oil poured it on Saul's head, and kissed him, and assured him of his election to be the first King of Israel. To this assurance he added prophetic intimations of incidents which would occur on Saul's return homewards, and which could not fail still further to confirm him in the conviction that his sudden elevation was indeed of the Lord. Two men would meet him at Rachel's sepulchre, and inform him that the asses were found, and that his father's anxieties now centred on himself; at the "plain," or rather the "oak" of Tabor (1 Sam. x. 3) he would meet three men going to Bethel carrying gifts of kids, bread, and a skin bottle of wine; they would salute him, and offer him two loaves of bread, which he was to receive at their hand; then, thirdly, on reaching *the hill of God*, probably Gibeah, where the Philistines had posted a garrison, he would meet a company of the prophets coming down from the high place with psaltery, tabret, pipe, and harp, whose inspired strains would so affect him that he would join himself to them, and be turned into another man. After the fulfilment of these three signs, he was to go to Gilgal, and there tarry seven days till Samuel's arrival to offer sacrifices, and tell him what he should do (1 Sam. x. 8). Then the two men parted, each of the three signs came to pass, and God gave the son of Kish *another heart*. Convinced of his call to inaugurate the kingly period of Israel's history, his soul rose to the greatness of the occasion; the strains of the prophetic choir so wrought upon his spirit that he felt inspired to join them, and his appearance in their society became the occasion of a well-known proverb, *Is Saul also among the prophets?* (1 Sam. x. 12).

Meanwhile Samuel convened all the people to Mizpeh

of Benjamin, and after again rebuking them for their want of faith in thus hastily seeking a change of government, bade them present themselves before the Lord by their tribes and by their thousands, in order that the sacred lot might decide the election of the king. In solemn order the tribes passed before him, and the lot fell upon that of Benjamin. Then the same ceremony was successively repeated with the clans, the families, the individuals, and in a manner that none could dispute, it was indicated that Saul the son of Kish was the object of the Divine choice. But when search was made for him, he was not to be found. Still unwilling to accept the arduous duties of the kingdom, he had concealed himself in the circle of baggage round the encampment at Mizpeh. The search was renewed, and he was brought forth from his hiding-place. As he advanced into the midst his exalted stature struck the spectators with admiration, and a universal shout of *Long live the King* betokened the nation's acceptance of its new head (1 Sam. x. 24).

Left to themselves, the Israelites would, doubtless, have stood committed to the new form of government, without pausing to insist on any conditions from their Ruler, well content if he proved as absolute and irresponsible as those of the nations round about. But the far-seeing Samuel was wiser than they. Well knowing the bearing of the transactions of that day on the nation's future, he not only expounded to the people the manner of the kingdom as set forth by their great Lawgiver in the Book of Deuteronomy (xvii. 14—20), but for the sake of greater security committed the regulations thus accepted to writing, and laid them up in safe keeping before the Lord, and thus, "under Divine sanction, and amidst the despotisms of the East, arose the earliest example of a constitutional monarchy[1]."

[1] According to the law as laid down in the above quota-

This ceremony concluded, the people returned to their homes, and Saul retired to Gibeah. Though his elevation had been thus formally approved, there were not wanting those who, on the score, probably, of the obscurity of his tribe, and the fact that his capacities were as yet unknown, expressed much dissatisfaction at his promotion, questioned his ability to rule them, and brought him none of the usual presents (1 Sam. x. 27). With rare self-control, however, he held his peace, and in a short time was enabled to justify the confidence that had been reposed in him.

While living in retirement at Gibeah, he received intelligence which roused all his martial ardour, and for the first time revealed his talents as a military leader. The Ammonites, recovered from the defeat they had sustained from Jephthah, had under the leadership of their king NAHASH laid siege to Jabesh-gilead (See Judg. xxi. 8), the inhabitants of which place in their terror invited the heathen king to make a covenant with them, and agreed to serve him. This, with characteristic haughtiness he declined, except on the condition that he might put out their right eyes, and thus render them unfit for further military service. In this strait, the elders of the place requested seven days' respite,

tion from Deuteronomy, (i) The nomination of any Israelite king rested with Jehovah, whose Will would be made known through the High-priest, or the voice of a Prophet, or the sacred lot, a provision which could not fail to remind him that he was not an irresponsible autocrat, but the representative and viceroy of Jehovah: (ii) The monarch must be a native Israelite, not a foreigner, or even a proselyte: (iii) On his accession he must transcribe a copy of the Law, that he might know it and keep its Statutes: (iv) He was forbidden to maintain any large body of cavalry with a view to aggressive warfare: (v) He was to eschew the usual accompaniment of Oriental despotism, a numerous *Harem*, and the excessive accumulation of gold and silver, which could only be acquired by oppressive exactions from his subjects. Jahn's *Heb. Comm.* 64, 65.

and meanwhile sent messengers to their brethren imploring assistance. Saul was driving his herd homewards from the field, when the sound of wild lamentation in his native town revealed the danger which threatened the friendly[1] town of Jabesh-gilead. Immediately *the Spirit of the Lord came upon him* (1 Sam. xi. 6), filling him with courage and resolution for the emergency. Taking a yoke of oxen, he hewed them in pieces, and sent this war-token throughout all the tribes, summoning them under pain of eternal disgrace to rally round himself and Samuel and hasten to the rescue of their brethren. He then bade the messengers return to Jabesh-gilead with the assurance of succour, *before the sun was hot on the morrow.* His determined spirit quickly communicated itself to others, and 300,000 from Israel, and 30,000 from Judah gathered round him and the Prophet. Bezek, a place apparently within a day's march of Jabesh, was appointed their headquarters, and thence dividing his forces into three companies Saul executed a swift night-march, and burst upon the Ammonites in the morning watch, who panic-stricken by this unexpected onslaught were defeated with enormous loss, *so that not two of them were left together* (1 Sam. xi. 11).

This signal success had an instantaneous effect upon the people. The Israelites hailed Saul as the deliverer of their country, and even proposed to put to death those who had not at first acknowledged him as king. With continued self-command, however, he calmed their zeal, and declined to stain with innocent blood the memory of a day, on which, as he said with becoming modesty, *not he but Jehovah had wrought salvation in Israel.* At this juncture, the new ruler having been tried and not found wanting, Samuel suggested that the people should once more repair to Gilgal, and there

[1] See above, p. 232.

renew the kingdom. Accordingly after the sacrifice of
peace-offerings and amidst great rejoicings Saul was
solemnly inaugurated in his regal functions, while Samuel embraced the opportunity afforded by so large a
gathering to bid farewell to the people he had ruled so
prudently with all his power (1 Sam. xii.). *He had
hearkened*, he said, *to their voice; he had made a
king over them. For himself, he was old and grey-
headed, he had walked before them from his childhood
unto that day. Let them now testify if they had ought
against him. Had he defrauded any? Had he oppressed any? Had he taken any bribe to blind his
eyes? If so, he would make ample restoration.* With
one voice the whole people bore witness to the integrity
and uprightness of his public life. Then, like Moses and
Joshua, he gave them his parting counsels, and after
exhorting them by the memory of past mercies and past
deliverances to cleave fast to the Lord, and not forsake
His commandments, called on the Lord Himself to
ratify his words by an outward and visible sign. It was
the season of wheat-harvest[1], when thunder and rain
seldom or never occurred. But at the word of Samuel,
the sky became black with clouds, the thunder rolled
and the rain fell, bearing witness to the solemnity of the
Prophet's warnings; who having thus bidden farewell
to the people, henceforth retired from any share in the
government, which now devolved on Saul alone.

CHAPTER IV

THE BATTLE OF MICHMASH.

1 SAM. XIII. XIV.   B. C. 1093—1087.

IN dismissing Saul from Ramah after their first interview, Samuel, it will be remembered, had told him
that he would pass *a garrison of the Philistines* (1 Sam.

[1] See Calendar, p. 155.

x. 5 ; xiii. 3)   Recovering from their defeat at Ebenezer
this people had again renewed their old hostilities, and
pitched in the heart of the mountains of Benjamin.
Two years after his accession (1 Sam. xiii. 1), Saul resolved to throw off a yoke which pressed so severely on
the neighbourhood of his native place. Gathering round
him a small standing army of 3,000 men, he placed 1,000
under the command of his valiant son Jonathan at
Geba[1], while he himself with 2,000 took up a position at
Michmash (*Mŭkhmas*) about 7 miles north of Jerusalem,
and along the ridge of intervening heights in the direction of Bethel. Either at or close to Jonathan's position
was posted a garrison of the Philistines. For some time
the rival forces stood watching one another, and at
length Jonathan in a fit of youthful ardour fell upon the
garrison, and put it to flight.

Tidings of this event quickly reached the Philistines
in their rich southern plains, who forthwith swarmed with
a vast force up through the passes of Benjamin, while
Saul retired to Gilgal, and there summoned a general
gathering of the nation. But in face of the enormous
masses of their foes, the Israelites, seized with a sudden
panic, as in the days of Gideon (Judg. vi. 2), fled for
refuge to the natural hiding-places of the country, to
the dens, the inaccessible fastnesses, and the caves with
which it abounded, while some even crossed the Jordan
into the territory of Gad and Gilead (1 Sam. xiii. 7).

The Philistines now in their turn occupied Michmash, and their oppression of the Israelites was most
grievous. A regular disarmament was carried out, so
that none of the Hebrews had sword or spear save the
king and his son, and their immediate retainers; nay,
the very smiths were removed, and the Hebrews were
constrained to go down to their enemies to get their

[1] Now Jeb'a, see 1 Sam. xiii. 16 (*margin*); Robinson, *Bib.
Res.* I. 441, *n.*; Porter's *Handbook*, p. 214.

agricultural implements sharpened. In this terrible crisis Saul sent messages from Gilgal to Samuel at Ramah, who promised within seven days to join the king and celebrate solemn sacrifices, preparatory, probably, to some concerted plan of action. But the days passed away, and Samuel came not. The Philistines were collecting in constantly increasing numbers at Michmash, and the terrified Israelites dropped off more and more, leaving their king with barely 600 followers. The present posture of affairs imperatively demanded prudence and caution, and from Samuel the king would, doubtless, have learnt the Divine will, and He, who had enabled Gideon with only 300 men to conquer even more numerous foes, would have opened up some mode of deliverance. But Samuel came not, and Saul, unable to restrain his impatience, resolved to offer the sacrifices himself. He had scarcely done so when the Prophet arrived and sternly rebuked him for his impetuous zeal. *Thou hast done foolishly,* said he, *thou hast not kept the commandment of the Lord thy God,* and he proceeded to intimate that the kingdom, which might have been established in his family, would not continue, but would be transferred to another (1 Sam. xiii. 11—14).

Meanwhile the Philistines continued their oppressive and tyrannical exactions. Roving bands from their camp went forth in three directions[1], and committed disastrous depredations, while from the heights, where they were encamped, Saul and Jonathan, at the head of their little band, looked down upon a ravaged and

---

[1] "East, and west, and north, through the three valleys which radiate from the uplands of Michmash—to Ophrah on the north, through the pass of Beth-horon on the west, and down the ravine of the hyenas, 'toward the wilderness of the Jordan on the East.'" Stanley's *S. and P.* 204; Robinson, *Bib. Res.* I. 441.

terror-stricken country, unable and afraid to lift a hand
against its oppressors. At length Jonathan resolved
to strike another blow. Between the Israelite position
at Geba and the Philistine garrison at Michmash was
a distance of about three miles, part of which consisted
of a deep gorge, running between two sharp jagged
rocks, the one called Bozez (*Shining*), probably from
the white chalky cliffs, the other Seneh (*the Thorn* or
Acacia), so called probably from some solitary acacia
on its summit. Above this gorge[1] was the Philistine
garrison. Without informing his father, or communicating his design to any one, except the young man his
armour-bearer, Jonathan resolved to ascend the steep
sides of the ravine, and then to take the conduct of
the enemy as an omen for further operations. If the
Philistines came forth and threatened an attack, they
would remain in the valley; if they challenged them
to advance, they would take this as an augury of success, and press on. Upon their hands and feet, then,
the two climbed up, and at length were detected by
the Philistines. *Behold,* they cried in derision, *the
Hebrews come forth out of the holes, where they have
hid themselves. Come up and we will shew you a thing.*
The omen was favourable, and the two pressed on.

Strong as a lion, and swift as an eagle (2 Sam.
i. 23), Jonathan no sooner reached the summit than
he rushed upon his unexpecting foes, and aided by his
armour-bearer, slew at the first onset upwards of twenty

---

[1] The deep gorge of the Wâdy-Suweinît, or Harith.
"Immediately on leaving Jeb'a we descend by a rugged, zigzag track, apparently intended only for goats, into
Wâdy-es-Suweinît, here tolerably wide, though deep and
rocky. A few hundred yards to the right it contracts to a
narrow ravine, shut in by high, almost perpendicular cliffs,
above which on each side the ground is tolerably level. This
is doubtless the scene of Jonathan's adventure." Porter's
Handbook, I. 215; Robinson, I. 440, 441.

men. Thereupon a sudden and uncontrollable panic seized the garrison and spread to the camp, and even the marauding hordes in the neighbourhood. A simultaneous earthquake (1 Sam. xiv. 15) increased the confusion, and when Saul's watchmen at Gibeah looked towards the opposite end of the gorge of Michmash, they beheld the multitudes *melting away, going and beating down one another.* Unable to explain the cause of this sudden movement, the king ordered the High-priest Ahiah to enquire who had left the Israelite camp. On ascertaining that Jonathan was leading an attack upon the enemy, he would have a second time consulted the ark of God, but while he was talking, the noise in the Philistine host grew louder and louder. On this he bade the High-priest stay his enquiries, and putting himself at the head of his 600 followers, he rushed up the defile, and on reaching the opposite side found that a general panic had seized the foe, *every man's hand was against his fellow, and there was a great discomfiture* (1 Sam. xiv. 20).

It was the signal for a general rising. Even the Israelites in the Philistine camp turned against their captors, and were quickly joined by others of their brethren, who till now had remained concealed in the mountains of Ephraim. Onwards the pursuit swept over the high ground of Bethel and down the pass of Beth-horon to Ajalon[1]. In the excitement of the hour, and carried away by that rash impetuosity which henceforth seemed to mar all his actions, Saul cried to heaven, *Cursed be the man that eateth any food until evening, that I may be avenged of mine enemies* (1 Sam. xiv. 24). He had not yet encountered his heroic son, and the fasting people were spent and wearied. Soon the pursuit lay through a forest be-

[1] Smith's *Bib. Dict.*, Article *Jonathan;* Stanley's *S. and P.* p. 205.

dewed in divers places with the droppings of wild honey. Overcome with his exertions, which had brought such glory to the nation, and unaware of his father's rash adjuration, Jonathan put forth the end of his staff into a honeycomb, and therewith refreshed his parched lips. An Israelite saw what he had done, and revealed the terms of the royal curse. *My father hath troubled the land,* said he, and once more mingled in the pursuit (1 Sam. xiv. 24—32).

The day must now have been far advanced, and the host utterly unable to endure any longer the enforced fast flew upon the spoil, and taking sheep and oxen slew them on the ground, devouring the fresh carcases even with the blood[1]. When the news of this infraction of the law was announced to Saul, he directed that a large stone should be set up to serve as a kind of altar. Still eager and impetuous, late as it was, he wished to continue the pursuit and to spoil the Philistines till the morning light. The more prudent Ahiah suggested that the Divine Will should first be ascertained. Arrayed in his ephod (1 Sam. xiv. 3), he consulted, probably, the "Breastplate of Judgment[2]," while the king enquired of the Lord, *Shall I go down after the Philistines? Wilt Thou deliver them into the hand of Israel?* But no answer was vouchsafed, the Oracle was dumb. Suspecting there was something to intercept the Divine response, Saul proposed to ascertain the cause by appealing to the sacred lot, exclaiming with all his former rashness, *As the Lord liveth, though the sin be found in Jonathan my son, he shall surely die.* In solemn silence the chiefs of the host divided; Saul and Jonathan stood on one side, the people on the other. The lot was cast, and it was ascertained that the sin lay between the king and his son. Again the lot was cast, and this time Jonathan was taken. Ad-

[1] See above, p. 156.　　　[2] See above, p. 132.

jured by his father, the youthful conqueror confessed that with his staff he had taken and eaten some honey. Saul declared he would abide by his vow, and Jonathan would have fallen a victim to the royal rashness, had not the people interfered. With a determination he dared not oppose, they declared that not one hair of his head should fall to the ground. Thus Jonathan was saved; and Saul returned to his native hills, and the Philistines, defeated and disgraced, to their fertile lowlands (1 Sam. xiv. 24—46).

CHAPTER V

SAUL AND THE AMALEKITES. DAVID AND GOLIATH.

1 Sam. xv.—xvii.   B. C. 1079—1063.

THIS signal victory materially confirmed Saul's supremacy. Acting no longer merely on the defensive, he now directed expeditions against Moab, Ammon, Edom, and even the king of Zobah, a region east of Cœle-Syria and extending towards the Euphrates. While in the full tide of his success he received a visit from Samuel, who on the strength of a Divine command, entrusted him with a commission, which he was to execute to the very letter. The treacherous hostility of the powerful tribe of Amalek, when they fell upon the exhausted rear of the Israelites at their departure from Egypt, had not been forgotten by God (Ex. xvii. 8, 14; Num. xxiv. 20). Since then they had on more than one occasion evinced the same hostility[1]. They were now devoted to utter destruction. *Go and smite Amalek,* ran the Divine commission; *utterly destroy all that they have; spare them not; slay both*

[1] Comp. (i.) Num. xiv. 45; (ii.) Judg. iii. 13; (iii.) Judg. vi. 3.

man and woman, infant and suckling, ox and sheep, camel and ass (1 Sam. xv. 2, 3).

Thereupon Saul mustered a force of 210,000 at Telaim in southern Judah, and after warning the Kenites to betake themselves to a place of safety, he attacked the Amalekites and smote them from Havilah to Shur. All the people he utterly destroyed, but, in direct violation of the express instructions he had received, spared all the best of the spoil and Agag the Amalekite king. Returning from this expedition he set up a *place*, or, probably, a *monument* of his victory, at Carmel in the mountainous country of Judah, and thence repaired to Gilgal. A Divine intimation had already made known to Samuel how imperfectly the king had executed his commission, and with a heavy heart he went forth to meet him. With a haste which betrayed the misgivings of his conscience, Saul no sooner saw the Prophet than he boasted of his execution of the Divine mandate. But Samuel was not thus to be deceived. *The bleating of the sheep and the lowing of oxen* on all sides revealed but too clearly the lax interpretation which Saul had chosen to put upon his instructions, and he only increased his condemnation by trying to throw the blame of his own shortcomings upon the people, who, he declared, *had spared the best of the spoil to sacrifice to Jehovah.* The Prophet sternly reminded him that Jehovah had far more delight in obedience to His commands than in burnt-offerings and sacrifices, and for the second time intimated that the continuance of his dynasty was forfeited; he had *rejected the Word of the Lord, and the Lord had rejected him from being king* (1 Sam. xv. 12—23).

With much contrition Saul then confessed his error, and as the Prophet turned to depart, grasped the skirt of his mantle to induce him to stay. The mantle rent, and Samuel interpreted the omen; the Lord had *rent*

the kingdom from its unworthy head, and designed it
for *a neighbour of his,* who was better than he. Without denying the justice of the sentence, Saul entreated
the granting of one concession, imploring Samuel to
*honour him before the elders of his people, and turn
with him and worship Jehovah.* The prophet yielded,
and for the last time the two offered sacrifice together.
But if Saul had neglected his duty, Samuel could not
forget the captive king, whom the Divine decree had
devoted to death. He ordered Agag to be brought
before him. The king came forward *delicately,* re-
marking, as if to disarm hostility, *surely the bitterness
of death is past.* *As thy sword,* rejoined the Prophet,
*hath made women childless, so shall thy mother be
childless among women;* and he hewed him in pieces
before the Lord. The commission of Jehovah thus vindicated, Saul returned to Gibeah, and Samuel to Ramah, there to mourn for one, whose career, once so
hopeful, was now obscured with such dark forebodings
of coming doom (1 Sam. xv. 24—35).

The sorrow of Samuel for Saul's shortcomings was
real. But he was before long roused from his grief by
a Divine commission to take a horn of oil and go to
Bethlehem, there to anoint another king. Fear lest
the purport of his errand should reach Saul's ears would
have deterred him from venturing on the journey, but
he was bidden to take a heifer and invite the elders of
the town to a sacrificial feast. In obedience to this
command he left Ramah, and proceeded on his way.
As he ascended the long gray hill leading to the village,
his approach was discerned by the elders, who trembled
when they saw the venerable Prophet. *Comest thou
peaceably?* they enquired anxiously. *Peaceably,* was
the reply, and they were bidden to prepare to accompany him to the feast.

Amongst those invited on this occasion was JESSE,

sprung from one of the oldest families[1] in the place, the son of Obed, and grandson of the Moabitess Ruth. He was an aged man at this time, and the father of eight sons, of whom seven now accompanied him to the feast (1 Sam. xvii. 12). When they were all assembled, and waiting to commence, the Prophet looked upon the eldest, the tall Eliab, and thought that of a surety he beheld the Lord's anointed. But the Divine Voice bade him not look upon *his countenance*, or *the height of his stature*, for the Lord, *who looketh not upon the outward appearance but upon the heart*, had refused him. Then the old man's second son Abinadab passed before him, and his third son Shammah, and after them four other sons, but the Lord had chosen none of them. *Are here all thy children?* enquired Samuel. *There remaineth yet the youngest*, said Jesse, *and, behold, he keepeth the sheep. Send and fetch him*, rejoined the Prophet; *till he come hither, we cannot sit round* (1 Sam. xvi. 11, *margin*).

Accordingly a messenger was sent to the sheepfolds, and brought in the youngest, David (*the beloved, the darling*), the Benjamin of Jesse's house. With his shepherd's staff in his hand, his scrip or wallet round

---

[1] The family belonged to the greatest house in Judah, the descent being as follows: *Judah, Pharez, Hezron, Ram, Amminadab, Nahshon* (Num. i. 7), *Salmon*, who married Rahab the Canaanite, *Boaz, Obed, Jesse*. (Ruth iv. 18—22; 1 Chr. ii. 5—12.)

JESSE.

Eliab.		
Abinadab.	Zeruiah.	Abigail.
Shammah.		
Nethaneel.	Abishai, Joab, Asahel.	Amasa.
Raddai.		
Ozem.		

[*One not given.* 1 Chr. ii. 15.]
David.
[Comp. 1 Sam. xvi. 7—10 with 1 Chr. ii. 13—17.]

his neck (1 Sam. xvii. 40), a mere stripling beside the tall Eliab, ruddy or auburn-haired, with fair bright eyes[1], *comely and goodly to look to* (1 Sam. xvi. 12, 18), he stood before the Prophet. *Arise, anoint him, for this is he*, whispered the Divine Voice, and there in the midst of his brethren and the assembled elders, Samuel poured upon him the consecrated oil, on which the feast so long delayed was celebrated, and Samuel rose up and returned to Ramah. (See Ps. lxxviii. 70—72.)

Meanwhile the Spirit of God, which came upon David from that day forward, departed from Saul, and *an evil spirit troubled him* (1 Sam. xvi. 14). He became moody and liable to fits of sudden phrensy. To rouse him from this distressing state, his servants advised that a clever player on the harp should be sent for, that by the charms of his music he might soothe his spirit. When enquiry was made for such a minstrel, one of the royal servants mentioned the name of the son of Jesse as not only cunning in playing, but of tried valour, prudent in speech, comely in person, and prospered with the blessing of the Lord (1 Sam. xvi. 18). Saul thereupon sent for him, and Jesse dispatched him with a humble offering. Even the troubled spirit of the king was soothed by the music of the future Psalmist of Israel; he loved him, and made him not only his minstrel but his armour-bearer, and retained him about his person (1 Sam. xvi. 21).

When the paroxysms of Saul's malady abated, David would seem to have returned to his old occupations on the bleak downs of Bethlehem, where his faithfulness *in a few things* fitted him to become a ruler *over many things*. His shepherd life called into action some of the best qualities in human nature. Firmness, nerve, energy and constancy were all required of him, who would in

---

[1] Article *David* in Smith's *Bibl. Dict.*

true devotion to this calling, endure the heat by day
and the frost by night (Gen. xxxi. 40), climb narrow
ledges and scale lofty precipices in quest of pasture for
his flocks, and defend them against wild beasts, such as
lions and wolves, bears and panthers, or robbers of the
desert. All these tests David had stood. His strength
and courage were well known beyond the boundaries of
his native village. Once during his solitary shepherd
life a lion, and at another time a bear attacked his
father's flock. He fled not like a "hireling shepherd,"
but put his life in his hand, and went after them and
slew them (1 Sam. xvii. 34—37).

Meanwhile the ever active Philistines had once more
risen in arms against the Israelites. Gathering together
their forces they took up a position on a height, which,
probably from being the scene of frequent sanguinary
encounters, was known as Ephes-dammim (*the boundary
of blood*), situated on the frontier hills of Judah between
Socoh and Azekah. Separated from their foes by a
deep ravine or glen, Saul and his followers pitched
on the north side of the Valley of Elah [1] (*the terebinth*).
For forty mornings and evenings there descended into
this valley from the camp of the Philistines a giant
named Goliath of Gath. Of enormous height and clad
in complete armour, he openly defied any one of the
Hebrew host to mortal combat, and offered to stake the
supremacy of either people on the issue. Even the tall
majestic Saul declined the challenge, and, like his people, *was dismayed and greatly afraid* (1 Sam. xvii. 11)

While the two armies thus stood confronting each
other, early one morning David entered the camp, hav-

---

[1] Identified by Robinson with the *Wady es-Sümt.* "It
took its name Elah of old from the terebinth, of which the
largest specimen we saw in Palestine still stands in the vicinity; just as now it takes its name *es-Sumt* from the acacias
which are scattered in it."—*Bibl. Res.* II. 21.

ing been bidden by his father to visit his three eldest brothers, then serving in the army. As he drew near the outskirts of the camp, the host with the well-known war-cry was advancing to take up its daily position in battle-array. Hastily leaving with the keeper of the baggage the provisions which his father had sent as a present to their captain, he hurried within the lines, and was in the act of saluting his brethren, when the voice of the giant was audible calling across the ravine his morning challenge. David heard his words of haughty defiance, and lost in wonder at the despondency of the people, listened eagerly to the bystanders, as they recounted the reward, which the king had promised to bestow on any one who was willing to accept the giant's challenge, and slew him in the fight. Heeding nothing the taunts of his eldest brother ELIAB, who would have had him mind the few sheep he had left amidst the pastures of Bethlehem, instead of coming thither to see the battle, he went from soldier to soldier listening again and again to the account of the king's promised reward, till at length his bold defiance of the giant reached the ears of Saul (1 Sam. xvii. 31).

Summoned into the royal presence, David declared his readiness to go forth and encounter his gigantic foe, and at Saul's request tried on his armour, which, however, did not fit him, and he speedily put it off again. Then, choosing five smooth stones from the dry torrent-bed which ran through the ravine, he placed them in his shepherd's script, and with his staff in one hand, and a sling[1] in the other, drew near the Philistine. The latter enraged at the youthful appearance of his assailant cursed him by his gods, and threatened *to give his flesh to the fowls of the air and the beasts of the field.* Undismayed David returned threat for threat, and as

[1] In all ages the favourite weapon of the shepherds of Syria. See Thomson, *The Land and the Book*, p. 572.

his foe drew near, put his hand into his bag and took thence a stone, which he slang with all his might, and smote the Philistine in his forehead, *that the stone sank into his forehead, and he fell upon his face to the earth.* Then without delay he stood upon the prostrate body, and drawing the giant's huge sword from its sheath, finished the work by cutting off his head. The sight of their champion lying weltering in his blood filled the Philistines with consternation, and they commenced a precipitate flight. Raising their well-known war-cry, the Israelites then rushed across the ravine and up the opposite heights, and chased their foes to the gates of Ekron and Gath, and spoiled their tents. On their return the youthful warrior, who had in so signal a manner proved that the Lord saved not with sword and spear, bearing the head of his gigantic enemy in his hand, was conducted to Saul's tent by Abner the king's uncle and captain of the host. Some two or three years had probably elapsed since the days when David soothed Saul's melancholy with the strains of his harp, and in his altered visage the king did not recognise his former minstrel[1]. But he now took him permanently into his

---

[1] "We do not know how long a period intervened between the return of David to his father's house and his appearance before the king on the morning of the *duel* with Goliath. If it were two or three years, it is possible that David had, in the meanwhile, suddenly shot up from boyhood to youth, tall and robust, and his personal appearance might have so changed as to bear little resemblance to the ruddy lad who played skilfully on the harp. It is a fact that lads of this country, particularly of the higher classes, are often very fair, fullfaced, and handsome, until about fourteen years of age, but during the next two or three years a surprising change takes place. They not only spring into fullgrown manhood as if by magic, but all their former beauty disappears; their complexion becomes dark, their features harsh and angular, and the whole expression of countenance stern, and even disagreeable. I have often been accosted by such

service, and would let him no more return to his father's
house (1 Sam. xviii. 2).

CHAPTER VI

DAVID'S LIFE AS AN OUTLAW.

1 Sam. XVIII.—XXIII. B. C. 1063—1061.

THE victory over Goliath was the turning-point in
David's life. He was now no longer the obscure
shepherd of Bethlehem, but the recognised deliverer of
Israel, and the chief of Saul's men of war (1 Sam. xviii. 5).
Moreover he now became the devoted friend of Jonathan, the king's son. The hero of Michmash would naturally sympathise with the daring shepherd of Bethlehem,
and *his soul was knit with the soul of David* (1 Sam.
xviii. 1 ; Comp. 2 Sam. i. 26). The two ratified a solemn
vow of undying friendship, and Jonathan bestowed on
his new-found friend almost every article of his attire,
not only the costly robe that he wore, but even his
sword, his bow, and his girdle (1 Sam. xviii. 4).

But the hour of David's triumph was the signal for
the commencement of those embittered relations which
subsisted between him and Saul till the day of the
latter's death. As the royal party returned from the
Valley of Elah, they were met by companies of Hebrew
maidens, who in their songs expressed the discerning
feelings of the nation, singing, *Saul hath slain his thousands, and David his ten thousands.* To the king this
was gall and wormwood ; in the youthful warrior he
saw that *other more worthy than himself,* for whom

persons, formerly intimate acquaintances, but who had suddenly grown entirely out of my knowledge, nor could I,
without difficulty, recognize them." Thomson's *Land and
the Book,* p. 569.

the kingdom was designed, and *he eyed him from that day and forward* (1 Sam. xviii. 9).

As the king's armour-bearer David did not neglect his musical talents, and when Saul's fits of madness were upon him he soothed him with the strains of his harp. But more than once he did so at the peril of his life, for in a sudden paroxysm of rage the king flung at him the long spear he held in his hand, and would have pinned him to the wall, had he not escaped out of his presence (1 Sam. xviii. 11). Perceiving that the Divine favour was withdrawn from himself, Saul now became afraid of David, and in the hope of getting rid of him gave him the command of a thousand men (1 Sam. xviii. 13), and sent him on several expeditions; but David's uniform success and the prudence he displayed only won for him still more the favour of the people. The king then tried other expedients. He promised him his eldest daughter MERAB in marriage, on condition that he fought against the Philistines. David went, and instead of falling in battle, only covered himself with fresh glory, but when the time for the marriage came, Merab was given to another (1 Sam. xviii. 19).

Meanwhile MICHAL, the king's second daughter, had fallen in love with her father's armour-bearer. As if to bring his previous designs to a positive fulfilment, Saul named as her dowry proof that David had slain a hundred of the Philistines. At the head of his men David went, and slew twice that number, and brought the required proofs of their death. The marriage was celebrated, and David became captain of the royal body-guard, second only, if not equal, to Abner. But the king's jealousy of his successful rival was only the more increased, and he went so far as to propose to Jonathan and his servants that David should be put out of the way, and was only dissuaded by the moving intercession of Jonathan himself. A partial reconciliation with the king ensued, and David returned to court. But his life was not more secure. On one occasion his own vigilance in eluding the royal javelin, on another the devotion of his wife Michal, alone saved his life. On the last occasion, the officers charged to put him to death had actually penetrated into his chamber, but only to find in the bed, in place of the object of their search, an *image*, or household god, with the head enveloped in a net of goats' hair[1]. During the night his wife had let him down from the window. (Comp. Ps. lix.)

David now fled away to Naioth[2], the *huts or habitations* near Ramah, where he enjoyed a brief respite from danger and anxiety in the congenial society of the aged Samuel, whom he had not seen since the occurrence at Bethlehem, and of the company of prophets there gathered together under his superintendence. News of his hiding-place reached the ears of Saul, who forthwith sent messengers to take him. But the sight of the prophets performing their sacred functions under the eye of the venerable Samuel and their strains of sacred melody so wrought upon the messengers, that they could not refrain from joining in their religious exercises. A similar issue attended a second, and even a third deputation. At length Saul went in person to the great well or cistern of Sechu, not far from Ramah, and enquired for the Prophet and the fugitive. But as he drew near the place, he himself could not resist the prophetic impulse, and for the second time justified the enquiry, *Is Saul also among the prophets?* (1 Sam. xix. 24).

Thus the danger was for the time averted. But this state of suspense was intolerable, and David felt there was *but a step between him and death.* Probably by Samuel's advice, he now obtained a secret interview

[1] Used as a protection from gnats.
[2] See *Naioth* in Smith's *Bib. Dict.* It was now, probably, that he became acquainted with the prophets *Nathan* and *Gad.*

with Jonathan at Ezel, a well-known stone near Gibeah. In pathetic language he poured out his whole soul to his friend, and besought him to make an effort to ascertain once for all the real feelings of his father, which he might think had undergone a change after the incidents at Naioth. The morrow was a festival of the New Moon. Saul would hold a solemn feast, and at his table would sit Abner and Jonathan, but David's place would be vacant. The demeanour of the king on observing his absence was to be taken as an omen. If he acquiesced in Jonathan's explanation that David was absent at a similar festival under the family roof at Bethlehem, all would be well. If he was wroth, then it would be certain that the old grudge was not healed, and that evil was determined against him. A solemn compact was then ratified between the two. Jonathan undertook to ascertain his father's mind; David promised to shew kindness not only to Jonathan himself, but to all his posterity (1 Sam. xx. 5—10).

When this compact had been duly ratified, Jonathan suggested an expedient, whereby the news was to be made known to David. Within three days he would again repair to the " great stone " with his bow and arrows, and accompanied by a little lad. He would then shoot three arrows, as though he shot at a mark, and his words to the lad, which David would overhear, must decide the point. If he said to the lad, *Behold, the arrows are on this side of thee, take them,* then David might come forth, and know that all was well. If he said, *The arrows are beyond thee,* then he might go his way, certain that the wrath of the king could not be appeased. The day came, and David repaired to his hiding-place. In due time Jonathan and his little lad appeared, and the three arrows were shot as agreed upon, and as the lad ran to pick them up, he cried, *Is not the arrow beyond thee ?* Then David knew that he must fly, and, when the lad was gone to carry back the bow and arrows to Gibeah, rose from his hiding-place, and with passionate embraces and many tears parted from his friend, who once more commended his posterity to his care (1 Sam. xx. 35—42).

David now betook himself to Nob, a sacerdotal city in the tribe of Benjamin, and situated on an eminence near Jerusalem. Here the High-priest Ahimelech resided with the Tabernacle, and trembled when he saw the captain-general of the royal troops approaching alone, and unattended by his usual retinue. But David disarmed his suspicions by pretending a secret mission from the king, and in this character obtained, in the failure of other bread, the sacred[1] loaves of Shew-bread, which having served their turn in the weekly course, were about to be replaced by new loaves. With these and the sword of Goliath, which was brought forth from its receptacle behind the ephod, he fled away, resolved to seek refuge amongst his enemies the Philistines[2].

On his arrival at the court of Achish, king of Gath, he was recognised by the royal guards as the famous champion of Israel, and the sword he carried doubtless recalled bitter memories of the Valley of Elah. He was accordingly thrown into prison[3]. But in this dilemma he changed his behaviour, scrabbled on the doors of the gates, let his spittle fall upon his beard, and gave every sign of being insane. The oriental respect for madness[4] procured him his release, and he was suffered to depart.

From the Lowlands of the Philistines he now betook himself to the town of Adullam (Josh. xv. 35), at the foot of the mountain-range of Judea, and found a secure retreat in one of the extensive caves, with which the

---

[1] See Matt. xii. 3 ; Mark ii. 23 ; Luke vi. 3, 4.
[2] Compare the histories of Coriolanus and Themistocles.
[3] See titles of Psalms xxxiv. and lvi.
[4] Thomson, *The Land and the Book*, p. 148.

limestone cliffs of the neighbourhood are pierced[1].
News of his coming reached Bethlehem (1 Sam. xxii. 1),
and straightway his brethren and all his father's house,
feeling perhaps insecure from Saul's vengeance, came
down to his stronghold from the Judean hills. These
probably included his nephews, the sons of Zeruiah, JOAB
and ABISHAI; but besides these, were 400 men who joined him from various motives, some from distress, others
to avoid exacting creditors, others from some private
sorrow. Not considering, however, his aged father and
mother secure in this secluded spot, David hastily
crossed the Jordan, and conveyed them into the friendly
territory of Moab, and there consigned them to the
king, who agreed to protect them (1 Sam. xxii. 3, 4).

By the advice of his friend the prophet Gad, he now
retired to the forest of Hareth, not far from Adullam.
It was probably while he was here in hold that the sons
of Zeruiah performed the memorable exploit recorded
in 2 Sam. xxiii. 14—17, 1 Chr. xi. 16—19. A garrison
of the Philistines had established themselves even in
David's native town of Bethlehem. One day, sorely tried
by thirst, he expressed a longing for the delicious water
of its well near the gate. Upon the word the three
heroes burst through the Philistine forces, and returned with the much-coveted draught[2]. But their leader
would not drink of the blood of the men that *had gone
in jeopardy of their lives,* and poured it forth as a
libation before the Lord.

Other bands now joined him. Amongst these were
eleven mighty men, *their faces like the faces of lions,
their feet as swift as the roes upon the mountains*
(1 Chr. xii. 8), from the uplands of Gad beyond Jordan,
who swam that river when it had overflowed all its

---

[1] See Robinson, I. 481, 2; Van de Velde, II. 156.
[2] Comp. the story of Alexander in the Desert of Gedrosia.

banks (1 Chr. xii. 15), and found their way to his hold. They were followed by men, not only from the tribe of Judah, but from that of Benjamin, with their chief Amasai. This defection of members of Saul's own tribe at first excited David's suspicion, but the straightforward, honest words of their leader convinced him of their sincerity, and he associated them in the command of his band of six hundred faithful followers (1 Chr. xii. 16—18).

Meanwhile the Philistines attacked Keilah, a town of uncertain situation in the lowland district of Judah, and robbed the threshing-floors. At first David's men, in spite of a Divine assurance of success, feared to relieve the place, and so incur the hostility of their powerful foe. A second assurance restored their courage. Keilah was rescued, and the Philistines defeated with great slaughter. Whilst here David was joined by another and an important ally in the person of Abiathar, the son of the high-priest Ahimelech, bearing sad intelligence. On the day of David's visit to Nob, there was a stranger watching intently all that took place between him and the high-priest. This was Doeg, an Edomite, and the chief of Saul's herdmen (1 Sam. xxi. 7). When the king was deploring at Gibeah the defection even of his own tribe, Doeg poured into the royal ear *his* version of what had occurred at Nob. Transported with rage the king sent for Ahimelech, and all the priests of the line of Ithamar, and charged them with befriending his enemies. In vain the high-priest repelled the charge. Saul sentenced the entire body of the priests to instant death, and gave the signal to his guard to execute it. But they declined to imbrue their hands in such a bloody murder. Thereupon he called on Doeg, who straightway obeyed, and falling upon the unresisting priests slew in one day *fourscore and five persons that did wear a linen ephod.* Not content with this, the king put the entire population of the place to the sword, *both*

men and women, children and sucklings (1 Sam. xxii.
19). Such was the sad news which the solitary survivor
of the house of Ithamar now announced to David. *I
knew it,* replied the latter, *I knew it, that day when
Doeg the Edomite was there, that he would surely tell
Saul; I have occasioned the death of all the persons of
thy father's house*[1]. From this day forward Abiathar
remained with David, and having brought with him the
high-priest's ephod, was enabled by his oracular answers
materially to aid David's movements on occasions of
difficulty or danger. Meanwhile the entry of his rival
into a town that had gates and bars (1 Sam. xxiii. 7)
inspired Saul with the hope of at length capturing David.
Summoning his forces, as if for a regular military expedition, he marched down to Keilah, to besiege him and
his followers. Aware of the king's secret designs, David
consulted the Divine Will by means of the ephod, and
thus ascertaining the intention of the townspeople to
betray him, he and his men departed, *and went whithersoever they could* (1 Sam. xxiii. 13).

CHAPTER VII

DAVID AT ZIKLAG. BATTLE OF MOUNT GILBOA.

1 Sam. xxiv.—xxxi.   B. C. 1061—1056.

FROM Keilah David now removed to a stronghold in
the wilderness of Ziph[2], in the highlands of Judah,
between Carmel and Juttah, about three miles south of
Hebron. Hither Saul pursued him with ceaseless zeal,
but was utterly unable to discover his hiding-place.
Jonathan, however, sought him out and found him in a
neighbouring wood, *and strengthened his hand in God*,
assuring him of his belief that his father would never

[1] Compare Psalms cxl., cxlii.
[2] Robinson, *Bib. Res.* I. 492.

find him, that he would live to come to the throne, and that he himself should be next unto him. The former covenant was now for the third time ratified, and the two friends parted, never to meet again (1 Sam. xxiii. 16—18).

Meanwhile Saul returned to Gibeah, whither messengers from the Ziphites followed him with news of David's hiding-place, and offering to betray him into his hands[1]. Thereupon the king set out, and so close were the pursuer and pursued on one another's track, that while David was climbing down one side of a cliff in the waste pasture ground of Maon, in the extreme south of Judah, Saul and his men were posted to intercept them on the other. But the arrival of a messenger, with news of a sudden inroad of the Philistines, obliged the king to discontinue the pursuit, and the name of the spot Sela-hammahlekoth, *The Cliff of Divisions*, long commemorated David's narrow escape (1 Sam. xxiii. 28).

Engedi[2], or *The Spring of the Wild Goats*, a town on the western shore of the Dead Sea, was his next hiding-place, and the scene of an instance of magnanimity on his part, rare at all times, especially rare amongst Oriental nations. The panic of the Philistine invasion being over, Saul advanced to Engedi at the head of 3,000 men, and on one occasion entered one of the numerous caves of the neighbourhood. David and his men, seeing but not seen, were concealed in the

---

[1] See Psalm liv.

[2] Its original name was Hazazon-Tamar (*the pruning of the palm*), on account of the palm-groves which surrounded it (Gen. xiv. 7; 2 Chr. xx. 2). Wilton's *Negeb*, 120. "We were now in the 'wilderness of Engedi,' where David and his men lived among 'the rocks of the wild goats'......The whole scene is drawn to the life. On all sides the country is full of caverns, which might then serve as lurking-places for David and his men, as they do for outlaws at the present day."—Robinson, *Bib. Res.* I. p. 500.

dark recesses of the same retreat. Had he listened to
the advice of his men, he might now have surprised and
slain his unsuspecting foe, but he contented himself with
cutting off the skirt of the royal robe. Even for this,
however, his heart smote him, and bidding his men remember that the king was *his master* and *the Lord's
anointed* (1 Sam. xxiv. 6), he refused to permit them to
rise up against him. Presently Saul left the cave, and
then David followed, and cried after him, *My lord the
king!* Saul looked behind him, and David, bowing before him with his face to the ground, expostulated with
him in words of touching beauty, and in the skirt of his
robe bade him behold a pledge of his unwillingness to
do him any harm[1]. Even Saul himself was deeply
moved, and lifted up his voice and wept, frankly ac-
knowledging the generosity of his rival. He then owned
how well he knew David was to be the future king, and
made him solemnly swear not to visit his own ill-will on
his posterity, or destroy his name out of his father's
house. All this David faithfully undertook to perform,
but knowing well the capriciousness of the king did not
quit his stronghold. About this time the aged prophet
Samuel died, and *all the Israelites* were gathered together, and lamented him, and buried him within the
walls of his own house at Ramah (1 Sam. xxv. 1).

The relations of David towards the neighbouring
landholders is strikingly illustrated by an incident
which now took place. On the neighbouring range of
Carmel dwelt a rich sheep-master named NABAL. In
these troublous times his shepherds experienced more
than usual difficulty in safely keeping his 3,000 sheep
and 1,000 goats. The presence, therefore, of David's
valiant men was a matter of no small importance, for
instead of injuring or robbing them, *they were a wall
unto them both by day and by night* (1 Sam. xxv. 15—

[1] See Psalm lvii.

17). Hearing that Nabal was about to shear his sheep, an occasion of much festivity, David sent ten of his retinue to request a small reward for the kindness he had ever shewn to his shepherds. This Nabal, who was notorious for his churlish temper, flatly and insultingly refused. Enraged at such selfish insolence, David resolved on vengeance. Leaving 200 men to guard the baggage, he marched with the remaining 400 towards Carmel, and would certainly have inflicted severe punishment on the churlish sheep-master, had he not on the way encountered his beautiful and prudent wife ABIGAIL, who, informed of her husband's uncivil conduct, had come forth to meet him with a long train of asses laden with provisions. In language courteous and politic she deprecated his vengeance, frankly allowing that as for her husband, Nabal (*fool*) *was his name, and folly was with him* (1 Sam. xxv. 25). David consented to desist from his determined revenge, and Abigail returned to find her lord drinking to excess at the feast. The next morning she told him of the risk he had run, *and his heart died within him, and he became as a stone* (1 Sam. xxv. 37). Smitten with a sudden stroke he only lingered ten days, when he died. Thereupon David married Abigail, and besides her, his wife Michal having been bestowed by Saul upon another, he espoused Ahinoam of Jezreel (1 Sam. xxv. 43, 44), a town in the neighbourhood of the southern Carmel. (See Josh. xv. 56.)

Returning once more to the old hiding-place in the pasture country of Ziph, and the neighbouring hill of Hachilah, the secret of his retreat was again betrayed to Saul by the Ziphites[1], who at the head of 3,000 men went forth to capture David (1 Sam. xxvi. 3). Informed

---

[1] Psalms liv, lvii, lxiii. by their titles relate to this period, and it has been remarked that "probably these Psalms made the Psalter so dear to Alfred and to Wallace during their like wanderings."—Smith's *Bib. Dict.*, Art. *David.*

of his approach, David retired from the hill to the lower
ground, the wood which then covered the country concealing him from view[1]. Saul advanced to the hill, and
there pitched his tent, with Abner his captain-general,
and his forces round about him. Accompanied by his
nephew Abishai, David in the dead of the night penetrated through the lines to the spot where the king
slept within the baggage, his spear stuck in the ground
at his bolster[2]. Again Abishai bade him take advantage of the opportunity, and asked permission to smite
but once the sleeping king, promising not to smite a
second time. But again David refused, and contented
himself with taking the royal spear, and the cruse of
water from his bolster, and passing through the lines of
sleeping warriors went over to the other side, and
standing on the top of a hill afar off, called across the
long intervening space to Abner, who was sunk in heavy
sleep after the fatigues of the day. Roused by the
strange voice disturbing the still midnight air, Abner
awoke, and asked who called. Then David reproached
him for the little care he had taken of his master, and
in the well-known royal spear and the cruse of water
bade him see a second proof of his generosity towards

[1] See Smith's *Bib. Dict.*, Article *Hachilah*.
[2] " I noticed, at all the encampments which we passed, that
the sheikh's tent was distinguished from the rest by a tall
spear stuck upright in the ground in front of it ; and it is the
custom, when a party is out on an excursion for robbery or
for war, that when they halt to rest, the spot where the chief
reclines is thus designated......The cruse of water is in exact
accordance with the customs of the people at this day. No
one ventures to travel over these deserts without his cruse
of water, and it is very common to place one at the ' bolster,'
so that the owner can reach it during the night. The Arabs
eat their dinner in the evening, and it is generally of such a
nature as to create thirst, and the quantity of water which
they drink is enormous. The *cruse* is, therefore, in perpetual
demand."—Thomson's *L. and B.* 367.

an unrelenting foe. Presently Saul himself awoke, and recognised the voice of David. Again the fugitive pleaded in moving words with the pursuer, and again Saul, touched to the heart with admiration for his magnanimous rival, acknowledged his own guilt, and bestowed a blessing upon him (1 Sam. xxvi. 13—25).

This last occurrence seems to have convinced David that there was no hope of any permanent change in the king's feelings towards himself (1 Sam. xxvii. 1), and he therefore determined to seek refuge once more among the Philistines. No longer a solitary fugitive, but accompanied by his two wives, and his 600 followers with their households, he again presented himself before the king of Gath. In answer to his petition for a place in some town in the country[1], Achish assigned to him and his retinue the town of Ziklag, situated at some distance from Gath, towards the south or south-east of the Philistine frontier[2] (1 Sam. xxvii. 5). His stay here lasted over a year and four months, and during this period he and his men made an expedition against the Geshurites, Gezrites, and Amalekites, who roamed over the desert plateau overhanging the Philistian plain, and having carried off enormous booty, lest the truth should reach the ears of Achish, saved neither man nor woman alive. The king, however, did hear of the expedition, but in reply to his enquiries, was assured that it had been directed against the country south of Judah, and against the south of the Kenites. Satisfied with this proof of the fidelity of his vassal, he rejoiced that David had made *his own people Israel utterly to abhor him,* and deemed it an earnest of still greater services (1 Sam. xxvii. 8—12).

Before long the Philistines gathered their armies together for another and a decisive contest with the Israelites for the supremacy. Achish and his contingent

---

[1] Compare the story of the Persian king and Themistocles.
[2] Wilton's *Negeb,* p. 207.

prepared to take part in the expedition, and as his
vassal, David consented to accompany him with his 600
men. Aphek, near Jezreel, was fixed upon as the place
of rendezvous, and thither, probably along the sea-coast,
the hundreds and thousands of the Philistines poured up
from their fertile lowlands. As David passed on the way
to Aphek, seven valiant chiefs, captains of thousands of
the powerful tribe of Manasseh, instead of joining Saul's
army, preferred to throw in their lot with him and
share his fortunes (1 Ch. xii. 19—21). But the unsuspecting confidence of Achish in his new-found vassal
was not shared by the other Philistine chiefs, and they
protested against David's followers being allowed to
accompany them. Achish was, therefore, constrained
much against his will to dismiss him, and with the first
dawn David set out on his return to Ziklag (1 Sam. xxix.
11). On arriving there, no town was to be found, nothing but a mass of burning ruins. During his absence
the Amalekites had burst upon the place, burnt it to
the ground, and carried off David's wives and those of
his retinue, whose faith in their leader, now for the first
and only time, seems to have failed, and in the extremity
of their grief they even threatened to stone him to
death. It was a critical moment, but David's old trust
did not fail him, and he *encouraged himself in the Lord
his God* (1 Sam. xxx. 6). Abiathar was bidden to bring
the ephod and ascertain the Divine Will. *Shall I pursue after this troop?* David enquired. The reply was
favourable, and his six hundred men, accompanied by
the chiefs of Manasseh, set out in the direction of the
brook Besor, a wady somewhere in the extreme south
of Judah. Here 200 of his forces were so spent that
he was fain to leave them by the brook, while the remainder pressing on, found in a field an Egyptian at the
point of death, who had neither eaten bread nor drunk
water for three days and three nights. But being sup-

plied by David's men with food and drink he revived,
revealed that he was a slave of one of the Amalekite
chiefs, and on promise of his life consented to guide the
avengers to their foes. On coming up with them they
were found *spread abroad upon all the earth, eating,
drinking, and dancing* in honour of their late victory
(1 Sam. xxx. 16). The attack was instantly made, and
David smote them from the twilight of the early dawn
to the evening of the next day, till none remained, save
only 400 young men, who effected their escape on camels.
With all the captives recovered and enormous spoil[1]
the conqueror returned to Ziklag, and was now for the
first time enabled to requite the kindness of many of
his own tribe, who had protected him during the long
period of his wanderings, and distributed of the spoil to
the elders of many friendly towns (1 Sam. xxx. 26—31).

Two days after his return news arrived of the utmost
importance respecting the Philistine invasion. With
their chariots and horses the Philistines had pressed
forward towards the plain of Esdraelon and pitched
their camp by Shunem[2], on the southern slope of the
range now called Little Hermon, or *Jebel ed Dûhy,*
while Saul encamped his forces on the opposite heights
of Mount Gilboa, at *the fountain that is in Jezreel*[3], on

---

[1] "A lasting memorial of this battle was the law, which
traced its origin to the arrangement made by David, formerly
in the attack on Nabal (1 Sam. xxv. 13), and now again more
completely, for the equal division of the plunder amongst
the two-thirds who followed to the field, and the one-third
who remained to guard the baggage" (1 Sam. xxx. 21—25).
Smith's *Bib. Dict.*

[2] See Robinson, *Bib. Res.* II. 325. "Shunem (*Sulem*) afforded an admirable camping-ground for a large army, *Jebel ed
Dûhy* rising abruptly behind, and the top of it commanding a
perfect view of the great plain in every direction, so that there
could be no surprise, nor could their march be impeded, or
their retreat cut off."—Thomson's *Land and the Book*, 451.

[3] Probably the same as the Spring of Harod or *Trembling,*

the eastern side of the plain. As he beheld the masses
of his foes passing on by hundreds and thousands, the
Israelite king was filled with the utmost alarm (1 Sam.
xxviii. 5). In this dreadful crisis he felt himself utterly
alone. Samuel, his old adviser, had been sometime dead ;
the cruel massacre at Nob had alienated from him the
entire priestly body; he enquired of the Lord, but *the
Lord answered him not, neither by dreams, nor by
Urim, nor by prophets* (1 Sam. xxviii. 6). Alone, and dis-
trusted even by his own army, he bade enquiry be made
for a woman *that had a familiar spirit.* After diligent
search it was ascertained that by going a distance of
about 7 or 8 miles to Endor, he would find, in one of the
dark and gloomy caverns[1] with which the mountain
here is hollowed, a woman who might serve his purpose.
Disguising himself, therefore, and accompanied by two
of his retinue, the unhappy king set out under cover
of night. It was an undertaking perilous in the extreme, and nothing but the agony of despair would have
induced him to venture upon it. Stealing down the
mountain from the camp, the three crossed the shoulder
of the very hill on which the Philistines were entrenched, and made for Endor, which lay behind Shunem.
Reaching the cave, the king told the witch the object of
his coming. He longed to have one more interview
with his old adviser, the prophet Samuel, and desired
her by her arts to bring him up. At first the woman
demurred, and pleaded the danger of exciting the wrath
of the king, who in better days had distinguished him-

at which Gideon's three hundred lapped (see above, p. 247),
and "identical with the fountain of Jalûd, a few miles
to the east of the modern village of Jezreel." Hewitt's
Scripture Geography, p. 33.

[1] "The rock on which Endor is built has been hollowed
out by the hand of nature into large caverns, whose dark
and gloomy entrances brought involuntarily to my mind the
witch of the days of Saul." Van de Velde, II. 383.

self by his zeal against all magic and sorcery. But her
visitor calmed her fears. She exercised her arts, and
the awful form of Samuel, *an old man, and covered
with a mantle,* appeared. Bowing himself with his
face to the earth, Saul made known his deep distress.
The Philistines, said he, *make war against me : God
is departed from me, and answereth me no more,
neither by prophets, nor by dreams : I have called thee,
that thou mayest make known unto me what I shall
do* (1 Sam. xxviii. 15). In reply the Prophet could only
inform the king that the Day of Doom was near. *To-
morrow,* said he, *the Lord will deliver Israel with
thee into the hand of the Philistines : and to-morrow
shalt thou and thy sons be with me.* This awful sentence utterly prostrated the unhappy king. He fell *with
the fulness of his stature all along upon the earth*
(1 Sam. xxviii. 20, *marg.*). For a day and a night he
had eaten nothing, and now there was no more strength
in him. With the utmost difficulty the woman and his
two attendants succeeded in compelling him to partake
of food, and then he rose up, once more crossed the
shoulder of the hill, and reached the heights of Gilboa
(1 Sam. xxviii. 21—25).

The next morning broke, and the Philistines made
their onset. The Israelite leader, with his doom upon
him, could do little in such a crisis. His army was
driven up the sides of Gilboa, and as it fled from the
victorious Philistines, numbers were slain on the heights.
Resolved on striking a decisive blow, the Philistine
archers and charioteers followed hard after Saul and
his sons. Three of the latter, including the valiant
Jonathan, were slain outright, and Saul himself was sore
wounded. In this extremity he implored of his armour-
bearer to thrust him through with his sword, and put
an end to his sufferings. But his armour-bearer refused,
and Saul, taking his own sword, fell upon it and died,

and the other then followed his example. The rout of
the Israelites was now complete, and extended even to
the tribes beyond the Jordan. Even here the Israelites
fled from their cities, and *the Philistines dwelt in them*
(1 Sam. xxxi. 7).

On the morrow after this disastrous battle, the bodies
of Saul and his three sons were found by the Philistines,
when they came to strip the slain. With savage glee
they cut off his head, stripped him of his armour, and
sent it into their own land, to be placed as a trophy in the
temple of Ashtaroth, probably at Ashdod, and fastened
his body and those of his three sons to the wall overhanging the open space in front of the gate of the
Canaanite city of Beth-shan[1]. On the mountain-range
beyond Jordan in full view of Beth-shan[2] was the town of
Jabesh-Gilead, by his heroic relief of which Saul had
inaugurated his reign[3]. Hearing from the fugitives
what had occurred to their king, the grateful inhabitants, mindful of past services, determined that his remains should not continue thus dishonoured. Their
valiant men arose, crossed the Jordan, and under cover
of night took down his body and those of his sons,
buried them under the terebinth of their native town,
and fasted seven days (1 Sam. xxxi. 13).

[1] Beth-shan (now *Beisan*) was one of the Canaanite
strongholds which the Israelites had never taken. (See above,
p. 225.) Situated on a *tell* or hill, about 200 ft. high, on the
slope of the range of Gilboa, it was a very strong position,
with nearly perpendicular sides, and was abundantly supplied
with water. Thomson, 455. Stanley, *S. and P.* 346.

[2] Jabesh-gilead "was on the mountain-range east of the
Jordan, *in full view of Beth-shan,* and these brave men would
creep up to the *tell,* without being seen, while the deafening
roar of the noisy cascades leaping through the deep ravines
dividing the city would render it impossible for them to be
heard." Thomson, *The Land and the Book,* p. 445. Van de
Velde, II. p. 360.

[3] See above, pp. 283, 284.

Such was the news David now received at Ziklag from a young Amalekite, who had been present at the battle. Deeming himself sure of the reward that greeted the bearer of glad tidings, he had brought with him Saul's crown and the bracelet that was on his arm, and pretended to have slain him at his own request (2 Sam. i. 1—12). But David's wrath was kindled, and having sternly rebuked him for touching *the Lord's anointed,* he bade one of his young men put him to death, and then burst into a strain of passionate lamentation over Saul and Jonathan. Forgetting all that had passed between him and the fallen king, he remembered only the better features of his character, while towards Jonathan his whole soul gushed forth in expressions of the tenderest affection (2 Sam. i. 17—27).

BOOK IX

THE REIGNS OF DAVID AND SOLOMON.

CHAPTER I

DAVID'S REIGN AT HEBRON.

2 SAM. II.—IV. B. C. 1055—1048.

THE hour which the prophet of Ramah had long ago
foretold was now come. The long period of trial
and discipline was over. The brave shepherd, the conqueror of Goliath, the daring but prudent leader of
attached followers was the only one left, to whom the
Israelites could look for guidance in this great crisis of
their national history.

But though the way was open, David did not enter
upon it without seeking the Divine direction. *Shall I
go up into any of the cities of Judah?* he enquired of
the Lord; and the Lord bade him go up to Hebron, "the
ancient sacred city of the tribe of Judah, the burial-
place of the patriarch[1], and the inheritance of Caleb[2]."
Accordingly, leaving Ziklag, he repaired thither with
his two wives Ahinoam and Abigail, and his faithful
band of six hundred; and there the chiefs of Judah,
now after a long period of obscurity to become the ruling tribe, anointed him as their king. His first act after
his accession was to thank the men of Jabesh-Gilead for
their bravery in removing the corpses of Saul and his
sons from the walls of Beth-shan (2 Sam. ii. 1—7).

Of the family of the late king there now remained

---

[1] See above, p. 44.   [2] See above, p. 215.

only ISHBOSHETH his youngest son, and Mephibosheth
the son of Jonathan, a child but five years old. Ishbosheth, according to the law of Oriental succession, ascended the throne, and, under the protection of his kinsman, the powerful Abner, established his kingdom at
the ancient sanctuary of Mahanaim[1] on the east of the
Jordan, ruling over not only the eastern tribes, but
the territory of Asher, the plain of Esdraelon, central
Ephraim, his own tribe of Benjamin, and eventually
over all Israel (2 Sam. ii. 9), excepting only Judah, which
remained faithful to David.

The first of many skirmishes between the rival kings
took place at Gibeon, to the heights of which, in their
native Benjamin, Abner and his forces went out from
Mahanaim (2 Sam. ii. 12). Thither also, as if to watch
their movements, repaired the three nephews of David,
Joab, Abishai, and Asahel. On the east side of the
hill of Gibeon, at the foot of a low cliff, was a large pool
or tank, on either side of which the rival forces encamped, and, as if to try their respective strength, Abner
proposed that a select body from both sides should engage in combat. Joab accepted the challenge, and twelve
picked champions of the party of Ishbosheth met an
equal number of the warriors of David[2]. The struggle
was desperate; each combatant caught his fellow by the
head, and thrust his sword into his side, and thus all fell
dead together on a spot henceforth called Helkath-haz-
zurim, the *Field of Heroes.* This brought on a general
engagement, in which the forces of Ishbosheth were defeated, and Abner himself was fain to fly hotly pursued
by Asahel, the youngest of David's nephews, and *as
light of foot as a wild roe* (2 Sam. ii. 18). Abner recognised his fleet pursuer, and advised him to desist

---

[1] See above, p. 53.
[2] Compare the combat of the Horatii and Curiatii. *Livy,*
I. xxiv. xxv.

from the chase. But the youth, heeding not, pressed on, and Abner, turning back upon him, thrust him through with a spear.

The bleeding corpse lay in the middle of the road, and was quickly surrounded by the men of Judah, who as they came up stood still in mournful astonishment (2 Sam. ii. 23). But the sight of their brother's body only roused Joab and Abishai to greater fury, and they pursued after Abner as far as the hill of Ammah, by the way of the wilderness of Gibeon, which they reached at sunset. There the men of his own tribe of Benjamin rallied round the general of Ishbosheth, and stood on the top of the hill, while he cried to the pursuing Joab, and implored him not to push matters further. On this Joab gave the signal for a cessation of the pursuit, and drew off his men, and conveying his brother's corpse to Bethlehem, laid it in the ancestral tomb. Then at daybreak he rejoined David at Hebron, to whom he announced the loss of only 19 men in the late encounter. Meanwhile Abner returned to Mahanaim, whence he carried on a series of petty wars with the adherents of David, in which *David waxed stronger and stronger, and the house of Saul waxed weaker and weaker* (2 Sam. iii. 1).

In the course of time a quarrel with his kinsman and general precipitated the fall of Ishbosheth. Abner had married Rizpah, the daughter of Aiah, and a concubine of Saul. According to the notions of Orientals, this very nearly amounted to treason (Comp. 2 Sam. xvi. 21; xx. 3; 1 K. ii. 13—25), and as such Ishbosheth flung it in the teeth of his general. Abner replied in words of utmost anger, and reproaching Ishbosheth with the basest ingratitude, straightway began to open communications with David, who agreed to receive him at Hebron, on condition that Michal, his former wife, was restored to him. This condition was complied with, and after sounding the chiefs of Israel and of his own tribe, Abner with twenty men came to David at Hebron. A feast greeted his arrival, and he departed with the avowed intention of *gathering all Israel unto his lord the king* (2 Sam. iii. 17—21).

He had hardly departed from the royal presence, when Joab returned from a foray, and was informed of this unexpected visit. Jealous probably of a possible rival, and burning with rage against his brother's murderer, he remonstrated in no measured terms with David for his imprudence, as he termed it, in admitting the general of Ishbosheth to an audience and sending him away in peace. Then, unknown to the king, he sent messengers after Abner to call him back. Not suspecting treachery the latter returned to Hebron, and, as he entered the gate, Joab took him aside, and stabbed him to death, as he had stabbed his brother Asahel. News of this cruel and treacherous deed roused David's unbounded indignation. Unable to punish the assassin, he imprecated on the house of Joab the most fearful curses, and compelled him to attend the funeral of his murdered victim, robed in sackcloth, and wearing all the signs of mourning. He himself fasted till sunset, and as he followed the bier to the burial-place at Hebron, poured forth a solemn dirge. This incident gave David an insight into Joab's unscrupulous character, which he never forgot. *These men*, he said, *the sons of Zeruiah, be too hard for me, and I am this day weak though anointed king* (2 Sam. iii. 39).

The death of Abner was the signal for the dissolution of the tottering kingdom he had supported. On receiving the tidings of his kinsman's murder, Ishbosheth's *hands were feeble, and all the Israelites were troubled* (2 Sam. iv. 1). His body-guard was composed of men from his own tribe of Benjamin, but two divisions of it were commanded by two men, Baanah and

Rechab, who, though descendants of the Canaanitish natives of Beeroth[1], were reckoned among the Benjamites. In revenge, it has been suggested, for some injury they had received from Saul—possibly the slaughter of their Gibeonite kinsmen (Comp. 2 Sam. xxi. 1, 2)—and certainly with the hope of conciliating the new king at Hebron, these two resolved to take the life of Ishbosheth. *About the heat of the day* (2 Sam. iv. 5), therefore, they entered the palace under pretence of fetching some wheat piled up near the entrance (2 Sam. iv. 6), and finding Ishbosheth lying on his bed they stabbed him to the heart, and cut off his head. Then hurrying all that afternoon and all night (2 Sam. iv. 7) down the valley of the Jordan, they presented themselves before David at Hebron with the bloody head in their hands. But they met with no better reception than the pretended slayer of Saul. David sternly rebuked them for their cold-blooded *murder of a righteous person in his own house upon his bed,* and ordered their instant execution. Their hands and feet were cut off, and their bodies were suspended over the pool at Hebron, while the head of Ishbosheth was buried with all honours in the sepulchre of Abner (2 Sam. iv. 8—12).

CHAPTER II

DAVID'S REIGN AT JERUSALEM.

2 SAM. V.—VII. B. C. 1048—1042.

EVERY obstacle was thus removed that had hitherto prevented David's assuming the royal power over all the tribes. Ishbosheth was dead, Abner was dead, Mephibosheth, Jonathan's only surviving son, was barely 12 years of age. The son of Jesse had long waited for

[1] See above, p. 210, and Art. *Ishbosheth* in Smith's *Bib. Dict.*

his hour, and at length it was come. A deputation from all the tribes of Israel (2 Sam. v. 1) repaired to Hebron, and formally offered him the crown. A solemn league was then entered into, and for the third time David was anointed amidst great rejoicings. At Hebron he had reigned for $7\frac{1}{2}$ years over Judah; he was now king of all Israel. His band of six hundred faithful followers had rapidly swelled into a great host, *like the host of God* (1 Ch. xii. 22). And now not only Dan and Judah and Simeon, not only Benjamin and Ephraim, not only the tribes beyond the Jordan, Reuben, Gad, and the half tribe of Manasseh, flocked around his standard, but Issachar sent *men that had understanding of the times, to know what Israel ought to do* (1 Ch. xii. 32), and Zebulun and Naphtali sent not only men, but the peculiar products of their rich territory [1] (1 Ch. xii. 40), while a still more important accession consisted of 4,600 warriors of the Levitical tribe, and 3,700 of the house of Aaron, headed by Jehoiada, and the youthful but valiant Zadok (1 Ch. xii. 25—28). Upwards of 300,000 choice warriors of the flower of Israel were thus gathered together *to turn the kingdom of Saul to David*, and join in celebrating the three days' festival which greeted his accession to the throne (1 Ch. xii. 39).

His first act after his coronation was significant. Saul had been always content with the obscurity of his native Gibeah, and had cared little for any central point of union for the tribes. As sovereign over all Israel, both north and south, David resolved to move the seat of government from Hebron nearer to the centre of the country. No spot seemed to present so many advantages as the rocky mass on which rose the city of the Jebusites[2]. It was neutral ground, on the

---

[1] See above, p. 219.
[2] "The situation of Jerusalem is in several respects singular amongst the cities of Palestine. Its elevation is remark-

very meeting-point of his own tribe and that of Benjamin[1]. The lower city had been once taken by the warriors of Judah (Judg. i. 8)[2], but the fortress of the Jebusites, strong in its seemingly impregnable position, had never been reduced. The presence of so many warriors from all the tribes was favourable for making an attempt on so renowned a citadel, and at the head of all his forces David advanced against it, probably from the south. As before, the lower city appears to have been easily captured, but again the fortress held out against every attack[3]. Moreover, so convinced were the Jebus-

able, occasioned, not from its being on the summit of one of the numerous hills of Judæa, like most of the towns and villages, but because it is on the edge of one of the highest table-lands of the country. Hebron, indeed, is higher still, by some hundred feet; and from the south, accordingly, the approach to Jerusalem is by a slight descent. But from every other side, the ascent is perpetual; and, to the traveller approaching Jerusalem from the west or east, it must always have presented the appearance, beyond any other capital of the then known world—we may add, beyond any important city that has ever existed on the earth—of a *mountain city, enthroned on a mountain fastness.*" (Comp. Ps. lxviii. 15, 16; lxxxvii. 1; cxxv. 1; lxxvi. 1, 2; lxvi. 4.) But besides being thus elevated, Jerusalem was separated from the rocky plateau of which it forms a part by deep and precipitous ravines on its south-eastern, southern, and western sides, out of which the rocky slopes of the city "rose like the walls of a fortress out of its ditches, so that from them it must have appeared quite impregnable." "Something of the same effect is produced by those vast rents which, under the name of 'Tago,' surround or divide Ronda, Alhama, and Granada, on the table-lands which crown the summits of the Spanish mountains. But in Palestine, Jerusalem alone is so entrenched, and from this cause derived, in great measure, her early strength and subsequent greatness." Stanley's *Sinai and Palestine,* p. 172. Robinson's *Bib. Res.* I. 258—260.

[1] Stanley's *Sinai and Palestine,* p. 176.
[2] See above, p. 225, and Kitto's *Daily Bible Illustr.* III. 340.
[3] Joseph. *Ant.* VII. 3. § 1. See Article *Jerusalem* in Smith's *Bib. Dict.* Kurtz's *Sacred History,* p. 183.

ites of the strength of their castle and of the ancient
"everlasting gates" of its rocky ravines, that they merely
manned its walls with *the lame and blind* (2 Sam. v.
6), deeming them amply sufficient for the defence. Their
taunts roused the wrath of David, and he promised that
whoso first scaled the rocky sides of the citadel and
smote the Jebusite garrison, should have the post of
captain-general of the forces. Thereupon the agile Joab
climbed up first, and as the conqueror of the fastness
of Jebus was rewarded with the post of commander-
in-chief, the same office that Abner had held under Saul.
Then, without loss of time, David took measures for se-
curing his new possession. He enclosed the whole city
with a wall, and connected it with the newly-captured
fortress, and there took up his abode, and thus the
Jebusite stronghold became the *City of David*.

The effect of the conquest of this celebrated fortress
was very great. The news no sooner reached the court
of HIRAM, king of Phœnicia[1], than he despatched messengers to David with offers of artificers and materials
for constructing a palace, which was accordingly built,
and hither David removed his wives from Hebron, and
increased his already numerous household (2 Sam. v. 13
—16). In other quarters the news was very differently
received. The Philistines made two distinct attempts
to crush the new king, of whose powers they were well
aware. On the first occasion they came and encamped
their numerous forces in the valley of Rephaim, or the
Valley of Giants, south-west of Jerusalem, and stretching
thence half-way to Bethlehem. After duly enquiring of

[1] "It was necessary for the commerce of Phœnicia that
she should enjoy the friendship of whatever power commanded
the great lines of inland traffic, which ran through Cœle-
Syria and Damascus, by Hamath and Tadmor, to the Euphrates." Rawlinson's *Bampton Lectures*, p. 97. Kenrick's *Phœnicia*, pp. 201—205. Heeren's *Researches*, II. pp. 116, 117.

the Lord, David marched out against them, and swept them away, as though with a "burst of waters," whence he named the spot Baal-perazim, *the Plain of Bursts* or *Destruction* (2 Sam. v. 17—20). A second attempt of the same pertinacious foe met with no better success; they were entirely routed, and the fame of David *went out into all lands, and the Lord brought the fear of him upon all nations* (1 Chr. xiv. 17).

His next care was to consecrate his new capital with religious associations. After consultation with the chiefs of the nation, he assembled 30,000 from all Israel (2 Sam. vi. 1; 1 Chr. xiii. 1), and went to Kirjath-jearim, *the Village of Forests,* where the Ark seems to have remained all through the reign of Saul in the custody of the Levite Abinadab (1 Sam. vii. 1, 2). The sacred coffer was placed in a new cart drawn by oxen, and with Uzzah and Ahio the sons of Abinadab preceding it, was escorted towards Jerusalem amidst great rejoicings, and the sound of psalteries, cornets, timbrels, and cymbals. On reaching the threshing-floor of Chidon or Nachon (1 Chr. xiii. 9, *margin*), the oxen stumbled, and Uzzah put forth his hand to hold the ark. In a moment he fell dead (2 Sam. vi. 7). This untoward event filled David with alarm; the spot itself was henceforth known as Perez-uzzah, *the breaking* or *disaster of Uzzah* (1 Chr. xiii. 11), and it was resolved to desist from any further attempt at present to remove the sacred coffer. Accordingly it was carried aside to the house of Obed-Edom the Gittite, that is, probably, a native of Gath-Rimmon, a town of Dan, allotted to the Kohathite Levites, of whom Obed-Edom was one, where it remained three months (2 Sam. vi. 10, 11; 1 Chr. xiii. 13).

Meanwhile David prepared a new Tabernacle at Jerusalem, and hearing that the presence of the Ark had brought a blessing to the house of Obed-Edom, he assembled the Levites, and Zadok and Abiathar the two representatives of the Aaronic family, and bade them prepare for the duty of removing the sacred symbol. Solemn purifications, neglected on the previous occasion (1 Chr. xv. 12—14), were now performed, and the Levites, arranged in orderly divisions with singers and musicians, the elders of Israel, and captains of the host, set out for the house of Obed-Edom. On this occasion the Levites, as enjoined in the Law, lifted it with the long staves passing through the rings of the ark[1], and raising it upon their shoulders, commenced the joyous procession (1 Chr. xv. 15).

When they had advanced six paces (2 Sam. vii. 13), it was clear that the Lord was this time helping them, and the procession paused to offer a sacrifice of seven bullocks and seven rams in token of thankfulness for this proof of the Divine favour. Then the march was resumed amidst shouting and the joyful sounds of all kinds of music, headed by David himself in an ephod of linen, and by the singers and Levites arrayed in white vestments. As they ascended the path leading upwards to the ancient fortress of the Jebusites, the king, carried away by the associations of this great day, not only played on a stringed instrument, but accompanied the music with leaping and dancing. At length the city was reached, and the gates of the ancient fortress lifted up their heads, as the symbol of the presence of Jehovah, *the King of Glory, the Lord strong and mighty,* entered in (Ps. xxiv. 8, 9), and was placed within the awnings of the new Pavilion-Tent that had been prepared for it. A series of burnt-offerings and peace-offerings were then celebrated, and the king blessed the people, and dismissed them to their homes with ample presents. A single untoward incident marred this the greatest day in David's life. As the procession passed under the

---

[1] See above, p. 124. Blunt's *Coincidences,* p. 130.

windows of her apartments, Michal, the daughter of Saul, deeming David's dance undignified, *despised him in her heart* (2 Sam. vi. 16), and when at the conclusion of all the gorgeous ceremonial he entered his house to bless his family (2 Sam. vi. 20), she came out to meet him, but in place of congratulations taunted him with his indecorous appearance that day. David replied with great bitterness to this untimely scoffing, and *Michal had no child unto the day of her death* (1 Sam. vi. 23).

The construction of his own palace and the reception of the Ark within the folds of a new Tabernacle in Zion, now awoke in the king the desire to build a more ample and permanent Temple for Jehovah. The design received the Divine approval, but it was intimated to him by Nathan the prophet, that as *he was a man of war and blood* (1 Chr. xxviii. 3), so peaceful a work would be better reserved for another. The refusal, however, was accompanied by a promise of the permanence of his dynasty; the mercy of Jehovah should not be taken from him as it had been from Saul; a son of his own should carry on the work, and his throne should be established for ever (2 Sam. vii. 12—17; 1 Chr. xvii. 3—15).

CHAPTER III

DAVID'S ARMY, HIS CONQUESTS, HIS SIN.

2 SAM. VIII.—XII. 1 CHRON. XVIII.—XX. B.C. 1040—1033.

THUS assured of the continuance of his kingdom, David began by a series of conquests to extend his power beyond the immediate boundaries of his own people, and to found an imperial dominion, which for the first time realized the prophetic description contained in the Promise made to his forefather Abraham (Gen. xv. 18—21).

As instrumental to these conquests the military organization[1] of the Israelites was now materially developed, and David was enabled within ten years after the reduction of the fortress of Jebus to push his conquests far and wide, and *get him a name like unto the name of the great men that are in the earth* (2 Sam. vii. 9).

i. On the South-west he turned his arms against his old enemies the *Philistines,* and subdued them,

---

[1] *The Army.* In early times all males above twenty and under fifty years of age were required to serve in the wars, and formed a kind of national militia (Deut. xx. 5—9). A standing army, as we have already seen, was first formed at the early part of Saul's reign (1 Sam. xiii. 2; xiv. 52). Under David the national forces were divided into twelve divisions of 24,000 men, each division commanded by its own officer, and liable to be called on to serve in their respective months (1 Chr. xxvii. 1—15). Unlike the armies of the surrounding nations, that of the Israelites was composed only of infantry, and but few chariots were as yet introduced (2 Sam. viii. 4). Over the entire force of the nation JOAB was commander-in-chief by right of his services before Jebus, and whenever the king was absent, he led the troops to battle.

ii. *The Royal Body-guard,* or *the Cherethites and Pelethites.* To defend the person of the king a force was now for the first time organized, consisting of foreign mercenaries, the command of which was entrusted to the Levite BENAIAH, the son of the high-priest Jehoiada. (For whose exploits, see 2 Sam. xxiii. 20, 21; 1 Chr. xi. 22—25.)

iii. *The Heroes* or *Mighty Men.* Round the king when a fugitive in the cave of Adullam had gathered, as we have seen, a body of six hundred men. This number David always preserved, but elevated it to a sort of military Order, with the special title of the GIBBORIM, *Heroes* or *Mighty Men.* This body was divided into 3 divisions of 200 each, and 30 divisions of 20 each. The lowest rank in this order consisted of the captains of the 30 divisions, who were known as *the Thirty;* then came the captains of the three larger divisions, who were known as *the Three;* and lastly, the commander of the whole force, who was known as *the Captain of the Mighty Men,* and was at this time ABISHAI, David's nephew (2 Sam. xxiii. 8—39; 1 Chr. xi. 9—47). See Articles *David* and *Army* in Smith's *Bibl. Dict.* Kitto's *Bibl. Illustr.* III. pp. 301—304.

capturing Gath with its *daughter towns*[1] (1 Chr. xviii. 1).

2. On the South-east the *Edomites* felt the weight of his arms. Together with Joab he carried on a campaign of six months against them (Comp. 2 Sam. viii. 14 with 1 K. xi. 15), during which period he put vast numbers to the sword, established garrisons in the country, and thus became master of the Eastern arm of the Red sea, and the caravan-routes to the marts and harbours of Arabia[2]. (Comp. Gen. xxvii. 29, 37, 40; Ps. lx. 6—12.)

3. On the North-east the kingdom of *Zobah* had acquired considerable influence under Hadadezer, son of Rehob. David attacked him as he went to *recover his border at the river Euphrates* (2 Sam. viii. 3), and defeated him with a loss of 1,000 chariots, 700 cavalry, and 20,000 infantry. Hadadezer's allies, the Syrians of Damascus, then marched to his assistance, but they were routed with a loss of 22,000 men, and became David's vassals. The wealth of Zobah was considerable. Several of Hadadezer's officers carried *shields of gold* (2 Sam. viii. 7), that is, probably, "iron or wooden frames overlaid with plates of the precious metal;" these David brought to Jerusalem, as also large stores of brass from other Syrian cities (1 Chr. xviii. 7, 8).

4. On the East of Jordan he had hitherto maintained the most amicable relations with the king of *Moab*[3] (1 Sam. xxii. 3, 4), but now from some unexplained cause, he not only attacked and defeated, but well-nigh extirpated the nation. Two-thirds of the people were put to death, the rest were reduced to bondage, and paid regular tribute, while the spoils were treasured up in Jerusalem (2 Sam. viii. 2; 1 Chr. xi. 22). This campaign, in which the valiant Benaiah greatly dis-

---

[1] See above, p. 258, note 2.   [2] See above, pp. 49, 50.
[3] See above, p. 304.

tinguished himself (2 Sam. xxiii. 20), fulfilled the prophecy of Balaam; *a Sceptre had risen out of Israel, and smitten through the princes of Moab*, and destroyed the city of *Ar*, that is, Rabbath-Moab, the capital of the children of Lot (Num. xxiv. 17)[1].

5. It was, however, from the kindred people of *Ammon* that the royal conquests experienced the greatest resistance. During the period of his wanderings David had received much kindness from Nahash the king of Ammon, and on his death he sent a royal embassy to offer his condolences to the new king Hanun. But Hanun's courtiers persuaded him that this embassy was really dictated by a wish to spy out his land, and probably add it to the many others that David had conquered. Accordingly on the arrival of the ambassadors, Hanun treated them with the utmost indignity. He shaved off the one half of their beards, cut off their garments in the middle, and so sent them away (2 Sam. x. 1—3; 1 Chr. xix. 1—4).

As soon as David was informed of this aggravated insult, he bade his ambassadors remain at Jericho till the traces of the indignities they had suffered were removed, and then made preparations for sending Joab with the "Mighty Men" and the host to take summary vengeance on the Ammonites. Truly divining the consequences of their folly, the latter prepared for the impending war by raising a mercenary force of 32,000 men from the Syrians of Beth-rehob and Zoba, from those owning fealty to the king of Maacah, a region in the valley of the Jordan south of Zoba, and from the land of Tob[2]. Aided by these allies the Syrians awaited the onset of the Hebrews.

On his arrival Joab, perceiving that he was confronted by two very considerable armies, divided his forces,

---

[1] See above, p. 192.   [2] See above, p. 256.

and assigned to his brother Abishai the task of assaulting the Ammonites, while he himself with a picked body of troops attacked the Syrians, situated a little to the south of Heshbon. At Medeba the latter were quickly routed, and the Ammonites, in alarm at their speedy defeat, fled to their capital, Rabbah[1], now called *Ammân*, situated on a very advantageous position, and well supplied with water.

Meanwhile the Syrians beyond the Euphrates, under the command of Shophach or Shobach, a general of Hadarezer, assembled their forces with the intention of avenging the repulse sustained by their kindred, the allies of the Ammonites. Crossing the Euphrates they joined the Syrians at Helam, the site of which is unknown. The occasion was deemed of sufficient importance to justify the personal interference of David. Gathering all Israel and passing over Jordan, he attacked the Syrians, and defeated them with great slaughter. Shobach himself was slain, and the allied princes quitted the Syrian confederacy, and became the tributary vassals of the Hebrew monarch (2 Sam. xi. 15—19; 1 Chr. xix. 10—19).

Early in the following year the campaign against the Ammonites was resumed, and the command of the forces, including the royal body-guard (2 Sam. xi. 1), and the troops of Ephraim and Benjamin as well as Judah (2 Sam. xi. 11), was again entrusted to Joab, and the army was for the first time since the disastrous battle of Aphek accompanied by the Ark and its Levitical

---

[1] Already mentioned as the place where the bedstead of the giant Og was deposited (see above, p. 186). It was on the road between Heshbon and Bosra, on the edge of the desert, near one of the sources of the Jabbok. Afterwards from Ptolemy Philadelphus (B.C. 285—247) it received the name of *Philadelphia,* and in the Christian era became the seat of a bishop and one of the 19 sees of "Palestina Tertia." Smith's *Bib. Dict.,* Article *Rabbah.*

guard[1] (2 Sam. xi. 11). On this occasion Rabbah was the main object of the attack, and after ravaging the country, Joab drove the Ammonites into their citadel, and commenced a regular siege, which lasted very nearly two years (2 Sam. xi. 1).

Meanwhile, critical as was the nature of the campaign, instead of accompanying the Ark, David lingered behind at Jerusalem, and there wrought that "deed of shame," which has left so dark a blot upon his character, and which threw a gloom over all the rest of his life. One day on rising from his afternoon repose, he saw from the roof of his palace a woman of extraordinary beauty, for whom he instantly conceived a most violent passion. On making enquiry, he discovered that her name was BATHSHEBA, the daughter of Eliam or Ammiel, and wife of URIAH the Hittite, who was at that time serving in the army against Rabbah, as one of the famous "Thirty" (2 Sam. xxiii. 39; 1 Chr. xi. 41). The fact that she was the wife of one of his most distinguished officers did not make David hesitate, he sent for her, and committed adultery with her. As time went on, he found it would be no longer possible to screen her from the death-punishment of an adulteress. Accordingly, after vainly trying other and most unworthy expedients to cover his own guilt, he sent a letter to Joab, bidding him expose this chivalrous and high-minded officer where the contest was hottest, so as to ensure his death. The unscrupulous Joab did as he was told, and Uriah fell happily unconscious of his wife's dishonour. Joab then sent a trusty messenger to David to inform him that Uriah was dead, and the days of mourning for her husband were no sooner over, than the king sent for Bathsheba, and she became his wife (2 Sam. xi. 14—27).

[1] See above, p. 271.

But though David had done all this secretly, an all-seeing Eye had watched each step in this dreadful crime, and punishment quickly appeared at the door. The prophet Nathan was sent to him, and with wonderful tact roused the royal attention by the well-known Parable of the *Rich man and the Poor man's ewe lamb.* Unsuspecting its purport, David's wrath was kindled, and he denounced death as the penalty of the rich man, and the restoration of the property fourfold[1]. Then turning to the king the prophet sped his winged arrow, saying, *Thou art the man,* and announcing the awful penalty. As David had measured unto others, so should it be measured to him; evil was to rise up against him out of the bosom of his own family, and *the sword should never depart from his house* (2 Sam. xii. 10).

Unlike other kings of Israel and Judah, unlike any common Eastern despot, David did not slay or ill-treat the messenger of judgment, he acknowledged his sin and the justice of the sentence. On this Nathan went on to tell him that *the Lord had put away his sin,* and he himself was not to die. But an earnest of future judgments soon appeared. The Lord struck the child that Uriah's wife bare unto him, and it died[2]. But in the midst of judgment God remembered mercy; and in the course of time a second son was born to Bathsheba, whom Nathan named JEDIDIAH, *beloved of the Lord,* but David himself called him SOLOMON, *the peaceful one* (2 Sam. xii. 15—25).

Meanwhile Joab had been pushing forward the siege of Rabbah, and eventually succeeded in capturing the *city of waters,* that is, the lower town, which " contained the perennial stream, which rises in, and still flows through it[3]." But the citadel, a place of great strength,

[1] See above, p. 165.
[2] To this sad period belong Psalms xxxii. li.
[3] "The ruins which now adorn the 'royal city' are of a

still held out. The possession of the perennial stream
was, however, the next step to the capture of the stronghold, and Joab sent messengers to David bidding him
gather the rest of the people, and come himself, unless he
wished him to have the honour of capturing the place,
and calling it after his own name. Accordingly the king
set out, and the fortress was speedily taken. Enraged,
it is not improbable, at the obstinacy of the siege, he
wreaked a terrible vengeance on the inhabitants, some
were decapitated, others sawn asunder or crushed beneath iron instruments, others were passed through the
fire in brick-kilns[1] (2 Sam. xii. 31). The royal crown,
"the crown of Milcom," weighing a talent of gold with
the precious stones, was then placed on David's head,
and he and his army returned in triumph to Jerusalem
with abundant spoil.

CHAPTER IV

THE REBELLION OF ABSALOM.

2 Sam. xiii.—xx.   B. C. 1032—1022.

THE reduction of Rabbah was the last of David's
conquests. His kingdom had reached the limits
foretold to the patriarch Abraham, and vied in extent
with some of the great empires of that age. But from
this point dark clouds began to gather round his own
personal history, and the doom denounced by the prophet found its fulfilment. The terrible secret of his
adultery and murder may at first have been known only

later Roman date; but the commanding position of the citadel
remains, and the unusual sight of a living stream, abounding
in fish, marks the significance of Joab's song of victory—
*I have fought against Rabbah, and have taken the city of
waters.*" *Sinai and Palestine*, p. 323.
  [1] See Kitto's *Daily Bibl. Illustr.* III. 395.

to a few, but its results were soon proclaimed upon the housetops. Out of the numerous harem which, in defiance of the law of the kingdom, he had multiplied to himself, out of his own household, came the instruments of his punishment. First, his daughter Tamar was outraged by her half-brother and his eldest son AMNON. Two years afterwards Amnon fell a victim to the wrath of Tamar's own brother ABSALOM (*father of peace*), who caused him to be murdered at a sheep-shearing festival, and then, apprehensive of the resentment of David, fled to the court of Talmai his grandfather, the king of Geshur, a district on the east of the Jordan south of Mount Hermon (2 Sam. xiii. 36).

Here he remained secure in its rocky fastnesses for three years, during which time the soul of David was *consumed* (2 Sam. xiii. 39, *margin*) with longing for his favourite son. Perceiving this, Joab availed himself of the services of a wise woman of Tekoa[1], who sought an interview with the king, and addressing him in an apologue similar to that which Nathan had employed, succeeded in obtaining permission for the exile's return. Joab, therefore, went to the court of the king of Geshur, and thence brought back the young prince, who took up his abode at Jerusalem, but was not suffered to see his father's face. Twice he sent a message to David's general, begging him to intercede in his behalf with the king, but Joab deemed he had done enough, and would take no further steps in the matter. Thereupon Absalom caused a barley-field belonging to Joab, which was near his own estate, to be set on fire, and the latter, probably fearing further outrage, informed the king, who consented to see his son, and gave him the kiss of peace (2 Sam. xiv. 23—33).

But the ungrateful son was no sooner thus restored,

---

[1] A village about six miles to the south of Bethlehem, the birthplace of the prophet *Amos* (Am. i. 1).

than he began to form plots against his father. First he surrounded himself with a small body-guard, with chariots and horses, and fifty men to run before him. Then, to ingratiate himself with the people, he took his stand by " the way of the gate[1]," a duty which David appears to have neglected, and conversed with suitors coming up to the city for judgment, lamented the delays they would encounter in obtaining· a hearing of their causes (2 Sam. xv. 3), and insinuated how different would be the aspect of affairs if *he* was made judge in the land. Young, handsome beyond compare in Israel (2 Sam. xiv. 25), sprung from a royal house both on his father and his mother's side (2 Sam. iii. 3), he made a deep impression on the people, and his insinuating manners and unusual condescension stole away their hearts (2 Sam. xv. 6). Since the dark sin of which he had been guilty, the hold of the king upon the nation appears to have been weakened, and he had become less fitted for the more personal and more energetic duties of his position. And now the powerful tribe of Judah, fretting, it has been suggested, under their absorption into one great kingdom, or looking for some greater degree of power under the supremacy of a prince like Absalom, showed signs of a want of confidence in their sovereign, and in the course of two years Absalom perceived that matters were ripe for a revolt[2].

Under pretence, therefore, of a vow which he had vowed to the Lord (2 Sam. xv. 7—9), he succeeded in obtaining from David permission to go to Hebron, the old capital of the tribe of Judah, and repaired thither accompanied by 200 men from Jerusalem, probably of the chief families, who were, however, entirely ignorant of his designs. To the same place also he summoned

---

[1] See above, p. 238.
[2] See the dates in margin, 2 Sam. xv.

22

Ahithophel the Gilonite, the *familiar friend* and *counsellor* of his father, whose advice was deemed to have the value of a Divine oracle[1].

While Absalom was taking these measures, news of the conspiracy and of the popular feeling reached the royal palace. Instantly, without offering any resistance, or striking a single blow in defence of his crown, David resolved on flight. Accompanied by the royal body-guard and the 600 Gittites, and a vast concourse of people, he left Jerusalem, and early in the morning crossed the brook Kidron. As far as the city boundaries he was also followed by the Levites, and the high-priests Zadok and Abiathar with the Ark. But David had no wish to expose the sacred symbol to any risk, and the two chiefs of the Levitical tribe might do him better service at Jerusalem; accordingly they were bidden to turn back. Then crossing the ravine of the Kidron, with head covered and unsandalled feet, his retinue manifesting every sign of profound sorrow, the king ascended the slopes of Olivet, and as he went received intelligence that his privy counsellor Ahithophel had gone over to the ranks of his rebellious son. In the defection of this man, his *equal*[2], his *guide*, his *own familiar friend*, he instantly saw his danger, and prayed that the counsel of Ahithophel might be *turned into foolishness* (2 Sam. xv. 31).

Reaching the summit of the hill, he encountered Hushai the Archite[3], *the king's friend*, with torn robe

---

[1] What was Ahithophel's motive for this defection is not stated; but it is to be remembered that he was the grand-father of Bath-sheba (Comp. 2 Sam. xx. 3 and xxiii. 34), and was doubtless well aware of the sad fate of Uriah, his son Eliam's brother-officer. See Blunt's *Coincidences*, p. II. x. pp. 136, 137. Art. *Ahithophel*, Smith's *Bib. Dict.*

[2] See Ps. xli. 9; lv. 12, 13, 20.

[3] Probably an inhabitant of Erech, a place of uncertain site. See Smith's *Bib. Dict.*

and dust upon his head. In him David saw a fitting instrument for counteracting the influence of Ahithophel, and persuaded him to return to Jerusalem, and undertake the dangerous task of pretending a devotion to the cause of Absalom, while really, in conjunction with Zadok and Abiathar and their two sons, he kept a strict watch over all that occurred. Hushai accordingly turned back, and David descended the further slopes of Olivet. Here he met Ziba, the wily servant of Mephibosheth, the son of his old friend Jonathan, with welcome supplies of wine, bread, and fruit. Ziba represented that his master was staying behind at Jerusalem, awaiting any change in his fortunes which the rebellion might bring, and, as a reward for his services, obtained a ready grant of his estates. At Bahurim, a little further down the hill, David encountered Shimei, a Benjamite of the house of Saul, who flung stones at the royal retinue, and imprecated on them the most furious curses, in which he perhaps expressed the long pent-up hatred of the family of Saul, as well as the popular feeling against the author of Uriah's death. The impetuous Abishai would have instantly cut off his head, but David stayed his hand, *Let him curse*, said he, *for the Lord hath bidden him* (2 Sam. xvi. 10—12). The way now led into the Jordan valley, and for the first time the weary retinue halted, and refreshed themselves with Ziba's welcome supplies.

Meanwhile Absalom, with Ahithophel and a numerous retinue, had reached Jerusalem. There he met Hushai, who saluted him with the words, *Long live the king.* Even Absalom was startled, and reproached him for his apparent treachery, but kept him by him. The first step of the usurper, suggested by Ahithophel, was to take possession of his father's harem[1], and so render all reconciliation impossible (Comp. 2 Sam. iii. 7, 8).

[1] Compare the account of Abner and Rizpah above, p. 320.

The course to be next taken was anxiously debated. Ahithophel was for instant measures, and offered with 12,000 men to head a pursuit after David that very night, while he was weary and weak-handed. If he smote the king, he felt sure the whole people would side with Absalom, and his triumph would be complete. The advice found favour with the usurper, and the elders about him. But first he resolved to call in Hushai, and ascertain his opinion. Hushai pronounced the plan imprudent in the extreme. To attack the king while surrounded by his *mighty men, all chafing in their minds, as a she bear robbed of her whelps,* was very dangerous. From a partial defeat the prince had everything to fear, and the king everything to gain. He counselled, therefore, delay, and the mustering of the entire national forces from Dan to Beer-sheba. Absalom approved of this plan, and Ahithophel, probably seeing the certain effects of such delay, and chagrined at the adoption of another's counsel in preference to his own, retired to Giloh, *put his household in order, and hanged himself* (2 Sam. xvii. 23).

Without a moment's delay Hushai now sought out Zadok and Abiathar, related all that had occurred in the council, and urged that a messenger should be instantly sent to David, to bid him not linger in the Jordan valley, but cross the river with all speed. The two sons of the high-priests were in concealment at the fountain of En-rogel, ready for such an errand. A female slave was sent thither to bid them instantly carry the message to David. They forthwith started, but narrowly escaped detection. At Bahurim a lad saw them and conveyed the news to Absalom, and it was only by hiding in a well that they escaped the vigilance of their pursuers, and announced their errand to David. Though it must have been midnight, the king instantly crossed the river, and before the dawn of the following day not one of his retinue remained on the western side of the Jordan[1]. Mahanaim, the former capital of Ishbosheth, now became his head-quarters, and here he mustered his forces, and placed them under the command of Joab, Abishai, and Ittai, and received a welcome supply of provisions from Shobi, the son of his old friend Nahash of Rabbah, from Machir of Lodebar, and Barzillai a wealthy Gileadite.

Meanwhile Absalom also had mustered his forces, and having entrusted the command to AMASA, the son of Ithra or Jether by Abigail David's sister (2 Sam. xvii. 25), he too crossed the Jordan. The decisive engagement, which was not long delayed, took place not far from Mahanaim, in the dense forest of Ephraim, a region still "covered with thick oaks, and tangled bushes, and thorny creepers growing over rugged rocks and ruinous precipices[2]." Here the army of Absalom was utterly routed. Entangled in the thick undergrowth, crushing each other in remediless ruin, upwards of 20,000 perished in that fatal wood, which *devoured more people that day than the sword devoured* (2 Sam. xviii. 8). Amidst the crowd of fugitives Absalom also fled, and as he rode on his mule where "the strong arms of the trees spread out so near the ground that one cannot walk erect beneath them[3]," his long hair caught in an oak, and he hung suspended from the tree. A man chanced to see him, and forthwith told Joab. He himself had forborne to touch the prince, having heard the strict injunctions of the loving David to his three captains before the battle *to deal tenderly with the young man.* But Joab had no such scruples; with three darts in his hand he went to the spot and transfixed him while yet alive. A great pit was then dug, and into it the corpse was flung,

---

[1] To this period belong Psalms iii., iv., xlii.
[2] Thomson, *The Land and the Book*, p. 490.   [3] Ibid.

and covered with a great heap of stones. With the death of the usurper Joab knew the rebellion was at an end, he therefore sounded the signal of recall, and the battle closed.

Meanwhile David, who had been sitting at the gate of Mahanaim anxiously awaiting tidings of the battle, no sooner heard that his son was dead, than he gave way to the most violent grief. Joab alone dared to confront him, bidding him bestir himself if he would not see another popular revolt. Roused at last, the king consented to present himself at "the gate." But he could not forget who had given the death-blow to his favourite son, and even vowed to transfer the chieftaincy of the troops to Amasa, though he had led the forces on the other side, and "in this was laid the lasting breach between himself and his powerful nephew, which neither the one nor the other ever forgave." The rebellion ended, the rightful monarch could return to his kingdom. With a self-control rare in Western no less than Eastern history, every step in his progress was marked by forgiveness. Shimei was forgiven, Mephibosheth, proved to have been faithful, was partially reinstated, and Barzillai rewarded with ample gifts (2 Sam. xix. 16—43).

But the danger was not yet over. In bringing about the king's return, his own tribe of Judah had the largest share. This provoked the old jealousy of the other tribes[1] (Comp. Judg. viii. 1; xii. 1), while the Benjamites even took up arms, and placed themselves under the leadership of Sheba, son of Bichri, a man of Mount Ephraim. Many others also rallied round him, and when Amasa, the

---

[1] "Now for the first time called *Israel*, as distinct from Judah. But it is likely that, although it now first appears, this distinction had actually grown up while David reigned over Judah only, and Ishbosheth over the other tribes." Kitto, *Bibl. Illustr.* III. 424.

new general-in-chief failed within three days to muster
the forces of Judah, David was afraid lest more harm
should come of this fresh rising than had come from
that of Absalom. Accordingly Abishai with the "Mighty
Men" was dispatched to quell the insurrection, and
to pursue after Sheba before he reached any fortified
towns. Taking with him the royal body-guard, Abishai,
accompanied by Joab, set out, and at the great stone
of Gibeon encountered Amasa. Joab's robe was girded
round his waist, and in the folds was a sword, which
"by accident or design protruded from the sheath."
Art thou in health, my brother? he saluted Amasa,
and took him by the beard as if to kiss him. The
other rushed into his embrace, and was instantly stabbed to the heart, his blood spirting out upon his cousin's
girdle and sandals. Leaving the body in the road,
Joab hurried on after Sheba, who, rousing the tribes
as he passed, had made for Abel Beth-Maachah[1], a
town of some importance far up in the north by the
waters of Merom. Thither Joab rushed in pursuit, threw
up an embankment, and battered the walls. A wise
woman saved the town from destruction. Approaching
the wall, she gained a parley with the angry general,
who promised to leave the place, if Sheba was put to
death. Thereupon she returned to her people, and the

---

[1] Sometimes called Abel-maim, *Abel on the waters* (2 Chr.
xvi. 4). "Taking advantage of an oblong knoll of natural
rock that rises above the surrounding plain, the original inhabitants raised a high mound sufficiently large for their city.
With a deep 'trench' (2 Sam. xx. 15) and strong wall, it
must have been almost impregnable. The country on every
side is most lovely, well watered, and very fertile. The
neighbouring fountains and brooks would convert any part of
this country into a paradise of fruits and flowers; and such,
no doubt, was Abel, when she was called a 'mother in Israel.'" (2 Sam. xx. 19.) Thomson, *The Land and the Book*
p. 217.

head of the rebel was soon flung into Joab's camp, who straightway sounded a trumpet, and with his troops returned to Jerusalem (2 Sam. xx. 22).

CHAPTER V

CLOSE OF DAVID'S REIGN.

2 Sam. xxi.—xxiv.   i Kings i. ii.   B. C. 1022—1015.

SHORTLY after David's restoration, his kingdom was visited for three years with a grievous famine. Enquiry was made of the Divine Oracle, and it was discovered to be a punishment for an act of faithlessness on the part of Saul, who had broken the solemn covenant made by Joshua with the Gibeonites (Josh. ix. 3—27). In a fit of sudden zeal for the children of Israel and Judah he had killed some of them, and devised a general massacre of the rest (2 Sam. xxi. 2, 5). The Gibeonites were now asked what atonement they were willing to receive for the wrongs they had suffered. In reply, they demanded neither silver nor gold. Blood had been spilt, and blood they would have, and nothing would satisfy them but permission to take seven of Saul's sons and hang, or rather crucify, them at Gibeah. Accordingly the two sons of Rizpah, the daughter of Aiah, and the five sons of Michal, whom they had borne to Saul, were delivered up, and the Gibeonites crucified them on the hill of Gibeah. This was done in April, at the beginning of barley-harvest[1] (2 Sam. xxii. 9), and there the bodies remained till the periodical rains in October *dropped upon them out of heaven* (2 Sam. xxii. 10). All this while, spreading on the rock a coarse sackcloth robe, Rizpah watched over the blackening corpses, and

---

[1] See Calendar, p. 155, and Article *Rizpah*, in Smith's *Bib. Dict.*

suffered neither the birds of the air to rest on them by day, nor the beasts of the field by night. The tale of her devoted love at length was conveyed to David, who had the remains removed, and at the same time directed that the bones of Saul also and of Jonathan should be taken from Jabesh-Gilead, and buried in the ancestral sepulchre of Kish, *after which God was intreated for the land* (2 Sam. xxi. 14).

Meanwhile, in consequence probably of the intestine feuds of the Israelites, the Philistines had recovered sufficient strength to venture on once more attacking them. David himself went with the host to battle, and in mortal combat with another descendant of the giant race was near falling a victim to his rashness, when he was succoured by the valiant Abishai, and the people, fearful lest *the light of Israel should be quenched* (2 Sam. xxi. 17), prevailed upon him to desist from accompanying them to battle in future. Other attempts were afterwards made by the Philistines, but the valour of David's captains served to keep them in check (2 Sam. xxi. 18—22).

The Hebrew kingdom had now attained its farthest limits, even those which God had revealed many centuries before in vision to Abraham (Gen. xv. 18). Not only had David given a capital to his people, but he had conquered all the nations on the immediate frontier of his realm. His kingdom had become like one of the kingdoms of the world[1]. It had its court, its palace, its splendour, its tributaries. In this hour of his prosperity the monarch was tempted (1 Chr. xxi. 1) to yield to pride and self-exaltation, and gave directions to Joab to carry out a general census of the people from Dan even to Beer-sheba. His object, it has been supposed, was either the levying of a poll-tax or the formation of a standing

---

[1] See Rawlinson's *Five Great Monarchies,* ii. 333, *n.*

army with a view to foreign conquests[1]. Whatever was
his precise motive, it excited the repugnance of the captains of the host, and even of Joab himself, who not only
warned the king against being *the cause of a trespass
in Israel*, but regarded the royal proposition as actually
abominable (1 Chr. xxi. 6). When, however, he found
that nothing would turn the king from his fixed purpose, he set out, and after the lapse of 9 months and 20
days reported 800,000 in Israel as fit for military service, and 500,000 in Judah. But before he had numbered Benjamin or Levi (2 Sam. xxiv. 10) David's heart
smote him, and Gad, the seer, was commissioned to offer
him the choice of 7 years' famine, or 3 months' defeat
before his enemies, or a 3 days' pestilence. David chose
*to fall into the hands of God rather than into the
hands of man*. Thereupon the plague began, and during
three days swept off upwards of 70,000. But when the
hand of the destroying angel was uplifted over Jerusalem, the Lord, *whose mercies are great* (2 Sam. xxiv. 14),
repented of the evil, and on the intercession of the king
the angel desisted, when he was by the threshing-floor of
Ornan or Araunah, a wealthy Jebusite. By the advice
of Gad David now bought the site of the threshing-floor
and a yoke of oxen, erected there an altar, and offered
thereon burnt-offerings and peace-offerings. Fire descended in testimony of the acceptance of the sacrifice,
and with the cessation of the plague consecrated the
rocky site of the future altar of Solomon's Temple on
Mount Moriah (2 Chr. iii. 1).

The remaining years of David's life were spent in
amassing treasures and materials, and making preparations for the erection of the Temple (1 Chr. xxii. 5, 14).
But even now the truth of the prophet's words was
forced upon him, that his foes should be those of his

---

[1] Jahn's *Hebrew Commonwealth*, p. 76.

own household. The three eldest of his sons, Amnon, Chileab, and Absalom being dead, the fourth—ADONIJAH —resolved to put forth his pretensions to the kingdom. Like Absalom, whom he resembled in personal beauty, he began by surrounding himself with chariots and horsemen, and succeeded in drawing over to his side not only the high-priest Abiathar, but even Joab, the commander-in-chief, whose loyalty at last wavered. Confident in the support of such old servants of the king, the pretender proclaimed a great sacrificial festival at the *Stone of Zoheleth*, south of Jerusalem, near the fountain of En-rogel, and invited to it all the royal princes, except Solomon, and not a few of the captains of the royal army (1 K. i. 5—9).

While they assembled at Zoheleth, Nathan the prophet persuaded Bath-sheba to seek an interview with the king, and inform him of what was going on. Bath-sheba did so, and had hardly concluded her tale, when Nathan himself entered, confirmed her account, and demanded to know whether Adonijah's actions had the royal approval. Though old and feeble, David had sufficient energy to rise to the present emergency, and solemnly assured Bath-sheba of his unalterable determination that Solomon should succeed to the throne. Then summoning Zadok and Benaiah he bade them, together with Nathan, convey Solomon in state down to Gihon, and there formally anoint and proclaim him king. Accordingly these officers, accompanied by the royal guards, escorted Solomon thither, mounted on the royal mule (1 K. i. 38), and there Zadok anointed him with oil from the sacred horn of the Tabernacle, amidst the sound of trumpets and loud shouts of *God save the King*. Thence the new monarch was escorted in triumph back through the city, and sat on the royal throne amidst general applause, in the sight of his aged father, who blessed God that during his own lifetime he had

been permitted to behold his successor (1 K. i. 45—48).
Intelligence of these transactions was conveyed to the
conspirators, in the midst of their festivities at En-rogel,
by Jonathan the son of Abiathar. They had already heard
the noise of the people shouting as Solomon passed in
procession through the city, and no sooner learnt the
cause than, seized with alarm, they instantly dispersed,
and *every man went his way* (1 K. i. 49). Dreading the
vengeance of the new king, Adonijah now fled to the
Tabernacle, put himself in sanctuary by grasping the
horns of the altar, and refused to quit the spot till Solomon had promised with an oath to spare his life. The
young and politic monarch, on being informed of this,
abstained from binding himself by any oath, and simply
assured Adonijah of safety *so long as he shewed himself
a worthy man,* but threatened him with death, *if
wickedness should be found in him* (1 K. i. 49—52).
On these conditions he quitted his place of refuge, and,
having made obeisance to the new king, returned to the
privacy of his own house (1 K. i. 53).

The days of David were now rapidly drawing to
a close. He therefore convened a solemn assembly of
all the chiefs and elders of his people, the royal princes,
the captains of his army, and his public officers, and
standing up, aged as he was, gave them his last charge,
and exhorted his son to constancy in the service of
Jehovah. He then solemnly delegated to him the accomplishment of the desire of his life, the erection of
the Temple, and committed to him in trust the abundant materials he had amassed for this purpose, as well
as a pattern of the building, and of everything belonging
to it. This address, confirmed as it was by the sight of
the gold and silver, the brass and iron and precious
stones, which the royal prudence had collected, had a
great effect upon the people, and they also joyfully contributed to the execution of their sovereign's design.

Then, in language of unequalled pathos and beauty, the
aged monarch solemnly thanked God for all His goodness, and prayed that He would bestow upon his son
" a perfect heart," enabling him to keep His testimonies
and statutes, and build the Temple for which he had
made provision. Amidst sacrifices of unusual abundance and great feastings and rejoicings, Solomon was
then for the second time anointed king, and received
the formal submission of all the royal princes, and the
chiefs of the nation. In another and more secret interview David gave his son his last counsels, not only concerning his own deportment as ruler, but also respecting
Joab and Shimei, who were committed to his vigilance,
and Barzillai the Gileadite, who was entrusted to his
regard. Then after a reign of $7\frac{1}{2}$ years at Hebron, and
of 33 years at Jerusalem, *in a good old age, full of
years, riches, and honour*, the son of Jesse, the Shepherd, the Warrior, the King, the Psalmist, was gathered
to his fathers, and buried in the city which had been
once the fortress of the heathen Jebusites, but was now
the capital of an empire that realised the loftiest ideal
of prophecy, stretching from the " river of Egypt " to
the Euphrates, and from the range of Lebanon to the
gulf of Akaba[1].

[1] The life of David admits of a fivefold division.   (i) His
shepherd life at Bethlehem ; (ii) His courtier life with Saul
at Gibeah ; (iii) His life as an outlaw ; (iv) His Kingly life at
Hebron during $7\frac{1}{2}$ years, and (v) at Jerusalem during 33 years,
in all 40. His history will be ever memorable, whether we
regard *the work he achieved*, or *his own personal character*.
    (i) *His work.* " He had succeeded to a kingdom distracted
with civil dissension, environed on every side, or occupied by
powerful and victorious enemies, without a capital, almost without an army, without any bond of union between the tribes. He
left a compact and united state, stretching from the frontier
of Egypt to the foot of Lebanon, from the Euphrates to the
sea. He had crushed the power of the Philistines, subdued

CHAPTER VI

ACCESSION OF SOLOMON.

1 Kings II.—VIII.　1 Chron. I.—IX.　B. C. 1015.

THE new king was hardly seated on the throne before he was called upon to repress with a high

or curbed all the adjacent kingdoms; he had formed a lasting and important alliance with the great city of Tyre. He had organized an immense disposable force: every month 24,000 men, furnished in rotation by the tribes, appeared in arms, and were trained as the standing militia of the country. At the head of his army were officers of consummate experience, and, what was more highly esteemed in the warfare of the time, of extraordinary personal activity, strength, and valour *." He had also given especial attention to the management of public worship, as the most efficacious means of promoting religion and morality, and, consequently, obedience to the Invisible, Supreme Monarch. The solemn transfer of the Ark of the Covenant, at which almost all the people were present, had made a deep impression on their minds, and had awakened them to a sincere adoration of Jehovah. These favourable dispositions he had upheld and strengthened by suitable regulations in the service of the priests and Levites, and especially by the instructive and animating Psalms, which were composed partly by himself, and partly by other poets and prophets †. "In comparison with the hymns of David, the sacred poetry of all other nations sinks into mediocrity. They have embodied so exquisitely the universal language of religious emotion that they have entered, with unquestioned propriety, into the ritual of the holier and more perfect religion of Christ. The songs which cheered the solitudes of the desert caves of Engedi, or resounded from the voice of the Hebrew people as they wound along the glens or the hill-sides of Judea, have been repeated for ages in almost every part of the habitable world, in the remotest islands of the ocean, among the forests of America or the sands of Africa ‡."

(ii) *His character.* Obedience to the Divine commands

---

* Milman's *History of the Jews,* I. 305.
† Jahn's *Hebrew Commonwealth,* p. 75.
‡ Milman's *History of the Jews,* I. 307.

hand a second and dangerous attempt of Adonijah to
obtain the kingdom.   As is usual in Oriental countries,
the influence of Bath-sheba the queen-mother was very

was ever with David the axiom of his life, and in every step
he took he shewed the greatest anxiety to act as God's servant (2 Sam. ii. 1 ; 1 Sam. xxiii. 2, 4). All deliverance from
danger, and all victories from first to last, he ascribed to the
Divine aid, and neither in the hour of danger, nor the more
trying hour of prosperity, did he go after "strange gods," or
introduce any idolatrous rites. It was, probably, to this feature of his administration that God referred, when He described him as *a man after His own heart* (1 Sam. xiii. 14,
Comp. Acts xiii. 22), rather than to his private virtues. And
yet these were of no mean order. "Shepherd, soldier, poet,
king, the romantic friend, the chivalrous leader, the devoted
father," he was eminent alike for his exalted piety, and his
noble patriotism. "During a war of seven years he never
lifted his sword against a subject, and at the end of it he
punished no rebels, and remembered no offence but the murder of his rival (2 Sam. iv. 10—12)." The adultery with
Bath-sheba, the murder of Uriah, the numbering of the people, with a view, probably, to foreign conquests, are the deep
blots on his fame, and the chief instances in which he forgot
alike himself and his God. "And yet when we look at the
piety of his youth, the depth of his contrition, the strength of
his faith, the fervour of his devotion, the loftiness and variety
of his genius, the largeness and warmth of his heart, his eminent valour in any age of warriors, his justice and wisdom as
a ruler, and, above all, his adherence to the worship and will
of God, we may well regard him as a model of kingly authority and spiritual obedience*."

Moreover, not only was he the ancestor of Christ after the
flesh, not only was the blessing of the Promise expressly
transferred to his family, but in his humiliation and exaltation, as the king of the people of God, and as the vanquisher
of heathen nations, he was a type of HIM whose coming he
foretold in many of the Psalms, and who is not called the
son of Abraham, or of Jacob, or of Moses, but the "*Son of
David.*" Kurtz's *Sacred History*, p. 189; Article *David*, in
Smith s *Bib. Dict.*

Angus, *Bible Handbook*, p. 437; Jahn's *Hebrew Commonwealth*, p. 76; Chandler's *Life of David*, pp. 582—587.

great. To her Adonijah preferred a request that she would intercede with the king in obtaining for him the hand of ABISHAG the Shunammite, his father's latest wife (1 Kings ii. 17). Bath-sheba sought an interview with Solomon, who instantly saw in this petition a design upon the throne, and declaring that Adonijah had forfeited his claim to the indulgence extended to him after the late rebellion, directed that he should be put to death by the hand of Benaiah. But he divined that others were concerned in the insinuating request, and notably the high-priest Abiathar, and Joab the commander-in-chief. The former, in consideration of his past services, was not put to death, but simply degraded from his high office, and ordered to live in retirement at Anathoth, a Levitical city, about 3 miles north of Jerusalem, whereby the word of the Lord concerning the house of Eli was fulfilled (1 Sam. ii. 31—33). News of these events no sooner reached the ears of Joab than he fled for refuge within the curtains of the Tabernacle at Gibeon, and caught hold of the horns of the altar. Thither, however, Solomon sent Benaiah with orders to put him to death. Benaiah went and told his old companion-in-arms the king's command. But Joab refused to stir from sanctuary, and the other returned to the king for fresh instructions. Solomon bade him not spare, but fall upon him even at the altar, urging his execution as a just recompense for the murder of Abner and Amasa. Thereupon he returned once more, and fell upon him at the altar, and obtained the important post of commander-in-chief, while Zadok succeeded to the high-priesthood (1 K. ii. 28—34).

Though David had spared the life of Shimei, he had on his death-bed cautioned Solomon against him, and now, possibly owing to some unrecorded symptoms of disaffection, the young king renewed the concession, but on condition that Shimei confined himself to the city of

Jerusalem, and did not stray beyond the brook Kidron, which separated him from the road to his old home at Bahurim. For three years Shimei carefully complied with this condition. But two of his slaves fleeing to Achish king of Gath, he went thither and brought them back. This sealed his fate. Intelligence of what he had done was conveyed to Solomon, who sent for him, and ordered his execution by the hands of Benaiah (1 K. ii. 36—46).

Shortly before this last event the king convened a general assembly of all the notables of the realm at Gibeon, where was not only the venerable Tabernacle of the Wanderings, but the brazen altar of burnt-sacrifice (2 Chr. i. 3, 5). There accordingly were gathered together all the great officers of state, the judges, the governors, and the chief of the fathers, and a thousand burnt-offerings were consumed on the Altar. On the night following this solemn ceremonial, the Lord appeared in vision to Solomon as he slept, and bade him prefer any petition he desired. Impressed with the magnitude of the office to which he had been called, as yet *humble in his own sight*, and mindful of the mercy bestowed upon his father, the young king prayed not for riches, or honour, or long life, or the life of his enemies, but *for a wise and understanding heart*, that he might know how to rule his people. His prayer pleased the Lord, and because he had requested nothing for himself, He, who is wont to give to the sons of men "more than they ask or think," not only promised him wisdom and knowledge, but assured him that all the blessings he had not asked should be "added unto him," including length of days, if he, for his part, took heed to observe the statutes and commandments of Jehovah, as his father had done before him (1 K. iii. 6—14). Returning to Jerusalem the king offered burnt-offerings and thank-offerings to the Lord before the Ark of the Covenant,

and celebrated a sacrificial feast with his whole court
(1 K. iii. 15).

Very shortly he was called upon to give proof of
that sagacity and clearness of judgment, especially in
judicial cases, so much prized by Orientals. Of two
women inhabiting one house together, each had an infant child. The mother of one overlaid hers while
she was asleep, and rising at midnight, laid it in the
bosom of the other woman, taking her live child in its
place. In the morning the latter discovered the deception that had been practised upon her, and demanded
the living infant. This the other woman refused, claim-
ing it for her own, and both of them appealed to Solomon, who commanded the living child to be divided
into two halves, one of which should be given to each.
The anguish of the real, and the cruel acquiescence of
the pretended mother in this sentence, decided the point
in a moment, and proved the sagacity of the king. But
besides judicial sagacity, Solomon was eminent for his
attainments. He was deeply versed in all the knowledge
of his age, his *wisdom excelled the wisdom of all
the children of the East country, and all the wisdom
of Egypt* (1 K. iv. 30). In the course of his life he
spake 3,000 proverbs, of which a considerable portion
remain in the "Book of Proverbs," and his Songs, of
which the "Song of Songs" alone survives, were a thousand and five. He spoke or wrote also of trees, from
the lofty cedar of Lebanon to the humble hyssop *that
springeth out of the wall, of beasts, of fowl, of creeping
things, and of fishes.* His fame spread abroad among
surrounding nations; and there came of all people to
hear his wisdom (1 K. iv. 34).

CHAPTER VII

THE BUILDING OF THE TEMPLE.

1 Kings v.—viii. 2 Chron. ii.—vii. B. C. 1012—1005.

MINDFUL of the repeated instructions of his father, Solomon no sooner received the congratulations of Hiram, king of Tyre, upon his coming to the throne, than he sent to that monarch requesting that he would let him have Sidonian artisans, and a supply of cedar wood from the forests of Lebanon, for the construction of the Temple. Hiram responded with alacrity to the request, and a regular treaty was entered into between the two kings. Solomon bound himself to send yearly 20,000 cors[1] of wheat, and 20 cors of oil to the Phœnicians, while Hiram undertook to float cedar trees and fir-trees to Joppa, and to send a number of skilled artificers to Jerusalem. For the purpose of felling the timber, a levy of 30,000 Israelites was made, who were placed under Adoniram; 10,000 were employed at a time, and relieved each other every month, spending a month in the mountains of Lebanon, and the other two months at their own homes (1 K. v. 13, 14). Besides these, 70,000 were employed as porters, and 80,000 as hewers in the various quarries. These latter were bondslaves, remnants of the Canaanites, who had not been expelled from the land. Under the eye of Tyrian master-builders, they hewed, and squared, and bevelled the stupendous blocks, some measuring even 17 and 18 feet, for the foundation of the sacred edifice.

---

[1] See *Table of Weights and Measures* in the *Appendix*, pp. 492, 493. "Each country needed what the other could supply. The wheat of the plains of Galilee and the oil of the hill-country of Judah maintained the royal household of Hiram (Comp. Acts xii. 20); the skill of the Phœnician artists supplied the want of it among the Israelites."—Kenrick's *Phœnicia*, p. 355.

23—2

The site, which had been already selected by David, was the eminence of Moriah, on the east of the city, rendered sacred at once as the spot where Abraham had offered up Isaac, and where the plague had been stayed during the last reign[1]. "Its rugged top was levelled with immense labour ; its sides, which to the east and south were precipitous, were faced with a wall of stone, built up perpendicular from the bottom of the valley, so as to appear to those who looked down, of most terrific height; a work of prodigious skill and labour, as the immense stones were strongly mortised together and wedged into the rock."

On this site, after 3 years of preparation, in the 4th year of Solomon's reign, and the 480th after the departure from Egypt, the foundations were laid. No sound of hammer or axe, or any tool of iron, was heard as the structure rose (1 K. vi. 7). Every beam already cut and squared, every stone already hewn and bevelled, was laid silently in its appointed site,

Like some tall palm the noiseless fabric sprung[2].

Within a quadrangle formed by a solid wall was an open court, afterwards known as the *Court of the Gentiles.* Within this, surrounded by another wall and on a higher[3] level, was the *Court of the Israelites,* and within this, and on a still higher level, the *Court of the Priests.* The Temple itself was built on the model of the ancient Tabernacle, but of more costly and durable materials, and like it consisted of the Porch, the Holy Place, and the Holy of Holies[4].

---

[1] See above, p. 346. Milman's *History of the Jews,* I. 311.
[2] Milman's *History of the Jews,* I. 315.
[3] "These successive terraces were an imitation of the Assyrian style of architecture, which at this time prevailed more or less all over Syria, and particularly at Tyre." Lewin's *Jerusalem,* p. 255; Art. *Palace* in Smith's *Bib. Dict.*
[4] The chief architect of the Temple was Hiram (1 K. vii.

(1) The *Porch* or Hall, which faced the East, was 10 cubits deep from E. to W., by 20 in width from N. to S., and 30 cubits high[1]. Either within, or, as some think, on either side of it, rose two brazen Pillars, the one called JACHIN (*durability*), the other BOAZ (*strength*), their capitals ornamented with network, chainwork, and pomegranates. (2) *The Holy Place*, the dimensions of which were exactly double those in the Tabernacle[2], was 40 cubits long, by 20 wide, and 30 high. Its walls were of hewn stone, wainscotted with cedar and overlaid with gold[3], and adorned with beautiful carvings representing cherubim, fruit, and flowers. It was entered by folding doors, similarly overlaid with gold and richly embossed. The floor was of cedar, boarded over with planks of fir or cypress; the ceiling was of fir, but both, as indeed every part, overlaid with gold in the richest profusion. In the Holy Place, as in the Tabernacle, stood the golden Altar of Incense, the Table of Shew-bread, and the Candlesticks of pure gold, five on the right, and five on the left. (3) A rich veil of the brightest colours separated the Holy Place from *the Holy of Holies*, which was a perfect cube of 20 cubits. Here was the original Ark overshadowed by two colossal Cherubim of olive wood overlaid with gold, 10 cubits in height. These stood at each end, N. and S., and faced each other, each having two wings expanded, so that one wing of each touched over the Ark, and the other touched the wall. Outside the Holy Place stood a great Tank or "Sea" of

13, 40), called also Huram in 2 Chr. ii. 13 ; iv. 11, 16, an Israelite on his mother's side, of the tribe of Dan or Naphtali, by birth a Tyrian.

[1] In 2 Chron. iii. 4, the height is said to have been 120 cubits. See Milman's *History of the Jews*, I. p. 313.

[2] See above, p. 122.

[3] "Such a copious use of gold was a practice known to the Phœnicians, the Assyrians, and the Babylonians." Rawlinson's *Bampton Lectures*, p. 107.

molten brass, 10 cubits in diameter, 30 round, 5 high, and capable of holding 2000 baths. It was supported on 12 oxen, three turned each way, and its rim was ornamented with blossoms. Besides this there were 10 Lavers, for the purpose of ablutions, which stood on moveable bases of brass; each side of these was formed in three panels, and adorned with figures of oxen, lions, and cherubim. The great Brazen Altar of Burnt-sacrifice, 20 cubits long and 10 high, stood on the exact site of the threshing-floor of Araunah.

At length, by the 7th month in the 11th year of Solomon's reign, the work was completed, and the king invited the chiefs of the different tribes, all the notables of the realm, as also the entire priestly and Levitical body[1], to the solemn dedication. He himself took his seat on a raised throne of brass ; the sacrificers stood before the Altar of Burnt-offering, surrounded by the choir arrayed in white robes, and playing on cymbals, psalteries, and harps ; while the assembled nation crowded the courts without. Countless sheep and oxen were first laid on the brazen altar. Then from under the covering, where David had placed it, the priests solemnly brought the Ark of the Covenant to the folding-doors of the Temple. These were opened, and then past the Table of Shew-bread, and the golden Candlesticks, and the Altar of Incense, it was conveyed through the Veil to its appointed place, and the Cherubim spread

---

[1] The functions of the priests and Levites had already been duly arranged by David. (i) The Priests were divided into 24 courses (1 Chr. xxiv. 1—19; 2 Chr. xxiii. 8; Luke i. 5), each of which served in rotation for one week, the special services of the week being assigned by lot (Luke i. 9). (ii) Of the Levites 24,000 were over the work of the temple ; 6,000 were officers and judges ; 4,000 were porters or sentries, and as such bore arms (1 Chr. ix. 19 ; 2 Chr. xxxi. 2); 4,000 formed the choir of singers and musicians. See Arts. *Priests* and *Levites* in Smith's *Bib. Dict.*

over it their wings, and "received it, as it were, under
their protection." At this moment the choir lifted up
their voices *with the trumpets and cymbals, and instruments of music, and made one sound to be heard
in praising and thanking the Lord*[1]*, whose mercy en-
dureth for ever*, and simultaneously the Temple was
filled with a cloud (1 K. viii. 10, 11), the "Glory" of the
Lord descended, and Jehovah took possession of His
new abode. Thereupon the king, rising on his brazen
throne, and kneeling down upon his knees, spread forth
his hands toward heaven, and offered up a solemn and
sublime prayer. As he concluded with the petition,
*Arise, O Lord God, into Thy resting-place, Thou and
the Ark of Thy strength*, fire flashed forth from the
"Glory" already filling the Temple, and consumed the
burnt-offerings and the sacrifices (2 Chr. vii. 3), while
the priests stood without, blinded with the excess of
splendour, and the people bowing with their faces to
the ground, worshipped and praised the Lord. The
ceremony of dedication lasted seven days, and was succeeded by the Feast of Tabernacles, which was continued
for two weeks, or twice the usual time[2]. During it, upwards of 22,000 oxen and 120,000 sheep were partly offered in sacrifice, and partly made the materials of a
great sacrificial feast, from which, on the 23rd day
of the 7th month, the king sent the people away, *glad
and merry in heart for the goodness that the Lord had
shewed unto David, and to Solomon, and to Israel His
people* (2 Chr. vii. 10).

[1] Comp. Psalms xxiv, xlvii, xcvii, xcviii, cvi.
[2] See above, p 153.

CHAPTER VIII

SOLOMON'S REIGN CONTINUED.

2 Kings ix.—xi.   2 Chr. viii. ix.   B. C. 1005—975.

BEFORE the Temple was thus completed, Solomon had proceeded to construct other magnificent buildings. Amongst these was a sumptuous palace for himself, surrounded with beautiful pleasure-grounds, which stood within the city opposite to the Temple, and occupied 13 years in building (1 K. vii. 1). Another palace he built for Pharaoh's daughter, whom he had espoused, and besides it the house of the forest of Lebanon [1], 175 ft. long, half that measurement in width, and 50 ft. high. The roof, which was made of cedar, was supported by 4 rows of cedar columns, and the whole received light from 3 rows of windows on each side. Adjoining it were the women's apartments, a banqueting-hall, and spacious and luxuriant gardens.

Other works were designed for use and security; among these were artificial reservoirs for supplying the city with water, and the strengthening or repairing of a fortress called Millo (1 K. ix. 15), already begun by David (2 Sam. v. 9). Solomon also fortified Baalath [2],

---

[1] So called from its cedar pillars. Similarly the halls of the Nimroud palace " were supported by rows of pillars, not of stone, but of wood, and the Hall of Lebanon was supported by 3 rows of cedar pillars, 15 in a row, making 45 in the whole." Lewin's *Jerusalem*, p. 270. Rawlinson's *Bampton Lectures*, p. 106.

[2] Baalath was a town of Dan near the Philistine plain. For the two Beth-horons, see above, p. 212. "The importance of the road on which the two Beth-horons are situated, the main approach to the interior of the country from the hostile districts on both sides of Palestine—Philistia and Egypt on the west, Moab and Ammon on the east—at once explains and justifies the frequent fortification of these towns at dif-

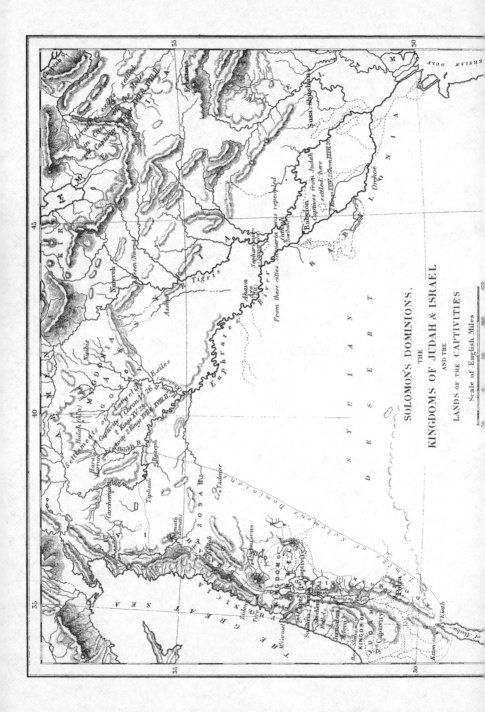

SOLOMON'S DOMINIONS.

THE

KINGDOMS OF JUDAH & ISRAEL

AND THE

LANDS OF THE CAPTIVITIES

Scale of English Miles

Gezer[1] and the two Beth-horons on the great road towards the sea-coast; the strong and important post of
Hazor[2] to defend the entrance from Syria and Assyria:
Megiddo to guard the Esdraelon plain; while, for the
protection of his eastern caravans, he built Tadmor,
afterwards called *Palmyra*, in the Syrian wilderness,
and Tiphsah or *Thapsacus*[3] on the Euphrates (2 Chr.
viii. 3—6).

His reign was a period of great commercial activity.
On the North-west the important kingdom of Phœnicia
was united with him by the bonds of a strict alliance.
Once only did Hiram, king of Tyre, express any dissatisfaction with the dealings of his powerful friend. Solomon had bestowed upon him twenty cities which he had
conquered in the land of Galilee, on the borders of
Asher. But when the Tyrian king came forth to see
them, he was much dissatisfied. One of them named

---

ferent periods of the history. This road is still, as in ancient
times, the great road of communication and heavy transport
between Jerusalem and the sea-coast." Robinson's *Bibl. Res.*
II. 252. Smith's *Bib. Dict.*, Art. *Beth-horon*.

[1] The exact site of Gezer has not been found, but it
must have been between the lower Beth-horon and the sea,
on the regular coast-road of communication with Egypt.
Smith's *Bibl. Dict.*

[2] For Hazor see above, pp. 201, 214. For Megiddo (now
el-Lejjûn), see p. 240. It was a principal station on the caravan route from Egypt to Damascus, "and for a long while
possessed a large khan, mentioned by Maundrell and many
travellers after him." Van de Velde, I. 353.

[3] Tiphsah (= πόρος, "a ford"), the Thapsacus of the Greeks
and Romans, "must have been a place of considerable trade,
the land-traffic between the East and West passing through
it, first on account of its fordway (which was the lowest upon
the Euphrates), and then on account of its bridge, while it
was likewise the point where goods were both embarked for
transport down the stream, and also disembarked from boats
which had come up to it, to be conveyed on to their final
destination by land." Smith's *Bib. Dict.*

Cabul, now *Kabûl*, about 8 or 9 miles east of *Akka*, in his own Phœnician tongue denoted *displeasure*, and this name he gave to them all (1 K. ix. 10—13).

1. But Phœnician enterprise was turned to account in other directions. Having possession of the Eastern shore of the Red Sea, Solomon strengthened the ports of Elath and Ezion-geber (*the giant's backbone*), and with the assistance of Tyrian shipwrights, constructed a fleet, which sailed to Ophir[1], and returned with gold, silver, ivory, and other products (1 K. ix. 26—28).

2. The Tyrian alliance opened up also the traffic of the Mediterranean. On every shore washed by this sea Phœnician energy had founded colonies, and opened trading ports, of which the chief was Tarshish, or Tartessus—"the Peru of Tyrian adventure[2]"—on the southern coast of Spain, at this time abounding in gold and silver mines. Hither Solomon's fleet sailed in company with that of Hiram, and brought back every three years of its precious products (1 K. x. 22).

3. Another important outlet for trade was supplied by Egypt. Not only had Solomon espoused a daughter of Pharaoh, but in defiance of the Mosaic Law (Deut. xvii. 16) he exchanged the produce of his own country

---

[1] "A region variously identified with (i) the south of Arabia, (ii) Sofala on the coast of Africa opposite to Madagascar, and (iii) India; the first was probably its locality, though the Jewish fleets may also have visited India." Kenrick's *Phœnicia*, p. 357.

[2] Milman's *History of the Jews*, I. 322. "Notwithstanding the long export of silver from the mines of Tartessus by the Phœnicians, who drew from them the wealth by which they founded so many powerful colonies, the Carthaginians, who succeeded the Phœnicians in their possession, derived from them the revenues by which they were enabled to pay their mercenary armies. Even in the Roman times 40,000 men were employed as miners within a circuit of 400 stadia near Carthagena, and the workings yielded a revenue to the republic of 20,500 drachmas daily." Kenrick's *Phœnicia*, p. 211.

for the horses and chariots of Egypt, as also for the
linen-yarn, spun from the flax which the Nile valley
yielded in abundance (1 K. x. 28, 29).

4. Last, but not least important, was the inland
trade of the Arabian peninsula. Caravans of the native
tribes transported on camels the spices, incense, gold,
precious stones, and valuable woods of the country, especially the almug or sandal, and brought them into the
dominions of Solomon, or, if they were intended for his
Tyrian allies, to Gezer and Beth-horon, whence they
were transported to the port of Joppa.

But though these several branches of commerce
opened up to the Hebrew kingdom many and various
sources of national prosperity, and tended to multiply
the luxuries and magnificence of the court, this prosperity was on the surface only. Hidden beneath its
external splendour were several cankers, which surely
though secretly undermined the true life of the nation.
First of all, this massing of gold and silver, as doubtless
the Jewish Lawgiver had foreseen, could only be brought
about by a process of severe taxation. And while forced
to bear burdens heavy and grievous, the nation saw the
tide of commercial profits, instead of being fairly distributed among the people, flowing only into the royal exchequer. Secondly, these commercial alliances seriously
affected the nation's allegiance to Jehovah. In imitation
of other Oriental empires Solomon surrounded himself
with a numerous harem, having 700 wives and 300 concubines (1 K. xi. 1—3). Besides the daughter of Pharaoh,
he espoused women of the Moabites, Ammonites, Edomites, Zidonians, and Hittites and, as he grew old, they
turned away his heart from the worship of the true God.
Three times, indeed, during the year he celebrated the
Festivals of Jehovah (1 K. ix. 25), but the licentious
worship of Baal and Ashtaroth, of Moloch and Chemosh,
found its way even into the Holy City, and their hideous

orgies were enacted "hard by the oracles of God" (1 K. xi. 5—8).

At first, perhaps, there may have been few signs of weakness in a fabric so vast and so magnificent. In the figurative language of the sacred record, *silver was in Jerusalem as stones, and cedar-trees as sycamores; Judah and Israel were many, as the sand which is by the sea in multitude, eating and drinking and making merry;* in the enjoyment of profound peace, *every man dwelt safely under his vine and under his fig-tree.* Princes administered the government of various portions of the empire (1 K. iv. 1—6); officers deputed for the purpose provided victual for the royal table, and barley and straw for Solomon's 40,000 chariot-horses, his 12,000 war-horses (1 K. iv. 26), and his swift mules; kings and princes of subject-provinces brought in their tribute at a fixed rate year by year (1 K. x. 25); and when the queen of Sheba came with her great train from distant Yemen in Arabia to prove the king with hard questions, and beheld his palace, *and the meat of his table, and the sitting of his servants, and the attendance of his ministers, and their apparel, and his cup-bearers,* and the ascent from his own palace to the Temple[1], there was no spirit left in her, and she confessed that the half of his fame and magnificence had not been told her (1 K. x. 1—9).

Before long, however, clouds began to gather portending the coming storm. Once at Gibeon, on the oc-

---

[1] "The Palace of Solomon was below the Temple Platform, and in laying the solid foundations of Millo, provision had been made for a double passage from the Palace to the Temple, about 250 ft. long and 42 ft. wide, formed of bevelled stones, and rising by a gentle incline to one of the gates of the Inner Temple. This marvellous subterranean approach, impregnable from its nature to the ravages of time, still remains, though painfully disfigured; it is called to this day the Temple of Solomon." Lewin's *Jerusalem*, p. 270.

casion of his accession, again after the dedication of the Temple (1 K. iii. 5 ; ix. 2), the Lord had appeared to Solomon, and on condition that he continued to walk in the ways of his father, had promised to crown him with prosperity, and establish his dynasty, but at the same time had warned him that any apostasy would bring down severe punishment. But promise and warning had been alike forgotten, and when the Lord appeared for the third time, it was to announce that the kingdom should be rent from him (1 K. xi. 9—13).

    i. The quarter, whence danger first threatened, was on the south, in the land of Edom. When Joab invaded that country during the late reign, and for six months directed an indiscriminate massacre of the male population, HADAD, who was of the blood royal, and at that time a little child, was carried off into Egypt, where he was hospitably received by the reigning Pharaoh, and rapidly rising in the royal esteem, obtained the hand of Tahpenes, the sister of the Egyptian queen. On the death of David and of Joab, he returned from Egypt, and thirsting to break off the hard yoke of Jacob from the neck of Esau, organized a revolt in his native land, and began to threaten Solomon's communication with the Elanitic Gulf (1 K. xi. 15—22).

    ii. A second adversary appeared in the north-eastern provinces of the empire. REZON, the Syrian, the son of Eliadah, flying from the defeat which his feudal lord Hadadezer, king of Zobah, had sustained at the hands of David, put himself at the head of a band of adventurers and seized Damascus. Here he set up a petty kingdom, and *became an adversary to Israel all the days of Solomon*, and an impediment to the king's commerce with Tadmor and the Euphrates (1 K. xi. 23—25).

    iii. But a far more formidable adversary appeared nearer home. When Solomon was constructing the fortifications of Millo under the citadel of Zion, he observed

the industry and activity of Jeroboam, already known
as a man of valour, the son of an Ephraimite, named
Nebat. Perceiving his worth, the king not only employed him on the works, but elevated him to the rank of
collector of the taxes from his native tribe. On one
occasion as he was going out of Jerusalem, Jeroboam
encountered the prophet Ahijah of the ancient sanctuary of Shiloh, and accompanied him to a neighbouring
field. When they were alone, the prophet rent the new
outer robe in which he was attired into twelve pieces,
and gave ten of them to Jeroboam, assuring him at the
same time that he should reign over ten of the tribes,
and that if he proved faithful to His laws God would
establish his dynasty as he had done that of David
(1 K. xi. 26—39). News of this mysterious intimation
in some way reached the ears of Solomon, and he sought
to put Jeroboam to death, but the latter fled for refuge
to the court of Shishak (*Sheshonk* I.), a powerful monarch,
who was bent on restoring Egypt to its former greatness. Here he remained during the rest of Solomon's
reign. Departing from his earlier policy the king had
laid the burden of compulsory labour not only on the
remnant of the Canaanites, but on the Israelites themselves (1 K. v. 13, 14). This increased the old jealousy
of the great house of Joseph, and a man like Jeroboam
was certain at any time to rally round him all the
national discontent and ill-feeling against the once prosperous monarch.

While the signs of coming danger were thus becoming more and more evident, Solomon's reign of 40 years
came to a close, B.C. 975. The hopes he might have inspired
when first elevated to the throne had not been fulfilled.
He had, indeed, built the promised Temple; he had
adorned Jerusalem with sumptuous palaces; his wisdom
and learning had attracted the notice and roused the
envy of distant monarchs; but he had not been mindful,

save for a short time, while the example of David and the instructions of his preceptor Nathan were fresh in his memory, of the vocation to which he had been called. His kingdom exhibited some of the worst faults of other Oriental monarchies. He had violated each and all of the fundamental principles of the kingdom as laid down by the great Lawgiver of his nation. He had encouraged the worst forms of idolatry, had multiplied wives, had amassed enormous wealth, had laid heavy burdens on the people, and sated with pomp and splendour and selfish luxuries, he had confessed the vanity of his life (Eccles. i. 12—18). The kingdom which Abraham had seen in vision stretching from the river of Egypt to the gates of Damascus had, indeed, been realized, but its unity was not destined to survive the reign of the son of David[1].

[1] See Milman's *History of the Jews*, I. 326—328; Art. *Solomon* in Smith's *Bib. Dict.*; Jahn's *Hebrew Commonwealth*, 78, 79; Kitto's *Daily Bible Illustrations*, IV. 127—132.

BOOK X

KINGDOMS OF JUDAH AND ISRAEL.

PART I

Period of mutual hostility.

CHAPTER I

THE REVOLT OF THE TEN TRIBES.

1 Kings xii. 2 Chron. x. B. C. 975.

REHOBOAM, the successor of Solomon, was 41 years of age when he came to the throne. Though his title does not seem to have been disputed at Jerusalem, he deemed it right to obtain a more general and public recognition, and probably as a concession to the powerful house of Joseph, convened a solemn assembly of the tribes at Shechem, its ancient but ruined[1] capital. On his arrival there he encountered JEROBOAM, who had been summoned from his retreat in Egypt, and now boldly appeared at the head of a deputation from all the tribes requesting a remission of the taxes and other heavy burdens, which had been laid upon the nation during the late reign. Thus directly appealed to, Rehoboam requested a space of three days for deliberation, and during this period first consulted the old advisers of his father. They unanimously suggested that he should accede to the nation's request, and lighten its burden. But besides these experienced counsellors there were

---

[1] See above, p. 254.

young men of rank, who had been the king's companions, and were now about his court. They could ill brook any line of policy that seemed likely to lower the power of their patron, and advised him to take up the matter with a high hand, and by a firm denial of the nation's request put down once and for all any similar demand. In an evil hour Rehoboam listened to their counsel, and at the end of the three days, when the envoys, again headed by Jeroboam, were summoned into his presence, announced to them his final resolve. *My father made your yoke heavy,* said he in the true spirit of an Oriental despot, *and I will add to your yoke; my father chastised you with whips, but I will chastise you with scorpions* (1 K. xii. 1—15).

This senseless reply was no sooner made known to the tribes than it roused a general spirit of rebellion. *What portion have we in David?* exclaimed the great tribe of Ephraim, *and what inheritance in the son of Jesse?   To your tents, O Israel; now see to thine own house, David* (comp. 2 Sam. xx. 1). The assembly broke up in confusion, and each man returned to his home. But Rehoboam did not yet discern the full force of the rising storm.   He was unwise enough to send Adoram, who had been chief receiver of the tribute during the reigns of his father and grandfather (2 Sam. xx. 24; 1 K. v. 14), to levy the usual dues. But the fate of his envoy proved the strength of the popular feeling. *All Israel stoned him with stones, that he died,* and the king himself was obliged to fly in haste to Jerusalem. His first impulse on his return was to punish the rebellious tribes, and for this purpose he gathered together an army of 180,000 men.   But his preparations for a civil war were forbidden by Shemaiah, a man of God, who declared it to be the will of Jehovah that all hostilities should be laid aside, for the rending of the kingdom *was from Him* (1 K. xii. 18—24). Thereupon the

24

projected war was given up, and the rebellion was complete[1].

According to the new division of the land, (i) *The kingdom of Judah* included that tribe itself, together with Benjamin, which transferred to it its allegiance

[1] The disunion of the kingdom of Solomon, though apparently sudden, had been brought about by many pre-disposing causes. From the earliest period there had been a jealous rivalry between the powerful tribes of Ephraim and Judah, like that between the houses of York and Lancaster in our own history.

For upwards of 400 years the leadership of the nation had been practically in the hands of Ephraim. From this tribe had come the great hero Joshua; to it belonged, at least by his place of birth, the great prophet Samuel; and though from "little Benjamin" had come the first king, yet hereditary ties as well as geographical position had united it to the house of Joseph. Within the boundaries, moreover, of Ephraim had been the sanctuaries of Shechem and Shiloh, which would naturally make it the resort of numbers from all parts of the country. Hence the spirit of jealousy this tribe was ever ready to evince if any exploit was performed or advantage gained in which it had not the lion's share. Hence its complaints against Gideon*, against Jephthah†, against David‡.

But its influence, hitherto so great, began to wane when the victories of the latter prince exalted the tribe of Judah to its proud pre-eminence. For seven years Ephraim supported Ishbosheth's rival throne at Mahanaim, but when he died, and David captured Jebus, gave to the nation a fortress and a capital, and transferred thither the Tabernacle, the glories of Shechem and of Shiloh began to vanish away. For a time David's personal influence preserved the semblance of union, and many Ephraimites were in high favour about his person (1 Chr. xii. 30; xxvii. 10, 14), but the restoration of the king after the rebellion of Absalom was the signal for an outburst of the old rivalry, which well-nigh precipitated a disruption (2 Sam. xx. 1), and when the smouldering feelings of jealousy were fanned into exasperation by the oppressive taxation of Solomon and the insane folly of his son, a leader only was required, like Jeroboam, to make the separation complete. See Blunt's *Script. Coincid.* 164—175.

* See p. 249.   † See p. 257.   ‡ See p. 342.

probably because Jerusalem was within its borders, and, at least eventually, a part if not all of the territory of Simeon and of Dan. For the present Edom appears to have remained its faithful vassal, and guarded the caravan trade with Ophir, while Philistia continued, for the most part, quiet. (ii) *The kingdom of Israel,* on the other hand, included that of the remaining eight tribes, *i. e.* Ephraim, and half Manasseh, Issachar, Zebulun, Asher, and Naphtali, as well as the coast line between Accho and Joppa, on the west of the Jordan; Reuben, Gad, and the remaining half tribe of Manasseh on the east of that river. Its vassal states were Moab (2 K. iii. 4), and so much of Syria as had remained subject to Solomon (1 K. xi. 24)[1].

The first act of Jeroboam, on being declared ruler of the Ten Tribes, was to give a capital to his kingdom. For this purpose he rebuilt and fortified Shechem. His next step was to secure his dominions against his powerful northern neighbour, Syria. He, therefore, fortified Penuel[2] beyond the Jordan, which commanded the fords of Succoth, and was on the great caravan road leading over Gilead to Damascus. But it required little reflection to convince him, that so long as the yearly pilgrimages summoned their thousands and tens of thousands to Jerusalem, his authority was but nominal. The Levitical class would constantly require to go up to the City of David in the order of their courses[3], and the majority of them began to leave his kingdom for that of

[1] "The whole area of Palestine was nearly equal to that of the kingdom of Holland (13,610 sq. m.), or rather more than that of the 6 northern counties of England (13,136 sq. m.). The kingdom of Judah was rather less than Northumberland, Durham, and Westmoreland (3,683 sq. m.); the kingdom of Israel was very nearly as large as Yorkshire, Lancashire, and Cumberland (9,453 sq. m.)." See Smith's *Bib. Dict.,* Article *Kingdom of Israel.*

[2] See above, p. 250.   [3] See above, p. 358, n.

Judah. Without a Temple, without the Ark, without a Priesthood, he felt he could not maintain his power. Within the boundaries, however, of his realm were two sanctuaries, Bethel in the south, and Dan in the north. These, after some deliberation (1 K. xii. 28), he resolved to elevate into seats for national worship, which he hoped might rival the Temple at Jerusalem. Instead, however, of erecting altars there in honour of Jehovah, he made two calves of gold, figures probably of Apis or Mnevis, whose worship he had often witnessed during his residence in Egypt, and set them up at either sanctuary, with the address, *Behold thy gods, O Israel, which brought thee out of the land of Egypt* (1 K. xii. 28). Moreover, at both places he established a new order of priests, not taken from the sons of Levi, but from the lowest of the people, and therefore absolutely dependent on himself, and into this order any one could obtain admission on sacrificing a young bullock and seven rams (2 Chr. xiii. 9).

Having taken these measures, on the 15th day of the eighth month[1] he proclaimed a solemn Festival of Dedication, and went up to Bethel, to offer incense in person on the altar. But at this critical moment, as he was standing there, a man of God from Judah appeared, who boldly confronted the king, denounced the idolatrous service, and foretold the desecration of the altar by a future king of the house of Judah, Josiah by name, who would offer upon it the priests of the high-places, and burn men's bones upon it (See 2 K. xxiii. 15). Enraged at this out-spoken defiance, Jeroboam stretched forth his hand, and bade the bystanders seize the bold stranger. But at the moment his hand became suddenly paralysed, and at the same time the altar was rent asunder, and the ashes of the victims were poured out. Now thoroughly

---

[1] The month of the Vintage in Northern Palestine. See the Calendar above, p. 155.

alarmed, the king implored the prophet to intercede with the Lord for him, that the heavy judgment he had incurred might be removed. The other complied, and the king's hand was restored. Grateful for this signal favour, Jeroboam would now have hospitably entertained the man of God. But the latter had been sent on a special errand, and his commands had been precise, and peremptory, neither to eat bread, nor drink water in a place so openly profaned with idolatry, nor even to return thence by the same road that he had come. Accordingly he declined the royal invitation, and went his way (1 K. xiii. 10).

On the road, however, as he lingered under an oak, he was overtaken by an old prophet of Bethel, who had heard from his sons of the day's occurrences at the festival. His own guilty silence had wellnigh made him a partaker in the sins of the king, and the bold bearing of the stranger reminded him of what he himself should have done. Either, therefore, from a wish to win respect for himself once more by intercourse with such an accredited messenger of the Most High, or with the full intention of deceiving him, and so bringing discredit on his words, he hurried after him, and now announced himself as the bearer of a distinct Divine command that he should return to Bethel. Overcome by this solemn declaration, the other accompanied him to the town. But as they were seated at the meal, the Spirit of the Lord came upon the guilty host, and the Deceiver was constrained to pronounce the doom of the Deceived. The man of God had been faithless to the terms of his commission, and a certain death awaited him, nor should his body ever come into the sepulchre of his fathers. With his doom upon him he went his way, and a lion met and slew him (1 K. xiii. 24).

But though dead, he was yet to speak, and testify to the solemnity of the mission on which he had been sent.

When he was found lying dead on the road, the lion also was standing there, as well as the ass on which he had ridden; the beast of prey had not eaten the corpse, nor torn the ass. Thus the mysterious circumstances of the prophet's death confirmed that sign of his authority, which he had weakened during his life; and the old prophet of Bethel, by laying him in his own sepulchre with all honour, and charging his sons after his death to bury him beside the victim of his own deceit, preserved in Jeroboam's new religious capital a silent witness against the idolatries there practised (1 K. xiii. 30—32).

CHAPTER II

REHOBOAM AND ABIJAH, JEROBOAM AND NADAB.

1 Kings xiii.—xv.   2 Chr. xi.—xiii.   B. C. 975—955.

THIS warning, however, though confirmed by signs and wonders, had little or no effect on Jeroboam himself. He persisted in his evil courses, and his dynasty was destined to pass away, a fact before long revealed to him under very mournful circumstances. His son Abijah fell sick. In his anxiety to know the fate of the hope of his kingdom, Jeroboam bade his wife disguise herself, and repair to Shiloh, and there consult the now blind and aged prophet, who had foretold his own elevation to the throne. Though she was effectually disguised, and presented only the gift of an ordinary person, a few loaves, some cakes, and a cruse of honey, the prophet detected his visitor as soon as he heard the sound of her feet at the door, and confirmed her worst fears. In words of utmost sternness he denounced her husband's idolatries, and distinctly told her that her son would die. He, indeed, as one in whom *was found some good thing towards the Lord God of Israel,* would descend into the grave mourned and lamented by the whole people. But no other of his family would thus receive an honourable funeral, and his death would be but the prelude of the destruction of his father's dynasty. With a heavy heart the mother returned, and as she entered the town of Tirzah, Abijah sickened, and the blind prophet's words came true (1 K. xiv. 1—18).

Meanwhile, the relations between the rival kingdoms had been marked by continued hostility (1 K. xiv. 30; 2 Chr. xii. 15). The first step taken by Rehoboam, when the disruption of the kingdom was complete, was to fortify 15 cities in the neighbourhood of his capital, and in the southern and south-western portions of Judah (2 Chr. xi. 5—12). All these he stored with provisions and arms, and placed over them commandants. During the first three years of his reign he walked in the ways of the Lord, and was strengthened in upholding the principles of true religion by numerous bodies of priests and Levites, who flocked into the territory of Judah from that of Jeroboam, as also by many of the tribes of Israel, who still remained faithful to the Lord God of their fathers (2 Chr. xi. 13—17). But soon, like Solomon before him, he too was found wanting. Surrounding himself with a numerous harem, he took 18 wives and 60 concubines, by whom he became the father of numerous sons and daughters. Reserving the throne for Abijah, the son of Maachah daughter of Absalom, he dispersed the rest of the royal princes among his fortified cities, and in the splendour of his court and the security of his now established throne, forgat the law of the Lord (2 Chr. xii. 1), and set an evil example to his subjects, who speedily began to build high places, and set up *images and groves on every high hill, and under every green tree* (1 K. xiv. 22—24).

Five years, however, after his accession, his peace was rudely disturbed. Shishak the Egyptian king, instigated probably by Jeroboam, whom as we have already seen, he had befriended in exile, advanced against Judah with 1200 chariots, 60,000 cavalry, and an enormous host of Libyans, Nubians, and Ethiopians. Having made himself master of Rehoboam's fenced cities, he penetrated as far as his capital, and forced him to purchase an ignominious peace by delivering up the treasure of the royal palace and the Temple, even to the shields of gold, which Solomon had made for the purpose of being borne before him whenever he visited the Temple in state[1] (1 K. x. 16, 17). More than this the Egyptian monarch did not attempt, as Shemaiah the prophet had promised would be the case, if the king and his people displayed signs of real contrition for their idolatries. After this deep humiliation, the moral condition of Judah seems to have improved, and the rest of Rehoboam's reign is not marked by any remarkable event. He died, B.C. 957, at the age of 58, after a reign of 17 years, and was succeeded by his son ABIJAH.

The new king continued the war with Jeroboam, and made a determined effort to recover the ten tribes. At Mount Zemaraim, in the range of Ephraim, he confronted with 400,000 troops twice that number of the enemy; and previously to the battle endeavoured by a solemn address to win over the subjects of his rival to their former allegiance. He reminded them of the Divine election of David to the throne of the entire nation, and the emphatic manner in which the monarchy had been covenanted to him; he recounted the circumstances under which Jeroboam had usurped the regal power, and con-

---

[1] "This success is found to have been commemorated by Shishak on the outside of the great temple of Karnak; and here in a long list of captured towns and districts, which Shishak boasts of having added to his dominions, occurs the 'Melchi Yuda,' or kingdom of Judah, the conquest of which by this king is thus distinctly noticed in the Egyptian records." Rawlinson's *Bampton Lectures*, p. 126; Herod. II. p. 376.

trasted the idolatrous worship he had established with
the time-honoured ritual of the Temple, and its divinely-
ordained priests.   While he thus sought to awaken the
loyalty of the tribes, his rival had posted an ambuscade
behind the men of Judah, who found themselves entrap-
ped.   But, nothing daunted, they cried unto the Lord,
and, while the priests sounded with the silver trumpets,
raised a shout, and fell upon the foe.   The forces of
Jeroboam were utterly routed, and Abijah succeeded
in capturing the towns of Bethel, Jeshanah, and Ephraim
with the surrounding villages.   From this signal defeat
the king of Israel never *recovered strength again* (2 Ch.
xiii. 20), and soon after died, bequeathing his throne to
his son NADAB, while his rival Abijah, after a brief reign
of three years, also died, and was succeeded by his son
ASA, B.C. 954.

CHAPTER III

ASA AND BAASHA, ELAH, ZIMRI, OMRI.

1 KINGS XV. XVI.   2 CHR. XIV.—XVI.   B. C. 955—918.

THE reign of NADAB was very brief, lasting only two
years.   As he was besieging Gibbethon, a town
allotted to Dan (Josh. xix. 44), and afterwards given to
the Kohathite Levites (Josh. xxi. 23), but which was
now in the hands of the Philistines, BAASHA, the son of
Abijah, of the house of Isaachar, conspired against him,
and, usurping the throne, smote all the house of Jeroboam till he left none that breathed, thus fulfilling the
words of Ahijah, and destroying the first Israelitish
dynasty, B.C. 953.

Between the new king and Asa constant hostilities
were maintained.   The latter, mindful of the conditions
on which he held the kingdom, no sooner ascended the
throne, than he commenced a general religious reform
throughout his dominions.   He removed the idols his

father had set up, the high places, the images, and the groves; nor did he spare the idolatrous ritual even of his grandmother Maachah, who held the special dignity of queen-mother; he removed the symbol of her religion, and flung the ashes into the brook Kidron. Having thus restored the worship of Jehovah to something of its former purity, he strengthened his kingdom by fortifying the frontier towns, and raised and equipped a large army. He was thus in a condition to confront the enormous host with which his realm was invaded by Zerah, the Ethiopian, probably *Osorkon II.*[1], the successor of Shishak, and the inheritor of his quarrel with Rehoboam. The Egyptian host penetrated as far as Mareshah in the low country of Judah, where they were confronted by Asa, whose confidence in his God was rewarded by a complete victory, and the Egyptian host fell back routed as far as Gerar, leaving immense spoils in the hands of the men of Judah (2 Chr. xiv. 9—15).

After this signal success, encouraged by the assurances of the prophet Azariah, Asa resolved to continue his religious reforms, and on his arrival at Jerusalem convoked an assembly of the tribes of Judah and Benjamin, as well as of the strangers sojourning amongst them from Ephraim, Manasseh, and Simeon, and in the 3rd month of the 15th year of his reign, renewed with solemn sacrifices a national Covenant. *With a loud voice, and with shouting, and with trumpets, and with cornets,* the assembly swore fealty to their God and king, and vowed to put to death all who proved unfaithful to Jehovah (2 Chr. xv. 1—15).

The peace which his kingdom now enjoyed was soon disturbed by the hostility of Baasha, who marched against Asa, and having recovered the territory which he had lost, fortified Ramah, about 6 miles north of Je-

---

[1] Rawlinson's *Bampton Lectures,* p. 127.

rusalem, not only to annoy his enemy, and stop the tide of emigration from his own kingdom into that of Judah, but also to cut off Asa's communications with the central portion of Israel. On this that monarch resolved to purchase the aid of the king of Syria, Benhadad I.[1], and persuade him to break off his alliance with his rival. Sending, therefore, all the silver and gold left in the treasuries of the Temple to the Syrian monarch, he succeeded in inducing him to fling an army into northern Palestine, which smote Ijon, Dan, Abel-beth-Maachah, Cinneroth, and all the land of Naphtali. This forced Baasha to withdraw his forces, and retire to Tirzah; whereupon Asa summoned all Judah, and having destroyed the works at Ramah, used the stones and timber to fortify two towers, Geba and Mizpeh, as checks to any similar attempts in future. This is the first instance of a Hebrew king courting an alliance with a heathen power in a great crisis of the national fortunes, and it did not pass unnoticed by the prophetical order. Hanani the seer denounced such faithless leaning on an arm of flesh, and foretold that from henceforth he should have wars. The outspoken rebuke roused the anger of Asa. He flung the bold prophet into prison, and oppressed some of the people, who probably sympathised in his denunciations. In other respects he had ruled his kingdom with energy, loyalty, and piety, and after a severe attack of gout, died in the 41st year of his reign, and was committed to the tomb amidst general sorrow, bequeathing his throne to his son JEHOSHAPHAT (2 Chr. xvi. 7—14), B.C. 914.

Meanwhile there had been great vicissitudes in the kingdom of Israel. After destroying the whole house

---

[1] Hadad or Adad was a Syrian god, probably the sun, still worshipped at Damascus in the time of Josephus (*Ant.* IX. 4, 6), and from it several Syrian names are derived, as Hadadezer, i. e. *Hadad has helped*, Ben-Hadad, *worshipper of Hadad*.

of Jeroboam, Baasha made the beautiful city of Tirzah[1] his capital, and in spite of the warnings of the prophet Jehu the son of Hanani (1 K. xvi. 1—7), persisted in walking in the ways of Jeroboam, *wherewith he made Israel to sin.* His reign of 24 years was chiefly distinguished by his persistent hostility to his rival Asa, which cost him, as we have seen, several cities in the northern part of his dominions, in consequence of Asa's alliance with Benhadad. He was succeeded in the year B.C. 930 by his son ELAH ; who had barely reigned for the brief space of a year, when on the occasion of a riotous feast in the house of his steward at Tirzah, he was assassinated by ZIMRI, *the captain of half his chariots,* B.C. 929. The usurper signalized his accession by ruthlessly murdering every member of the family of Baasha, but had barely occupied the throne for seven days, when OMRI, captain of the army then besieging Gibbethon, attacked him at Tirzah. Despairing of aid Zimri anticipated the wishes of his rival by firing the palace over his head, and perished in the flames.

But the claims of the usurper to his blood-stained throne were not universally acknowledged. Half the people sided with him, and half with another aspirant, TIBNI the son of Ginath (1 K. xvi. 21). For 5 years the latter reigned as rival king, and the land was desolated with civil discord. At length the faction of OMRI pre-

---

[1] " In the territory of Ephraim, the fertile plains and to a certain extent wooded hills, which have been often noticed as its characteristic ornaments, at once gave an opening to the formation of parks and pleasure-grounds similar to those which were the 'Paradises' of Assyrian and Persian monarchs. One of these was Tirzah (*Tellûzah ?*) of unknown site, but evidently near Shechem, and of proverbial beauty, Cant. vi. 4. Stanley's *S. and P.* 243. It " was to Shechem what Windsor is to London, and had been the seat of a Canaanitish king before the conquest of the country by the Israelites" (Josh. xii. 24). Porter's *Handbk.* II. 348.

vailed, and Tibni dying, he became sole king of Israel, and founder of its third dynasty. For 6 years he made Tirzah, though now in ruins, his capital, and then in spite of its proverbial beauty (Cant. vi. 4) determined to remove his residence elsewhere. About 6 miles north-west of Shechem was "an oval-shaped isolated hill, rising by successive terraces 600 feet above the surrounding plateau, and combining in union not elsewhere found in Palestine, strength, beauty, and fertility." This hill Omri purchased of Shemer, its owner, for two talents of silver, and on its "long flat top" built a city, which instead of naming after himself, he called after the name of its owner *Shomrôn*, "the city of Shemer," afterwards corrupted into the Chaldee *Shemrin*, and thence into the Greek *Samaria*[1]. In his new capital Omri reigned 6 years more. A vigorous and unscrupulous ruler, he did evil in the eyes of the Lord more than all his predecessors on the throne. He not only courted an alliance with Benhadad I. and surrendered to him some border towns (1 K. xx. 34), and admitted a resident Syrian embassy[2] into Samaria, but gave his son and successor AHAB in marriage to JEZEBEL, the daughter of Ethbaal, king of Zidon (1 K. xvi. 31), thus introducing the worship of Baal as the recognised religion of his kingdom.

[1] "No better site for a capital could have been selected in the length and breadth of Palestine, combining a strong position, rich environs, central situation, and an elevation sufficient to catch the cool healthy breezes from the sea." Porter's *Handbook*, II. 345. "Situated on its steep height, in a plain itself girt in by hills, it was enabled, not less promptly than Jerusalem, to resist the successive assaults made upon it by the Syrian and Assyrian armies. The first were baffled altogether, the second took it only after a three years' siege, that is three times as long as that which reduced Jerusalem" (2 Kings xviii. 10). Stanley, *S. and P.* 244.

[2] The meaning of the expression - "making streets in Samaria," 1 Kings xx. 34.

KINGDOMS OF JUDAH AND ISRAEL.

PART II

Period of mutual alliance, and hostility to Syria.

CHAPTER I

REIGN OF AHAB. ERA OF ELIJAH.

1 Kings xvii.—xix.   2 Chr. xvii.   B. C. 918—915.

THE first act of Jehoshaphat, who succeeded Asa on the throne of Judah, was to fortify and garrison the fenced cities in his dominions, as well as the towns in Ephraim, which his father had captured (2 Chr. xvii. 2). With much zeal for the national faith he next endeavoured to put down the high places and groves, and sent a commission of princes, priests, and Levites to traverse the various towns, and instruct the people out of the Book of the Law (2 Chr. xvii. 6—9). His pious zeal did not go unrewarded. *The Lord established the kingdom in his hand,* and gave him peace round about. Not only his own subjects, but even the Philistines and Arabians brought him tribute (2 Chr. xvii. 5, 11), which enabled him to build castles and store-cities in Judah, and maintain a large standing army (2 Chr. xvii. 12—19).

Meanwhile, very different scenes were enacted in the rival kingdom of Israel.

Ithobalus or Ethbaal[1], the father of Ahab's queen, had once been a priest of the Phœnician goddess Astarte, and had usurped the throne of his brother Phalles[2].

---

[1] Ithobalus = *Baal with him*, Ethbaal = *with Baal*.
[2] Kenrick's *Phœnicia*, p. 362. The date of Ethbaal's reign may be given at about B. C. 940—908. Smith's *Bib. Dict.*

Jezebel inherited the spirit of her father, and quickly
acquired the most unbounded influence over her weak-
minded husband, so that he became a mere puppet in
her hands. The first effect of her influence was the
establishment of the worship of Baal on the most extensive scale. Near the palace at Samaria rose a temple
in honour of this Phœnician deity, and an oracular grove,
while 450 of the prophets of Baal, and 400 of Astarte,
were supported at the queen's table (1 K. xvi. 31, 32,
xviii. 19). She also resolved that a worship, now formally legalized, should be forcibly imposed on her husband's subjects, and so great was her severity towards
the prophets of Jehovah, that they were constrained to
conceal themselves in caves, and there eke out a pre-
carious existence (1 K. xviii. 13). While she thus per-
secuted the servants of Jehovah, her yielding husband
occupied himself chiefly with indulging a taste for splendid architecture. He erected several cities, and built
an ivory palace; and while Samaria remained his capital,
sought another Tirzah in the beautiful city of Jezreel,
the very name of which, *the seed-plot of God*, indicates
the fertility of the neighbourhood[1].

In this crisis of the Israelitish kingdom came forth,
sudden as the lightning, alarming as the thunder, one
of the most remarkable men that Israel ever produced.
From the wooded uplands across the Jordan, "from the
country of the rude soldier-judge Jephthah[2]," clad in the
austere garb of the prophets, consisting of a girdle of
skin round his loins, and a sheep-skin "mantle," his
"hair long and thick, and hanging down his back" (2 K. i.
8), appeared in the palace of Ahab, *Elijah the Tishbite,
of the inhabitants of Gilead.* Without a word of comment or introduction, he announced in the name of that
God, whom the monarch had insulted, a speedy and

---

[1] See above, p. 219.   [2] See above, p. 256.

awful judgment. *As the Lord God of Israel liveth,*
said he, *there shall be neither dew nor rain these years
but according to my word*[1]. Having thus boldly delivered his message, he fled for his life to the brook or
torrent-bed of the Cherith, either amongst his own native
hills, or on the west of Jordan and nearer to Samaria.
Here he was for some time miraculously supported by
ravens, which *brought him bread and flesh in the morning, and bread and flesh in the evening,* while he drank
of the water of the brook (1 K. xvii. 1—7).

After a while the slender streamlet was dried up.
Guided by the Divine direction the prophet now repaired to Zarephath or Sarepta (Lk. iv. 25—29), a Phœnician village on the sea-shore between Tyre and Sidon,
and in the very midst of Phœnician heathenism. As he
drew nigh the place he met the widow, with whom he
was to lodge, gathering sticks. Though she was so
poverty-stricken, that she had but a handful of meal in
a barrel, and a little oil in a cruse, and the sticks she
was gathering were to make a last meal for her child
and herself before they died, he yet bade her make a
little cake for him first, and assured her that the barrel
of meal should not waste, nor the cruse of oil fail, till the
rain returned. Strong in faith, the woman did as he
bade her, and found his words true. For a full year
(1 K. xvii. 15, *margin*) she and her house did eat, nor
did their supplies fail. But before long a sore trouble
visited her home. Her son sickened, and seemed at the
point of death. In the agony of her grief she imputed
this trial to the presence of the mysterious prophet.
But Elijah took the boy up to his chamber, and laid him

---

[1] That is, for 3 years and 6 months (Comp. Lk. iv. 25).
"The annals of Tyre record a drought of a year's duration in
the reign of Ithobaal, who continued to reign at Tyre during
a considerable portion of Ahab's reign in Israel." Kenrick's
Phœnicia, 362; Rawlinson's *Bampton Lectures,* 128, 129.

on his own bed; then he stretched himself three times upon him, and cried mightily to the Lord that his life might be restored to him. His prayer was heard; *the soul of the child came into him again, and he revived,* and the prophet restored him to his mother, who was now convinced that her guest was a man of God, and *that the word of the Lord in his mouth was truth* (1 K. xvii. 8—24).

Meanwhile, the kingdom of Israel was suffering the most grievous extremities from the prolonged drought. The earth lay cracked and parched and barren. Sheep, cattle, horses, perished from want of water, and from the failure of the crops. So great was the destitution, that Ahab left his luxurious palace at Samaria, and divided with Obadiah—his chief domestic officer, and who, at the peril of his life, remained faithful in his allegiance to Jehovah—the duty of examining every spring and "nook of the most shaded torrent-bed" to discover any sign of herbage, wherewith to *save the horses and mules alive, that they might not lose all the beasts.* While, then, Ahab went one way by himself, and Obadiah went another way by himself, suddenly the latter discerned the prophet standing in the midst of the path. At the Divine command Elijah had left his retreat at Zarephath, and now bade the minister of Ahab announce to his master his own return. At first Obadiah demurred. He feared lest, while he had gone on this mission, the Spirit of the Lord might summon the prophet in some other direction, and the king would slay him in his disappointment. But Elijah reassured him, and he went and told Ahab, and Ahab went to meet the servant of Jehovah. Few but pointed were the prophet's words, when he was confronted with the weak woman-governed king. After sternly denouncing his idolatries, he commanded him to summon instantly to the top of Carmel[1]

---

[1] Carmel, nearly always found with the definite article,

the 450 prophets of Baal, and the 400 prophets of Ashtaroth. Awed by the bearing of the seer, the monarch dared not disobey, and the prophets, followed by a large concourse of people, repaired to the appointed spot, at the extreme eastern point of the long Carmel range, " commanding the last view of the sea behind, and the first view of the great plain in front[1]."

It was the crisis in the history of the Ten Tribes. On that day it was to be proved, once for all, who was supreme, Baal or Jehovah. With his one attendant Elijah proceeded to the Place of Controversy, and proposed to the assembled multitudes a decisive test. Let two bullocks be chosen ; let one of them be slain by the priests of Baal, and cut in pieces ; let these be laid upon an altar, with no fire under; let them then call upon the name of their gods, and *the God that answered by fire let him be God.* The challenge was accepted. The altar was built ; the victim slain ; the pieces laid in order ; and the priests of Baal commenced their incantations. *But there was no voice, neither any that answered.* Morning passed, and noon came, and still there was no reply. Meanwhile Elijah suggested to them that they

= *the park*, or *the well-wooded place*, and is famous even now for its "impenetrable brushwood of evergreens and oaks." (See Isai. xxxiii. 9, xxxv. 2 ; Mic. vii. 14; Amos i. 2.) This well-known ridge, rising at the west end about 600, and the east about 1600 feet above the sea, stretches from the Mediterranean inland a little more than 12 miles, and separates the plain of Esdraelon from the plain of Sharon.

[1] Stanley's *S. & P.* 353. "We descended to the Mohrakah, or 'place of sacrifice.' It is a glade overlooking the plain, somewhat in the shape of an amphitheatre, and completely shut in on the north by the well-wooded cliffs down which we had come. No place could be conceived more adapted by nature to be that wondrous battle-field of truth. In front of the principal actors in the scene, with the king and his courtiers by their side, the thousands of Israel might have been gathered on the lower slopes, witnesses of the whole struggle to its stupendous result." Tristram's *Holy Land*, p. 117.

should *cry aloud, for*, said he, with cutting irony, *he is a god; either he meditateth, or he is pursuing, or peradventure he sleepeth, and must be awaked.* Stung to the quick, the priests redoubled their invocations. They cried aloud, *they cut themselves, after their manner, with knives and lancets, till the blood gushed out upon them.* But prayers, cries, lacerations were each and all in vain (1 K. xviii. 1—30).

The hour for the evening-sacrifice now drew near, and Elijah bade the people approach, and with twelve stones, according to the number of the tribes of Jacob, repaired an ancient altar on the mountain-top, which Jezebel probably had caused to be thrown down. Round about it he next caused a trench to be dug, and having slain his victim, laid it upon the altar. Then once, twice, and yet again he caused victim and altar to be drenched with water [1], till it filled even the trench. This done, the solitary prophet poured forth his whole soul to the God of Abraham, of Isaac, and of Israel, praying Him that He would that day prove that He was indeed the Lord, and that he himself had done all these things at His word. His prayer was answered. The Fire of the Lord descended, and consumed the *burnt-sacrifice and the*

---

[1] Obtained from a neighbouring fountain, Josephus *Ant.* VIII. 13, § 5, which even now is found close beneath *el-Mohrakah* ("the burning"), the spot pointed out as the scene of this event. "In the upper part of the amphitheatre to the left is an ancient fountain, overhung by a few magnificent trees, among them a noble specimen of the Turkey oak. The reservoir of the spring is stone-built and square, about 8 ft. deep, and the old steps which once descended to it may still be traced. The water is of some depth, and is perennial. This was corroborated by the existence of molluscs attached to the stones within the cistern. *In that three years' drought, when all the wells were dry, and the Kishon had first sunk to a string of pools, and then finally was lost altogether, this deep and shaded spring fed from the roots of Carmel remained.*" Tristram's *Holy Land*, pp. 117, 118.

*wood, and the stones and the dust, and licked up even
the water that was in the trench.* The effect on the
people was profound. Falling on their faces to the
earth, they with one accord confessed, *Jehovah, He is
the God; Jehovah, He is the God* (1 K. xviii. 30—39).

It was the moment for still more decisive measures.
Elijah had *bowed the hearts of the people as one man.
Take the prophets of Baal,* he cried, *let not one of them
escape;* and down the steep sides of the mountain they
were brought to the level plain below[1], where flowed the
Kishon. There these troublers of the nation's peace were
slain, and this stern act of duty done, the prophet bade the
king accompany him up the mountain to join in a sacrificial feast. Then, while Ahab ate and drank, he himself
ascended to a higher level, and on the bare ground, with
his face between his knees, remained wrapt in prayer,
having bidden his servant ascend yet higher, and look
towards the blue waters of the Mediterranean Sea. Six
times he came back to his master with the announcement
that he could see nothing. But the seventh time he returned, saying, *Behold, there ariseth a little cloud out
of the sea, like a man's hand.* It was the long-desired
sign, "the first that had for days and months passed
across the heavens," telling of the coming rain. Instantly the prophet bade the king descend the mountain,
prepare his chariot, and make for his palace. The king
obeyed, and meantime the little cloud had grown and
overcast the whole evening sky. Soon a wind arose and
shook the forests of Carmel, and the welcome rain poured
down in torrents. Across the bed of the Kishon Ahab

[1] "Immediately below [the Mokrakah], on the banks of
the Kishon, was a small flat-topped green knoll, 'Tell Cassis,'
the Mound of the Priests, marking in its name the very spot
where Elijah slew the prophets of Baal, when he had brought
them down to the brook Kishon." Tristram's *Holy Land,* pp.
117, 118.

urged his chariot along the road to Jezreel, while Elijah, girding up his loins and tightening his hairy mantle about him, ran before the chariot of his sovereign at least 16 miles to the entrance of the city[1].

Thus far the triumph of the Prophet was complete. But now, when victory seemed to be in the hollow of his hand, at the most critical moment of his life, his courage failed him. Jezebel, informed of what had taken place on Carmel, sent a messenger threatening him with certain death, and Elijah, who had boldly defied multitudes on Carmel, fled before the face of a woman, in a southerly direction towards Beer-sheba. There he left his attendant, and went alone a day's journey into the waste uninhabited country, which borders on the south of Palestine. Wearied, disappointed, he requested that he might die, and flinging himself under

---

[1] "This conduct of Elijah, when rightly understood, was full of important instruction. As God's minister he had overwhelmed the king with shame and confusion in the presence of his subjects. The natural tendency of this would be to lower him in their eyes, and lessen their respect for his authority. It was not the intention, however, to weaken the government, nor to encourage rebellion. The prophet was, therefore, divinely directed to give a testimony of respect and honour to the king, as public and striking as from necessity had been the opposition and rebuke to his idolatry. The mode of doing honour to Ahab, by running before his chariot, was in accordance with the customs of the East, even to this day. I was reminded of this incident more than 20 years ago at Jaffa, when Mohammed Aly came to that city with a large army to quell the rebellion of Palestine. The camp was on the sand hills south of the city, while Mohammed Aly stopped inside the walls. The officers were constantly going and coming, preceded by runners, who always kept just ahead of the horses, no matter how furiously they were ridden; and, in order to run with the greater ease, they not only 'girded their loins' very tightly, but also tucked up their loose garments under the girdle, lest they should be incommoded by them. This, no doubt, did Elijah." Thomson's *Land and the Book*, p. 485. Kitto's *Daily Bible Illustr.* IV. 271, 272.

a juniper-tree[1] fell asleep. Presently an angel awoke him, and pointing to a cake baked on the coals, and a cruse of water, bade him refresh himself, and in the strength of that meat go still further southward, to Horeb the Mount of God.

Arrived there, he remained at least one night in one of the caverns of the awful mountain-range, and in the morning heard the word of the Lord enquiring, *What doest thou here, Elijah?* In reply, the prophet urged his eminent services for the cause of Jehovah. The children of Israel had forsaken the covenant, thrown down the Lord's altars, and slain the prophets with the sword, he alone was left, and they sought his life to take it away. In this dejected, murmuring mood he was not fit to discharge the duties of his office. The Lord, therefore, bade him leave his cave, and stand before Him face to face upon the mountain, while He passed by "in all the terror of His most appalling manifestations." First, a mighty rushing wind rent the solid mountain, and brake in pieces the cliffs of Sinai, *but the Lord was not in the wind.* Then an earthquake shook the rocks, and the mountain trembled with the crash, *but the Lord was not in the earthquake.* Then a fire blazed forth, and burned with a consuming heat, *but the Lord was not in the fire.* Then all was quiet; the convulsion of nature was hushed; and presently there came *a still, small, Voice,* and as Elijah listened, his face wrapped in his mantle, he learnt that there was yet something left for him to do, that he was not the only instrument the Lord could employ. He was to return, and anoint HAZAEL king over Syria, JEHU the son of Nimshi king of Israel, and ELISHA of Abel-meholah as his successor in the pro-

---

[1] Or rather a species of *broom* very abundant in the desert of Sinai, and capable of "affording shade and protection, both in heat and storm, to travellers." Smith's *Bib. Dict.;* Thomson's *Land and the Book,* p. 611.

phetical office ; and whereas he had complained that he
was the only faithful servant of Jehovah, he now learnt
that the Lord had left him 7000 in Israel, *all the knees
which had not bowed unto Baal, and every mouth
which had not kissed him* (1 K. xix. 1—18).

CHAPTER II

WARS OF AHAB AND BENHADAD.

1 Kings xx. B. C. 901.

OF the three commands thus laid upon him, Elijah
straightway proceeded to execute the last. From
Horeb he journeyed to Abel-meholah[1] (*the Meadow of
the Dance*), in the northern part of the Jordan valley.
Here he met ELISHA, the son of Shaphat, apparently a
man of substance, plowing with twelve yoke of oxen
before him and he with the twelfth. Casting his well-
known mantle upon him, the prophet by this symbolic
action claimed him as his son, and called him to follow
him. Lingering only to bid farewell to his father and
mother, and to celebrate a parting feast with his people,
Elisha arose and hurried after the great Prophet, and
became henceforth his constant attendant.

Meantime Ahab, while he retained Samaria as the
capital of his kingdom, adorned with a palace and park
the beautiful city of Jezreel, in the Esdraelon plain.
But ere long this and other instances of his passion for
splendid architecture received a rude check. At the
head of a large army and aided by 32 vassal kings,
Benhadad II., king of Syria[2], laid siege to Samaria.

---

[1] See above, p. 249.

[2] "In the cuneiform annals of an Assyrian king we have
a very curious and valuable confirmation of the power of
Damascus at this time—of its being under the rule of a monarch named Benhadad, who was at the head of a great confederacy of princes, and who was able to bring into the field,

While this was in progress, with true Oriental haughtiness he made a formal demand of all the silver and gold, the wives, and children belonging to his enemy. Hoping to disarm hostility, the servile Ahab replied by a promise of faithful vassalage to the lord of Syria. But Benhadad, emboldened by this weak compliance, sent ambassadors with the announcement that on the following day he should enforce his demand by an actual search of Ahab's palace. Even the king of Israel was stung to the quick by this insulting message, and summoning all the elders of his kingdom he laid the matter before them. It was resolved to defend Samaria at all risks, and Benhadad was informed that his demand could not be entertained. On receiving this reply, the king of Syria sent another message to declare his intention of laying Samaria level with the ground. *Tell him*, rejoined Ahab, *Let not him that girdeth on his armour boast himself as he that putteth it off*, a spirited reply, which filled Benhadad with rage, and he ordered preparations to be made for an instant assault.

At this juncture a prophet stood forth, and assured Ahab of a complete victory over the vast host of his enemy, which should be achieved by a mere handful of men. In accordance with his suggestion, the king thereupon numbered the 232 attendants on the " princes of the provinces[1]," and prepared to send them against the

year after year, vast armies, with which he repeatedly engaged the whole force of Assyria. We have accounts of three campaigns between the Assyrians on the one side, and the Syrians, Hittites, Hamathites, and Phœnicians, united under the command of Benhadad, on the other, in which the contest is maintained with spirit, the armies being of a large size, and their composition and character such as we find described in Scripture." Rawlinson's *Bampton Lectures*, p. 130, and notes; Rawlinson's *Herod.* I. 464, 465.

[1] " Probably *local governors* or *magistrates*, who took refuge in Samaria during the invasion, while the 'young men' were their *attendants*."—Smith's *Bib. Dict.*

Syrian camp, while 7,000 of the regular troops followed
behind. The little band left the gates of Samaria and
proceeded towards the *pavilions,* or rather "the tents
and booths of branches, boughs, and brushwood, which
were erected for the Syrian chiefs in the camp, as they
are still erected for the Turkish pashas and agas in their
expeditions[1]." Though it was only high noon, Benhadad with his vassal chiefs was carousing over his wine-
cups. But he no sooner heard of the approach of the
little band from the city, than with drunken insolence
he ordered that they should be taken alive, whether
they came for peace or war. The force, however, sent
to execute this order found it no easy one, for the 232
"princes of the provinces" offered a strenuous resistance, and struck down all who opposed them. This, and
the sight of the 7,000 following behind, filled the Syrian
host with a sudden panic, and they fled precipitately,
headed by Benhadad himself on a fleet horse, and pursued by the victorious Israelites, who inflicted upon
them a great slaughter (1 K. xx. 1—22).

Thus Samaria was delivered. But the same prophet,
who had predicted the victory, now warned Ahab to be
on his guard, for with the return of spring the enemy
would renew the invasion, which duly came to pass.
Annoyed at their late humbling defeat, the Syrians had
concluded that it was owing to the fact that they had
attacked in a hilly region a people, whose gods *were gods
of the hills*[2]. They now resolved to fight in a more level
region, and in place of the vassal kings, who probably
had been the first to fly in the late battle, they had
substituted captains, and mustered an army as large as
the last. Accordingly, at the season named by the prophet, they advanced with a vast host to Aphek[3], a town

[1] See Keil on 1 K. xx. 16.
[2] See Kitto's *Daily Bible Illustr.* iv. pp. 286, 287.
[3] Now called *Fik,* a considerable village on the top of a

in the level country, east of the Jordan, on the military
road from Syria to Israel. Hither the army of Ahab
went forth to meet them, and encamped, appearing *like
two little flocks of kids* in comparison of their formidable foes, who filled the country round. But again a
prophet appeared to encourage Ahab, and assure him of
a second victory. The Syrians had imagined Jehovah
to be merely a god of the *hills,* they should know that
he was a god also of the *valleys* (1 K. xx. 28).

For seven days the two armies confronted one another, and then the battle was joined. The Syrians
were utterly routed, and fled in confusion to Aphek,
resolved there to make a stand. But the wall of the
town, in consequence probably of a sudden earthquake,
fell with a terrible crash and buried upwards of 27,000
in the ruins[1]. Benhadad himself with his immediate
attendants escaped, and was advised by them to throw
himself on the mercy of the conqueror. They proposed
to go forth with sackcloth on their loins and ropes on

mountain (Thomson, p. 388), at the head of the *Wady Fîk,*
6 miles east of the sea of Galilee, "the great road between
Damascus, Nablous, and Jerusalem, still passing through the
village." Smith's *Bib. Dict.*

[1] "This tremendous destruction was caused, as I suppose,
by an earthquake; and after having seen the effects of the
earthquake in Safed and Tiberias, I can easily understand
this narrative. We are not required to limit the catastrophe
to the falling of a single wall; or, if this be insisted on, we
have only to suppose that it was the wall of the city, and a
little consideration will convince any one familiar with Oriental fortifications that it might overwhelm a whole army. Those
ramparts were very lofty and massive. An open space was
always left along their base, and this would be packed, from
end to end, by the remnants of Benhadad's mighty host, and
escape from the falling towers would be impossible. Burckhardt informs us that the town is built round the base of a
hill, in the shape of a crescent, and this peculiarity of the site
would render the destruction only the more extensive and inevitable." Thomson's *Land and the Book,* p. 389.

their heads, and plead for their lives. Mounted in his chariot Ahab received the envoys, enquired after the welfare of his late dreaded enemy, and called him his *brother*. The word *brother* revived the courage of the Syrian ambassadors, and they were presently bidden to return and usher their master into Ahab's presence. Benhadad came, and was invited to take his place in the chariot by the side of his conqueror. Grateful for this unexpected clemency, he promised to restore to the king of Israel all the towns his father had taken from the Israelites, and to permit his subjects to have a quarter in the Syrian capital, similar to that which Benhadad's father had obtained in Samaria (1 K. xx. 34).

This impolitic clemency to an unrelenting national foe was sternly rebuked by one of the sons of the prophets. Having caused himself to be wounded and disguised with a headband, he awaited Ahab's coming along the road, and said, *Thy servant went out into the midst of the late battle; and, behold, a man turned aside, and brought a man unto me, and said, Keep this man: if by any means he be missing, then shall thy life be for his life, or else thou shalt pay a talent of silver; and as thy servant was busy here and there, he was gone.* Instantly Ahab decided the matter, and pronounced that he must bear the penalty. On this the headband was removed, and the king perceived not only that the speaker was a scholar of the prophets, but understood also the true meaning of his parable. Because he had spared a man, whom Jehovah had devoted to utter destruction, the punishment should fall upon him and his people, which he had failed to execute on Benhadad (1 K. xx. 35—43).

CHAPTER III

MURDER OF NABOTH—BATTLE OF RAMOTH-
GILEAD.

1 Kings xxi. xxii.   2 Chr. xviii.   B. C. 898.

SHORTLY after these events an incident occurred, which brought down upon Ahab and his house an awful doom. Adjoining his palace at Jezreel was a vineyard belonging to a native of the place named NABOTH. Eagerly desirous to add the vineyard to his palace grounds and convert it into a garden of herbs, Ahab proposed to its owner to purchase it, or give him in exchange another and even a better piece of ground. This Naboth stoutly refused to do, alleging his unwillingness to part with the inheritance of his fathers (Lev. xxv. 23; Num. xxxvi. 8). Annoyed at this rebuff, the king returned to his palace, and in his vexation flung himself on his bed, turned away his face, and would eat no bread. While in this mood he was visited by Jezebel, to whom he explained the cause of his vexation. She instantly resolved to take the matter into her own hands, and bade her lord trouble himself no more, *she would give him the vineyard.* Thereupon she wrote a warrant in Ahab's name, sealed it with his seal, and sent it to the elders of the city, directing that, as if on the occasion of some great calamity, a solemn fast should be proclaimed; that two men should be set up to charge Naboth with blasphemy against God and the king, and that then he should be stoned to death (Exod. xxii. 28; Lev. xxiv. 15, 16). It is a striking proof of the degeneracy of the nation at this period, that the elders of Jezreel never for one moment scrupled about carrying out this inhuman order. Naboth was dragged forth, arraigned, condemned, and stoned together with his sons (See

2 K. ix. 26), and the elders reported to the queen that the guilt of blasphemy against Jehovah and His anointed had been avenged[1]. The vineyard had now lapsed to the crown, and Jezebel bade her lord go down and take possession of it. But on proceeding thither, the king found himself confronted by no other than the great Elijah, who in words of utmost sternness denounced the late cruel murder, and declared the sentence of the Lord. The king and all his house should share the fate of Jeroboam and of Baasha; his queen should be eaten by the dogs at the wall of Jezreel, and dogs should lick up his own blood on the very spot where they had licked up that of Naboth. Appalled at this awful sentence, Ahab rent his clothes, put on sackcloth, fasted, and displayed all the signs of a sincere repentance. Such as it was, it was accepted, and Elijah was bidden to announce to him that the punishment should not be inflicted during his own lifetime, but in his son's days it would surely descend upon his house (1 K. xxi. 29).

Meanwhile the relations between the rival kingdoms of Israel and Judah had been more peaceful than at any other period, since they had parted 60 years before at Shechem. Not only were hostilities laid aside, but an alliance between the sovereigns was cemented by the marriage of JEHORAM, son of Jehoshaphat, with ATHALIAH, the daughter of Ahab and Jezebel. Moreover about the 16th year of his reign, B.C. 898, the king of Judah went on a visit to the court of Israel. He was received with every mark of distinction, and Ahab slew sheep and oxen in abundance for him and his retinue (2 Chr. xviii. 2). During this visit, the king of Israel took occasion to propose to his ally that they should undertake an ex-

---

[1] "The place of execution was by the large tank or reservoir, which still remains on the slope of the hill of Samaria, immediately outside the walls." Article *Naboth*, in Smith's *Bib. Dict.*

pedition for the purpose of recovering Ramoth-gilead[1],
a strong fastness and the key to an important district
east of Jordan, which Benhadad I. had wrested from
Omri. Jehoshaphat expressed his willingness to take
part in the expedition, but proposed that the will of Jehovah should first be ascertained. For this purpose
Ahab summoned about 400 of the prophets of his kingdom, who all advised him to go up, and assured him
that the Lord would deliver the place into his hands
(1 K. xxii. 6).

But this did not satisfy the king of Judah. He enquired if there was not a true prophet of Jehovah, at
whose mouth they might seek counsel. Ahab confessed
that there was one, MICAIAH, the son of Imlah, but
openly avowed that he hated him, because he never predicted good to him but only evil[2]. Jehoshaphat, however, overruled the objection, and Micaiah was summoned from his prison, where he had been confined by
Ahab, probably for some disagreeable prediction. Meanwhile the two kings, arrayed in their royal robes, sat at
the entrance of Samaria, and the 400 prophets standing
before them persisted in their predictions of success.
One of them, Zedekiah, the son of Chenaanah, even
made him horns of iron, and by this symbolic action
assured the kings that they would push the Syrians till
they had destroyed them. But Micaiah had the courage
to differ from all. At first, indeed, he ironically assured
the king of success, but, when Ahab adjured him to

---

[1] "Now *Es-Salt*, situated on a hill, isolated to a great extent from the loftier mountains round it by deep ravines on
the east and west, which unite on the south. Probably from
its commanding position in the territory of Gad, as well as its
strength, it was chosen by Moses as the City of Refuge for
that tribe (Deut. iv. 43 ; Josh. xx. 8; xxi. 38). Afterwards
it became the residence of one of Solomon's commissariat officers" (1 K. iv. 13). Smith's *Bib. Dict.*

[2] Comp. Homer, *Il.* I. 106.

speak the truth, he boldly affirmed that the prophets, in whom he trusted, were all filled with lying spirits, and that he was destined to fall in the campaign. This outspoken declaration brought down upon the faithful seer the mockery and scorn of the other prophets, and still greater severity from Ahab, who ordered him to be sent back to the city gaol, and there fed on the scantiest fare (1 K. xxii. 27).

Then the two kings set out on the expedition, and on crossing the Jordan found that Benhadad and his vassal princes were prepared to contest the possession of Ramoth. On this Ahab, the more surely to ward off a fate he too clearly divined, disguised himself, while the king of Judah went into battle in his royal robes. The contest began, and the 32 captains of Benhadad, acting on instructions they had received, bent all their efforts to slay Jehoshaphat, whom they mistook for the king of Israel. But his voice convinced them that he was not the man they sought, and they desisted from the pursuit. In spite, however, of his disguise Ahab could not escape his doom. *A certain man drew a bow at a venture,* and the arrow pierced the joints of his breast-plate. That the troops might not be discouraged, he was kept up standing in his chariot till the evening, when he died. From the battle-field the corpse was then borne to Samaria, and there interred, while the bloody chariot was washed in the pool[1] of the city, beside which Naboth and his sons had been murdered. Without a *shepherd* and without a *master,* the people were scattered abroad, and returned home defeated before their enemies, and the words of Elijah (1 K. xxi. 19), and of Micaiah (xxii. 17) were fulfilled.

---

[1] See above, p. 397, note.

CHAPTER IV.

*WARS OF JEHOSHAPHAT—TRANSLATION OF
ELIJAH.*

2 Kings i. ii.   2 Chr. xix. xx.   B. C. 896.

ON his return from a campaign, in which he had so
nearly lost his life, Jehoshaphat was sternly rebuked by one of the prophets (2 Chr. xix. 2) for the guilty
alliance he had formed with the court of Israel, and he
resolved henceforth to devote himself to the spiritual
and temporal welfare of his own subjects.   Accordingly
he went on a second personal tour through his dominions from Beer-sheba to Mount Ephraim, and strove to
reclaim his people to the worship of Jehovah.   He also
provided for the better administration of justice; placed
judges in all the fenced cities, and remodelled the tri-
bunals in his capital.   He next turned his attention to
foreign commerce, and at Ezion-geber constructed a
fleet for the purpose of trading in gold with Ophir.   In
this project he was aided by Ahaziah, who had succeeded Ahab on the throne of Israel.   But the unfor-
tunate issue of the enterprise determined him to decline
the proposal of his ally, that the attempt should be renewed (2 Chr. xx. 37; 1 K. xxii. 49, 50).

The remainder of his reign was not, however, destined
to be peaceful.   A vast host of the people of Moab,
Ammon, and Edom invaded his territory, and encamped
at Hazazon-tamar or En-gedi[1].   In his alarm, Jehoshaphat proclaimed a solemn fast throughout his kingdom,
assembled all Judah together with their wives and their
children, and offered up a pathetic petition for the Divine aid.   He had hardly concluded, when the Spirit of
the Lord came upon Jahaziel a Levite, and one of the

---

[1] See above, p. 307, note.

sons of Asaph then in attendance at the Temple, commissioning him to assure the pious king of a victory on the morrow, which he would only need to stand still and see. A Psalm of thanksgiving[1] was straightway sung, and on the morrow the army, preceded by choirs of Levites, left the Holy City, and at about 12 hours' distance from Jerusalem came to "the uneven table-land" of Tekoa, *Tekûa*, abounding in hidden caverns, clefts, and excavations[2], where David and his men had often hidden during the period of his wanderings. It was not a locality adapted to the "sons of the desert," and the ambushments, for which it afforded so much opportunity, sadly galled their wild hordes, and the children of Ammon and Moab turned their swords against their allies from Mount Seir, and then fell upon one another. On reaching the Watch-tower of Tekoa the warriors of Judah beheld only a mass of dead bodies, and busied themselves for three days in stripping them of their rich ornaments, and gathering up the riches and jewels they had flung away in their hasty flight. Four days afterwards a Psalm of thanksgiving once more ascended to Jehovah from the valley of Berachah (*blessing*)[3], and the

[1] See Psalm cxxxvi. 1. Comp. also Ps. xlviii. and xcii, Joel iii. 2, 12.

[2] Van de Velde, II. 30 ; Thomson's *Land and the Book*, p. 606. Tekoa was fortified by Rehoboam (2 Chr. xi. 6), was afterwards the birthplace of the prophet Amos (Am. i. 1), and gave its name to the adjacent desert on the east (2 Chr. xx. 20). Robinson, *Bibl. Res.* I. 486, 7. "It is remarkable that this is the usual route taken in the present day by such predatory bands from Moab as make incursions into southern Palestine. They pass round the southern end of the Dead Sea, then up the road along its western shore to *Ain-Jidy*, and thence towards Hebron, Tekoa, and Jerusalem, as the prospects of plunder seem most inviting." Smith's *Bibl. Dict.*

[3] "The name of *Bereikût* still survives, attached to ruins in a valley of the same name, lying between Tekoa and the main road from Bethlehem to Hebron, a position correspond-

26

army of Jehoshaphat returned in triumph to Jerusalem (2 Chr. xx. 26—28).

Meanwhile Ahaziah, during his short and troubled reign over Israel, began to feel the effects of the late disastrous campaign against Ramoth-Gilead. The Syrians, now masters of the country East of the Jordan, cut off all communication between his realm and his vassal the king of Moab. The latter, therefore, rebelled against Israel, and refused to send his yearly tribute of 100,000 lambs, and 100,000 rams (2 K. iii. 4). Before he could take measures for punishing this revolt, Ahaziah fell through a lattice in his palace at Samaria, and sustained much injury. A devotee to the Phœnician idolatries of his mother, he sent messengers to the Philistine city of Ekron to enquire of the oracle of Baal-Zebub (*the lord of flies*), whether he should recover. On their road thither the messengers encountered Elijah, who, after reproaching them for consulting a heathen deity instead of Jehovah, announced that their master would never leave his bed alive. Returning, they informed Ahaziah of this occurrence, who enquired what kind of man they had met. Their answer was decisive. In the hairy man, girt with a girdle of leather about his loins, the king recognised all too clearly his father's enemy, and, ill as he was, this only served to kindle his wrath. Dispatching a captain with 50 men to the recesses of Carmel, where the prophet seems to have taken up his abode, he demanded his instant surrender. The soldier went and found Elijah seated on the mountain. *Man of God,* said he, *the king hath said, Come down. If I be a man of God,* replied the other, *let fire come down from heaven, and consume thee and thy fifty men.* With the word the fire descended, and consumed the captain

ing accurately enough with the locality of the battle as described 2 Chr. xx." Smith's *Bibl. Dict.*

and his fifty. A similar force was then a second time dispatched by the king, and they too met the same fate[1].

A third captain, in an altered tone, implored the prophet to come down, and Elijah, assured by God of safety, descended and followed him into the presence of the king, and announced in person his approaching end; shortly after which Ahaziah died, and was succeeded by his brother JEHORAM (2 K. i. 2—17).

This was the last time Elijah confronted any of the family of Ahab. Once only is he recorded to have expostulated with any of the house of Judah. Hearing that the son of Jehoshaphat, who seems to have been entrusted with a portion of the regal power during his father's lifetime, was not walking in his father's ways, but in those of Ahab and the kings of Israel, he sent a letter to him, denounced his idolatries, and threatened him with sore judgments (2 Chr. xxi. 12—15).

Shortly afterwards, though how soon is not certain, he received intimation of his approaching removal from the earth. From Gilgal, probably somewhere on the western edge of the hills of Ephraim, accompanied by Elisha, whom he had vainly tried to persuade to remain behind, he proceeded to Bethel. There the two were met by certain of the sons of the prophets, who also had been warned of what was at hand, and now enquired of Elisha if he knew of the loss he was about to sustain. Elisha replied that he did, but bade them hold their

---

[1] "It was when our Lord and His disciples were on their journey through this very district from Galilee to Jerusalem, and when smarting from the churlish inhospitality of some Samaritan villagers, that—led to it by the distant view of the heights of Carmel, or, perhaps, by some traditional name on the road—the impetuous zeal of James and John, the 'sons of thunder,' burst forth, *Lord, wilt Thou that we command fire to come down from heaven and consume them, even as Elijah did?* For the answer of our Lord to this question see Lk. ix. 51—56." Smith's *Bibl. Dict.*

peace. Having again vainly tried to induce his faithful
attendant to remain at Bethel, the prophet repaired to
Jericho, where another company from the prophetic
school warned his companion, and were similarly enjoined to keep silence. From Jericho the two then held
on their way towards the Jordan, while 50 of the sons of
the prophets ascended the abrupt heights behind the
city [1], which command a view of the plain below, to watch
what would occur. Arrived at the river's brink, Elijah
took off his prophetic mantle, and, wrapping it together,
smote the waters, which divided "hither and thither,"
and the two went over on dry ground. Once on the other
side, the prophet was within the borders of his native
land, and he now enquired of his companion, what he
should do for him before he was taken away. The other
asked for a *double portion of his spirit.* He had asked
a hard thing: but still if he looked steadfastly on his
master while he was taken from him, he was told that
his request should be granted, but not otherwise. Still
conversing the two then walked on, till suddenly a chariot
of fire and horses of fire parted them asunder, and Elijah
was carried by a whirlwind into heaven. With a great
and bitter cry Elisha called after him as he ascended,
*My father, my father, the chariot of Israel, and the
horsemen thereof!* But he was gone, and he saw him
no more. In token of grief he thereupon rent his clothes,
and taking up the mantle of his master went back, and
once more stood by the banks of Jordan. Then wrapping the mantle, even as he had seen the other do, he
smote, saying, *Where is the Lord God of Elijah?* and
the waters again parted "hither and thither," and he
went over. Meanwhile the sons of the prophets, who had
stood watching, saw him coming towards Jericho, and
going down to meet him, bowed themselves to the ground
before him. Contrary to his advice they then insisted on

[1] See above, p. 202.

sending fifty "strong men" to search for Elijah, lest peradventure the Spirit of the Lord had taken him up, and
cast him upon some mountain, or into some valley. For
three days the search was continued, but they found him
not. The work of the most wonderful character Israel
ever produced was over, and he had been summoned to
another world (2 K. ii. 11—18).

CHAPTER V

JEHOSHAPHAT AND JEHORAM—ERA OF ELISHA.

2 Kings ii.—iv. B. C. 895.

FOR a time Elisha tarried at the now rebuilt Jericho,
and here he performed his second miracle. "Of
the two perennial springs which, rising at the base of
the steep hills behind the town, send their streams
across the plain towards the Jordan, scattering, even at
the hottest season, the richest and most grateful vegetation over what would otherwise be a bare tract of sandy
soil[1]," one at least was at this time noxious and unfit
for use. At the urgent request of the inhabitants Elisha
put salt into a new cruse, and poured it into the spring
at its source, and the waters were healed (2 K. ii. 19—
22). Thence he repaired to Bethel, which, though the
seat of the school of the prophets, was, it will be remembered, one of the centres of the Calf-worship. As the
prophet ascended the defile leading into the town, the
youths of the place came forth, and began to revile the
gentle successor of the terrible Elijah. *Go up, bald
head!* was their cry, alluding, probably, "to the contrast between his closely-trimmed hair and the shaggy
locks of Elijah." Turning round, the prophet looked

[1] Smith's *Bibl. Dict.* Art. *Elisha.* Ever since the time of
Josephus a large spring N. W. of the present town, and called
Ain-en-Sultân, has been pointed out as the spring in question.

upon them, and cursed them in the name of Jehovah, and from a forest hard by the road, and haunted by wild beasts, came forth two she-bears, which tare forty-two of them. Elisha meanwhile passed on to Carmel, the resort of his late master, and thence returned, and eventually took up his abode at Samaria (2 K. ii. 25).

Jehoram, who now reigned in that capital, persisted in his idolatrous courses, but, possibly owing to the late activity of Elijah, had removed the image of Baal, and recurred to the old Calf-worship. He now resolved to take that vengeance on the rebellious Moabites, which the death of his brother Ahaziah had postponed. Accordingly, having obtained the promise of the assistance of Jehoshaphat, he numbered his forces, and set out on the campaign. Instead of crossing the Jordan above the Dead Sea, and invading Moab from the North, it was resolved to pass round the southern end of that sea, and thence push forwards through the northern portion of the territory of Edom, whose king also promised his aid in the expedition. Accordingly a long and tedious circuit of 7 days was made, during which the armies suffered the greatest extremities from the want of water. In this crisis Jehoshaphat proposed that the advice of some prophet of Jehovah should be sought, and, enquiry being made, it was found that Elisha was present with, or in the near neighbourhood of, the armies. The three kings, therefore, went down to consult him. The prophet evinced no willingness to befriend the ruler of Israel, but in consideration of the presence of the pious king of Judah, he relented, and summoned a minstrel before him. The minstrel played, and in the usual prophetic ecstasy Elisha directed that dykes should be dug in the valley, which he foretold would speedily be filled with water sufficient for the host, and he moreover assured the kings of a speedy victory over their enemies.

On the next day at early dawn, the hour of offering
the meat-offering at Jerusalem, in consequence probably
of a great and sudden fall of rain in the eastern mountains of Edom[1], water came down and filled all the
dykes, which the armies had dug in the red soil of the
valley. To the Moabites, who had mustered all their
forces and awaited the attack in the border of their
territory, the water, glistening in the rays of the morning sun, appeared to have assumed a red colour like
blood. Thereupon concluding that the confederate
kings had turned their arms against one another, they
hastily marched on to gather up the spoil. But they
had no sooner reached their camp, than they were
attacked with great fierceness, and put to a complete rout. As they fled to their own cities, the confederate kings pursued them, felled their trees[2], stopped
up their wells, filled their choice pieces of land with
stones, and ravaged all their towns, save the impregnable fortress of Kir-haraseth[3] (*Kerak*), built on a high
steep rock and surrounded by a deep and narrow ravine. There the king of Moab made his last stand,
and with 700 picked men made a desperate attempt to
break through the besieging army. This last hope failing, he ascended the wall with his eldest son, the heir
to his throne, and in sight of the allied besiegers, killed

[1] See Keil on 2 K. iii. 20.
[2] Compare the conduct of the Lacedæmonians in the
Megarid, Thuc. I. 108.
[3] The modern *Kerak* lies about 6 miles from Rabbath-
Moab, and some 10 miles from the Dead Sea. "Its situation
is truly remarkable. It is built upon the top of a steep hill,
surrounded on all sides by a deep and narrow valley, which
again is completely inclosed by mountains rising higher than
the town, and overlooking it on all sides. It must have been
from these surrounding heights that the Israelite slingers
hurled their volleys of stones after the capture of the place
had proved impossible (2 K. iii. 25)." Smith's *Bibl. Dict.*,
Art. *Kir-Moab*.

and burnt him as a propitiatory sacrifice to his idol Chemosh. This frightful spectacle filled the allied hosts with such horror that they raised the siege and departed to their own land (2 K. iii. 20—27).

During the reign of Jehoram Elisha performed many miracles, the fame of which could not fail to strengthen the cause of true religion.

i. A widow of one of the sons of the prophets was in debt, and her creditor was coming on the morrow to take her two sons and sell them as slaves. In her extremity she applied to the prophet, and told him that the only thing she had in her house was a cruse of oil. This Elisha caused to multiply, till she had filled all the vessels she could borrow, and thus liquidated the debt (2 K. iv. 1—7).

ii. The little village of Shunem, in the tribe of Issachar, was a frequent resort of the Prophet, and a rich woman of the place, at whose house he stayed, on one occasion, persuaded her husband to permit a little chamber to be prepared for him, that he might turn in there, as often as he came that way. One day he came thither attended by Gehazi his servant, and lodged in the little chamber. Grateful for this kindness, Elisha enquired if there was anything he could do for his benefactress; *Should he speak for her to the king, or the captain of the guard?* Both these offers the woman declined, alleging that she *dwelt among her own people.* Thereupon Gehazi whispered that she had no son, and her husband was old. Elisha promised that in the ensuing year a son should be born to her. His words were fulfilled. the boy grew, and in the course of time went to join his father in the reaping-field. There struck by the fierce rays of the morning sun, he cried, *My head, my head!* and was carried home to his mother, on whose knees he died at noon. In this sad crisis she immediately took the dead body into the pro-

phet's chamber, and laid it on the bed. Then with a
single attendant, mounted on an ass, she set out for one
of the heights of Carmel, about 15 or 16 miles distant,
where Elisha then was. Her familiar form attracted
the prophet's attention as from the eminence he discerned her approaching, and he sent Gehazi to enquire
the reason. But her errand was not to be revealed to the
servant, and pressing on she drew near the spot where
the prophet himself was, and flinging herself before him
embraced his feet. The first word about her son revealed the state of the case, and Elisha instantly bade
Gehazi gird up his loins, and with his staff in his hand
hurry with all speed to Shunem. Gehazi went, and was
soon followed by Elisha, and the mother, who would not
leave him. As they drew near the town, they met Gehazi returning. He had laid the staff upon the face of
the child, *but there was neither voice nor hearing.*
Arriving at the house, Elisha ascended to the well-known
chamber, shut the door, and prayed mightily unto the
Lord. Then he stretched himself upon the dead body,
and the flesh of the child grew warm ; presently he
sneezed seven times and opened his eyes. Gehazi was
thereupon bidden to summon the Shunammite, who received her boy restored to life, and went her way (2 K.
iv. 8—37)[1].

[1] A few years after this event, and before the visit of
Naaman to Samaria (comp. 2 K. viii. 4 with 1, 2, 3), in consequence of a famine predicted by Elisha, the Shunammite
retired to the rich low lands of the Philistines. At the close
of the dearth she returned to her native place, to find her house
and fields in the possession of a stranger. Thereupon, with
her son, she repaired to Samaria, and as the king was listening to the story of *all the great things which Elisha had done,*
and especially the crowning miracle at Shunem, she drew
near, was recognised by Gehazi, and confirmed the wondrous
tale in person. The king, struck by the remarkable circumstances, ordered her land to be restored to her, with the value
of the fruits of it during her sojourn amongst the Philistines.

iii. Elisha is next found at Gilgal, at a time when there was a dearth in the land. The sons of the prophets sat before him, and he bade the great caldron be set on, and pottage be seethed. Into the caldron one of the company shred wild gourds and grapes, and when they found out the contents, all exclaimed, *there is death in the pot.* Thereupon Elisha bade meal be cast into it, and the pottage was rendered fit for food (2 K. iv. 38—41)·

iv. While still at Gilgal, Elisha was visited by a man from Baal-shalisha (See 1 Sam. ix. 4), with 20 barley-loaves, and roasted ears of corn in his scrip or bag[1]. This moderate supply he ordered to be distributed amongst the people who were present, to the number of one hundred, and in reply to his hesitating "servitor" assured him that there would not only be enough, but that the people *would leave thereof,* which came to pass ; and thus Elisha was enabled to anticipate the works of Christ (2 K. iv. 42—44).

CHAPTER VI

ELISHA AND NAAMAN—SIEGE OF SAMARIA.

2 KINGS v. vi.   B. C. 894—892.

BUT Elisha's fame was soon to overstep the limits of his own country. The captain of the army of Benhadad, king of Syria, at this time was named NAAMAN (See Lk. iv. 27). He had achieved many victories for his master, and for personal prowess was held in high honour, being in close attendance on his sovereign,

"It is still common for even petty sheikhs to confiscate the property of a person who is exiled for a time, or who moves away temporarily from his district; especially is this true of widows and orphans, and the Shunammite was now a widow." See Thomson's *Land and the Book*, p. 458.

[1] These were probably first-fruits and perquisites of the priests, see above, p. 134 (*a*), Numb. xviii. 8, 12: Deut. xviii. 3, 4.

but *he was a leper.* This frightful malady which, had he been an Israelite, would have cut him off from all intercourse with his fellows, does not appear to have laid him under the same disadvantages in Syria, and he still retained his post as commander-in-chief. In his harem, waiting on his wife, was a little Israelitish maid, who had been taken prisoner in one of the forays of the Syrians over the border. She knew what Elisha could do, and assured her mistress that, if only Naaman was *with the prophet that was in Samaria,* he would certainly be cured of his malady. Her words were told to Naaman, who communicated them to Ben-hadad[1]. The Syrian king thereupon wrote a letter to Jehoram, king of Israel, and sent his general with it, accompanied by a large retinue bearing 10 talents of silver, 6,000 pieces of gold, and 6 of the rich fabrics, for which Damascus had always been famous. On reaching Samaria Naaman presented the letter to Jehoram, who had no sooner read the curt words of the Syrian king, than he rent his clothes, and exclaimed, *Am I God, to kill and to make alive, that this man doth send unto me to recover a man of his leprosy?* He could only think of one motive for the letter; *Consider,* said he, *how this man seeketh a quarrel against me* (2 K. v. 7).

News of Naaman's arrival, of the purport of his coming, and of the dismay of the king was conveyed to Elisha, who straightway sent to Jehoram and bade him send his visitor to him, that he might know that there *was a prophet in Israel.* With his horses, his chariots, and entire cavalcade, Naaman thereupon came and stood before the door of the prophet's dwelling. But instead of coming forth himself, Elisha simply sent his servant to tell him to go down to the rapid waters of the Jordan and wash seven times, promising him a cer-

[1] Not "one," but "he," Naaman, went in and told his "lord," the king, 2 K. v. 4, as in the Vulgate.

tain cure. The prophet's independent tone, the neglect
to come out to him, above all his command that he, the
native of a city watered by such famous streams as the
Abana and Pharpar[1], should go and wash in Jordan, was
unbearable. Naaman *turned and went away in a rage.*
But his retinue, unwilling to throw up the hopes of their
long journey, succeeded in persuading him to make
trial of the prescribed cure. Naaman accordingly went
down and dipped himself seven times in the rushing
stream, and *his flesh came again like the flesh of a
little child, and he was clean.* Full of gratitude for so
priceless a boon, he then returned with his whole retinue to Samaria, and once more stood before the prophet's door. This time, however, he not only stood
there, but went in and gratefully acknowledged the
power of Israel's God, and urged the prophet to receive
the present he had brought. This, the latter absolutely
declined, and in spite of Naaman's urgency, persisted
in his refusal. But one thing the grateful soldier was
resolved to have. If Elisha would not accept his presents, he could not depart from a land where he had
received so great a benefit without two mules' burden
of its hallowed earth, for the construction, probably, of
an altar to Jehovah. But here a difficulty occurred to
him. If he became a servant of Jehovah, how could
he go to the house of Rimmon[2], and bow before the

---

[1] The ABANA, the Χρυσορρόας of the Greeks, and now the
Barada, was the chief river of Damascus and flowed through
it, and was the main source of its beauty and fertility, having
even now 14 villages and 150,000 souls dependent on it; the
PHARPAR, now the *Awaj*, is further from Damascus, "a small
lively river." Robinson, *Bibl. Res.* III. 448.

[2] "According to Movers (*Phœn.* I. 196, &c.) Rimmon was
the abbreviated form of Hadad-Rimmon (as Peor of Baal-
Peor), Hadad being the sun-god of the Syrians. Combining
this with the pomegranate, which was his symbol, Hadad-
Rimmon would then be the sun-god of the late summer, who
ripens the pomegranate and other fruits, and, after infusing

Syrian god? Elisha's simple reply was, *Go in peace*, and he went his way (2 K. v. 1—20).

The generous conduct, however, of his master had not escaped the notice of Gehazi, the attendant of Elisha, and the Syrian had not gone any great distance when he ran after his chariot. Naaman discerned him hurrying along the road, and alighting enquired if all was well. *All was well*, the other replied; *but already there had come to his master from Mount Ephraim, two young men of the sons of the prophets*, for whom he solicited *a talent of silver, and two changes of raiment.* The generous Syrian pressed upon him two talents and two changes of raiment, and sent two of his retinue to bear them to a secret place, whence Gehazi removed them into the house, and then presented himself before his master, denying, when questioned, that he had gone anywhere. But the prophet had marked his wickedness. His heart had gone after him the whole while, and with righteous sternness he now pronounced upon him the awful punishment from which Naaman had just been delivered; and *he went out of his presence a leper as white as snow* (2 K. v. 27).

Elisha is next found at Jericho. Here the habitation of the sons of the prophets had become so small, that they desired to construct a new dwelling near the Jordan. Accompanied by Elisha they proceeded towards the river, and began to fell trees in the wood which lined its banks. As they felled, the head of an axe, which one of them had borrowed, flew off and sank in the water. He appealed to Elisha, who bade a piece of wood be flung into the stream, when the iron re-appeared, and was restored to the borrower (2 K. vi. 1—7).

Shortly after this, in spite of the cure wrought upon

into them his productive power, dies, and is mourned with *the mourning of Hadad-rimmon in the valley of Megiddon*," Zech. xii. 11.   Smith's *Bibl. Dict.*

their general, the Syrians renewed their marauding incursions, and even encamped in spots which the king of
Israel was wont to frequent. Warned by Elisha, Jehoram was on more than one occasion able to escape the
ambuscades laid for him, which so annoyed Ben-hadad,
that he even suspected treachery among his own retinue.
But one of his servants pointed to the true cause. The
informer was no other than the healer of his general
Naaman, and his power was such that he could tell Jehoram the very words Ben-hadad uttered in his chamber.
Thereupon the king of Syria sent horses and chariots,
and a considerable force to Dothan[1], 6 miles north of
Samaria, to capture Elisha. The Syrian forces completely surrounded the village, and the prophet's servant came running in, crying, *Alas! my master, how
shall we do ?* Elisha calmed his fears with the assurance that *they which were with them were more than
they which were with the foe,* and the eyes of the young
man being opened he was enabled to discern the hill, on
which the village was built, filled with horses and chariots
of fire ready to protect his master. At the same moment the Syrian forces were smitten with blindness, and
were easily led away to Samaria; nor were their eyes
opened till they found themselves in the presence of Jehoram. The first impulse of the king of Israel was to
put them to death. But Elisha dissuaded him from
such unworthy conduct, and the men were sent back to
Ben-hadad, who drew off his army, and for a while desisted from the invasion (2 K. vi. 8—24).

But the Syrian king could not long brook such a
humiliating repulse. Mustering, therefore, all his troops,
he went up and besieged Samaria, B.C. 892, for a space of
3 years, during which period the inhabitants were reduced
to the direst extremities. Two mothers even agreed to
boil their children for food (Comp. Deut. xxviii. 53, 57).

[1] See above, p. 58, and note.

One actually did so, but the other hid her child lest it should suffer such an awful fate. This story was told Jehoram, as he one day passed by on the city wall, and in token of sorrow he put on sackcloth beneath his armour. But deeming Elisha in some way culpable for the nation's disasters, he threatened to take away his life, and sent a messenger to the prophet's house, where he sat surrounded by the elders of the city, to carry it into execution. Before however the messenger's feet had touched the threshold, Elisha, warned of his danger, had commanded that he should be held fast. At this moment Jehoram himself also entered, leaning on the hand of one of his officers. *This evil*, he burst forth, *is from Jehovah; why should I wait on Jehovah any more?* (Comp. Job xxi. 15; Mal. iii. 14). To which the prophet replied, *Hear the word of Jehovah; to-morrow about this time shall a measure of fine flour be sold for a shekel, and two measures of barley for a shekel, in the gate of Samaria.* *Nay,* interposed the royal officer, *if Jehovah would make windows in heaven, this could not be.* *It will,* replied Elisha; *thou thyself shalt see it with thine eyes, but shalt not eat a morsel thereof* (2 K. vii. 2).

These marvellous and prophetic words were fully verified. In the twilight of the selfsame evening four lepers who were wont to take their place at the gate of the city, despairing of life, resolved to enter the Syrian camp, and brave their fate. Reaching the edge of the encampment, to their great surprise they found no man there. Alarmed by a mysterious noise of chariots, horses, and a great host, the Syrians had concluded that the kings of the Hittites and Egyptians had come to the aid of the beleaguered city, and had hastily fled, leaving their camp and everything in it just as it was. Amidst the deepening gloom the lepers entered a tent, satiated the pangs of hunger, and then secretly hid a quantity

of silver, gold, and raiment. Entering a second they did
the same, and then fearing harm if they concealed such
joyous news, they hastily returned to Samaria, and announced to the warder at the barred gate (2 K. vii. 10)
that they had visited the Syrian camp, and found nothing but horses tied, and asses tied, and the tents as
they were. The warder carried the news to his chief,
and he communicated it to the king's household. Though
it was midnight Jehoram was roused, and informed of
the strange news. Fearful of a plot to draw the Israelites away from the city, he ordered two horsemen to
reconnoitre and discover whether it was really true.
They made their way towards the Jordan, and found
the road filled with garments and vessels, which the
Syrians had flung away in their precipitate flight. Their
return with this welcome news roused the whole city.
Starving and emaciated, the entire population rushed
forth to the gate, and thence made their way to the
Syrian camp. To preserve some degree of order, the
king entrusted the command of the gate to the officer
who had scoffed at the prophecy of Elisha, but so great
was the press and confusion that he was trodden to
death by the excited crowd, and before evening the words
of the prophet had been fulfilled to the letter. *Two
measures of barley were sold for a shekel, and a measure of fine flour for a shekel,* and Samaria was delivered (2 K. vii. 17—20).

KINGDOMS OF JUDAH AND ISRAEL.

PART III

Renewal of mutual hostilities; decline of both kingdoms before the power of the Assyrian Empire.

CHAPTER I

ACCESSION OF JEHU.

2 Kings viii.—x. B. C. 884.

AFTER this signal discomfiture Ben-hadad returned to Damascus, and before long lay prostrate with his last illness. At this time Elisha was present in the city, and the king being informed of it, sent Hazael, an officer in high position at his court, to enquire whether he should recover of his disease. With 40 camels' burden of the choicest products of the Syrian capital, Hazael presented himself before the prophet, and preferred his request in the most humble tones. Elisha replied that his master *might* indeed recover, but yet that he *would* not. Wondering at these ambiguous words, Hazael fixed upon him a long and searching glance, and the prophet burst into tears. *Why weepeth my lord?* enquired the other. And Elisha, who saw in him the destined successor of Ben-hadad, replied, *Because I know the evil that thou wilt do unto the children of Israel; their strongholds wilt thou set on fire, and their young men wilt thou slay with the sword, and wilt dash their children, and rip up their women with child.* But such a future had no sorrow for his listener, it was only too good to expect. *What is thy servant,* he replied, *dog that he is*[1], *that he should do this great*

[1] See Smith's *Bib. Dict.*, Art. *Hazael.*

27

thing? The prophet, without making any remark, simply announced the message Elijah had long ago been bidden to deliver, *Jehovah hath showed me*, said he, *that thou shalt be king over Syria* (2 K. viii. 7—13). With these mysterious words sounding in his ears Hazael returned to his master, and told him but the half of the prophet's answer. That day was the last of Ben-hadad's life. On the morrow he was found suffocated with a thick cloth dipped in water spread upon his face. Whether or no Hazael's hand had done the deed, his path was now clear[1], and he mounted the Syrian throne[2].

Meanwhile there had been changes in the kingdom of Judah. After an unsuccessful attempt to quell a rebellion of his vassal, the king of Edom (2 K. viii. 20; 2 Chr. xxi. 8—10; see Gen. xxvii. 40), Jehoram died, and was succeeded by AHAZIAH, B.C. 885, the issue of his father's ill-starred marriage with the daughter of Jezebel. True to the traditions of his mother, he signalized his accession by the grossest idolatries (2 Chr. xxii. 3), but soon, like his rival the king of Israel, began to feel the hand of the new monarch of Syria, who had already

[1] The cuneiform inscriptions "mention Hazael as king of Damascus immediately after Ben-hadad; and Jehu is the first Israelite king mentioned by name on any inscription hitherto discovered." Rawlinson's *Bampton Lectures*, p. 131; Layard's *Nineveh*, I. p. 396.

[2] "The cuneiform inscriptions show that towards the close of his reign Ben-hadad was exposed to the assaults of a great conqueror, who was bent on extending the dominion of Assyria over Syria and Palestine. Three several attacks appear to have been made by this prince upon Ben-hadad, who, though he had the support of the Phœnicians, the Hittites, and the Hamathites, was unable to offer any effectual resistance to the Assyrian arms. His troops were worsted in several engagements, and in one of them he lost as many as 20,000 men. It may have been these circumstances which encouraged Hazael to murder him and seize the throne, which Elisha declared would certainly one day be his." Smith's *Bib. Dict.; Rawlinson's Five Great Monarchies*, II. pp. 361, 362.

made an attempt to recover the stronghold of Ramoth-gilead. In intimate alliance the two kings now crossed the Jordan to defend the place, and an engagement ensuing, Jehoram was severely wounded, and forced to return to Jezreel, whither also Ahaziah followed him (2 K. ix. 28, 29).

During their absence Elisha, knowing that the time was now come for the doomed destruction of Ahab's family, sent a young man, one of the "sons of the prophets" to Ramoth-gilead, with a horn of oil and a commission to look out and anoint JEHU the son of Jehoshaphat, the son of Nimshi, king over Israel. As one of Ahab's guards, Jehu, in company with Bidkar, had ridden behind his master to the fatal plot of Naboth's vineyard, and heard the terrible warning of Elijah against his murderer (2 K. ix. 25). Since then, he had risen to a position of some importance, and was now well known for his vehemence and activity, as well as his rapid, furious driving. According to his instructions the young disciple of the prophets went to Ramoth-gilead, and finding Jehu seated in the midst of his officers, intimated that he had an errand for his ear alone. Together the two retired to an inner chamber, and there the youth having poured the oil on Jehu's head, and announced the Divine Will that he should be king over Israel, and utterly exterminate the whole family of Ahab, opened the door and fled.

Shortly afterwards Jehu came forth, and rejoined his comrades, who eagerly enquired the purport of the *mad fellow's* visit. At first he tried to evade the question, but soon revealed all that the other had said. Instantly the enthusiasm of his hearers was kindled. Recognising the truth of the prophetic call, they threw off each man his garment, and placing Jehu on a rude throne or carpet of state, blew the trumpets, and shouted *Jehu is king.* Then, for everything depended on the speed of his movements, without losing a moment Jehu drove his chariot towards the fords of Jordan, and thence direct to Jezreel. From the tower[1] of the latter city the watchman observed his hurrying chariot, and announced the fact to Jehoram, who straightway sent a horseman to enquire, *Is it peace?* The crafty conspirator detained the messenger. Then a second horseman was despatched, and he too was detained. By this time the watchman was better able to distinguish the advancing charioteer, and pronounced him to be no other than *Jehu, the son of Nimshi.* Thereupon the chariot of the king of Israel was made ready, and with Ahaziah, king of Judah, he set out to meet him, probably expecting tidings of the Syrian war. But he was quickly and terribly undeceived. His question, *Is it peace, Jehu?* was met by a furious denunciation of the idolatries of his mother Jezebel, and in an instant divining his danger, he turned his chariot towards Jezreel. But at that moment Jehu drew a bow with his full strength, and shot him to the heart. While he paused to charge Bidkar to take up his corpse and fling it into the portion of Naboth, Ahaziah, pursued by his soldiers, fled down the westward plain towards Beth-gan, or the village of Engannim[2], but was overtaken, and wounded, and died at Megiddo, whither he managed to escape.

Jehu's next step was to make for Jezreel. Here Jezebel, the queen-mother, still retained her influence, and hearing of the approach of the conspirator, she resolved to confront him in person. After the Oriental fashion, *she tired her head and painted her eyes* with

[1] "Jehu and his party could be seen for at least 6 miles, and there was time enough to send messenger after messenger to meet him." Thomson, *Land and the Book*, p. 460.

[2] In the E. V. translated "the garden-house." See Stanley, *S. and P.* p. 349. Robinson places it at *Jenin*, still surrounded by the "orchards" and "gardens" which gave its ancient name. See Van de Velde, I. p. 361.

antimony, and, as Jehu passed beneath the palace, cried
out from the latticed window, *Had Zimri peace, who
slew his master*[1]*?* On that Jehu looked up, and called
aloud, *Who is on my side? who?* and two or three
eunuchs looking out, he bade them throw her down;
and they threw her down before his chariot, and her
blood was sprinkled partly on the palace-wall and partly
on his horses, while with merciless severity he trode
her underfoot. Then he entered the palace, and ate
and drank. But remembering the fallen queen, he
commanded that she should be buried. His messengers
went forth to execute his commands, but when they
reached the open space before the city walls, they found
nothing but her skull, and feet, and the palm of her
hands. The dogs, which prowl about the streets of
Eastern cities, had devoured all the rest, and thus fulfilled the words of Elijah, *In the portion of Jezreel
shall dogs eat the flesh of Jezebel* (2 K. ix. 36).

The thoughts of the conqueror now turned towards
Samaria. Here resided the sons and grandsons of Ahab
to the number of 70 persons. To the elders of the city,
therefore, he wrote letters, bidding them select the best
and meetest of their master's sons, set him on his
father's throne, and fight for their master's house. This
proposition terrified the servile elders, and they replied
that they had no idea of setting up a rival king, and
were perfectly ready to submit in all things to the
usurper's will. On this, Jehu wrote a second letter,
proposing as a test of their fidelity, that they should
send to Jezreel on the next day the heads of the 70
descendants of Ahab, and then repair thither themselves. His commands were duly executed, the 70 heads
were sent to Jezreel, and by Jehu's command placed in
two heaps at *the entrance of the gate*, where they remained all night. In the morning the usurper went

[1] See above, p. 380.

forth, and acknowledged to the awe-struck crowd that he had conspired against his master, but threw the blame of the slaughter of Ahab's descendants on their guardians at Samaria, who had thus fulfilled the words of Elijah. He then proceeded to exterminate all the acquaintance of Ahab at Jezreel, the officers of his court, and the hierarchy of Ashtaroth, and finally set out in person for Samaria (2 K. x. 12).

On the road, he first met 42 sons or nephews of the late king of Judah, and discovering who they were, directed that they too should be put to death at the *Well of the Shearing-House,* between Jezreel and Samaria. A little further on he encountered Jehonadab the son of Rechab, of the race of the Kenites, who had bound his descendants[1] to drink no wine, to build no houses, to sow no seed, neither to plant nor possess vineyards, but to adhere to the old nomadic life and dwell in tents (Jer. xxxv. 6, 7). *Is thine heart right, as my heart is with thy heart?* exclaimed Jehu, when he saw him. The other assured him that it was, and was bidden thereupon to ascend his chariot and *come and see his zeal* for Jehovah. Thus side by side the two drove into the city, where the butchery of Ahab's relatives was renewed, till none were left remaining. But this was only preparatory to another and still greater blow. Convening an assembly of the people, Jehu announced his intention of inaugurating the worship of Baal on a scale of the greatest magnificence; *Ahab,* said he, *served Baal a little, but Jehu shall serve him much.* Then, under pain of death, he commanded the entire hierarchy of Baal and all his worshippers throughout Israel to assemble in the great temple, which Ahab had built in honour of this god (1 K. xvi. 32). On the appointed day they came, and the building was filled from end to end.

[1] Established, probably, "at or near the town of Jabez in Judah (1 Chr. ii. 55)." Smith's *Bib. Dict.*

The sacred vestments, probably of white linen, were brought forth, the worshippers arrayed in them, the temple cleared of any chance worshippers of Jehovah, and then Jehu and Jehonadab entered, and the king himself offered the burnt-offering. He had hardly ended, when eighty trusty warriors, who had secretly received their orders, rushed in, and commenced an indiscriminate slaughter of the unarmed and helpless assembly. The huge image of Baal was broken, the smaller images burnt, and the temple itself converted to the basest uses (2 K. x. 26, 27).

CHAPTER II

ATHALIAH AND JOASH. DEATH OF ELISHA.

2 Kings xi.—xiv.   2 Chr. xxii. xxiii.   B. C. 884—839.

THUS, after scenes hitherto unparalleled in the history of the Chosen Nation, Jehu established himself upon the throne, and reigned upwards of 28 years. Those years are almost a blank to us. All we know is, that though commended for the destruction of Ahab's worthless dynasty, and assured that his descendants to the fourth generation should sit upon the throne, he persisted in walking in the ways of Jeroboam, and retained the old calf-worship at Dan and Bethel. But his reign was not a peaceful one. *The Lord began to cut Israel short,* Hazael attacked his kingdom, and ravaged the territories of the tribes east of the Jordan (2 K. x. 33).

Meanwhile similar scenes of extermination had been enacted even in the southern kingdom of Judah. On the death of Ahaziah, B.C. 884, ATHALIAH, the queen-mother, who had probably been entrusted with the royal functions during his absence at Jezreel, resolved to seize the supreme power, and for this purpose put to death

all the members of the royal house who had not already
perished by the sword of Jehu. From the general massacre JOASH, the infant son of Ahaziah, alone escaped, and
was concealed by his aunt Jehosheba, wife of Jehoiada
the high-priest, in the house of the Lord for the space
of 6 years (2 Chr. xxii. 11, 12). During this period the
usurpation of Athaliah was endured, but in the seventh
year (B.C. 878) her foreign practices having probably dis-
gusted the nation, the high-priest deemed it an auspicious moment to bring about a change. Gathering round
him all the supporters of the family of David, he placed
a large force of priests and Levites in three bands
at the entrances of the Temple, and armed the "captains of hundreds" with the consecrated spears and
shields placed there by David. Then before them and
a number of the people who favoured his design, he
brought out the infant Joash, and in the presence of all
publicly crowned and anointed him, and presented him
with a copy of the Law. The noise of the people reached
the ears of the queen-mother, and she came into the
Temple only to see her grandson already placed on a
raised throne, and invested with regal functions. Jehoiada had given strict orders that she should not be
put to death within the sacred enclosure, and crying
treason, she was hurried from the ranges, and slain at
the entrance of the Horse-Gate by the royal palace (2
K. xi. 4—16; 2 Chr. xxiii. 12—15).

A covenant was then solemnly ratified between the
king, high-priest, and people, by which they bound
themselves to be faithful to Jehovah, and in proof
thereof attacked the temple of Baal, which Athaliah had
built, slew its attendant priest Mattan, and broke down
the altars and images. During the lifetime of his aged
counsellor, the youthful sovereign ruled his kingdom
prudently, and was blessed with a large measure of
prosperity. In the 23rd year of his reign he commenced

a complete repair of the Temple, which had suffered much during the late usurpation. Messengers were dispatched throughout his dominions to levy contributions for the work, which were willingly bestowed both by princes and people. But on the death of the high-priest, at the advanced age of 130 years, a change came over the policy and character of the king. At the suggestion of the princes of Judah, the worship of Baal and Ashtaroth was revived, and the service of Jehovah neglected. Prophets were sent to rebuke the king for this apostasy, but their protests were unavailing. One of them, ZECHARIAH, the son of the late high-priest, as a penalty for his bold outspoken honesty, was stoned to death between the Holy Place and the Altar of Burnt-offering[1] (Matt. xxiii. 35). His last words, *the Lord look upon it and require it*, were speedily fulfilled. The year had not ended before the Syrian army commanded by Hazael appeared before Jerusalem (2 K. xii. 17). It had lately been successful against the Philistine city of Gath, and now, though small in numbers, was able to defeat a large army of Judah, and was only prevailed upon to depart by being permitted to carry away to Damascus all the votive offerings and much of the Temple treasures. Nor was Joash destined long to survive this disgrace. Afflicted with a severe illness, probably in consequence of wounds received in the late engagement, he was suddenly attacked by two of his servants, and slain in his bed in the fortress of Millo, B.C. 839 (2 K. xii. 20, 21 ; 2 Chr. xxiv. 26).

In addition to their victories over the Philistines, the Syrians under Hazael had been equally successful against the king of Israel, JEHOAHAZ, the son of Jehu, reducing him to such a depth of subjection, that he was compelled to limit his army to 50 horsemen, 10 chariots,

[1] On the position of this Altar in reference to the Holy Place, see above, p. 120.

and 10,000 infantry. After an inglorious reign, he
bequeathed his throne to his son JEHOASH or JOASH,
B.C. 841, who in spite of the warnings the nation had
already received, persisted in practising idolatry. During
his reign the aged prophet Elisha fell sick, and Jehoash
went to his house and wept over him in the same words
that Elisha himself had used, when he beheld Elijah
carried up into heaven, saying, *O my father, my father,
the chariot of Israel, and the horsemen thereof!* But
other thoughts than the prophet's approaching end filled
the hearts of both. Hazael *was cutting Israel short,* and
ravaging the country far and near. The aged prophet
bade the king open the window eastward towards the
hated country, and place an arrow on the string of his
bow. Then, laying his own hands upon the king's
hands, he bade him shoot, and as the shaft sped from
the string, he followed it with the prophetic blessing,
*the arrow of the Lord's deliverance, and the arrow of
deliverance from Syria, thou shalt smite the Syrians
in Aphek till thou hast consumed them.* At the prophet's command the king next took the arrows and
smote them on the ground three times, and then
stayed. But he did it with no spirit or energy, and
the victories he might have achieved were limited to
three (2 K. xiii. 14—19).

Shortly afterwards Elisha died, but his wonder-
working power was not to cease with his life. He had
not been long laid in the tomb when marauding bands
of the Moabites invaded the land. A dead man was
about to be buried in the cemetery, which contained
the prophet's sepulchre. Seeing the band of spoilers
the mourners hastily thrust the corpse into the receptacle where the prophet lay, and no sooner did it touch
his remains than the *man revived and stood upon his
feet.* The victories, however, which Elisha had promised were realised. Three times was Jehoash enabled

to triumph over the Syrian armies, and recovered the cities which the Israelites had lost in previous wars (2 K. xiii. 25).

CHAPTER III

AMAZIAH AND JEROBOAM II. ERA OF JONAH.

2 Kings xiv. Jonah i.—iv. B. C. 840—758.

MEANWHILE Amaziah had succeeded to the throne of Judah. His first care after his accession was to punish the murderers of his father, which he did with unusual lenity, sparing their children, in accordance with the true spirit of the Mosaic law (Deut. xxiv. 16; Ezek. xviii. 4, 20). He next resolved to take vengeance on the revolted Edomites, and for this purpose summoned to his standard 300,000 of Judah, and, at the rate of 100 silver talents, hired 100,000 of Israel (2 Chr. xxv. 6). Warned, however, by a prophet against leading any of the idolatrous Israelites into battle amongst his own forces, he was induced to dismiss his mercenaries, who returned home in great anger. With his own army he then marched against the Edomites, and defeated them with great slaughter in the Valley of Salt, south of the Dead Sea, capturing also their rocky fortress-capital Petra or Sela, and flinging 10,000 of his captives headlong from their native cliffs. But with strange perversity he now set up in Jerusalem the idols of the very nation he had just subdued, and paid them religious honours (2 Chr. xxv. 14). For this apostasy a prophet threatened him with speedy vengeance, and misfortunes quickly thickened around him.

The Israelite mercenaries, in revenge for the loss of booty they had sustained, on their way homewards ravaged many of the towns of Judah. Smarting under this insult Amaziah was foolish enough to challenge his

rival, the king of Israel, to battle. Jehoash replied by the
contemptuous parable of the *Thistle and the Cedar*, and
bade Amaziah not provoke a contest. The other, however, would not yield, and the rival armies met at Beth-
shemesh[1], on the borders of Dan and Philistia, and the
men of Judah were utterly defeated. Jehoash even took
his rival prisoner, and conveyed him as a captive to Jerusalem, the walls of which he broke down on the side
nearest to his own kingdom to the extent of 400 cubits,
and after rifling the Temple of its treasures and exacting hostages returned to Samaria. Shortly after this,
however, he died, and bequeathed his throne to his
son JEROBOAM II., B.C. 825, while Amaziah survived him
15 years, at the close of which period a conspiracy was
formed against him, from which he fled to Lachish,
where he was assassinated, and was succeeded by his
son AZARIAH or UZZIAH, B.C. 810 (2 K. xiv. 19, 20).

The reign of Jeroboam II. which lasted 41 years[2],
was the most prosperous the kingdom of Israel had ever
known. The new king did not simply content himself
with repelling the attacks of the Syrian invaders, but
carried the war into their own country, captured their
capital Damascus, and recovered all the old dominion of
Israel from Hamath to the Dead Sea, together with the
territory of Moab and Ammon. These successes had
been predicted (2 K. xiv. 25) by the earliest of the prophets, whose writings as well as words have come down
to us, JONAH, the son of Amittai, of Gath-hepher in
Zebulun. The idolatries, however, of the king called
forth the protests of HOSEA, a prophet of uncertain tribe
and birth-place (Hos. i. 1), and AMOS a herdsman of
Tekoa[3] (Am. i. 1). Those of Amos were keenly resented
by Amaziah the high-priest of Bethel (Am. vii. 10), and

[1] See above, p. 273.
[2] Or 52 years, if the Interregnum be included.
[3] See above, pp. 401 and notes.

he reported him to the king as having predicted the destruction of the royal house and the captivity of the nation (Am. vii. 11—17), which, though not fulfilled in his reign, were only deferred[1].

AZARIAH or UZZIAH, the new king of Judah, retained the sceptre for upwards of 52 years, and was successful in several warlike expeditions. He subjugated the Philistines, and dismantled Gath and Ashdod, reduced the Arabians and Mehunims to obedience, and recovered Elath, the famous port on the Red Sea (2 Chr. xxvi. 2, 7). He also improved the internal resources of his kingdom, restored the fortifications of Jerusalem, built military engines, and established a powerful army. Moreover he devoted himself to the encouragement and protection of husbandry, building towers and wells for his numerous herds in the low country and in the plains, and growing vines on the terraces of the mountains (2 Chr. xxvi. 9—15). But in the hour of prosperity *his heart was lifted up to his destruction.* Assuming priestly functions, he entered the Holy Place in the Temple for the purpose of offering incense on the Golden Altar. This flagrant violation of the Law was resolutely opposed by the high-priest Azariah and others of the Levitical body, and drew down upon the king signal punishment. As he stood censer in hand by the Altar, the leprosy *rose up in his forehead,* and he hurried in alarm from the sacred enclosure. He was now incapable of discharging the regal functions[2], and till the day of his

---

[1] From both these latter prophets we gain several important hints respecting the moral condition of the kingdom of Israel at this time. The calf-worship was celebrated with all its former splendour at Bethel, which was the site of the royal sanctuary (Am. vii. 13), while the nation was distinguished for licentiousness, drunkenness, and oppression of the poor and needy (Am. ii. 7, 8, iv. 1; Hos. i. 2, iv. 12—14, xiii. 6). See Dr Pusey's *Introduction to Hosea.*

[2] See above, p. 157.

death lived in a separate house, while Jotham his son was entrusted with the regency, and eventually succeeded him B.C. 758 (2 K. xv. 5; 2 Chr. xxvi. 16—22).

Meanwhile the great Empire, destined to be the instrument of punishing the apostate kingdom of Israel, was advancing with gigantic strides in the path of universal conquest. Beyond the territory of the Syrians— the scourge of Jehu and his dynasty—was the far more powerful Empire of the Assyrians, including the whole region watered by the Tigris and Euphrates, and already augmented by important conquests in Cappadocia, Armenia, and Babylonia. To Nineveh, its celebrated capital, the prophet Jᴏɴᴀʜ, already mentioned, was directed to go and denounce its approaching doom, unless its people repented of their sins. The prophet shrunk from this arduous commission, and instead of crossing the Syrian desert, went down to Joppa, and there took ship for Tarshish, probably Tartessus[1] on the southern coast of Spain (Jon. i. 3). But during the voyage an awful storm arose, and in their alarm the mariners threw him at his own request into the sea, where a large fish took him up, and after three days and three nights flung him forth alive on the dry land (Matt. xii. 40, xvi. 4; Lk. xi. 30). Thus miraculously delivered he was a second time bidden to undertake the arduous journey, and now not daring to disobey arose and went. Suddenly appearing in the midst of Nineveh[2], clothed in his rough prophet's robe, he cried through corridor, and lane, and square, *Yet forty days, and Nineveh shall be overthrown!* His mysterious words filled the hearts of all with fear and

---

[1] See above, p. 362.

[2] In our Version the date of this visit is placed in B.C. 860. Others would place it in the later part of the reign of Jeroboam II., or about B.C. 780; Rawlinson even later, B.C. 760— 750, during a temporary depression of the Assyrian power; see the *Five Great Monarchies*, pp. 390—392, and notes.

consternation, and before long reached the palace, where
the king sat "on his royal throne in the great audience-
chamber, surrounded by all the pomp and magnificence of
his court[1]." The words of the unknown prophet touched
even his heart, and *he arose from his throne, and laid
aside his robe from him, and covered himself with
sackcloth, and sat in ashes* (Jon. iii. 6). Then -he proclaimed a decree that all his people, from the greatest
even to the least, should be covered with sackcloth, and
that even the beasts should be put in mourning[2]. His
decree was obeyed, a fast was observed, and the people
of Nineveh, laying aside their revelry and feasting, assumed the garb of mourning, humbled themselves, turned
from their evil way, and offered up petitions for mercy
to the Most High. Their repentance was accepted, God
had pity on the great city, with its 120,000 *persons that
could not discern between their right hand and their
left,* and deferred the judgment. In vain the prophet
sat in his booth of woven boughs, at the east side of the
city, waiting for the doom he had denounced. In vain
he complained of the deferring of the punishment. God
was more merciful than man, and for more than another
century Nineveh was to stand unharmed (Jon. iv. 5—11)

[1] Rawlinson's *Five Great Monarchies,* Vol. II. p. 391.
[2] "There is a remarkable parallel to this in a Persian
practice mentioned by Herodotus, IX. 24. In the mourning
for Masistius, a little before the battle of Platæa, the Persian
troops not only shaved off their own hair, but similarly disfigured their horses and their beasts of burden." Rawlinson's
Five Great Monarchies, II. 276, note.

CHAPTER IV

DECLINE AND CAPTIVITY OF THE KINGDOM OF ISRAEL.

2 Kings xv.—xvii.   B. C. 773—721.

THE death of Jeroboam II., b.c. 783, was the signal for a frightful state of anarchy in the kingdom of Israel. At length, after an interregnum of 11 years, ZACHARIAH his son succeeded to the throne (b.c. 773). His brief reign of six months served only to exhibit his addiction to idolatrous practices, when he was assassinated by SHALLUM, and with him the dynasty of Jehu came to an end. The reign of the usurper was briefer still. For one month only did he retain the royal power, and then was deposed in his turn by MENAHEM, the son of Gadi b.c. 772. Either at the beginning, or at a somewhat later period, during his reign of 10 years, the new king ordered a promiscuous massacre of the inhabitants of the country between Tirzah and Thapsacus, probably for the purpose of inspiring terror into the hearts of many who were unfavourable to his cause [1] (2 K. xv. 14). A more significant circumstance during his reign was the appearance of the Assyrians on the north-eastern frontier of his kingdom. PUL [2], king of Assyria, having been successful in his expedition against Damascus, advanced also against Israel, and was only induced to draw off his forces by a timely gift of 1000 talents of

[1] See Kiel *in loc.*, and Art. *Menahem* in Smith's *Bib. Dict.*

[2] Called in the Septuagint Phalôch or Phalôs, and in the Assyrian records *Phal-lukha* and *Iva-lush;* the annals of this monarch are scanty; but "in the most important record we possess of his reign, there is a notice of his having taken tribute from *Beth-Khumri*, or Samaria, as well as from Tyre, Sidon, Damascus, Idumæa, and Philistia." Rawlinson's *Bampton Lectures*, p. 133.

silver, which Menahem wrung from his people by an
assessment of 50 shekels a head from 60,000 Israelites
(2 K. xv. 20).

Menahem died in peace, bequeathing his throne to his
son PEKAHIAH, B.C. 761, who only reigned for 2 years, and
was then assassinated in his palace by PEKAH, son of
Remaliah, a captain of his body-guard, B.C. 759. The new
king displayed far greater energy than his immediate predecessors. The enormous tribute levied by the King of
Assyria had greatly exhausted the resources of his kingdom. He resolved, by way of compensation, to ally himself with Syria, and attack the rival kingdom of Judah.
During the vigorous reign of JOTHAM he does not seem
to have been able to carry out the latter part of this
design, but on the death of that monarch, and the accession of his weak son AHAZ, B.C. 742, he advanced
against Jerusalem in alliance with Rezin, king of Syria,
and took a vast number of captives, who were, however, restored by the advice of the prophet Oded
(2 Chr. xxviii. 8—15). So far as the Syrians were concerned, the expedition was successful. Rezin captured
the port of Elath, drove the Jews out of the place, and
settled there a Syrian colony. But in other respects
the unnatural alliance of Israel and Syria was calami-
tous. In his extremity, Ahaz resolved to seek the assistance of TIGLATH-PILESER, the successor of Pul on the
Assyrian throne, and for this purpose sent him a large
and valuable present from the Temple treasures (2 K.
xvi. 7). The Assyrian monarch readily embraced the opportunity of crushing the formidable alliance of Syria
and Israel. Marching against Damascus, B.C. 740, he
captured the Syrian capital, slew Rezin[1], and carried off
his subjects to Kir (2 K. xv. 29). Then turning his arms

---

[1] This was the occasion of the important prophecy of
Isaiah vii. 1—16.

28

still further westward, he fell upon the northern towns in Pekah's dominions, Ijon, Abel-beth-maachah, Hazor and others, and carried off the inhabitants to remote districts within his own dominions[1]. Pekah was now reduced to the position of a humble vassal of the great Lord of Assyria, and was obliged to abstain from any further hostilities against Ahaz.

But that king had purchased this temporary relief at a great cost. Not only was he obliged to yield up the Temple treasures as tribute to Tiglath-Pileser, but he had to appear also in person at Damascus as a vassal of that monarch, and did homage to his protector, and even to his protector's gods. *Because*, said he, *the gods of the kings of Syria help them, therefore will I sacrifice to them, that they may help me*, and he not merely conformed to heathen rites, but actually sent to Urijah, the high-priest at Jerusalem, the pattern of an altar he had seen in the Syrian capital, and desired that another should be made like it. The high-priest obeyed, and the idolatrous altar was placed within the sacred precincts of the Temple, and the king himself offered sacrifice thereon. Moreover, every city in his dominions shared in the idolatries of the capital. Everywhere Ahaz *made high places to burn incense to other gods*, introducing the worst superstitions of the remotest East, practising necromancy and witchcraft (Isai. viii. 19), causing his children to pass through the fire in the valley of Hinnom to Moloch (2 K. xvi. 3), dedicating sacred horses to the Sun, and raising altars on the house-tops for the worship of the heavenly bodies (2 K. xxiii. 12; 2 Chr. xxviii. 2—4).

---

[1] This was the first captivity of any considerable portion of Israel. See Map. The captives were located in Upper Mesopotamia on the affluents of the *Bilikh* and the *Khabour*, from about Harran to Nisibis, the Gozan of Scripture. Rawlinson's *Five Great Monarchies*, II. 398.

While the Southern kingdom thus seemed bent on rivalling that of Israel in idolatrous excesses, the fortunes of the latter kingdom had become more and more gloomy. After a reign of 20 years, Pekah was assassinated B.C. 737 by HOSHEA the son of Elah, who, after several years of anarchy, was strong enough to secure the sceptre for himself, B.C. 730. His reign, indeed, was not so sinful as that of his predecessors (2 K. xvii. 2), but the doom of Israel was nigh at hand. He had been on the throne but a few years when Shalmaneser, the successor of Tiglath-Pileser, invaded his territory, and reduced Israel to vassalage. This induced Hoshea to open a secret correspondence with So, *Sabaco I.*, king of Egypt. But news of his defection reaching the ears of the Assyrian monarch, he summoned Hoshea to Damascus to explain his conduct, and there placed him in prison. Then mustering his forces, he invaded his territory, and laid siege to Samaria, B.C. 723. Its natural strength enabled that city to hold out for three years, during which period Shalmaneser appears to have been obliged to return to Damascus, in consequence of a successful revolt headed by Sargon, to whom he forfeited his crown[1]. But this change brought no respite to the beleaguered capital of Israel. After a protracted resistance it was captured, B.C. 721, and thus Sargon completed the conquest which Shalmaneser had begun. Vast numbers of the remaining tribes were now removed into captivity[2], and located partly in Gozan or

[1] Rawlinson's *Five Great Monarchies*, II. 423; *Herodotus*, Vol. I. p. 473. See Chron. Table in the *Appendix*, p. 488.

[2] "It has been usual to ascribe the capture of Samaria to Shalmaneser; and this is certainly the impression which the Scriptural narrative leaves. But the assertion is not made expressly (comp. 2 K. xvii. 3, and xviii. 10), and if we may trust the direct statement of Sargon, the successor of Shalmaneser upon the throne, we must consider that he, and not Shalmaneser, was the actual captor of the city. Sargon relates that he took Samaria in his first year, B.C. 721, and

Mygdonia[1], and partly in the cities lately taken from the Medes. Their place was filled by a foreign population from the more inland districts of the empire, and colonies from Cuthah, Hamath, and Sepharvaim, possessed Samaria, and dwelt in the cities of Israel, whose existence as an independent kingdom now came to an end for ever.

CHAPTER V

REIGN OF HEZEKIAH.

2 Kings XVIII.—XX.   2 Chron. XXIX.—XXXII.

B. C. 726—698.

WHILE the kingdom of Israel thus came to an end, that of Judah seemed to have taken a fresh lease of vitality. At the close of the wicked reign of Ahaz, his son Hezekiah succeeded to the throne, B.C. 726, and proved one of the best of the monarchs of the line of David. His first act after his accession was to set on foot a thorough religious reformation. He removed the high places, brake down the images, and even destroyed the Brazen Serpent, the ancient relic of the Wanderings, which had become an object of idolatrous worship, under the name of *Nehushtan*[2] (2 K. xviii. 4). He then cleansed and purified the Temple, and re-opened it with splendid sacrifices, conducted by the reinstated priests and Levites (2 Chr. xxix. 20—36), and resolved to cele-

---

carried into captivity 27,280 families. It would appear, therefore, that Shalmaneser died, or was deposed, while Hoshea still held out, and that the final captivity of Israel fell into the reign of his successor." Rawlinson's *Hdtus.* I. 472. No king employed so generally or on so large a scale, the practice of wholesale deportation of his subjects as Sargon. See Rawlinson's *Five Great Monarchies*, II. p. 423.

[1] "As Gaza in Greek became Cadytis, Achzib Ecdippa, so M'gozan became Mygdonia." Smith's *Bib. Dict.*

[2] See Smith's *Bib. Dict.*, Art. *Nehushtan.*

brate a peculiar Passover, and invite to it all throughout the land of Palestine, who bore the Hebrew name (2 Chr. xxx. 1—10).

To this end he dispatched messengers throughout Judah, and northwards through Ephraim and Manasseh as far as Zebulun. The remnant of the once powerful house of Joseph treated his invitation with scorn, but all Judah and many of the smaller tribes assembled at Jerusalem, and took part in the great national rite, which was celebrated at an unusual but not an illegal period[1], and lasted upwards of 14 days. The associations awakened by this ancient ordinance roused the people to a becoming zeal for the true God, and on their return from Jerusalem a general destruction of idolatrous images and temples was set on foot throughout Judah and Benjamin, and even some portions of the northern kingdom (2 Chr. xxxi. 1).

Seconded in his pious efforts by the noble-minded prophet Isaiah, the king proceeded to carry out other religious reforms, and was rewarded for his zeal by a large measure of prosperity. Venturing to assume the offensive against the Philistines, he not only recovered the territory which his father had lost, but gained other important advantages (2 K. xviii. 7, 8). This success emboldened him to throw off the Assyrian yoke, and to decline forwarding the usual tribute. The late capture of Samaria by the Assyrians would render probable a speedy vengeance for this defection. But the wealthy city of Tyre, now the head of the Phœnician kingdom, was first to feel the weight of the Assyrian arms, and its inhabitants made such a stubborn resistance, that after operations extending over 5 years[2], the design was given up as impracticable.

---

[1] See Calendar, p. 155.
[2] Kenrick's *Phœnicia*, p. 378; *Five Great Mon.* II. 405.

The time thus gained was not thrown away by Hezekiah. He used every effort to strengthen his capital against the expected invasion; repaired the walls; built towers; set captains over the host; stopped up the wells; diverted the water-courses (2 Chr. xxxii. 3, 4); forged weapons of war; and while most of his people trembled at the certain coming of the great Assyrian conqueror, and many of his advisers would have made an alliance with Egypt, the monarch was exhorted by Isaiah not to lose his confidence in God. At length in the 14th[1] year of his reign (2 K. xviii. 13), the invader appeared[2]. Sennacherib, the successor of Sargon, *came up against all the fenced cities of Judah and took them* (2 K. xviii. 13). Thereupon Hezekiah thought it prudent to avert his wrath by a promise of submission, and consented to pay 300 talents of silver and 30 talents of gold, to raise which enormous sum he was obliged to spoil the Temple of many of its treasures, and even to strip the gold from the gates (2 K. xviii. 14—16). The respite thus obtained was only temporary. Two years had barely elapsed before Sennacherib, resolved to conquer the now flourishing kingdom of Egypt, commenced a second expedition through the dominions of Judah. While one of his generals attacked and captured Ashdod, he himself marched through Palestine, and laid siege to Libnah and Lachish, cities in the maritime lowland of Judah, and at this time subject to Egypt. From Lachish, however, he sent the *Tartan* or his "commander-in-chief," the *Rab-saris* or his "chief eunuch," and the *Rab-shakeh*, his "chief cupbearer," with a large force to Jerusalem, to

---

[1] Or perhaps the 27th, B.C. 700; see Rawlinson's *Hdtus.* I. 479 *n.*

[2] The route of the Assyrians may be traced in the vivid language of Isai. x. 28—34. The annals of Sennacherib contain a full account of this campaign; see Rawlinson's *Bampton Lectures*, pp. 142, 143; *Five Great Monarchies,* II. p. 425.

demand its surrender. On this occasion, the "chief cup-bearer" seems to have been at the head of the embassy. Standing by *the conduit of the upper pool* and speaking in the Hebrew tongue, he proclaimed to the advisers of Hezekiah and the people assembled on the city walls the message of the king of Assyria, exhorting them not to look for deliverance from Egypt, or even to place any confidence in their God, for what god had yet been able to deliver his land and people out of the hand of his master? (2 K. xviii. 33, 34).

By command of Hezekiah his scornful message was received in profound silence. The king himself, on being informed of the purport of the Assyrian embassy, with clothes rent and robed in sackcloth, repaired to the Temple, and sent his minister similarly attired to Isaiah, to entreat him in his perilous hour to lift up his prayer in behalf of his people. That undaunted prophet in reply bade his master defy boldly all the efforts of the enemy. That God, whom the Assyrian had blasphemed, would avenge His insulted honour; He would *send a blast upon him, and he should hear a rumour, and should return to his own land, there to fall by the sword.* These trustful words encouraged both king and people, and the Assyrian ambassadors finding it impossible to terrify the capital of Judah into subjection returned to Sennacherib, whom they found at Libnah, having taken or raised the siege of Lachish (2 K. xix. 8).

But while he was thus employed, news reached the ears of that monarch that Tirhakah, or *Tarakos*, a powerful king of Ethiopia, was on the march against him. On this he resolved to make one more effort to terrify Hezekiah into submission, and sent a second embassy to him, with a letter demanding in the most peremptory terms the surrender of the city, recapitulating the cities whose gods had been powerless to deliver them out of his hands, and bidding him dismiss the notion that he could escape. On receiving this vaunting letter, Hezekiah again repaired to the Temple, and there spread it before the Lord, entreating in words of singular pathos and beauty the aid of the God of Israel, *Who dwelt between the Cherubims* (2 K. xix. 15).

His prayer was heard. Isaiah was commissioned to assure the king that the *Virgin, the daughter of Zion,* might laugh to scorn all the efforts of the invader. True it was that the Assyrian monarch had laid waste many cities into ruinous heaps, but it was only because Jehovah Himself had so willed it, and had raised him up to be an instrument for the accomplishment of His own purposes. And now He would *put His hook*[1] *in* the Assyrian's *nose, and His bridle in his lips,* and turn him back by the way he had come, nor suffer him even to approach the city, or shoot an arrow there, or cast up a bank against it (2 K. xix. 32).

His words were destined to have a speedy and terrible fulfilment. Having reduced Libnah, Sennacherib appears to have pushed forward towards Pelusium[2], anxious to crush an Egyptian army under a native prince, named Sethos, before the dreaded Ethiopian monarch Terhak or Tirhakah could come to his aid. Within sight of each other the Assyrian and Egyptian hosts lay down, awaiting the morrow's battle, but that very night the angel of the Lord, probably by a sudden pestilence, or some more awful manifestation of Divine power, poured contempt on all the pride of the Assyrian monarch. As they slept, a sudden destruction fell upon his hosts, and

[1] " Properly a *ring*, such as in our country is placed through the nose of a bull, and similarly used in the East for leading about lions and other animals, as also prisoners, as in the case of Manasseh (2 Chr. xxxiii. 11; A.V. *in the thorns*). See Isai. xxxvii. 29; Ezek. xxix. 4, xxxviii. 4." Smith's *Bib. Dict.*

[2] See for the view here taken, Rawlinson's *Five Great Monarchies,* Vol. II. p. 442 ; *Bampton Lectures,* p. 143.

when he awoke next morning, behold 185,000 corpses
lay dead in his camp[1]! On this Sennacherib fled with
the shattered remnants of his forces to his own land,
where, 17 years after, or B.C. 680[2], he was assassinated
by his sons Adrammelech and Sharezer, as he was wor-
shipping in the temple of Nisroch his god, leaving his
throne to another son Esarhaddon (2 K. xix. 37).

At some period after, or as some think, before[3] this
signal deliverance, Hezekiah was seized with a serious
illness and was warned by the prophet Isaiah *to put
his house in order*, for the decree had gone forth that
he must die. This announcement caused the greatest
distress to the good king. He had striven to set a good
example while he lived, and had done much to reform
his people and their religion, and now in the very midst
of his work he must die! With many tears, therefore,
he turned his face to the wall, and pleaded his case
with God, praying that the prophet's words might not be
so immediately fulfilled. His prayer was heard. Isaiah
was bidden to assure him that his life would be prolonged for a space of 15 years, and as a sign to confirm
this assurance, the shadow on the great dial of his father
Ahaz went 10 degrees backwards, and by the application
of a plaster of figs, often used medicinally in such cases,
his malady was healed. News of his recovery, and of
the astronomical marvel accompanying it, was conveyed
into many lands, and various ambassadors with letters
and gifts came to his court. Amongst the rest came

---

[1] The Egyptians naturally ascribed their deliverance to
the interposition of their own gods. Rawlinson's *Hdtus*. Vol.
II. p. 141.

[2] *Five Great Mon.* Vol. II. p. 445; comp. 2 K. xix. 36.

[3] In the opinion of some, Hezekiah's illness preceded the
first invasion of Sennacherib by several years, and Merodach-
Baladan's visit is placed by them about the year B.C. 713, the
14th of Hezekiah (Comp. 2 K. xx. 6; Is. xxxviii. 5). Smith's
Bib. Dict.; Rawlinson's *Hdtus*. Vol. I. p. 479 *n.*

those of Merodach-Baladan[1], king of Babylon, who with
their retinue were escorted over the royal treasures. For
the pride and ostentation with which he displayed his
rich stores, Hezekiah was rebuked by Isaiah, who foretold that a day was coming, when all these treasures
would be carried away into the country of the very king
whose ambassadors had now come to congratulate him,
and that his sons would be compelled to serve as eunuchs
in the Babylonian court (2 K. xx. 17—19).

The remainder of Hezekiah's reign appears to have
been spent in peace and security. His treasury was
full; the agricultural resources of the country were developed; various new and useful improvements were
carried out in his capital; and on his death, lamented
by all Judah and Jerusalem, he was buried with especial
honour *in the chiefest of the sepulchres of the sons of
David*, b.c. 698 (2 Chr. xxxii. 27—33).

CHAPTER VI

REIGN OF MANASSEH. REFORMS OF JOSIAH.

2 Kings XXI.—XXIII.   2 Chron. XXXIII.—XXXV.

B. C. 698—623.

ON the death of Hezekiah, his son Manasseh succeeded to the throne at a very early age, having
been born in all probability twelve years before his

---

[1] "From the time of Sargon, Merodach-Baladan and his
family were the champions of Babylonian independence, and
headed the popular party in resisting the Assyrian monarchs."
"The real object of the mission was most likely to effect a
league between Babylon, Judea, and Egypt (Is. xx. 5, 6), in
order to check the growing power of the Assyrians. Hezekiah's exhibition of 'all his precious things' would thus have
been not a mere display, but a mode of satisfying the Babylonian ambassadors of his ability to support the expenses of a
war." Smith's *Bib. Dict.;* Rawlinson's *Herod.* I. 503.

father's death, B.C. 710. His mother, whose name was
Hephzibah[1] (*the delightsome one*, Isai. lxii. 4), was descended from one of the princes of Jerusalem. His
own name is remarkable, and was borne by no one else
in the history of the kingdom of Judah. It is the name
of the tribe second only to Ephraim in hostility to
Judah, and has been supposed to have been given to
him in remembrance of the fond hope of his father to
unite the remnants of Manasseh and other northern
tribes in a common worship and faith[2].

The accession of this king at the early age of 12
years was the signal for an entire revolution in the religious policy which his father had so consistently carried
out. It has been suggested that the idolatrous party,
which had sided with Ahaz, and had only been repressed
during the reign of Hezekiah, now recovered its old
ascendancy, and exercised a baneful influence over the
youthful monarch. Whether this was so or not, the spirit
of loyalty to Jehovah which Hezekiah had evinced was
exchanged for a more general adoption of heathen
modes of worship than had disfigured even the idolatrous
days of Ahaz. Not only were the high places restored,
but the worst enormities of Ahab were introduced into
Jerusalem. Altars were erected in honour of Baal and
Ashtaroth and all the host of heaven, even within the
sacred precincts of the Temple (2 Chr. xxxiii. 4, 5). The
king himself, not *only observed times, and used enchantments, and witchcraft, and dealt with a familiar
spirit, and with wizards* (2 Chr. xxxiii. 6), but even dedicated some of his sons in the fire to Moloch, and slaughtered others (Ez. xxiii. 37—39). The cries of human
victims offered in honour of this hideous deity of the
Ammonites re-echoed throughout the valley of Hinnom,
and the sins of Sodom and Gomorrah were practised

[1] See Blunt's *Scriptural Coincidences*, Pt. III. 5.
[2] Smith's *Bib. Dict.*, Art. *Manasseh;* and see above, p. 436.

with impunity in that city where Jehovah had said
that he would put His Name for ever (2 Chr. xxxiii. 4).
The consequent moral degeneracy was fearful. The
old faith was everywhere neglected and despised. The
altar of Jehovah was broken down (2 Chr. xxxiii. 16),
even the ark was displaced (2 Chr. xxxv. 3), and so
systematic was the destruction of the Sacred Books,
that fifty years later the discovery of the Book of the
Law was an event exciting wonder and astonishment
(2 K. xxii. 8), while the Sabbath, the sign between the
elect nation and Jehovah, was polluted (Isai. lvi. 2;
lviii. 13), and under the influence of the king and his
idolatrous advisers, the people *did more evil than did
the nations whom the Lord destroyed before the children of Israel* (2 K. xxi. 9).

Meanwhile the voice of the prophets was not hushed.
Heedless of the doom they incurred, the Lord's true
servants bore their faithful testimony against the deeds
of the king. They predicted the coming of such judgments on Judah and Jerusalem, that whoever heard of
them, *both his ears would tingle* (2 K. xxi. 12). *The
line of Samaria and the plummet of the house of
Ahab should be stretched over* the capital of Judah,
and it should *be wiped as a man wipeth a dish*, and
its people should be *delivered into the hands of their
enemies* (2 K. xxi. 13, 14). These outspoken rebukes met
with their natural reward. It was now, according to the
ancient Jewish tradition, that the aged Isaiah was *sawn
asunder*[1], while of other less known but no less faithful
servants of Jehovah, such numbers were murdered, that
the streets of Jerusalem ran with blood (2 K. xxi. 16).

Such a policy brought its inevitable punishment.
Risings of the Philistines, Moabites, and Ammonites

---

[1] Comp. Heb. xi. 37: but see Art. *Isaiah* in Smith's *Bib.
Dict.*

(Zeph. ii. 4—15; Jer. xlvii.—xlix.), were speedily followed by an invasion of the territory of Judah by the Assyrians (2 Chr. xxxiii. 11). The captains of Esarhaddon, who had crushed the rebellion of Merodach-Baladan, invested Jerusalem[1], took Manasseh captive, and carried him off to Babylon[2], where loaded with fetters he was cast into prison. But in the solitude of his dungeon the Jewish king repented of the awful wickedness he had committed, and humbled himself greatly before the God of his fathers, who in His infinite mercy listened to his petitions for forgiveness. His defection was pardoned by Esarhaddon[3], and he was permitted to return to Jerusalem (2 Chr. xxxiii. 13). The lessons learnt in captivity were not forgotten by the restored monarch. He set himself to effect so much of a religious reformation as his previous character would allow. The worship of Jehovah was renewed, sacrifices were once more offered in His honour, and the heathen altars within the sacred

[1] Either shortly before or after this visit to Jerusalem, Esarhaddon invaded Egypt, defeated Tirhakah, took his capital, and became master of the country as far as Thebes or Diospolis, the No or No-Amon of Scripture. Rawlinson, *Five Great Monarchies*, II. p. 475.

[2] "One is greatly surprised at first hearing that the generals of an *Assyrian* king, on capturing a rebel, carried him to *Babylon* instead of Nineveh. 'What has a king of Assyria to do with Babylon?' one naturally asks. The reply is, that Esarhaddon, and he *only of all the Assyrian kings*, actually was king of Babylon; that he built a palace, and occasionally held his court there; and that consequently a captive was as likely to be brought to him at that city as at the metropolis of Assyria-Proper." Rawlinson's *Bampton Lectures*, p. 145, and *Hdtus.* Vol. I. p. 482.

[3] After the example of Sargon, Esarhaddon "gathered men from Babylon, Orchoë, Susa, Elymais, Persia, and other neighbouring regions, and entrusting them to an officer of high rank, 'the great and noble Asnapper,' had them conveyed to Palestine and settled over the whole country, which until this time must have been somewhat thinly peopled." Comp. Ezra iv. 2, 9, 10; Rawlinson's *Five Great Monarchies*, II. p. 477.

precincts of the Temple were destroyed. But the change
was naturally but partial (2 Chr. xxxiii. 17). During his
long reign of 55 years the evil he had done had sunk
too deeply to be easily removed. The recollection of the
innocent blood he had shed was never forgotten, and at
his death he was not laid in the sepulchres of the kings,
but *in the garden of his own house, in the garden of
Uzza*, B.C. 643 (2 K. xxi. 26).

AMON his son now succeeded to the throne, and,
after a short reign of 2 years, fell a victim to a conspiracy and was slain in his own palace. The people, however, put the conspirators to death, and secured the
throne for his son JOSIAH, now only 8 years of age, B.C.
641. Young as he was, the new king displayed a remarkable spirit of loyalty to Jehovah, and surpassed
even the best of his predecessors in his zeal for the
true faith. In the 12th year of his reign (2 Chr. xxxiv.
3), B.C. 629, he commenced a great reform. In Jerusalem itself he removed the altars dedicated to Baal
and all the host of heaven, and burnt the symbol of
Ashtaroth at the brook Kidron, and the sacred horses
that had been dedicated to the Sun. He then commenced
a personal tour, not only throughout his own dominions,
but throughout Simeon, Ephraim, Manasseh, and even
distant Naphtali (2 Chr. xxxiv. 6). At Bethel he visited
Jeroboam's chapel, and agreeably to the remarkable prophecy of the disobedient Prophet, uttered 300 years before[1], broke down the altar and high places that king had
set up, exhumed the bones from the sepulchres in the
neighbouring mount, and scattered them over the altars.
A little further, one of the sepulchres attracted his
attention, and in answer to his enquiries, he learnt that
it contained the remains of the old prophet of Bethel
and his victim the man of God from Judah. On this he

---

[1] See above, p. 372.

directed that the sepulchre should be spared, and the
venerable relics carefully preserved (2 K. xxiii. 15—19).

Returning to Jerusalem, in the 18th year of his
reign he empowered a special commission to restore
the Temple, and to levy contributions for this purpose.
In the course of the repairs, Hilkiah the high-priest
found a roll containing the Book of the Law, probably
the Book of Deuteronomy, which he delivered to Sha-
phan the scribe, or royal secretary. By him portions
were read in the ears of the king, who struck with alarm
at its awful denunciations, rent his clothes, and directed
that the Divine Will should be instantly consulted, that
the wrath of heaven might not descend on the apostate
nation. The High-priest and the rest thereupon sought
the advice of a prophetess named HULDAH, the wife of
Shallum, keeper of the royal wardrobe, who resided in
one of the sacred cloisters of the Temple. In reply, she
assured them that the Divine judgments would certainly be fulfilled, not indeed in the reign of Josiah,
whose early piety had found favour with Jehovah, but
after he had been gathered to his fathers. This answer
was in due course returned to the king, who instantly
repaired to the Temple, and caused the awful denunciations on idolatry to be publicly read in the ears of
the assembled people. The effect was very great.. The
people, conscience-stricken and appalled, made a solemn
covenant, and promised to adhere thenceforward to the
worship of the true God, and agreed to a still more
thorough reformation. After a restoration of the ancient
Levitical service in the Temple, a national celebration
of the Passover was decreed, and was carried out with
a grandeur and magnificence exceeding anything that
had been seen on any former occasion (2 K. xxiii. 21—23).

CHAPTER VII

DEATH OF JOSIAH. CAPTIVITY OF JUDAH.

2 Kings XXIII. XXIV.   2 Chron. XXXV. XXXVI.

B. C. 623—588.

BUT the religious reformations of the pious king could not ward off the destined destruction of his kingdom. At this period the great Assyrian empire had considerably declined[1], while the kingdom of Egypt under a powerful monarch named Necho[2], had recovered much of its ancient glory. This king now resolved to gain possession of Carchemish[3], which commanded the passage of the Euphrates. From motives which cannot be certainly divined, Josiah resolved to oppose his progress through his own territory, and, in spite of an

---

[1] Partly from dissensions with the *Medes* (B.C. 634—603), who were attempting to seize the dominion over the East, but still more in consequence of the great *Scythian* invasion, about B.C. 630, described by Herodotus (I. civ.—cvi.), Assyria had been greatly weakened, her cities being desolated, and her palaces dismantled or destroyed. These Scythian hordes penetrated into Palestine as far as Ashdod, but were repulsed by Psammetichus, and on their return a portion, probably attracted by the situation of Beth-shan (See above, p. 313), settled there, whence its Greek name Scythopolis, "the city of the Scythians." Milman's *History of the Jews*, I. 391 ; Rawlinson's *Herod.* Vol. I. 485, *Five Gt. Mon.* II. 512.

[2] Called by Manetho *Nechao*, by Herodotus Νεκώς, on the monuments *Neku*, the son and successor of the first Psammetichus. His defeat of the Syrians in a great battle is mentioned by Herod. II. 159, and is said to have taken place at Magdŏlus (=*Migdal-el*, in the tribe of Naphtali, Josh. xix. 38), which is identified with the *Magdala* of Matt. xv. 39, probably in consequence of a confusion between this name and Megiddo. Rawlinson's *Herod.* II. 246 *n.*

[3] Not the classical Circesium, but higher up the Euphrates, "occupying nearly the site of the later *Mabog*, or Hierapolis." Smith's *Bib. Dict.; Dict. Geog.* Art. *Hierapolis.*

embassy from the Egyptian monarch begging him not
to interfere, drew up his forces at Megiddo, and, as
though with a presentiment of his doom, disguised himself before entering into the battle. His fears were
verified ; struck by the Egyptian archers, he was removed from the field to die before he reached Jerusalem, where he was committed to the grave amidst the
profoundest grief of his people, and especially of the
prophet JEREMIAH, who composed a funeral elegy over
this last and best of the kings of Judah, B.C. 610 (2
Chr. xxxv. 25; Lam. iv. 20).

His son and successor JEHOAHAZ or SHALLUM (Jer.
xxii. 11), only held the throne for 3 months. On his
return from Carchemish, Necho condemned the land to
pay a tribute of 100 talents of silver, and a talent of
gold, and sending for the new king to Riblah[1] in the land
of Hamath, put him in bonds, and thence removed him
to Egypt, where he died (2 K. xxiii. 34). His brother
ELIAKIM was now permitted by the Egyptian monarch
to ascend the throne, and in obedience to the same
authority changed his name to JEHOIAKIM. In the 4th
year of his reign, or B.C. 606, NEBUCHADNEZZAR, placed
by his father Nabopolassar at the head of the Assyrian
armies, marched forth to avenge the Egyptian invasion.
In a pitched battle at Carchemish (Jer. xlvi. 1—13) he utterly defeated Pharaoh-Necho, and recovered Cœlesyria,

---

[1] "At the upper end of the valley of Lebanon, some 35
miles beyond Baalbec, and about 10 days' journey from Jerusalem," on the great road between Palestine and Babylonia.
Describing the advantages of its position, Dr Robinson says
that it lies "on the banks of a mountain-stream in the midst
of a vast and fertile plain, yielding the most abundant supplies of forage. From this point the roads were open either by
Aleppo and the Euphrates to Nineveh, or by Palmyra to
Babylon...by the end of Lebanon and the coast to Palestine
and Egypt, or through the Bŭkâa and the Jordan valley to
the centre of the Holy Land." Robinson's *Bib. Res.* III. 545.

Phœnicia, and northern Palestine. Then advancing into Judæa he drove all who had no fenced cities—and amongst the rest the Rechabites (Jer. xxxv. 11)—to Jerusalem, captured that city, placed Jehoiakim in fetters, rifled the Temple, and carried off to Babylon some of the sacred vessels, and many of the principal Hebrew nobles, including Dᴀɴɪᴇʟ and his three friends, Hananiah, Mishael, and Azariah (Dan. i. 1—6).

On promise, however, of faithfulness to his liege lord Jehoiakim was suffered to retain his kingly dignity, at least in name, for 3 years longer. At the close of this period he had the hardihood to try and throw off the yoke, and rebelled against his suzerain. But this only involved his kingdom in deeper misery[1]. Unable to take the field in person, Nebuchadnezzar sent a numerous force against him from his now subject provinces of Chaldæa and Syria, as well as Moab and Ammon (2 K. xxiv. 2). These overran the whole country, and reduced it to the lowest degree of wretchedness and misery.

During the period of degradation that now ensued, Jehoiakim, either in a contest with some of his many foes, or owing to a rising of his oppressed subjects, came to a violent end. His body lay ignominiously exposed upon the ground, and was buried *with the burial of an ass*, without pomp or ceremony, *beyond the gates of Jerusalem*, ʙ.ᴄ. 599 (Jer. xxii. 18, 19; xxxvi. 30).

Jᴇʜoɪᴀᴄʜɪɴ his son, also called Jᴇᴄoɴɪᴀʜ and Coɴɪᴀʜ, was now placed upon the throne (2 Chr. xxxvi. 9), but after a reign of 3 months and 10 days, Nebuchad-

---

[1] For the moral and religious degradation of the country at this period, see Jer. xix.; Ezek. viii.; for the king's vindictive persecution of righteous prophets, Jer. xxvi.; for his impiety in cutting up the roll containing Jeremiah's prophecy, Jer. xxxvi.; for his luxury and tyranny, as also his selfishness in building splendid palaces while his kingdom was so impoverished, Jer. xxii. 13—17.

nezzar's army appeared before Jerusalem, and the young king and his court surrendered at discretion. The Temple was again pillaged of such vessels that yet remained, the king himself, the nobles, and chief artisans were removed to Babylon[1], and none, save the poorest of the population, were left behind (2 K. xxiv. 8—16). MATTANIAH, the uncle of the captive king, was now placed by the Babylonian monarch in charge of the exhausted kingdom, and took the name of ZEDEKIAH. In defiance of the dictates of common prudence, and of the advice of the prophet Jeremiah (Jer. xxvii. xxviii.; Comp. Ezek. xvii. 12—21), he was foolish enough to court an alliance with Pharaoh-Hophra, or Apries, a new and enterprising monarch in Egypt[2]. Instantly the Babylonian armies were put in motion, and overran all Judah, while Jerusalem together with Lachish and Azekah alone held out. A temporary delay was caused by an effort of the king of Egypt to relieve his ally, and the necessity of first repulsing the Egyptian forces. This achieved, the Chaldæans again presented themselves before the walls of the Holy City, and besieged it for upwards of 16 months. The wretched inhabitants were reduced to the most fearful straits. Famine prevailed throughout the city (2 K. xxv. 3); *the tongue of the sucking child clave to the roof of its mouth for thirst, the young children cried for bread, and no man brake it unto them* (Lam. iv. 4); nobles that had ever before *fed delicately,* searched even *dunghills* for any remnants of food that might be found (Lam. iv. 5); and mothers *boiled their own children* (Lam. iv. 10). The Lord at last poured

---

[1] In 2 K. xxiv. 14, 16, the numbers are given as 7,000 soldiers, 1,000 artificers and smiths, and 2,000 others, whose occupation is not mentioned.

[2] Rawlinson's *Herod.* Vol. I. 515. For the prophecies of Jeremiah during the reign of Zedekiah, see chaps. xxi. xxiv. xxvii. 12—22, xxviii. xxix. xxxii. xxxiii. xxxiv. xxxvii. xxxviii.

upon the city the cup of His fierce anger for all its iniquities, and its Day of Doom was come. At length the Chaldæan armies effected a breach in the strong walls, and made their way into the city. With a few of his troops Zedekiah effected his escape to Jericho, but was pursued, captured, and sent to Nebuchadnezzar at Riblah. Judgment was then passed upon him (2 K. xxv. 6), and his sons having first been put to death before his face, his eyes were thrust out[1], and laden with fetters he was removed to Babylon, B.C. 588.

Punishment having thus been inflicted on the king, Nebuzar-adan, an officer high in the confidence of the Babylonian monarch, was dispatched to Jerusalem, to carry out the complete destruction of the city. By his orders, the Temple, the royal palace, the houses of the wealthy, were set on fire; the walls were broken down; the sacred vessels of the once glorious House of Jehovah were plundered; the brazen pillars were broken up; the chief priests were put to death; and the rest with the greater part of the inhabitants were removed to Babylon. A scanty remnant was permitted to remain in their native land to be *vine-dressers and husbandmen* (Jer. lii. 16), under the superintendence of GEDALIAH, who with a Chaldæan guard (Jer. xl. 1, 2, 5) was stationed at Mizpeh[2] (2 K. xxv. 23; Jer. xl. 6), a strong fortress 6 miles north of Jerusalem. Declining the offer of a retreat at Babylon, Jeremiah resolved to share the lot of this miserable remnant in his own land (Jer. xl. 6). But even the late terrible misfortunes could not calm the spirit of faction. Gedaliah was assassinated under circumstances of revolting treachery by ISHMAEL, a man of royal blood, together with some of the Chaldæan guard

---

[1] Thus were fulfilled the apparently contradictory prophecies in Jer. xxxii. 4, and Ezek. xii. 13.

[2] Or Mizpah. For notices of this place on previous occasions, see above, pp. 272, 280, 375.

(See 2 K. xxv. 25 ; Jer. xli. 1—10). Johanan, one of the captains of the army of Judah, who had in vain warned Gedaliah of his danger (Jer. xl. 13—16), gathered a force and pursued the assassin as far as Gibeon, but he effected his escape beyond Jordan to the country of the Ammonites (Jer. xli. 15). Then the little remnant of Jews, fearful of the vengeance of the Babylonian monarch, contrary to the advice of Jeremiah (Jer. xlii. 7—22), fled into Egypt, and after first settling at Tahpanhes (Jer. xliii. 7), were scattered throughout the country at Migdol, Noph, and Pathros (Jer. xliv. 1), whither also Jeremiah accompanied them, to share their fortunes and to die[1].

---

[1] Before passing on, a few remarks may here be subjoined respecting the kingdoms of Judah and Israel, which now came to an end.

I. *Their respective duration.* The kingdom of Israel lasted from B.C. 975 to B.C. 721, or 254 years. The kingdom of Judah lasted from B.C. 975 to B.C. 588, or 387 years, thus outliving her more populous and powerful rival by 133 years.

II. *Their mutual relations.* These, as we have seen, were dictated by three different lines of policy:—

(i) *Mutual animosity from* B.C. 975—918.

The first three kings of Judah, Rehoboam, Abijah, and Asa, persisted in the hope of regaining their authority over the Ten Tribes, and for nearly 60 years there was war between the two kingdoms.

(ii) *Close alliance, and united hostility to Syria,* B.C. 918 —884.

With the accession of Jehoshaphat there sprang up an alliance between the two kingdoms, cemented by intermarriage, and prompted probably by the necessity of joint action in resisting the encroaching power of Syria.

(iii) *Fresh animosity, and the gradual decline of both kingdoms before the advancing power of the Assyrian Empire,* B.C. 884—588.

The alliance between the kingdoms was rudely shattered by the accession of Jehu to the throne of Israel. He put Ahaziah to death, and the hostility thus begun reached its highest pitch under Amaziah, Jehoash, and Pekah.

III.   *Their contrasts.*

1.   *In the kingdom of Judah,* (*a*) There was always a fixed capital and a venerated centre of religion; (*b*) the army was always subordinate; (*c*) the succession was interrupted by no revolution; (*d*) the priests remained faithful to the crown.

2.   *In the kingdom of Israel,* (*a*) There was no fixed capital, and no real religious centre; (*b*) the army was often insubordinate; (*c*) the succession was constantly interrupted, so that out of 19 kings there were no less than 9 dynasties, each ushered in by a revolution; (*d*) the authorized priests left the kingdom in a body, and the priesthood established by Jeroboam had no Divine sanction and no promise; it was corrupt in its very source.   Hence in the kingdom of Israel the *prophets* were the regular ministers of God, and, especially during the second of the two periods above mentioned, their ministry was distinguished by far more extraordinary events than in the kingdom of Judah, whose annals offer no prophetical deeds like those of Elijah and Elisha. See Arts. *Kingdom of Judah and Israel* in Smith's *Bib. Dict.;* Jahn's *Hebrew Commonwealth.*   For the *Table* of Kings and Prophets, see the Appendix.

BOOK XI

FROM THE CAPTIVITY TO THE CLOSE OF THE CANON.

CHAPTER I

DANIEL AND NEBUCHADNEZZAR.

DAN. I.—III.   B. C. circ. 606—570.

"NOTHING," it has been remarked, "could present a more striking contrast to their native country than the region into which the Hebrews were now transplanted. Instead of their irregular and picturesque mountain-city, crowning its unequal heights, and looking down into its deep and precipitous ravines, through one of which a scanty stream wound along, they entered the vast, square, and level city of Babylon, occupying both sides of the broad Euphrates; while all around spread immense plains, which were intersected by long straight canals, bordered by rows of willows. How unlike their national temple—a small but highly finished and richly adorned fabric, standing in the midst of its courts on the brow of a lofty precipice—the colossal temple of the Chaldæan Bel, rising from the plain, with its eight stupendous stories or towers, one above the other, to the perpendicular height of a furlong! The palace of the Babylonian king was more than twice the size of their whole city: it covered eight miles, with its hanging gardens built on arched terraces, each rising above the other, and rich in all the luxuriance of artificial cultivation. How different from the sunny cliffs of their own land, where the olive and the vine grew spontaneously, and the cool, shady, and secluded valleys, where they could always find shelter from the heat of the burning noon! No wonder, then, that in the pathetic words of their own hymn, *By the waters of Babylon they sat down and wept, when they remembered thee, O Zion*[1]" (Ps. cxxxvii. 1).

Thus far removed from their native land, amidst a strange people and strange rites, and exposed to all the influences of contact with their conquerors, we might, in the usual order of things, have expected that the Jews would have ceased to remain a nation at all. But with them it was not thus to be. The ten tribes, indeed, are never heard of more, but the remnant of Judah and Benjamin in Babylonia so far from blending its national life with that of its conquerors, remained a separate people, and preserved its national institutions. We shall very much misunderstand their condition, if we suppose that the Jews became bondsmen or serfs[2]. They were " colonists rather than captives;" they received grants of land, agricultural or pastoral, out of the conquered territories at the disposal of Nebuchadnezzar; and so valuable were their services considered that not a few rose to high eminence (Dan. ii. 48), and held confidential positions next to the person of the sovereign. While, moreover, they increased in numbers and wealth, they retained an internal jurisdiction over their own members; they kept up amongst themselves distinctions of rank; they preserved their genealogies (Neh. vii. 5, 6, 64); and although from the absence of any common centre of worship they could only observe the Mosaic Law in part[3], still they retained the rite of circumcision, the

[1] Milman's *History of the Jews*, I. 407, 408.

[2] See Jahn's *Hebrew Commonwealth*, pp. 112, 113.

[3] The Psalms which appear to belong to this period are, Psls. x. xiii.—xv. xxv.—xxvii. xxxvi. xxxvii. xlix. l. liii. lxvii. lxxvii. lxxx. lxxxviii. lxxxix. xcii. xciii. cxxiii. cxxx. cxxxvii.

distinction of meats, and other points (Comp. Dan. i. 8 ; Esth. iii. 8). Nor did the Providence, which had hitherto watched over them, fail them in the land of exile. The voice of Prophecy, so far from being hushed, now swelled into louder strains. While JEREMIAH[1] warned and exhorted them at the outset of this sad period in their history, EZEKIEL did not fail for 30 years to carry on the same work in the land of exile itself, while another and one of the most illustrious of their number rose to the very highest position, and proved the "Moses of the Captivity," and the fourth of the greater Prophets.

In the fourth year of Jehoiakim, B.C. 606, as we have already seen[2], Nebuchadnezzar had ordered the Chief of the Eunuchs to remove to Babylon certain select youths of royal descent, who from their talents seemed likely to be of service in his court. Of these one was DANIEL, apparently of the blood royal (Dan. i. 3), and gifted with no common talents (Dan. i. 4). With three other companions of the tribe of Judah, HANANIAH, MISHAEL, and AZARIAH, he was removed to the Babylonian court, and there trained for the king's service in *the learning and language of the Chaldæans* (Dan. i. 4). Moreover, in accordance with a common custom, his name was changed, and he and his three companions were now known as BELTESHAZZAR, SHADRACH, MESHACH, and ABEDNEGO. During the three years of their training they were not forgetful of the Law and Religion of their fathers, and with unusual firmness of character declined to partake of the daily allowance of meat and wine supplied them from the royal table, either probably because it was ceremonially unclean, or had been offered in sacrifice to the Assyrian gods. Preferring to live on the simplest fare, they yet proved as comely and well-favoured as though they had been fed on the rarest dainties, and when brought before Nebuchadnezzar were

[1] See above, p. 452.   [2] See above, p. 449.

pronounced to excel in wisdom and knowledge the wisest men in his empire, and were rewarded with high positions about his court (Dan. i. 15).

While they were thus employed, a remarkable circumstance took place. Nebuchadnezzar dreamt a dream, which exceedingly troubled his spirit. Summoning the magi and astrologers, he demanded that it should be instantly interpreted. They promised the interpretation, if they might be told the dream. But though this had escaped the monarch's memory, he reiterated his command; and when told that to obey it was impossible, issued an edict commanding the instant destruction of all the wise men throughout his realms. This despotic order was made known to Daniel by Arioch the "captain of the executioners," who was charged to see it carried out. The Jewish exile instantly sought an audience with the monarch, and having succeeded in gaining time for a fuller consideration, summoned his three friends, who with fervent prayer to HIM, "from whom no secrets are hid," besought a revelation of the dream. Their prayers were heard, and at a second audience Daniel disclosed the Vision of the Night. *The monarch had beheld a great Image, the form of which was terrible. The head was of fine gold, the breast and the arms of silver, the belly and sides of brass, the legs of iron, the feet partly iron and partly clay. The excellent brightness of this Image the monarch had watched, till he suddenly saw a stone cut out of a mountain without hands smite the feet of the Image till it broke in pieces, and became like the chaff of the summer threshing-floors, while the stone became a great mountain and filled the whole earth.* Such was the Vision which Daniel then proceeded to interpret. "The king himself was this head of gold. To him the God of heaven had given a kingdom, power, and strength, and glory. After him should arise another kingdom inferior to his; after that a third kingdom of brass, which should bear rule over all the earth; to which would succeed a fourth kingdom strong as iron, breaking in pieces and subduing all things. That kingdom, with its feet and toes, part of iron and part of clay, would be partly strong and partly brittle, and its subjects would mingle themselves with the seed of men, but they would not cleave one to another, even as iron is not mixed with clay, and would make room for another kingdom, which God Himself would set up, to break in pieces and consume all the previous kingdoms, and itself stand for ever[1]" (Dan. ii. 36—45).

The great Babylonian monarch was profoundly affected by this proof of superhuman knowledge. He fell down on his face and worshipped Daniel; commanded that *an oblation and sweet odours* should be offered unto him; bestowed on him costly presents, and made him viceroy over the whole province of Babylon, and supreme over all the wise men of his empire. In the hour of his prosperity Daniel did not forget his three companions. By his intercession similar honours were bestowed upon them, while he himself retained the pre-eminence *in the gate of the king* (Dan. ii. 46—49).

Though on this memorable occasion the new viceroy had been pre-eminently faithful to the God of his fathers, and by his ascription of all his wisdom to a higher Power, had made the great monarch he served acknowledge that there was a God of gods and Lord of lords, the lesson does not seem to have made a very lasting impression on Nebuchadnezzar's mind. In the vast empire he had won by his arms there were many different nations, with different gods, and different modes of worship. Over all he was supreme, and with the true feel-

---

[1] An interpretation now generally understood to indicate (i) the Chaldean, (ii) Medo-Persian, (iii) Macedonian, and (iv) Roman empires, which last gives way to (v) the kingdom of Messiah.

ing of an Oriental despot it seemed to him only right
that they should all acknowledge his chief deity. This
was the great Bel, or Bel-Merodach[1], "the supreme
chief of the gods," "the king of the heavens and the
earth," the Jupiter of the Babylonian Pantheon. It was
possibly an image of this god[2], 60 cubits high and 6 broad,
and overlaid with golden plates[3], which he now proceeded to set up on the plain of Dura, with the command that at the sound of instruments of music, all his
subjects, from the highest to the lowest, should fall
down and worship it, on penalty of being flung into a
burning fiery furnace (Dan. iii. 5, 6).

In accordance with this edict, all the officers of the
court of Babylon, and the governors of the different provinces who had been summoned to assist at the ceremony, flocked to the plain of Dura, and with one consent,
as soon as the music sounded, prostrated themselves
before the great dumb image which their lord had set
up. But Daniel's three friends, Shadrach, Meshach, and
Abednego, in this hour of trial remained faithful to the
religion of their fathers, neither falling down nor wor-
shipping with the rest. This act of disobedience to their
master was quickly perceived by many of the native Chaldæans, who were already filled with jealousy at the
elevation of the exiles, and they were not slow in report-
ing it to Nebuchadnezzar. On hearing it, that monarch's

---

[1] Rawlinson's *Bampton Lectures*, notes, p. 439; *Herod.*
Vol. I. pp. 628, 629.

[2] Smith's *Bib. Dict.*, Art. *Nebuchadnezzar*. Dr Pusey, on
the other hand, writes, "Whether the image was formed in
reminiscence of that emblem of human might, which Nebuchadnezzar had seen in his dream, and of which the head was
declared to represent himself, or whether it was himself whom
he intended to be worshipped in it, it was plainly some test of
allegiance required of all peoples, nations, and languages, in
his whole empire." *Lectures on Daniel*, p. 440.

[3] Ibid. p. 442, and the note.

wrath knew no bounds. He summoned them before him; he reiterated the command he had already issued ; he warned them that in spite of their high position they should certainly suffer the penalty of their disobedience. But his words were wasted. These three mighty ones in "the noble army of martyrs" replied that they were not careful to answer him in this matter ; their God could, if such was His will, deliver them from the fiery furnace, and even if He did not, they would not serve the monarch's god, or bow before the Image he had set up (Dan. iii. 16—18).

This outspoken refusal filled Nebuchadnezzar with still greater fury. *The form of his visage was changed,* he bade *the furnace be heated seven times more than it was wont to be heated,* and ordered the mightiest captains in his army to bind the three, and fling them into the fire. His words were obeyed, but at the cost of the lives of his captains, who fell victims to their zeal, being caught by the raging flames. Moreover, when he looked to see the three martyrs speedily reduced to ashes, behold they were observed *loose, walking* unscathed in the midst of the fire, accompanied by a Celestial Being, in whom the monarch discerned none other than a "Son of God!" Thereupon he drew near to the mouth of the furnace, and bade his intended victims come forth. And they came forth, and on their bodies, as all attested, the fire was seen to have *had no power, neither was a hair of their head singed, neither had the smell of fire passed over them.* Filled with admiration for their heroic faith, the monarch issued a decree that all men, far and wide, throughout his empire should revere the God of these Hebrews, and that every people, nation, or language that spake word against their God, should *be cut in pieces, and their houses made a dunghill* (Dan. iii. 29).

CHAPTER II

REIGNS OF NEBUCHADNEZZAR, BELSHAZZAR, AND DARIUS.

DAN. IV.—VI. B. C. 570—538.

THOUGH from the incident just recorded Nebuchadnezzar had learnt to know the greatness of the God of Israel, a still sterner lesson was needed to teach him his own position in reference to the Most High. He was by far the greatest of the Babylonian monarchs. His name was known, his power was dreaded throughout the entire Eastern world. He was the conqueror of Syria, of Phœnicia, of Tyre, of Palestine. He was the adorner and beautifier of his native land. He built noble cities; he raised stately temples; he renovated, fortified, almost rebuilt Babylon; he constructed quays and breakwaters[1], reservoirs, canals, and aqueducts on a scale of grandeur and magnificence surpassing everything of the kind recorded in history[2]. Perhaps no single man ever left behind him as his memorial, one-half the amount of building which was erected by this king. The palace he built for himself in Babylon with its triple walls, its hanging gardens, its plated pillars, was regarded in his day as one of the wonders of the world, while even at the present hour[3] it is his name

---

[1] Along the shores of the Persian Gulf. Rawlinson's *Herod.* Vol. I. p. 513.

[2] Rawlinson's *Bampton Lectures*, p. 160 and notes; *Herod.* Vol. I. pp. 512, 513; Smith's *Bib. Dict.*, Art. *Nebuchadnezzar.*

[3] "I have examined," says Sir H. Rawlinson, "the bricks *in situ*, belonging perhaps to a hundred different towns and cities in the neighbourhood of Baghdad, and I never found any other legend than that of Nebuchadnezzar, son of Nabopolassar, king of Babylon." Nine-tenths of the bricks amidst the ruins of Babylon are stamped with his name. Compare his own words as recorded in Dan. iv. 30: "Is not this great Babylon, *which I have built?*"

which is stamped upon well-nigh every brick found amidst the ruins of his capital. Amidst all this earthly grandeur he had grown and become strong ; *his greatness reached unto heaven, and his dominion to the end of the earth.* Inflated with pride, he became a god unto himself, and knew not that he was but an instrument in the hand of Him, *who ruleth in the kingdom of men, and giveth it to whomsoever He will* (Dan. iv. 17).

This was the lesson he had' now to learn, and he learned it on this wise. One night he dreamed a dream which none of his wise men could interpret. Daniel, therefore, was once more summoned before him, and listened while the monarch revealed the Vision of the Night. *I saw, he said, and behold a Tree in the midst of the earth, and the height thereof was great, reaching unto the heaven, and the sight thereof to the end of all the earth. The leaves thereof were fair, and the fruit much, and the beasts of the field had shadow under it, the fowls of heaven dwelt in the boughs thereof, and all flesh fed of it. And, behold! there came down from heaven a Watcher and a Holy One, who cried out, Hew down the Tree, and cut off his branches, but leave the stump of his roots in the earth, even with a band of iron and brass, and let it be wet with the dew of heaven, and let his portion be with the beasts, and let his heart be changed from man's, and let a beast's heart be given him, and let seven times pass over him.* Such was the Vision. What was the interpretation? Daniel did not disguise it from the monarch. "The Tree was no other than himself. For him there was a great trial in store. A day was near, when he would be cast down from his place of power, would be driven from the society of men, would have his dwelling with the beasts of the field, until seven times had passed over him and he revived and knew for a truth that not he, but the Most High ruled in the kingdom of heaven, and

gave dominion and power to whomsoever He would"
(Dan. iv. 1—27).

Thus a warning was given him, but it was disregarded. Nebuchadnezzar did not, as Daniel bade, *break
off his sins by righteousness, and his iniquities by shew-
ing mercy to the poor.* Twelve months afterwards he
was walking in that glorious palace which he had made
for himself, and in a moment of overweening pride he
cried, *Is not this great⋅ Babylon, that I have built for
the house of the kingdom by the might of my power,
and for the honour of my majesty?* The words had
hardly been spoken, when his doom came upon him.
The thick pall of madness[1] settled down upon him ; the
mind of a man departed from him, and that of a beast
entered in. Casting off his robes, he refused the food
and habitation of men ; mingling with the cattle in the
fields, he remained exposed to the weather day and
night, *till his hair was grown as eagles' feathers, and
his nails like birds' claws*[2] (Dan. iv. 33).

Meanwhile, as seems most probable, his queen Ni-
tocris administered his kingdom, and at length, after
an interval of four, or perhaps seven years, as he did

[1] Probably what the Greeks called Lycanthropy (λυκαν-
θρωπία), wherein the sufferer fancies himself a beast, quits the
haunts of men, and leads the life of a beast. For instances
and details, see Dr Pusey's *Lectures on Daniel,* pp. 425—435;
Rawlinson's *Bampton Lectures,* p. 165; *Herod.* Vol. I. p. 516.

[2] A sickness of this monarch is mentioned by Berosus,
and in the "Standard Inscription" of Nebuchadnezzar he
himself appears to allude to this mysterious passage of his
life: *For four years...the seat of my kingdom...did not rejoice
my heart, in all my dominions I did not build a high place of
power, the precious treasures of my kingdom I did not lay up.
In Babylon, buildings for myself and for the honour of my
kingdom I did not lay out. In the worship of Merodach, my
lord, the joy of my heart, in Babylon the city of his sovereignty,
and the seat of my empire, I did not sing his praises, I did not
furnish his altars with victims, nor did I clear out the canals.*
Rawlinson's *Bampton Lectures,* p. 166, and notes.

not scruple to declare in a proclamation addressed to
his people, he came to himself. His understanding
came back to him; he lifted up his eyes to heaven, and
blessed the Most High, and praised and honoured Him
that liveth for ever. With his reason, the glory also of
his kingdom returned. His counsellors and his lords
sought him and brought him back to his palace, *and
excellent majesty was added unto him.* Resuming his
great works which had been suspended, he "added fresh
wonders in his old age to the marvellous constructions
of his manhood," and after a reign of 43 years died,
B.C. 561, at the advanced age of 83 or 84, and was succeeded by his son Evil-Merodach. Shortly after his
accession the new king released JEHOIACHIN, king of
Judah, from the prison where he had been confined for
38 years, set his throne above the throne of the other
captive princes at Babylon, and gave him a daily allowance from the royal table (2 Kings xxv. 27—30). But in
the course of one or two years he was assassinated, and
one of the conspirators, Neriglissar or Nerigassolassar
usurped the throne, B.C. 559, and held the government
for 3 years and a half, bequeathing it to his son La-
borosoarchod, B.C. 556. In the course of nine months, he
was succeeded by Nabonadius[1], or Labynetus, B.C. 555.

Meanwhile the neighbouring kingdom of Media had
been the scene of a great revolution, in which Babylon
eventually became involved. Mandane a daughter of
Astyages, who mounted the Median throne B.C. 595,
married Cambyses, a Persian of the royal family of the
Achæmenidæ, and became the mother of CYRUS *the
Great*[2]. Alienated by his tyranny and wearying of his

---

[1] Nabonadius or Nabonnedus = *Nabu-nit* or *Nabu-nahit*,
i. e. *Nebo blesses* or *makes prosperous*, known amongst the
Greeks as Labynetus.
[2] Recognised by Isaiah as "a shepherd" of the Lord, an
"anointed king" (Is. xliv. 28; xlv. 1).

rule a large body of the subjects of Astyages transferred their affections to this prince, who heading a revolt, defeated and captured the Median king near Pasargadæ, B.C. 559, and obtained the supremacy over the combined Medo-Persic empire. At first the conqueror did not march against Babylon, and Nabonadius formed an alliance with Crœsus king of Lydia, and employed himself diligently in strengthening his capital, storing up provisions, and erecting defensive works.

But Cyrus gained a complete victory over the Lydian king B.C. 546, and at the end of about six years appeared before Babylon. After a single engagement he drove the Babylonians within their defences (Jer. li. 30), and commenced a regular siege. At this time Nabonadius does not appear to have been present in his capital, having fled to Borsippa after the late engagement. But he left behind him a son whom he had a few years before admitted to a share in the government[1]. This was *Bil-shar-uzar,* the *Belshazzar* of the Scripture narrative. This prince made a great feast for a thousand of his nobles, his wives and concubines, and high estates of the realm, in the midst of which, heated with wine, he commanded that all the gold and silver vessels, which his grandfather[2] Nebuchadnezzar had taken from the plunder of Jerusalem, should be brought forth, and from them the assembled guests drank in honour of their various gods. But in the midst of their festivities the Fingers of a Man's Hand were seen to write mysterious words on the plaister of the palace wall. Instantly all the brightness of Belshazzar's countenance vanished, *his thoughts troubled him, his knees smote one against an-*

---

[1] Pusey's *Lectures on Daniel,* p. 120; Rawlinson's *Bampton Lectures,* p. 170.

[2] On his accession Nabonadius, it is thought, may have married a daughter of Nebuchadnezzar. See Pusey, *Lectures on Daniel,* p. 402; Rawlinson's *Bampton Lectures,* p. 170.

other. With loud voice he bade the astrologers and soothsayers be brought before him, and promised honour, place, and power to any that would interpret the mystic words. But this none of the wise men of his realm could do. Amidst the alarm and confusion, the Queen-mother now entered, and advised that they should consult Daniel, who seems at this time to have been living in close retirement. Accordingly he was brought in, and after declining all the monarch's promised rewards, sternly rebuked him, for that though he knew all that his grandfather's pride had brought down upon him, he had yet lifted up himself against the Lord of Heaven, and in impious triumph profaned the sacred vessels once dedicated to that God who now had sent him this message, MENE, *God hath numbered thy kingdom and finished it;* TEKEL, *thou art weighed in the balances and found wanting;* PERES, *thy kingdom is divided and given to the Medes and Persians* (Dan. v. 25—28). That very night the Prophet's words were fulfilled. Having diverted the course of the Euphrates, Cyrus assaulted the city from the dry bed of the river, captured it, and slew Belshazzar, B.C. 538, thus fulfilling the prophecies of Isaiah (xxi. 9; xlv. 1) and Jeremiah (li. 31—39).

Hastening on to other conquests, Cyrus entrusted the captured city to a viceroy[1], known in Scripture as *Darius the Mede*[2]. He signalized his accession to power by setting over the kingdom of Babylon Proper, either as a body of councillors or provincial go-

---

[1] On the delegated authority of this Darius, see Pusey's *Lectures on Daniel*, pp. 122, 123; Rawlinson's *Bampton Lectures*, p. 171, and notes, p. 445.

[2] See Art. *Darius*, in Smith's *Bib. Dict.* Some identify him with Astyages; others with Cyaxares II., a son of Astyages; others with Neriglissar, or with Nabonadius; "each of these views," observes Prof. Rawlinson, "has its difficulties, and perhaps it is the most probable view that he was a viceroy set up by Cyrus, of whom there is at present no trace in profane history," *Bampton Lectures*, p. 171.

vernors, 120 princes, subject to the authority of three presidents, of whom Daniel, now far advanced in life, was chief (Dan. vi. 2). Old and grey-headed, he still remained faithful to the God of his fathers. And now moved with jealousy at his elevation, the other nobles resolved to compass his ruin. Unable to accuse him of any failure in the administration of the kingdom, they persuaded Darius to pass an irrevocable decree, like the law of the Medes and Persians, ordaining that for a space of 30 days no one should offer up any petition to any god or man save to the monarch himself, on penalty of being flung into a den of lions. This decree Daniel regarded not; steadfast in the religion of his fathers, he opened the windows of his chamber towards Jerusalem, and three times a-day, as had been his wont, offered up his prayers to his God. The nobles now had the opportunity they had coveted, and they reported his conduct to the king. Sorely against his will, and after fruitless efforts to deliver him from their malice, Darius bade the sentence be executed. The aged prophet was flung into the den, the mouth thereof was closed, and sealed with the royal signet, and the signet of the lords and princes. Fasting and sleepless the monarch passed the night, neither were instruments of music brought before him. Rising early in the morning he sought out the lions' den, and to his great joy found that Jehovah had protected His faithful servant, had sent His angel, and shut the lions' mouths. Thereupon he ordered him to be brought forth, and then issued instructions for the immediate execution of his accusers, who, according to the cruel but usual Oriental custom, were with their wives and children flung into the den and torn in pieces. Not content with this, he proclaimed that throughout his vast empire adoration should be paid to the God of Daniel, *the living God, steadfast for ever, who worketh signs and wonders in heaven, and hath delivered His servant from the power of the lions* (Dan. vi. 27).

CHAPTER III

REBUILDING OF THE TEMPLE. ESTHER AND AHASUERUS.

EZRA I.—IV. ESTHER I.—X. B. C. 536—479.

AT the time when Cyrus thus became the ruler of an empire greater even than Assyria itself, seventy[1] years had elapsed since the capture of Jerusalem in the reign of Jehoiakim (Dan. ix. 1, 2). The prosperity he had already enjoyed under so many sovereigns Daniel still retained under the new monarch, and it was probably through his influence that in the first year of his reign, or B.C. 536, Cyrus issued a decree giving permission to the Jews to return to their native land and rebuild their Temple. To aid them in so doing he restored to them the sacred vessels which Nebuchadnezzar had carried off from Jerusalem, and instructed the pashas throughout the various provinces to afford them every facility for their return (Ezra i. 1—6).

The majority, however, of the Jews who had for years been comfortably settled in the land of exile, and had there risen to affluence and high positions, preferred to retain their settlements[2], and only 42,360 attended by 7,337 servants were found willing to return to their native land. Over this body ZERUBBABEL, the head of the house of Judah, and grandson of King Jehoiachin, was invested with the supreme authority. He had held some office in the Babylonian court, and had received the Chaldæan name of Sheshbazzar. Appointed by Cyrus

---

[1] Dating, according to Prideaux and Davison (*Lectures on Prophecy*, VI. 1), from B.C. 606.

[2] The Jews who remained and kept up their national distinctions were called "The Dispersion" (John vii. 35; 1 Pet. i. 1; James i. 1), and "in course of time they served a great purpose in diffusing a knowledge of the true God, and in affording a point for the commencement of the efforts of the Evangelists of the Christian faith." Smith's *Bib. Dict.*

to the governorship of Jerusalem, and accompanied by
the high-priest JESHUA, and possibly the prophets HAG-
GAI and ZECHARIAH, with copious presents of silver and
gold (Ezr. i. 7—11), he set out at the head of the returning colonists and before long reached Jerusalem[1].

Seven months after their return, the Altar of Burnt-
sacrifice was re-erected on its ancient site, and the priests
and Levites offered burnt-offerings and sacrifices. This
done, preparations were made by the *Prince of the Captivity* for his great work, the rebuilding of the Temple.
A grant of money for this purpose having been already
received from Cyrus, cedar trees were brought from
Lebanon to Joppa; masons and carpenters were hired;
and in the 2nd month of the 2nd year of their return,
the foundations of the second Temple were laid, with all
the pomp and ceremonial that circumstances admitted.
*The priests in their apparel with trumpets, the Levites
the sons of Asaph with cymbals* (Ezr. iii. 10, 11), sang the
same Psalms, to the sound of which the first Temple had
been dedicated, and the people responded with a great
shout, which, however, was well-nigh drowned by the
sobs and lamentations of many, especially the older men,
who had beheld the glories of the former Temple.

But the good work was not to proceed unopposed.
Informed of their design, the Samaritans requested to
be allowed some share in its promotion. This Zerubbabel and Jeshua unwisely rejected, and the Samaritans
thereupon exhausted every artifice to prevent the completion of the work. After putting them to various other

---

[1] The chief effects of the Captivity upon the Jews were
these: (i) The old tendency to idolatry had been eradicated
(Comp. Ezek. xxxvi. 24—28); (ii) There had sprung up a deep
reverence for the letter of the Law, and for their great Lawgiver Moses; (iii) The love of agriculture had declined, and
had given place to a taste for commerce and trade; (iv) The
vernacular language had also undergone a change (Neh. viii.
8), the old Hebrew giving place to the Chaldee.

annoyances, they hired counsellors to misrepresent them
at the court of Persia, and eventually succeeded in pre-
venting any further progress during the reign of Cyrus,
and of his successors Cambyses and Smerdis, B.C. 525
—521 (Ezr. iv. 11—24).

But in the second year of Darius Hystaspes, B.C. 520,
the stirring words of the prophets HAGGAI and ZECHA-
RIAH (Hag. i. 1—8; Zech. i. 1—6) roused once more
the spirits of Zerubbabel and Jeshua, and a fresh and
determined effort was made to complete the work. The
Persian satraps of the province, Tatnai and Shetharboz-
nai, came to Jerusalem, and after an inspection of the
work applied to the Persian court for instructions whether
it was to be permitted to go on (Ezr. v. 6—17). Darius
caused the archives at Ecbatana to be searched, and at
length the original decree of Cyrus being discovered, he
reissued it, and at the same time commanded the Persian satraps instead of offering any molestation to the
Jewish colony, to promote the work to the utmost of
their power (Ezr. vi. 5—13). Thus aided, the Jews pressed forward with such vigour that, in the 8th year of the
reign of Darius, the Temple was completed and ready
for dedication, B.C. 516. This ceremony was performed
with every solemnity, numerous sacrifices were offered,
the priests were redistributed into courses, and the Passover was celebrated with great rejoicings (Ezr. vi. 15—22).

During the remainder of the long reign of Darius, the
Jews enjoyed a continuance of peace and tranquillity.
But in the year B.C. 485, AHASUERUS[1], the XERXES of

---

[1] "The name Ahasuerus is undoubtedly the proper Hebrew
equivalent for the Persian word which the Greeks represented
by Xerxes,...and we are at once struck with the strong resemblance which his character bears to that assigned by the
classical writers to the celebrated son of Darius. Proud, self-
willed, amorous, careless of contravening Persian customs;
reckless of human life, yet not actually bloodthirsty; impetuous, facile, changeable, the Ahasuerus of Esther corresponds

profane history, ascended the Persian throne. When he had reigned three years, this capricious despot made a feast for all his nobles at Susa, and on the seventh day of the revels ordered Vashti his queen to grace the banquet with her presence. With a due concern for her own dignity the queen declined, which so enraged her lord that he issued a decree deposing her from her royal station, and ordering a general levy of beautiful virgins, that he might select from them a new queen (Esth. ii. 1—4). At this time there was living at Susa a Jew named Mordecai, of the tribe of Benjamin (Esth. ii. 5). Having no child of his own, he had adopted his cousin HADASSAH or ESTHER, a beautiful orphan. Together with the other virgins she was brought into the royal harem, and found such favour with the monarch that in the seventh year of his reign, without enquiring into her kindred or people, he ordered her to be crowned in place of the deposed queen (Esth. iii. 16).

By virtue of his relationship Mordecai, too, shared in the prosperity of his niece, and became one of those who *sat in the king's gate* (Esth. ii. 41). In this capacity he discovered a plot of the eunuchs to assassinate the king, which he duly divulged, and they were executed, while a record of his services was entered in the royal chronicles. But Mordecai had a rival for the royal favour in the person of HAMAN, an Agagite, *i.e.* probably a descendant of the ancient Amalekite kings. Rapidly outstripping all his other competitors, the new favourite was advanced to the highest position in the kingdom, and was treated with the utmost reverence by everyone, save Mordecai only. Stung to the quick at this slight, and having discovered the secret of his rival's

in all respects to the Greek portraiture of Xerxes, which is not the mere picture of an Oriental despot, but has various peculiarities which distinguish it even from the other Persian kings." Rawlinson's *Bampton Lectures*, p. 186.

lineage, Haman resolved to strike a blow against the
nation to which Mordecai belonged. Accordingly he
represented to his royal master that the Jews, scattered
and dispersed throughout the provinces of his empire,
were a dangerous and turbulent race, of alien habits and
religion, who ought to be put to death; and from the
confiscation of their property he promised to place in
the royal coffers upwards of 10,000 talents of silver.
The prospect of so large an increase to his dilapidated
fortunes was eagerly favoured by the reckless despot,
and assenting to the cruel scheme, he placed his signet-
ring in the hands of Haman, who quickly saw that a decree was issued for the wholesale destruction of the
Jewish exiles throughout the Persian dominions, without regard to sex or age (Esth. iii. 8—15).

News of what was designed before long reached the
ears of Mordecai. Knowing that he himself was the
main cause of this bloodthirsty decree, he was filled with
the utmost alarm, and sat down arrayed in sackcloth
and ashes at the king's gate. His strange conduct
being reported to Esther, she sent to her relative to
ascertain the cause, and then for the first time learnt
the contents of Haman's edict. In this awful crisis she
resolved to *put her life in her hand,* and to intercede
with the king in behalf of her people. Meanwhile, at
her suggestion, all the Jews at Susa maintained for
three days a solemn fast, and then, arrayed in her royal
apparel, and radiant in her beauty, she presented herself before the king. The captivated monarch stretched
forth the golden sceptre, and invited her to prefer her
petition. Let the king and Haman, she begged, come to
a banquet of wine. They came, but declining to make
known her petition for the present, she invited the two
to a similar feast on the following day (Esth. v. 8).

Overjoyed at these special marks of honour, Haman
eagerly recounted them to his wife and family, but

declared that they availed him nothing so long as his rival was permitted to retain his place at the king's gate. They, therefore, advised that a gallows 50 cubits high should be erected, and that he should request the king's permission to hang Mordecai thereon. But that night, the monarch, unable to sleep, ordered certain of the chronicles to be read before him, and now for the first time learnt the service the Jewish exile had rendered by revealing the plot against his own life. In answer to his enquiries, he had just ascertained that no mark of the royal approval had been bestowed upon his benefactor, when Haman entered the court in the early morning to request that execution might be carried out upon his hated rival. The king enquired what ought to be done to the man he delighted to honour. Imagining that none but himself could be intended, the favourite suggested that he should be clad in royal apparel, crowned with the king's diadem, and mounted on the royal mule, be conducted through the streets of Susa by one of the king's most noble friends. The monarch approved, and bade him straightway confer all these marks of honour on no other than Mordecai. Not daring to disobey, he arrayed his rival in the gorgeous robes of the king, and conducted him through the streets of the city. Then with a heavy heart he returned home, and recounted to his family the strange events of the day. A presentiment of coming doom came over his relatives, but a hasty summons to the royal banquet cut short their deliberations. For the second time the monarch desired to learn the queen's petition, and Esther now revealed the danger of her nation, and denounced the wicked conspirator. Filled with wrath Ahasuerus ordered his instant execution, and at the suggestion of one of the eunuchs he was hanged on the very gallows he had constructed for his rival (Esth. vii. 7—10).

But the execution of Haman was but a step in Mor-

decai's designs for the delivery of his nation. The edict
for the massacre was still in force, and couriers had
already gone forth with it to the various provinces of
the empire. Its revocation was forbidden by Persian law,
but a second edict empowered the Jews to assume the
defensive against their adversaries, of whom, banding
themselves together, they slew 800 at Susa (Esth. ix. 6, 15),
and 75,000 in the various provinces, while Haman's ten
sons shared their father's fate (Esth. ix. 12, 16). In
memory of this signal deliverance the Jews to this day
celebrate the Feast of PURIM or *Lots*, in ironical commemoration of their great enemy, who had resorted to
this mode of augury for ascertaining an auspicious day
for executing his bloody design against their nation.
Preceded by a strict fast on the 13th of Adar[1], the festival is celebrated on the 14th and 15th with great rejoicings. According to modern usage the book of Esther
is read in the Synagogue, and when the reader comes to
the name of Haman, the entire assembly shout, *Let his
name be blotted out, let the name of the ungodly
perish;* and the conclusion of the service is followed
by feasting and merriment.

CHAPTER IV

TIMES OF EZRA AND NEHEMIAH. CLOSE OF THE CANON.

EZRA VII.—X. NEH. I.—XIII. B. C. 457—415.

IN the year B.C. 464 Artaxerxes Longimanus succeeded to the Persian throne. His reign was favourable
to the Jews, and was signalised, B.C. 458, by a fresh
migration to Jerusalem headed by EZRA, a descendant
of Hilkiah the high-priest in the time of Josiah. A
royal ordinance empowered him not only to receive
contributions from his own nation scattered through-

[1] See Calendar, p. 155.

out Babylonia for the adornment of the Temple at Jerusalem, but also to establish magistrates and judges throughout all Judea, and to claim assistance from the various pashas of the provinces through which he would pass (Ezr. vii. 11—26). Thus aided and encouraged, Ezra persuaded about 6,000 of his countrymen to take part in this second migration, amongst whom were many of the priesthood, both of the higher and lower orders. After a fast of three days at the river Ahava[1], to supplicate the Divine blessing on the enterprise, the expedition set out, and, though not escorted by a royal guard, reached Jerusalem in safety (Esth. viii. 32).

Ezra was well received by the Jewish governors, but was pained to find much to blame in the conduct of his countrymen. Forgetful of the commands of the Law, they had in many instances intermarried with the surrounding heathen tribes. He therefore devoted himself with all zeal to the correction of these abuses; proclaimed a fast by way of atonement for past transgressions, and succeeded in inducing many to put away their strange wives. At the same time he commenced a more complete reorganization of the people according to the Mosaic Law and the institutes of David, and, it is not improbable, a revision and rearrangement of the sacred Books (Ezra x. 1—17).

But though the Persian monarchs had not been unwilling to render aid in the rebuilding of the Jewish Temple, their policy had hitherto forbidden the re-erection of the city itself, which still lay exposed and defenceless, *its walls broken down and its gates burned with fire* (Neh. i. 3), the Temple, and a few private dwellings, being the sole result of 80 years of effort. In

---

[1] Identified by the latest researches with the modern *Hit*, on the Euphrates, due East of Damascus, afterwards known as the Ihi, or Ihi da-kira, "the spring of bitumen." Smith's *Bib. Dict.*

the 20th year, however, of Artaxerxes, or B.C. 444, there arrived at Shusan a deputation from Jerusalem, with a sad account of the condition of the city, which they laid before NEHEMIAH, a Jew, probably of the tribe of Judah, who held a high position amongst the royal cup-bearers. Nehemiah instantly conceived the patriotic design of quitting the comforts of his present position, and aiding his countrymen in their difficulties. With fasting and prayer he sought the blessing of the Most High on his design, and shortly afterwards, in reply to the enquiries of the king *why his countenance was so sad*, poured forth the deep desire of his heart, and begged that he might be allowed to go to Judea, and rebuild the city of his fathers. Artaxerxes consented[1], on condition that he returned within a certain period; and having appointed him Tirshatha or governor of Judea, gave him letters to the pashas of the provinces through which he would pass, as also to Asaph the keeper of the royal forests, directing him to supply timber and other necessaries for the work (Neh. ii. 1—8).

Thus empowered and guarded by a troop of cavalry, Nehemiah set out on his journey. On his arrival at Jerusalem he for three days kept silence as to his intentions, but after a midnight survey of the ruined condition of the city, openly proclaimed the purport of his visit, and the royal commission under which he was acting. He advised the instant rebuilding of the city

---

[1] "The power of Persia had received by the Athenians a fatal blow in the victory obtained at Salamis in Cyprus, B.C. 449. The Great King was obliged to submit to a humiliating peace, among the articles of which were the abandonment of the maritime towns, and a stipulation that the Persian army should not approach within three days' journey of the sea. Jerusalem being about this distance from the coast, and standing so near the line of communication with Egypt, became a port of the utmost value." Milman's *History of the Jews*, I. p. 435. Jahn's *Heb. Comm.* p. 142.

walls, till which was done the colony could not but be a reproach to the surrounding tribes, with their city almost deserted, and the Temple itself falling into decay (Neh. ii. 12—20).

His project was received with acclamation, and a resolution was formed to press on with the work without delay. But the coming of the new governor had reached the ears of the Samaritans, and Sanballat the Horonite[1], Tobiah an Ammonite, and Geshem an Arabian, employed every artifice to defeat his designs. Nehemiah, however, was not to be daunted. His object was to finish the walls in the shortest possible time, and he therefore directed that while one half of the people wrought at the work, the other should stand by armed and ready to defend them, and that the workmen should hold in the one hand a weapon, and in the other their tools. Thus by dint of incredible exertions, within the brief space of 52 days Jerusalem was again girded and enclosed, the walls were rebuilt, the ancient towers set up, and the gateways were ready for the doors to be swung upon them (Neh. iv. 13—23).

Unable to impede by open violence the progress of the enterprise, Sanballat and his friends resorted to various stratagems to get Nehemiah out of the city. They began by proposing a conference with the governor in one of the villages of the plain of Ono in Benjamin. Four times was the proposition made, and as often declined. Then resort was had to a still more cunning artifice. Sanballat sent to Nehemiah an apparently friendly letter, announcing the prevalence of a rumour among the heathen nations settled in Samaria that he intended Jerusalem to become the capital of an independent kingdom, and had suborned prophets to pro-

---

[1] Either of Horonaim a town of Moab, or of Horon, *i. e.* Bethhoron; he appears to have held some office at Samaria under Artaxerxes. Smith's *Bib. Dict.*

phesy of himself, *There is a king in Judah.* Such
rumours were sure to reach the Persian court, but might
be dissipated by a friendly conference. At the same time
Noadiah a prophetess and others were bribed to represent to the governor the risk he was running, and to
persuade him to take refuge in the fortress of the
Temple. But Nehemiah saw through their designs, and
refused to give them any pretext for accusing him of
conscious guilt (Neh. vi. 1—14). In addition to these
plots the governor had to be on his guard against
treachery within the city itself, where many of the
Jewish nobles were carrying on a secret correspondence
with Tobiah, and even espoused his cause. But in spite
of all obstacles the work went on, and the essential part
of the governor's design, the building of the gates, was
accomplished.

Having thus provided for the external security of
the city, Nehemiah applied himself with equal zeal to
the correction of internal abuses. One of these was the
high rate of usury, which those who had any money at
their command, exacted from their poorer brethren.
To such an extent was this the case, that some mort-
gaged their fields, vineyards, and houses; others sold
or pledged the freedom of their children; while many
borrowed at the most exorbitant rates sufficient to pay
the royal taxes (Neh. v. 1—14). The discovery of this
nefarious system roused the governor's indignation.
Himself noble, generous, and highminded, he declined
even the usual supplies for his own table which former
governors had received; defrayed many expenses out of
his own purse; and even entertained the poorer classes
of his countrymen at his own table (Neh. v. 14—19).
With righteous sternness, therefore, he rebuked the
nobles who connived at this disgraceful traffic, and con-
voking an assembly demanded that his enslaved country
men should be set free, their debts remitted, and the

enormous interest foregone. His rebukes had their effect. The assembly unanimously announced their willingness to accede to his demands, and abstain from such conduct in future. Other measures for the internal welfare of the city were then proceeded with. The doors having been set up in the gates, the custody of the city was committed to Hanani, a relative of the governor; a register of the people was taken, the Law was solemnly read in their hearing by Ezra (Neh. viii. 1 —16), and the Feast of Tabernacles was celebrated with due solemnities, from the 15th to the 22nd of the month Tisri[1]. Two days afterwards a Fast was proclaimed, and the people made a formal confession of their national sins, and enumerated the gracious dealings of the Most High with them, from the Call of Abraham to the return from the Captivity (Neh. ix. 6—37). At the same time they ratified a solemn covenant to serve the Lord with all their heart, and keep the ordinances of the Lord; to avoid intermarriages with heathens; to observe the Sabbaths and other holy days, and neither buy nor sell goods thereon; to keep the seventh or Sabbatical year, and remit all debts during it; to contribute each man one-third of a shekel towards the support of the Temple-service, and to maintain the customary first-fruits and tithes (Neh. x. 29.—39).

Having in co-operation with Ezra thus restored the national institutions, Nehemiah returned to the Persian court, B.C. 432. During his absence the old abuses again began to creep in; the people contracted alliances with foreigners, neglected the Sabbath, and forgot the covenant they had so lately sworn to observe. As soon as he was informed of this, Nehemiah sought and obtained permission to revisit once more the scene of his former labours, and as Tirshatha was invested with renewed powers. Returning after an absence of about nine years,

[1] See Calendar, p. 155.

he found that Eliashib the high-priest had permitted
Tobiah the Ammonite to occupy a large chamber in the
Temple, which had before been used as a store for the
frankincense, the holy vessels, and the tithes of corn,
wine, and oil. Thereupon he insisted on the expulsion
of the intruder, and the restoration of the ejected vessels and stores, over which he appointed a Levitical
guard (Neh. xiii. 1—15). He next introduced measures
for the prevention of traffic on the Day of Rest, and the
celebration of mixed marriages, alike amongst the lower
and the higher orders of the people, even deposing
from his sacred functions the high-priest Eliashib for
permitting his son Joiada to ally himself with a daughter
of Sanballat the Horonite (Neh. xiii. 15—28). Having
thus completed his second administration, this truly
patriotic and upright governor in all probability returned
to Persia about B.C. 413, and there died.

With this date closes the History contained in the
Scriptures of the Old Testament. While the mass of
the Hebrew people was scattered among the nations,
carrying with them, wherever they went, their Law and
their Institutions, we have seen a remnant, as had indeed been foretold, restored to their own land, their
holy Temple rebuilt, their glorious City raised from its
ruins. Very different, indeed, was their position now
from that which the nation had occupied during the
palmy days of Solomon, when their kingdom stretched
from "the river of Egypt" to the Euphrates, from the
mountains of Lebanon to the Red Sea. Different, too,
and far less costly was their Temple in comparison with
that which the artisans of Hiram had built for the Son
of David, but in its moral and spiritual condition the
remnant of the nation far excelled the contemporaries
of its greatest king. In the furnace of affliction it had
been thoroughly purified from all tendencies to idolatry.
The dreary years, when *their harps hung upon the*

31

willows by the waters of Babylon, had not been without their salutary effect upon the people.

There was no division now in the objects of their worship. No high places were to be seen crowned with temples dedicated to Baal or Chemosh; no groves screened with their leafy covert the impure orgies of Astaroth; no drums and cymbals drowned with their horrid clang the wail of infants in the valley of Ben-Hinnom, as they were passed through the fire to appease the cruel Moloch. These "oracles" were "dumb." The Jew was no longer an idolater. The Divine Unity was now the central truth of his creed. The Law once neglected was now read, copied, studied. While Nehemiah had earnestly applied himself to the civil administration, Ezra[1], and others after him, with no less zeal devoted their energies to collecting, transcribing, arranging the Sacred Books. These were ultimately classed under three divisions; (i) *The Law*, containing the five Books of Moses; (ii) *The Prophets*, which included the historical and prophetical writings; (iii) *The Psalms*, or Hagiographa (*sacred writings*), comprising the poetical works.

Meanwhile varied as had been the fortunes of the Chosen People, the Assurance of a Saviour, of God's purpose of love in the promised Seed, had never been forgotten. As first made known to man in Paradise, it did perhaps, as we have seen[2], little more than assure him of a future interposition in his behalf, without informing him whether his Redeemer should be one or many, the collective race, or a single deliverer. But once given, the realization of the Promise becomes the goal of Sacred History.

Through one of the sons of Noah[3], it is limited to a

---

[1] Westcott's *The Bible in the Church*, pp. 298, 299.
[2] See above, pp. 8, 9.   [3] See above, p. 18.

particular race; through the call of Abraham[1] to a particular nation; through Judah to a particular tribe. When the people flee away from the terrors of Sinai, Moses predicts the coming of a greater *Prophet*[2], and a mightier Mediator. When the Sceptre rises from Judah[3], and David sits upon his throne, he himself speaks of a Greater King[4], of ONE he calls his Lord, *who shall sit upon his throne, and of whose kingdom there shall be no end.* When the mournful close of Solomon's reign proves that he could not be the destined king, when his kingdom is rent in twain, and his subjects become a prey to their enemies, and are carried off into far distant lands, even then the very sadness of the Captivity only serves to correct the idea of the Messiah, and the "Son of David" gives place in the writings of Daniel to the "Son of Man[5]." Thus each crisis of the nation's history serves to bring the Promise within narrower limits, and to illustrate it with fresh details.

Meanwhile, as time rolls on, and one prophet after another brings out some new particular, foreshadowing the birth-place[6], or the offices[7], or the works of the Messiah, another Voice begins to be heard in the Temple of Prophecy. It is not jubilant and glad, telling of triumph and of glory, of the subjugation of nations, or the setting up of a kingdom. It is subdued and mournful. It whispers of suffering and rejection, of a triumph indeed, but not the triumph of an earthly conqueror. It speaks of the coming[8] of *a man of sorrows and acquainted with grief;* of His being *wounded for trans-*

---

[1] See above, pp. 26, 28.   [2] See above, p. 71.
[3] See above, pp. 109, 110.
[4] Psalm cx; ii; xlv.
[5] Dan. vii. 13. Westcott's *Introduction to the N. T.* p. 87. Davidson *On Prophecy,* p. 205.
[6] Mic. v. 2; Isai. vii. 14.   [7] Zech. vi. 13; Isai. lxi. 1.
[8] Isai. liii. Comp. also ix. 6; xl. 1, 12; xlii. 1, 4; xlix. 5—7; lii, liv.

gressions and bruised for iniquities; of His being *cut off, but not for Himself*[1].

The earliest prophecy had declared that the seed of the woman should *bruise the Serpent's head,* but had whispered that the Serpent would *bruise his heel.* The latest declared that the Messiah should *triumph,* but also that He should *die.* Thus gradually, but harmoniously, was the person and work of man's Redeemer unfolded.

And at length in *the fulness of time*[2] a Babe was born in Bethlehem, and laid in a manger. Seed of the Woman, of the race of Shem, of the descendants of Abraham, of the tribe of Judah, of the lineage of David, He lived, He died, He rose again. Prophet like unto, but infinitely greater than Moses, He gave us a law which shall never pass away[3]; Priest like unto, but not as Aaron *compassed about with infirmity,* He offered up on the Altar of His Cross a full, perfect, and sufficient sacrifice, atonement, and satisfaction for the sins of the whole world; King like unto, but infinitely higher than David, He sitteth at the right hand of God, clad in the glorified nature of the race He came to save, the predicted Redeemer of the Old, the revealed Deliverer of the New Testament, in *whom there is neither Jew nor Gentile, neither male nor female, neither bond nor free*[4].

---

[1] Dan. ix. 26, see Pusey *in loc.*   [2] Gal. iv. 4.
[3] See Butler's *Analogy,* Part II. ch. v.   [4] Gal. iii. 28.

APPENDIX

I

THE PATRIARCHS AND THEIR DESCENDANTS.

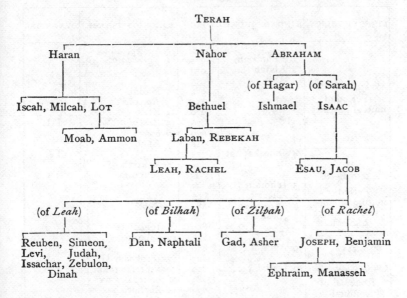

```
                              TERAH
                                |
        ┌───────────────────────┼───────────────────┐
      Haran                    Nahor              ABRAHAM
        |                        |            ┌───────────┐
        |                        |        (of Hagar)  (of Sarah)
        |                        |            |           |
  Iscah, Milcah, LOT          Bethuel      Ishmael      ISAAC
        |                        |                        |
   Moab, Ammon            Laban, REBEKAH                  |
                              |                           |
                       LEAH, RACHEL               ESAU, JACOB
                                                          |
   ┌──────────────┬──────────────────┬──────────────────┐
(of Leah)     (of Bilhah)        (of Zilpah)        (of Rachel)
   |              |                   |                  |
Reuben, Simeon, Dan, Naphtali    Gad, Asher    JOSEPH, Benjamin
Levi,   Judah,                                         |
Issachar, Zebulon,                            Ephraim, Manasseh
     Dinah
```

II

LEVI AND THE PRIESTHOOD.

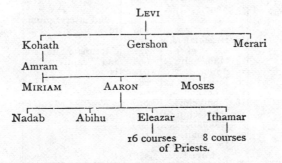

```
                         LEVI
                          |
        ┌─────────────────┼─────────────────┐
     Kohath            Gershon            Merari
        |
     Amram
        |
   ┌────┼──────────────────────┐
 MIRIAM        AARON         MOSES
                 |
   ┌────────┬────┴─────┬──────────┐
 Nadab    Abihu     Eleazar     Ithamar
                       |           |
                  16 courses   8 courses
                     of Priests.
```

III

KINGS OF JUDAH AND ISRAEL.

KINGS OF ALL ISRAEL.

B. C.

Saul 1095
David 1055
Solomon 1015

Division of the Kingdom, B.C. 975.

KINGDOMS OF JUDAH AND ISRAEL.

LINES OF POLICY.	KINGS OF JUDAH.	B.C.	KINGS OF ISRAEL.	DYNASTIES
I. B. C. 975—918 Period of mutual hostility.	1 Rehoboam .. 2 Abijah ...... 3 Asa	975 958 955 954 953 930 929 929 918	1 *Jeroboam* 2 Nadab 3 *Baasha* 4 Elah 5 *Zimri* 6 *Omri* 7 Ahab	I. II. III.
II. B. C. 918—884 Period of mutual alliance, and hostility to Syria.	4 Jehoshaphat 5 Jehoram .... 6 Ahaziah .... 7 (*Athaliah*) .. 8 Joash	914 898 896 892 885 884 878 856 841	 8 Ahaziah 9 Jehoram 10 *Jehu* 11 Jehoahaz 12 Jehoash	IV. V.
III. B. C. 884—588 Renewal of mutual hostilities, gradual decline of both kingdoms before the power of Assyria.	9 Amaziah .... 10 Uzziah ...... 11 Jotham .... 12 Ahaz........ 13 Hezekiah.... 14 Manasseh ... 15 Amon ...... 16 Josiah ...... 17 Jehoahaz.... 18 Jehoiakim... 19 Jehoiachin or Coniah..... 20 Zedekiah.... Jerusalem destroyed	839 825 810 783 773 772 772 761 759 758 742 737 730 726 721 698 643 641 610 610 599 599 588	 13 Jeroboam II. 1st interregnum of about 11 years* 14 Zachariah 15 *Shallum* 16 *Menahem* 17 Pekahiah 18 *Pekah* 2nd interregnum 19 *Hoshea* Capture of Samaria and captivity of Israel.	 VI. VII. VIII. IX.

* See Clinton's *Epitome*, p. 133.

IV

THE PROPHETS.

GENERAL DIVISION.	PROBABLE CHRON. ORDER.	PERIOD ILLUSTRATED BY THEIR PROPHECIES.		
		B. C.	KINGS OF ISRAEL.	KINGS OF JUDAH.
MAJOR PROPHETS.	PROPHETS.			
Four.	i. *Before the Babylonian Captivity.*			
1 Isaiah	*1 Jonah	840—784	Jehoash, Jeroboam II.	Joash, Amaziah
2 Jeremiah	2 Joel	810—795	Jeroboam II.	Joash
3 Ezekiel	3 Amos.....	810—785	Jeroboam II.	Uzziah
4 Daniel	4 Hosea....	800—725	Jeroboam II.—Hoshea	Uzziah, Jotham, Ahaz
———	5 Isaiah	758—699	Pekahiah—Captivity	Ahaz, Hezekiah
	6 Micah	765—698	Menahem—Captivity	Uzziah, Jotham, Ahaz, Hezekiah
MINOR PROPHETS.	ii. *Near to and during the Captivity.*			
Twelve.	1 Nahum ...	720—698	Captivity of Israel	Manasseh, Amon, Josiah
1 Hosea	2 Zephaniah	640—609		Josiah, Jehoahaz
2 Joel				
3 Amos	3 Habakkuk	612—598		Josiah—Zedekiah
4 Obadiah	4 Jeremiah..	628—585		Jehoahaz—Captivity
5 Jonah	5 Daniel	606—534		The Captivity Captivity of Judah
6 Micah	†6 Obadiah ..	588—583		
7 Nahum	7 Ezekiel ...	595—574		Zedekiah, Captivity
8 Habakkuk	iii. *After the return from the Captivity.*			
9 Zephaniah				
10 Haggai	1 Haggai...	520—518		The Rebuilding of the Temple.
11 Zechariah	2 Zechariah.	520—510		Rebuilding and Dedication
12 Malachi	3 Malachi ..	420—397		2nd Reformation of Nehemiah Close of the Canon

* The order of the first six Prophets is much disputed, but the one above given seems to receive most support.

† By some the prophecies of Obadiah are referred to the reign of Hezekiah, B. C. 726—698.

V

ISRAEL IN CONNECTION WITH THE SURROUNDING NATIONS.

I. THE LATER ASSYRIAN EMPIRE.

B.C.	CONTEMPORANEOUS KINGDOMS.				
	ASSYRIA.	BABYLON.	EGYPT.	JUDAH.	ISRAEL.
742	TIGLATH-PI-LESER invades Babylon	Nabonassar			
741	. . . . .	. . . .	. . . .	AHAZ	PEKAH
740	Takes tribute from PEKAH Defeats Rezin	. . . .	. . . .	. . . .	Pekah tributary
737	. . . . .	. . . .	. . . .	Pays homage to Tiglath-Pileser at Damascus	PEKAH slain
733	. . . . .	Nadius			
730	. . . . .	. . . .	. . . .	. . . .	HOSHEA
726	Accession of SHALMANESER	Elulæus	. . . .	HEZEKIAH	Submission to Shalmaneser (2 K. xvii. 3)
725	. . . . .	. . . .	Sabaco I.? So	. . . .	Alliance with So (2 K. xvii. 4)
723	Siege of Tyre	. . . .	. . . .	. . . .	Siege of Samaria
722	Rebellion of SARGON				
721	SARGON takes Samaria	Merodach Baladan	. . . .	. . . .	Samaria taken
715	Attacks Arabia	. . . .	Sabaco II.? Wars with Sargon	. . . .	CAPTIVITY of ISRAEL
713	. . . . .	. . . .	. . . .	HEZEKIAH'S illness Embassy of Merodach Baladan (See p.434 n.)	
711	Takes Ashdod	Attacked by Sargon			
702	SENNACHERIB expels Merodach Baladan	Belybus			

1. *Continued.*

B.C.	CONTEMPORANEOUS KINGDOMS.				
	ASSYRIA.	BABYLON.	EGYPT.	JUDAH.	ISRAEL.
700	Advances against Philistia and Egypt	. . . .	. . . .	First attack of Sennacherib on Jerusalem—makes HEZEKIAH tributary	CAPTIVITY of ISRAEL
699?	Defeated before Pelusium	Asshur-Nadin	. . . .	Second attack	
698	. . . . .	. . . .	. . . .	MANASSEH	
690	. . . . .	. . . .	Tirhakah		
680	Accession of ESARHADDON (2 K. xix. 37)	Esarhaddon			
676?	. . . . .	Manasseh brought to Babylon (See p.438 n.)	. . . .	The captains of Esarhaddon remove MANASSEH to Babylon	
660?	Assur-bani-pal	Saosduchinus			
664	. . . . .	. . . .	Psammetichus		
647	Asshur-emitili	Cinneladanus			
643	. . . . .	. . . .	. . . .	AMON	
630	Scythian invasion	. . . .	. . . .	JOSIAH	
625	Destruction of Nineveh by Cyaxares	Nabopolassar			

** This and the following Tables are framed from those given in Rawlinson's *Herodotus,* Vol. I. pp. 489, 530, Clinton's *Epitome,* and Prideaux's *Connection of Sacred and Profane History.*

2. BABYLONIAN EMPIRE.

B.C.	BABYLONIA.	MEDIA.	EGYPT.	LYDIA.	JUDAH.
625	Nabopolassar	8th year of Cyaxares	39th year of Psammetichus	Alyattes	15th year of JOSIAH
615	. . . . .	Cyaxares attacks Lydia	. . . .	Attacked by Cyaxares	
610	Makes peace between Cyaxares and Alyattes	. . . .	NECO (2 K. xxiii. 28)	Peace made	
609	Attacked by Neco	. . . .	Invades Syria Defeats JOSIAH	. . . .	JEHOAHAZ JEHOIAKIM
606	Sends Nebuchadnezzar against Neco	. . . .	Defeated at Carchemish	. . . .	Submits to Nebuchadnezzar
604	NEBUCHADNEZZAR	.			
602	. . . . .	. .	. . . .	. . . .	Rebels
599	Besieges Tyre				
597	Besieges Jerusalem	Assists Nebuchadnezzar	. . . .	. . . .	JEHOIACHIN 3 mo. ZEDEKIAH
595	. . . . .	Astyages			
594	. . . . .	. . . .	Psammetichus II.		
588	Second siege of Jerusalem	. . . .	Apries (Ezek. xvii. 15)	. . . .	Attacked by Nebuchadnezzar
586	Takes Jerusalem	. . . .	. . . .	. . . .	Taken prisoner
585	Takes Tyre	.			
581	Invades Egypt	. . . .	. . . .	. . . .	CAPTIVITY of JUDAH
570	Second Invasion of Egypt	. . . .	Deposed by Nebuchadnezzar (Jer. xliv. 30. Ezek. xxix. xxx. xxxii.)		
561	EVIL-MERODACH	. . .	. . . .	. . . .	JEHOIACHIN released
560		. . . .	. . . .	Crœsus	
559	Neriglissar	Defeated by Cyrus at Pasargadæ			
556	Laborosoarchod				
555	Nabonadius, Alliance with Crœsus				
546	. . . . .	. . . .	. . . .	Defeated by Cyrus	
539	Associated with BELSHAZZAR				
538	Conquered by CYRUS				

3. THE PERSIAN EMPIRE AND GREECE.

B.C.	JUDEA.	PERSIA.	GREECE.
537		Supremacy of Cyrus	
536	Return of the Jews	Decree for the return	
	The Altar set up	of the Jews	
534	Interruption of the		
	Samaritans		
529	. . . .	Death of Cyrus	
525	. . . .	Accession of CAM-	
		BYSES	
522	. . . .	DARIUS HYSTASPES	
520	Prophecies of Haggai		
	and ZECHARIAH		
	Building of the Tem-		
	ple resumed		
516	Temple dedicated		
510	. . . .	. . . .	Expulsion of the
			Pisistratidæ
499	. . . .	Burning of Sardis by	
		the Ionians	
493	. . . .	Darius declares war	
		against Greece	
490	. . . .	. . . .	Battle of Marathon
485	. . . .	Accession of XERXES	
		(*Ahasuerus*)	
480	. . . .	. . . .	Battle of Salamis
479	. . . .	Returns defeated	
		from Greece	
		Era of *Esther* and	
		Mordecai	
466	. . . .	. . . .	Battles at the Eury-
			medon
465	. . . .	Death of Xerxes	
464	. . . .	Accession of ARTA-	Themistocles goes to
		XERXES	Persia
458	EZRA comes to Jeru-		
	salem		
	Last prophecies of		
	ZECHARIAH		
449	. . . .	Artaxerxes makes	Victory of the Athe-
		peace with the	nians at Salamis in
		Athenians	Cyprus
444	NEHEMIAH rebuilds		
	the walls of Jeru-		
	salem		
	Opposition of San-		
	ballat		
433	. . . .	Nehemiah returns to	
		Persia	
432	. . . .	. . . .	Peloponnesian war
			begins
428	Return and further		
	reformations by		
	NEHEMIAH		
423	. . . .	Accession of DARIUS	
		NOTHUS	
420	Prophecies of		
	MALACHI		
413?	. . . .	Final return of Nehe-	
		miah	

VI

TABLES OF WEIGHTS, MEASURES AND MONEY.

1. *Jewish Weights reduced to English Troy Weight.*

	lbs.	oz.	dwts.	grs.
The gerah, $\frac{1}{20}$th of a shekel	0	0	0	12
Bekah, $\frac{1}{2}$ a shekel	0	0	5	0
The shekel.	0	0	10	0
The maneh = 60 shekels	2	6	0	0
The talent = 50 maneh = 3000 shekels	125	0	0	0

2. *Scripture Measures of Length reduced to English Measure.*

								Eng. feet.	inches.
A digit, Jer. lii. 21								0	0·912
4	A palm, Exod. xxv. 25							0	3·648
12	3	A span, Exod. xxviii. 16						0	10·944
24	6	2	A cubit, Gen. vi. 15					1	9·888
96	24	12	4	A fathom, Acts xxvii. 28				7	3·552
144	36	18	6	1½	Ezekiel's reed, Ezek. xl. 3—5 . .			10	11·328
192	48	24	8	2	1⅓	An Arabian pole . . .' .		14	7·104
1920	480	240	80	20	13	10	Schœnus, or Measuring line, Ezek. xl. 3.	145	11·040

3. *The Long Scripture Measures.*

					Eng. miles.	paces.	feet.
A cubit					0	0	1·824
400	A stadium or furlong, Luke xxiv. 13				0	145	4·6
2000	5	A Sabbath day's journey, Acts i. 12 . .			0	729	3·0
4000	10	2	An eastern mile, Matt. v. 41 . . .		1	403	1·0
12000	30	6	3	A parasang	4	153	3·0
96000	240	48	24	8	A day's journey	33	172	4·0

4. *Scripture Measures of Capacity for Liquids, reduced to English Wine Measure.*

						gal.	pints.
A caph						0	0·625
1⅓	A log, Lev. xiv. 10					0	0·833
5⅓	4	A cab				0	3·333
16	12	3	A hin, Exod. xxx. 24			1	2
32	24	6	2	A seah		2	4
96	72	18	6	3	A bath, or ephah, 1 Kings vii. 26; John ii.	7	4
960	70	180	60	30	10	A kor or homer, Ezek. xlv. 14; Isaiah v. 10.	75	0

5. *Scripture Measures of Capacity for things Dry reduced to English Corn Measure.*

							pks.	gals.	pints.
A gachal							0	0	0'1416
20	A cab or chœnix, 2 Kings vi. 25; Rev. vi. 6						0	0	2'8333
36	1⅘	An omer, Exod. xvi. 36					0	0	5'1
120	6	3⅓	A seah, Matt. xiii. 33				1	0	1
360	18	10	3	An ephah, Ezek. xlv. 11			3	0	3
1800	90	50	15	5	A letech, Hos. iii. 2		15	1	7
3600	180	100	30	10	2	A homer or kor, Num. xi. 32; Hosea iii. 2	31	1	6

6. *Jewish Money reduced to English Standard.*

					£	s.	d.
A gerah, Exod. xxx.					0	0	1'3687
10	A bekah, Exod. xxxviii. 26				0	1	1'6875
20	2	A shekel, Exod. xxx. 13; Isa. vii. 23			0	2	3'375
1200	120	60	A maneh or minah Hebraica		6	16	10'5
60000	6000	3000	50	A talent	342	3	9
A solidus aureus, or sextula, was worth					0	12	0½
A siculus aureus, or gold shekel, was worth					1	16	6
A talent of gold was worth					5475	0	0

In the preceding table, silver is valued at 5*s.* and gold at £4 per oz.

INDEX

A.

AARON, his parentage, 81; appointed spokesman to Moses, 85; fashions the calf, 112; rebuked by Moses, 113; made the first Highpriest, 130; rebels against Moses, 171; priesthood of his race confirmed, 178; excluded from the Promised Land, 180; his death on Mount Hor, 182

Abana, river, 412

Abdon, the judge, 258

Abednego at Babylon, 457; in the fiery furnace, 456

Abel, his sacrifice, 10; death of, 11

Abel Beth-Maachah, death of Sheba at, 343; its position, 343

Abel Meholah, meaning of, flight of the Midianites to, 249; residence of Elisha, 391

Abiah, son of Samuel, 275

Abiathar, the priest, joins David, 305; has charge of the Ark, 326, 338; rebels against David, 347; degraded from the Priesthood, 352

Abigail, David's wife, 309, 318

Abihu, the sin of, 131

Abijah, king of Judah, 376; defeats Jeroboam, 377

Abimelech made king of his tribe, 252; destroys Shechem, 254; his death, 255

Abiram, rebellion of, 176, 177

Abishai, David's nephew, 304, 310, 319; captain of the mighty men, 329, 343; saves David's life, 345

Abner, Saul's general, 310; supports Ishbosheth, 319; kills Asahel, 320; joins David, 320; killed by Joab, 321; effect of his death, 321

Abraham, the call of, 26, 36; his descent and abode, 27; promises to him, 28, 34, 37; sets out for the Promised Land, 28; arrives at Shechem, 31; builds his first altar there, 32; removes to Bethel, 32; goes down to Egypt, 33; returns to Bethel, 33; separates from Lot, 34; removes to the oak of Mamre, 34, 44; rescues Lot,

35; blessed by Melchizedek, 36; solemn covenant to him, 37; his name changed, 38; entertains three angels, 39; pleads for Sodom and Gomorrah, 40; his offering of Isaac, 43; his subsequent history, 44; death, and burial at Machpelah, 45; summary of his character, 76

Absalom murders Amnon, 336; forgiven by David, 336; his rebellion, 337; enters Jerusalem, 339; his defeat and death, 341

Achan, his transgression and death, 208

Achish, his policy towards David, 303, 311

Achor, valley of, 208

Adam, the creation of, 3; placed in Paradise, 3; his life there, 4; his disobedience, 6; the curse upon him, 7; the Promise to him, 8; his expulsion, 10; his sons and descendants, 10, 11; their longevity, 12; their general wickedness, 12

Adoni-bezek, his capture, 226

Adonijah rebels against David, 347; his life spared, 348; his rebellion against Solomon, 350, 351; put to death, 352

Adoram stoned to death, 369

Adullam, David at, 303

Agag, chief of the Amalekites, 103; spared by Saul, 292; slain by Samuel, 293

Ahab, king of Israel, married to Jezebel, 381; effects of her influence on him, 383; the drought during his reign, 385; denounced by Elijah, 383, 385, 397; his wars with Benhadad, 391—395; his death, 399; slaughter of his descendants, 421

Ahasuerus, the Xerxes of history, 471; chooses Esther for queen, 472; exalts Mordecai, 474

Ahaz, king of Judah, 433; his idolatry, 434

Ahaziah, king of Israel, 400; summons Elijah, 403

—— king of Judah, 418

THE END.